THE *OTHER* COLLEGE GUIDE

JANE SWEETLAND, PAUL GLASTRIS,

and the Staff of the *Washington Monthly*

///

THE NEW PRESS

NEW YORK
LONDON

THE *OTHER* COLLEGE GUIDE

A ROAD MAP to the Right School for You

The publisher is grateful for permission to reprint the following material:
"The Considerator" on page 10 is reprinted with permission from California Competes.

"So Where Are You Going?" on page 24 is reprinted with permission from the Washington State Workforce Training & Education Coordinating Board.

The "Career Clusters Interest Survey" on pages 26-30 is reprinted with permission from the National Association of State Directors of Career Technical Education Consortium (NASDCTEc).

The "Request for Admission Application Fee Waiver" on page 50 is reprinted with permission from the National Association for College Admission Counseling (NACAC).

The illustrations on pages 89–90, and 92–93 are adapted from College Results Online with permission from The Education Trust.

The "College App Map" on page 207 is reprinted with permission from the King Center Charter School in Buffalo, NY.

The "Student Consent for Release of Information" form on page 246 is reprinted with permission from the California State University, Sacramento, Office of the University Registrar.

The "Cost Comparison Worksheet" on page 295 is reprinted with permission from the National Community Tax Coalition.

Requests for permission to reproduce selections from this book should be mailed to: Permissions Department, The New Press, 120 Wall Street, 31st floor, New York, NY 10005.

Published in the United States by The New Press, New York, 2015
Distributed by Perseus Distribution

ISBN 978-1-62097-006-5 (PBK.)
ISBN 978-1-62097-035-5 (E-BOOK)
CIP DATA IS AVAILABLE

The New Press publishes books that promote and enrich public discussion and understanding of the issues vital to our democracy and to a more equitable world. These books are made possible by the enthusiasm of our readers; the support of a committed group of donors, large and small; the collaboration of our many partners in the independent media and the not-for-profit sector; booksellers, who often hand-sell New Press books; librarians; and above all by our authors.

www.thenewpress.com

Book design and composition by Lovedog Studio
This book was set in Sabon
Printed in the United States of America

10 9 8 7 6 5 4 3 2 1

To L.E. and K.G. for every day.

CONTENTS

Ready?

1.

CHOOSING TO GO:

AN INTRODUCTION TO THIS GUIDE

Goals
Knowledge
Seek
Resources
Choose
Think
Connected
Employment
Future
Skills
Journey
Advice

Choosing to go to college is one of those major, super-important, really, really critical decisions in life. After all, college could be the most valuable investment you ever make in your future. It could also be where you meet your closest group of friends, or where you decide what your career is going to be. Of course, college isn't for everybody, but since you picked up this book, our guess is that it's for you.

But here's the thing. Choosing to go to college is just the very first step. The next steps—choosing the right college for you and then getting there, and getting through all the way to graduation—are even more important. And that's where things really start to get exciting, scary, intimidating, thrilling, and, yeah, downright confusing.

It's a journey—an exploration, really. Remember reading about the explorers who were the first Europeans to encounter North America? Sailors who couldn't swim sailing across an ocean full of monsters to a New World they weren't sure existed? In some ways, you're like an explorer on a journey and you're not sure exactly where it will lead because it's sailing into the future and who can really know about that? The sheer amount of information can make you feel like you're in the noisy, swirling center of a disorienting storm. But here's the good news: you have a chart, marking the known obstacles and signaling where you're likely to hit a current that may be pushing you in the wrong direction. Our goal for this guide is to demystify the process of going to college. We want you to know about the resources that are free and available, and we want you to know the questions you can—and should—ask. We want you to avoid currents that seem convenient but will push you off course, we want you to build a network that will help you in every stage of your life, and we want you to pay as little as possible and graduate with a degree that matters.

This book will help you do all that successfully, in ways no other college guidebook on the market can, because it is different from those other books in four fundamental ways:

> Other books cater (though they don't come right out and say so) mostly to students from well-to-do families trying to get into the most exclusive, priciest schools. *The* Other *College Guide* is for every student. Whether you're rich, poor, or in the middle, or get straight As or mostly Cs, this book will help you find a challenging, high-quality school that's right for you.

> Other books, like *U.S. News & World Report Best Colleges*, rank schools based on how many students they turn away, or how much money they raise and spend, or how other college presidents rate them. But these metrics tell you next to nothing about how much actual learning goes on

in the classroom. They are mostly measures of *inputs*, not *outcomes*. So *The* Other *College Guide* ignores such criteria and instead ranks colleges based on the best available data about what really matters (or should matter) to *you*. Which schools will charge you a fair price and not bury you in debt (hint: you need to look beyond the sticker price)? Which schools help students like you graduate (going to college but not getting a degree is an almost complete waste of your time and money)? Which provide degrees that allow you to earn a decent income (at least enough to pay off your student loans, and hopefully a whole lot more)?

> Other books are full of happy talk about how wonderful America's higher education system is and how every college has something to offer. Baloney! There are a lot of terrible

colleges out there. We'll name names and help you avoid them. The system is confusing, complicated, full of trap doors, and often unfair. We'll guide you through it safely.

> Other books only profile the most prestigious colleges or the "Best Party Schools." We offer detailed profiles of 50 great schools that will maximize *your* chance of succeeding, academically and in life (the profiles begin on page 348).

From Imagination to Reality: Chapters 2–7

Chapter 2 asks you to imagine your future. Where is your future self? What are you doing for a living? How much do you earn? Imagining your future is all on you because no one can help you dream, but we can tell you this: most successful people have been reflective about their future career, and they figure out what they need to do to get there. Then they're strategic about picking a college that will help them gain the skills, abilities, knowledge, certification, and degrees that matter.

In Chapter 2, you will be guided through steps that match your interests and talents (the ones you have and the ones you will grow) with possible careers. It's important to be honest as you work through this process, but also have fun as you ask yourself what you *like* to do. The truth is, there is no single, straight-line path to success, but as you use the tools to explore your personality and interests, patterns will emerge, and they are likely to bunch together into a few career clusters.

The forces that change the world—technology, global politics, scientific advancements, catastrophes, demographics—are also changing the skills people need to engage in meaningful work. We'll guide you to experts who will give you a snapshot of the future job market, including the careers that will have the greatest demand and the educational preparation needed to break into the field that interests you. This section includes information on majors, careers, employment possibilities, and average earnings so that you can begin to translate your dreams (and it's okay if they're a little vague and shapeless at this point!) into goals that are specific and measurable.

Transforming an idea into reality means critically thinking about the steps you need to take to get there. That's why Chapter 3 includes a checklist to help you determine the kind of school that is right for you, which depends on who you are and your career goals. Students come from all backgrounds, with different needs, expectations, and goals, and there is no one-size-fits-all college that will meet all of them. In fact, there are so many different types of colleges (two-year and four-year, private and public, online and on the ground, and lots of blends in between) that it's downright intimidating. We'll guide you through this maze to help you find the type of degree you need for what you want to do and then find the college that will get you there.

Chapter 4 is *Washington Monthly*'s rankings chapter and includes four lists. The Best-Bang-for-the-Buck rankings include over 1,500 colleges sorted by region and answer a question we think you should be asking: What colleges will charge you the least and give you the highest chance of graduating with a degree that will actually get you a job? There are lots of choices out there, and though hardly anyone will tell you this, some of the colleges that will work hardest to recruit you are looking for paying students and may give you the least bang for your buck. The second ranking, Affordable Elite Colleges, includes only 224 colleges that are highly selective, and the third is a short list of the 50 best community colleges in the country.

Many people, notably among them African American students, factor in an additional consideration: *Should I go to a school with a history of service to a particular racial, cultural, or religious com-*

munity? To help with that decision, our fourth list ranks nearly eighty historically black colleges and universities (HBCUs), because if you're interested in an HBCU, you should approach your search with the same eye for fit and value as you would with any other category of school.

Chapter 5 is dedicated to the challenges that you'll face at a two-year college if your goal is a bachelor's degree. It's not an impossible bridge to cross, but there are some disconnects that we think you should be prepared for.

Chapters 6 and 7 are designed to help you take stock of where you are now. One of our experts in college preparation and planning told us: "I have met many students who have wasted a lot of time applying to colleges even though they have not met that college's requirements. Either they don't have the GPA or they have not taken courses needed to make them competitive."[1] With a lot of expert advice, these chapters will help you avoid that mistake and prepare for a successful college experience.

The Dreaded Admission and Financial Aid Processes: Chapters 8–10

It takes time to build a final list, and the chapters in this section are designed to help you add and subtract colleges, plan, and talk to parents and teachers. By fall of your senior year, you'll be ready to take the steps that will lead to admission, and you'll have a pretty good idea where you can get the best education for the best price. The path to admission and a favorable financial package is a slog because it takes a lot of energy and knowledge, but it's worth it. There are good questions that people in the know are asking, and we want you to be among them.

Some of you will be embarking on this journey with a supportive family or a group of friends who share your goal to go to college and are willing to do everything they can to help you get there. Some of you don't have that kind of support. Some of you may not be able to think of a single person in your family who's ever *been* to a college campus, much less gone through the harrowing application process. But no matter who you are or what your background is, don't be intimidated. Whether or not you can count on support from parents or family, think about the teachers you've had for all these years. Every single one of them successfully navigated the college process, and we're betting that somewhere along the line, there was one particular teacher you connected with. Go ahead. If you need a little perspective and encouragement, head on back to that fourth-grade classroom (you'll be amazed at how small the desks are). If you thought highly of a teacher, tell her that; we know she would be pleased. And even though she may not be able to guide you herself, she may be able to connect you with a network of college graduates who can. We also recommend that you use local public college resources (even if you don't plan to enroll there), and we'll give you some hints on how and when to approach them.

Chapters 8 and 9 provide advice and checklists to filter out some of the noise surrounding the application process. All colleges have posted deadlines, and you need to stay organized if you're going to stay on track. As the Chinese philosopher Laozi wrote twenty-five centuries ago: "The journey of a thousand miles begins with a single step." That step is yours to take.

Chapter 10 is a biggie. It's about paying for college, and while most experts say that college can be one of the wisest investments you can make, there's a caveat (that's a fancy word that means "warning") here: for that investment to pay off, you actually need to graduate—and you need to graduate without a crushing mountain of debt. It's unfortunate, but there are some institutions that will suck every penny of financial aid you have coming and leave you shipwrecked without a degree (or with limited skills) and with big debt. To complicate matters, comparing costs is not simple, since

The Considerator:

Go to College to Get a Better Job...
and for *a Lot* of Other Reasons

Exploring new and different academic disciplines and topics.

Being exposed to leaders and experts in science, the arts, and other fields

Learning to get along with others.

Having fun (parties, pranks, music, games, hanging out).

Becoming a more cultured person.

Preparing to make a positive difference in the world.

Finding opportunities to develop leadership skills.

Developing lifelong friendships and connections.

Developing a personal identity

Deepening and/or testing a spiritual commitment.

Getting to know people who are different from me.

Finding more people who are like me.

Developing a meaningful philosophy of life.

Participating in sports, clubs, and/or other extracurricular activities.

Experiencing a different place or living away from home.

every college will package financial aid differently, with some giving you lots of "free" (grant and scholarship) money and others giving you more loans. This chapter is designed to guide you through this treacherous gauntlet, pointing out trapdoors and shortcuts to help you figure out the best school for you that will challenge and reward you while keeping you from being lured by the siren song of false promises.

Making the Most of Your College Years: Chapters 11–13

Chapter 11 gives you some tips about how to make every college year count, from the first day of class freshman year to walking down that aisle wearing a cap and gown. We include lists of resources that are out there to help you succeed in school—especially in that crucial first year—and arm you with questions you should ask. (Spoiler alert: making it count isn't *only* about getting good grades.) Chapter 12 takes a look at how to line yourself up for future employment while you're still in college and how to think about what success means to you. In Chapter 13 our experts tell you how to make the most of your college years *and* set yourself up for a career through public, volunteer, or military service. Building skills while doing something that helps others reaps both social and personal benefits.

As you read this book, consider this: We know that one of the reasons many of you want to go to college is because you know that most of the jobs you might like require a college degree. But college is much more than a path to a good gig. It is an opportunity to be in a place where you will grow your talents, connect with others who share your goals, and learn to be a leader in your family, your community, and in the world. Take a look at the list of other reasons people go to college. As you think about your college choices, think about *your* reasons for going to college. Then think about where you want to be as you grow in knowledge, expand your network, and learn to engage with the world in a way that will get you where you want to go.

2.
MOVING UP
IN THE
WORLD

SETTING GOALS

AND

IMAGINING

YOUR FUTURE

Grow

Personality

Interests

Planning

Life

Investigate

Together Design

Support

Work

Money Business

Ideas

You plan to go to college, and that's good, because studies show that people who have college degrees are happier, healthier, and wealthier than people who don't.[3] Really! Another study puts a dollar figure on it—adults with bachelor's degrees earn 84 percent more over their lifetime than those with only a high school diploma.[4] That could be a million bucks!

These are all good reasons to go to college, but let's be honest: right now you're probably focused on just the next few years. A million dollars is a lot of money, but there's also a solid economic argument that it's less than that because while your friend is out there making money right out of high school, you're at college incurring debt. So you start out in a bit of a hole and it takes a while to

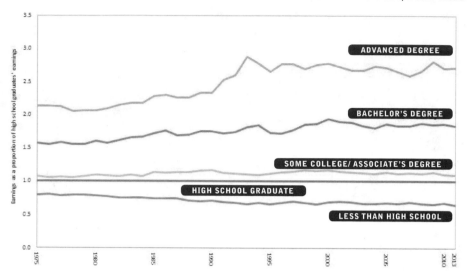

AVERAGE EARNINGS OF FULL-TIME, YEAR-ROUND WORKERS AS A PROPORTION OF THE AVERAGE EARNINGS OF HIGH SCHOOL GRADUATES BY EDUCATIONAL ATTAINMENT, 1975–2013

No matter what career you pursue, you are likely to earn more than you would have if you stopped your education at high school.

(UNITED STATES CENSUS BUREAU. 1975–2002 MARCH CURRENT POPULATION SURVEYS. 2005–2013 ANNUAL SOCIAL AND ECONOMIC SUPPLEMENT OF THE CURRENT POPULATION SURVEY.)

backfill. Then there are people who went to college and haven't landed in their dream job . . . yet. With a college degree you are likely to earn more in the long run and move into management positions that aren't available to those without a degree, but a college degree is not just about the job. It has to be about more than that, because it's something you earn, and it doesn't come easy or without some level of sacrifice. In fact, 35 percent of students who go to a four-year public college don't stay for their second year.[5] The ones who do make it have a purpose. That's what this chapter is about.

Start with Your Interests

Let's begin by delving into what interests you, because it's your interests that will carry you through life. When you meet someone who just *loves* what they do, it's not because what they're doing is easy.

Power Up for Success
While You're in High School

1. Take the most rigorous academic courses available including all the AP and honors courses you can.

2. *Pass Algebra 2 and take math all four years even if it's not your favorite subject.*

3. Stay continuously enrolled unless you are strategically taking a gap year.

4. *Maintain all As and Bs.*

5. Prepare to take the PSAT in October of your junior year, and the ACT and/or SAT in May or June of your junior year. And by prepare, we mean study up. Guides are available; sample questions are online. Put yourself in the driver's seat and prepare to do as well as you can. Check the College Board requirements online to see if you qualify for ACT and/or SAT fee waivers.

6. *If you have at least a 3.5 cumulative GPA, then get involved in extracurricular activities (but learn to prioritize so your academics don't suffer). If you're not pulling a 3.5, work on your grades.*

7. Volunteer in fields that reflect your career interests. Find out whether your school has partnerships with area employers or job shadow programs.

8. *Figure out the finances. (Use Chapter 9.)*

9. Have a purpose. Why are you going to college? What goal is going to get you through the hard parts?

Note: Some points are from the White House Initiative on Educational Excellence for Hispanics, "Graduate! A Financial Aid Guide to Success."[6]

In fact, it's probably not easy. They love it because it holds their attention. They keep chipping away at whatever they're doing because something about it excites them: they like to investigate or they enjoy analyzing documents, they like the thrill of the performance or the smile they bring to someone's face. They remain committed to what they're doing because they're interested in the outcome even if they don't love every task required to get the job done.

In this section, we connect your interests to possible careers with a six-step process:

1. **Reflect. Think quietly about who you want to be when you grow up.**

2. **Take inventory of your interests: they're what drive success.**

3. **Connect your interests with occupational personality types that have been developed by industrial psychologists.**

4. **Peruse careers that complement your personality.**

5. **Look at national research that shows the average earning power of degrees.**

6. **Put it all together.**

Step One: Reflect

Before you go for Google guidance, take a few minutes to be reflective. You, and everybody else these days, live in a world where everything's buzzing and beeping and there are so many pressures from the outside that it's hard to find a quiet space even inside your own head. But try. Turn everything off and spend some time visualizing your future.

Where are you living? What does your home look like? Describe your surroundings. Where are you working? What kind of work are you doing? Think about your daily routine. Does your work take you outside on occasion, or is it primarily in the field? If you're inside, what does your space look like? Where are your co-workers, and what are they doing? Are you working in a team or primarily alone? Close to home or far away? Imagine that you get recognized for an achievement. What did you do?

You may find the daydreaming part of this thought experiment kind of fun, but the real positive side effect of this kind of thinking is the next step: figuring out how you plan to get there. Steve Piscitelli at Florida State College gives his students a rubber bracelet with "H.T.R.B." on it: "hit the reset button." His message: If nothing is changing in your life and you're not headed where you want to go, hit the reset button![7]

Step Two:
Profile Your Interests

This next step brings you back to the present and introduces a tool developed by researchers that will help you get to that future you imagined. Our experts' advice to students at the front end of their educational journey is pretty straightforward: know your own personality, have a strategy, and start with an interest profile. Success begins when you build on what you're interested in.

Let's start with the interest profile. What is it and how do you get one? Basically, it is a series of questions that asks you whether you like performing a certain task. The Department of Labor's O*NET Interest Profiler is free and available on its My Next Move website (www.mynextmove.org), and it will generate bar charts showing how your interests span different occupational measures. If your high school uses college-planning software, there will be a link to an interest profiler on that site. There are dozens, but they all lead to the same six categories.

Step Three:
Link Your Interests with Occupational Personality Types

Industrial psychologists have come up with six basic categories that your interests, as measured by the profiler, lead to: Realistic, Investigative, Artistic, Social, Entrepreneurial, and Conventional. Each one of us is a unique blend of all of these types, so the personality mix that the Bureau of Labor Statistics O*Net Online profiler[8] gives you is like a view from thirty thousand feet—it's a picture that lacks specific details that make up who you are, but it's a good place to start.

Realistic. People with realistic interests like work that includes practical, hands-on problems and answers. Often people with realistic interests do not like careers that involve paperwork or working closely with others. Realistic people like working with plants, animals, and real-world materials such as wood, tools, and machinery. They often like outside work.

Investigative. People with investigative interests like work that has to do with ideas and thinking rather than physical activity or leading people. Investigative types like searching for facts and figuring out problems.

Artistic. People with artistic interests like work that deals with the artistic side of things, such as acting, music, art, and design. They like to have creativity in their work, and they like work that can be done without following a set of rules.

Social. People with social interests like working with others to help them learn and grow. They like working with people more than working with objects, machines, or information. Social interests often lead people to enjoy careers such as teaching, giving advice, helping, and being of service to others.

Enterprising.
People with enterprising interests like work that has to do with starting up and carrying out projects. These people like taking action rather than endlessly thinking about things. They like persuading and leading people, making decisions, and taking risks.

Conventional.
People with conventional interests like work that follows set procedures and routines. They prefer working with information and paying attention to details rather than working with ideas. They like working with clear rules and following a strong leader.

You're probably a blend of several of these categories. Some people have a little of everything and may be drawn to professions that require a range of talents. On the other hand, some people lean pretty heavily toward one type or another; you can see that in your friends. The person you'd call to help you build a website might not be the same person you'd call to help you plan a party or be the lead actor on a video project. Then again, it might be.

Step Four:
Link Your Personality Types with Career Goals

Getting from your general type to a specific career is definitely not a straight line. In fact, you'll likely have more than one career in your lifetime. College graduates who were born in the early 1980s had, on average, six or seven different types of jobs before they were twenty-six. Humans went to the moon for the first time during your parents or grandparents' lifetimes, and it's now possible for ordi-

CREATE A BOARD OF DIRECTORS FOR LIFE

In an ideal world, we'd all have awesome college counselors and sage teachers we could turn to. But most of us don't. Many of us don't even have parents we can turn to because they work all the time, or they never had the opportunity to go to college themselves, or they were never around to begin with. But that doesn't mean we don't have knowledgeable people in our lives whose advice we really, really trust. Who is that person for you? An aunt? A teacher? A pastor? A godparent? A coach? A cousin? A best friend? A former boss? Try to find at least three people in your life whom you respect and whose opinion you trust, and then do the same thing that successful CEOs do to stay on track and accountable: ask them to be on your own board of directors. Every time you need to make a major decision in life, call them up, email them, or simply ask, *What do you think I should do?* You don't have to follow their advice all the time (and sometimes you shouldn't!), but getting their opinions and really listening to their point of view will help keep you on track when life gets overwhelming or confusing.

nary (though very rich) people to take a shuttle up to space. People will think about cars needing drivers the same way you think about floppy discs. There's no limit to what you might accomplish if you're able to adapt to change and you're willing to put in the time and effort to develop your abilities. But no matter where you go or how much technology changes the way you think, you're going to carry your interests with you, which is why they're part of your personality type. Psychologists have taken the process one step further: from personalities to occupations that can be clumped into career clusters (pages 26–32) that are likely to be attractive to you based on your interests.

Do you like designing spaces? With plants, rocks, concrete, or recycled plastic? Would you like to counsel or teach people? Take care of animals? Think about what your favorite classes have been and why you liked them, or think about the television show you watched last night or the movie that you keep remembering. What careers intrigue you?

As you associate what you like to do with possible occupations, think about people who have inspired you. They can be real people, fictional characters, or people who have very public lives. If you aspire to be like them, think about what their daily lives are like, what skills they use, and what it is that you admire about them.

Talk to family and friends, teachers, counselors, and coaches, because sometimes other people see talents in you that you take for granted. You might not notice how patient you are with your grandmother who has Alzheimer's, but your mother or uncle sees it. You might not be aware that you really inspired a ten-year-old when you tutored him, but his teacher knows you're his hero. You might think that being good at art isn't a marketable skill, but several careers require a keen eye for color or the ability to quickly sketch an idea.

At this stage, don't think about whether or not you have the education or training to do the kind of job you're fantasizing about. You're not there yet, but one of the reasons you're going to college is to gain a whole new set of abilities, deepen your knowledge, and put all of this into practice doing something that interests you.

If you don't know exactly what career you want to pursue after college, you're certainly not alone. In fact, most high school students don't have a clue, and even many of the students who think they know end up changing course at least once. But that doesn't mean that you head off to college with a blindfold on. On the contrary, choosing the right college means that you have taken steps to direct the course of your life—even if the final destination isn't clear yet or it changes down the road, you have a general idea of why college is the next step.

So

WHERE ARE YOU GOING?

1. **Interests.** Do you like working with people . . . or numbers, or objects, or all of the above? Do you like to be in charge or would you rather report to someone else? Are you scientific or technical? Do you like detail work? Do you enjoy expressing yourself through art or music?

2. **Talents.** Do you have good writing and speaking skills? How about spatial perception and an understanding of how things fit together, or the ability to work with your hands? Are you good with numbers? What are your special talents?

3. **Personality.** Do you like to work under stress or under frequent deadlines? Do you like to do a variety of things or focus on one area? Are you generally upbeat and outgoing or more reflective and quiet?

4. **Education.** Are you a hands-on learner? Do you enjoy listening to lectures, or would you rather read? Do you like to put things together and take them apart? How do you like to learn?

5. **Working conditions.** Can you handle a noisy workplace or an intensely quiet one? Do you prefer to sit or stand? Do you like working indoors or outdoors? Could you work in a job where there is a risk of injury? Can you work in a health care setting, where people are sick or hurt?

6. **Pay and work hours.** How much money would you like to earn? Are you willing to travel? Are you willing to work the night shift, weekends, or overtime? Are you comfortable in a competitive, commission-only job? Or do you prefer a steady paycheck?

Source: Washington State Workforce Training and Education Coordinating Board, Where Are You Going? 2013–2015, www.wtb.wa.gov/Documents/CareerGuideweb.pdf.

After you've thought about these questions, take the Career Clusters Interest Survey.[9] The boxed questions on the quiz correspond to the career clusters listed on the pages that follow.

CAREER CLUSTERS INTEREST SURVEY

Name _____

School _____ Date _____

Directions: Circle the item in each box that best descibe you. You may make as many or as few circles in each box as you choose. Add up the number of circles in each box. Look to see which three boxes have the highest numbers. Find the corresponding Career Clusters on the pages immediately following this survey to see which Career Clusters you may want to explore.

BOX 1

Activities that describe what I like to do:

1. Learn how things grow and stay alive.
2. Make the best use of the earth's natural resources.
3. Hunt and/or fish.
4. Protect the environment.
5. Be outdoors in all kinds of weather.
6. Plan budget and keep records.
7. Operate machines and keep them in good repair.

Personal qualities that describe me:

1. Self-reliant
2. Nature lover
3. Physically active
4. Planner
5. Creative problem solver

School subjects that I like:

1. Math
2. Life Sciences
3. Earth Sciences
4. Chemistry
5. Agriculture

Total number circled in Box 1

BOX 2

Activities that describe what I like to do:

1. Read and follow blueprints and/or instructions.
2. Picture in my mind what a finished product looks like.
3. Work with my hands.
4. Perform work that requires precise results.
5. Solve technical problems.
6. Visit and learn from beautiful, historic, or interesting buildings.
7. Follow logical, step-by-step procedures.

Personal qualities that describe me:

1. Curious
2. Good at following directions
3. Pay attention to detail
4. Good at visualizing possibilities
5. Patient and persistent

School subjects that I like:

1. Math
2. Drafting
3. Physical Sciences
4. Construction Trades
5. Electrical Trades/ Heat, Air Conditioning and Refrigeration/ Technology Education

Total number circled in Box 2

BOX 3

Activities that describe what I like to do:

1. Use my imagination to communicate new information to others.
2. Perform in front of others.
3. Read and write.
4. Play a musical instrument.
5. Perform creative, artistic activities.
6. Use video and recording technology.
7. Design brochures and posters.

Personal qualities that describe me:

1. Creative and imaginative
2. Good communicator/ good vocabulary
3. Curious about new technology
4. Relate well to feelings and thoughts of others
5. Determined/tenacious

School subjects that I like:

1. Art/Graphic design
2. Music
3. Speech and Drama
4. Journalism/Literature
5. Audiovisual Technologies

Total number circled in Box 3

THE **OTHER** HELPFUL TOOL COLLEGE GUIDE

BOX 4

Activities that describe what I like to do:

1. Perform routine, organized activities but can be flexible.
2. Work with numbers and detailed information.
3. Be the leader in a group.
4. Make business contact with people.
5. Work with computer programs.
6. Create reports and communicate ideas.
7. Plan my work and follow instructions without close supervision.

Personal qualities that describe me:

1. Organized
2. Practical and logical
3. Patient
4. Tactful
5. Responsible

School subjects that I like:

1. Computer Applications/ Business and Information Technology
2. Accounting
3. Math
4. English
5. Economics

Total number circled in Box 4

BOX 5

Activities that describe what I like to do:

1. Communicate with different types of people.
2. Help others with their home-work or to learn new things.
3. Go to school.
4. Direct and plan activities for others.
5. Handle several responsibilities at once.
6. Acquire new information.
7. Help people overcome their challenges.

Personal qualities that describe me:

1. Friendly
2. Decision maker
3. Helpful
4. Innovative/inquisitive
5. Good listener

School subjects that I like:

1. Language Arts
2. Social Studies
3. Math
4. Science
5. Psychology

Total number circled in Box 5

BOX 6

Activities that describe what I like to do:

1. Work with numbers.
2. Work to meet a deadline.
3. Make predictions based on existing facts.
4. Have a framework of rules by which to operate.
5. Analyze financial information and interpret it to others.
6. Handle money with accuracy and reliability.
7. Take pride in the way I dress and look.

Personal qualities that describe me:

1. Trustworthy
2. Orderly
3. Self-confident
4. Logical
5. Methodical or efficient

School subjects that I like:

1. Accounting
2. Math
3. Economics
4. Banking/Financial Services
5. Business Law

Total number circled in Box 6

BOX 7

Activities that describe what I like to do:

1. Be involved in politics.
2. Negotiate, defend, and debate ideas and topics.
3. Plan activities and work cooperatively with others.
4. Work with details.
5. Perform a variety of duties that may change often.
6. Analyze information and interpret it to others.
7. Travel and see things that are new to me.

Personal qualities that describe me:

1. Good communicator
2. Competitive
3. Service-minded
4. Well-organized
5. Problem solver

School subjects that I like:

1. Government
2. Language Arts
3. History
4. Math
5. Foreign Language

Total number circled in Box 7

THE *OTHER* HELPFUL TOOL COLLEGE GUIDE

BOX 8

Activities that describe what I like to do:

1. Work under pressure.
2. Help sick people and animals.
3. Make decisions based on logic and information.
4. Participate in health and science classes.
5. Respond quickly and calmly in emergencies.
6. Work as a member of a team.
7. Follow guidelines precisely and meet strict standards of accuracy.

Personal qualities that describe me:

1. Compassionate and caring
2. Good at following directions
3. Conscientious and careful
4. Patient
5. Good listener

School subjects that I like:

1. Biological Sciences
2. Chemistry
3. Math
4. Occupational Health
5. Language Arts

Total number circled in Box 8

BOX 9

Activities that describe what I like to do:

1. Investigate new places and activities.
2. Work with all ages and types of people.
3. Organize activities in which other people enjoy themselves.
4. Have a flexible schedule.
5. Help people make up their minds.
6. Communicate easily, tactfully, and courteously.
7. Learn about other cultures.

Personal qualities that describe me:

1. Tactful
2. Self-motivated
3. Works well with others
4. Outgoing
5. Slow to anger

School subjects that I like:

1. Language Arts/ Speech
2. Foreign Language
3. Social Sciences
4. Marketing
5. Food Services

Total number circled in Box 9

BOX 10

Activities that describe what I like to do:

1. Care about people, their needs, and their problems.
2. Participate in community services and/or volunteering.
3. Listen to other people's viewpoints.
4. Help people be at their best.
5. Work with people from preschool age to old age.
6. Think of new ways to do things.
7. Make friends with different kinds of people.

Personal qualities that describe me:

1. Good communicator/ good listener
2. Caring
3. Non-materialistic
4. Intuitive and logical
5. Non-judgmental

School subjects that I like:

1. Language Arts
2. Psychology/Sociology
3. Family and Consumer Sciences
4. Finance
5. Foreign Language

Total number circled in Box 10

BOX 11

Activities that describe what I like to do:

1. Work with computers.
2. Reason clearly and logically to solve complex problems.
3. Use machines, techniques, and processes.
4. Read technical materials and diagrams and solve technical problems.
5. Adapt to change.
6. Play video games and figure out how they work.
7. Concentrate for long periods without being distracted.

Personal qualities that describe me:

1. Logical/analytical thinker
2. See details in the big picture
3. Persistent
4. Good concentration skills
5. Precise and accurate

School subjects that I like:

1. Math
2. Science
3. Computer Tech/ Applications
4. Communications
5. Graphic Design

Total number circled in Box 11

THE *OTHER* HELPFUL TOOL COLLEGE GUIDE

BOX 12

Activities that describe what I like to do:

1. Work under pressure or in the face of danger.
2. Make decisions based on my own observations.
3. Interact with other people.
4. Be in positions of authority.
5. Respect rules and regulations.
6. Debate and win arguments.
7. Observe and analyze people's behavior.

Personal qualities that describe me:

1. Adventurous
2. Dependable
3. Community-minded
4. Decisive
5. Optimistic

School subjects that I like:

1. Language Arts
2. Psychology/ Sociology
3. Government/History
4. Law Enforcement
5. First Aid/First Responder

Total number circled in Box 12

BOX 13

Activities that describe what I like to do:

1. Work with my hands and learn that way.
2. Put things together.
3. Do routine, organized, and accurate work.
4. Perform activities that produce tangible results.
5. Apply math to work out solutions.
6. Use hand and power tools and operate equipment.
7. Visualize objects in three dimensions from flat drawings.

Personal qualities that describe me:

1. Practical
2. Observant
3. Physically active
4. Step-by-step thinker
5. Coordinated

School subjects that I like:

1. Math-Geometry
2. Chemistry
3. Trade and Industry
4. Physics
5. Language Arts

Total number circled in Box 13

BOX 14

Activities that describe what I like to do:

1. Shop and go to the mall.
2. Be in charge.
3. Make displays and promote ideas.
4. Give presentations and enjoy public speaking.
5. Persuade people to buy products or to participate in activities.
6. Communicate my ideas to other people.
7. Take advantage of opportunities to make extra money.

Personal qualities that describe me:

1. Enthusiastic
2. Competitive
3. Creative
4. Self-motivated
5. Persuasive

School subjects that I like:

1. Language Arts
2. Math
3. Business Education/ Marketing
4. Economics
5. Computer Applications

Total number circled in Box 14

BOX 15

Activities that describe what I like to do:

1. Interpret formulas.
2. Find the answers to questions.
3. Work in a laboratory.
4. Figure out how things work and investigate new things.
5. Explore new technology.
6. Experiment to find the best way to do something.
7. Pay attention to details and help things be precise.

Personal qualities that describe me:

1. Detail-oriented
2. Inquisitive
3. Objective
4. Methodical
5. Mechanically inclined

School subjects that I like:

1. Math
2. Science
3. Drafting/ Computer-Aided Drafting
4. Electronics/Computer Networking
5. Technical Classes/ Technology Education

Total number circled in Box 15

THE *OTHER* HELPFUL TOOL COLLEGE GUIDE

BOX 16

Activities that describe what I like to do:

1. Travel.
2. See well and have quick reflexes.
3. Solve mechanical problems.
4. Design efficient processes.
5. Anticipate needs and prepare to meet them.
6. Drive or ride.
7. Move things from one place to another.

Personal qualities that describe me:

1. Realistic
2. Mechanical
3. Coordinated
4. Observant
5. Planner

School subjects that I like:

1. Math
2. Trade and Industry
3. Physical Sciences
4. Economics
5. Foreign Language

Total number circled in Box 8

Disclaimer: *Your interests may change over time. These survey results are intended to assist you with informal career exploration. Consider more formal assessments and other resources or services to help you plan your career. This survey does not make any claims of statistical reliability.*

This survey does not make any claims of statistical reliability and has not been normed. It is intended for use as a guidance tool to generate discussion regarding careers and is valid for this purpose. (SOURCE: ADAPTED FROM THE GUIDANCE DIVISION SURVEY, OKLAHOMA DEPARTMENT OF CAREER AND TECHNOLOGY EDUCATION (2005))

Now

Career Clusters Linked to Your Interests

After you've taken the Career Clusters Interest Survey, you'll be able to match your interests with some of the careers listed in the groups below.

1. Agriculture, Food, and Natural Resources.

The production, processing, marketing, distribution, financing, and development of agricultural commodities and resources, including food, fiber, wood products, natural resources, horticulture, and other plant and animal products/resources.

2. Architecture and Construction. Careers in designing, planning, managing, building, and maintaining the built environment.

THE *OTHER* HELPFUL TOOL COLLEGE GUIDE

3. Arts, A/V Technology, and Communications.
Designing, producing, exhibiting, performing, writing, and publishing multimedia content, including visual and performing arts and design, journalism, and entertainment services.

4. Business Management and Administration.
Careers in planning, organizing, directing, and evaluating business functions essential to efficient and productive business operations.

5. Education and Training.
Planning, managing, and providing education and training services and related learning support services, such as administration, teaching/training, administrative support, and professional support services.

6. Finance.
Planning and related services for financial and investment planning, banking, insurance, and business financial management.

7. Government and Public Administration.
Planning and executing government functions at the local, state, and federal levels, including governance, national security, foreign service, planning, revenue and taxation, and regulations.

8. Health Science.
Planning, managing, and providing therapeutic services, diagnostic services, health informatics, support services, and biotechnology research and development.

9. Hospitality and Tourism.
Management, marketing, and operations of restaurants and other food/beverage services, lodging, travel and tourism, recreation, amusement, and attractions.

10. Human Services.
Planning, managing, and providing services that relate to families and human needs, such as counseling and mental health services, family and community services, personal care, and consumer services.

11. Information Technology. Designing, developing, supporting, and managing hardware, software, multimedia, and systems integration services.

12. Law, Public Safety, Corrections, and Security. Planning, managing, and providing legal services, public safety, protective services, and homeland security, including professional and technical support services.

13. Manufacturing. Planning, managing, and performing the processing of materials into intermediate or final products and related professional and technical support activities such as production planning and control, maintenance, and manufacturing/process engineering.

14. Marketing. Planning, managing, and performing marketing activities to reach organizational objectives such as brand management, professional sales, merchandising, marketing communications, and market research.

15. Science, Technology, Engineering, and Mathematics. Planning, managing, and providing scientific research and professional and technical services (e.g., physical science, social science, engineering), including laboratory and testing services and research and development services.

16. Transportation, Distribution, and Logistics. The planning, management, and movement of people, materials, and goods by road, pipeline, air, rail, and water, plus related professional and technical support services such as transportation infrastructure planning and management, logistics services, and mobile equipment and facility maintenance.

Step 5:
To Meditate (or Not) on Money

Another reason to take a look at the jobs that will be out there when you graduate is that unless you're a bazillionaire, chances are that making money will be an important part of your life. But how important? It's a safe bet that when you imagine your future, you are likely not living in your parents' basement and eating Top Ramen for every meal. You might, however, be imagining that you land in a fairy tale with a gigantic salary that, while not impossible, is statistically unlikely—like being a professional athlete or a famous actor. You might make it (and a handful do), but it helps to be honest with yourself. According to NCAA statistics, for example, fewer than 1 percent of the men and women who play baseball, football, ice hockey, basketball, or soccer in high school will ever be drafted by a professional league, and only a few them will ever make the team. Even those lucky few only play a few years. Then they, like everyone else, need to find a career, too.

The point here is not to trample your dreams but to give you the information you need to make an informed decision about the education you need to lead the kind of life you want.[10] When you think about your future career, think about what fields are growing, where the jobs are going to be, and what sort of things you're good at. But also think about what you want your daily life to look like. Where do you live? What skills, abilities, or knowledge do you want the people you're working with to have? Do you like the idea of working in a hospital? A greenhouse? A lab? At a computer? In an office? In a classroom? In remote backcountry? Would you choose a job that you hate just because it pays well?

Maybe.

While the lure of a high income is one reason students pursue higher education, it is not the only reason. Many are looking to make a living while doing something personally meaningful and that often involves serving causes larger than themselves. Sometimes

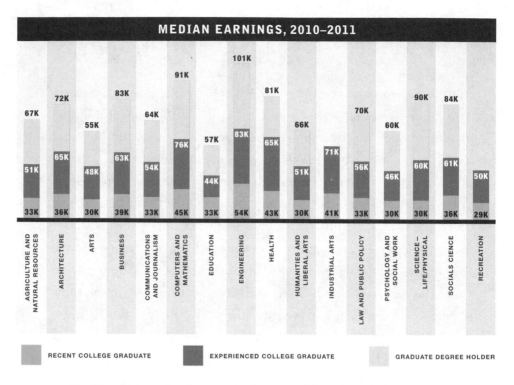

MEDIAN EARNINGS, 2010–2011

Field	Recent	Experienced	Graduate
Agriculture and Natural Resources	33K	51K	67K
Architecture	36K	65K	72K
Arts	30K	48K	55K
Business	39K	63K	83K
Communications and Journalism	33K	54K	64K
Computers and Mathematics	45K	76K	91K
Education	33K	44K	57K
Engineering	54K	83K	101K
Health	43K	65K	81K
Humanities and Liberal Arts	30K	51K	66K
Industrial Arts	41K	71K	70K
Law and Public Policy	33K	56K	70K
Psychology and Social Work	30K	46K	60K
Science—Life/Physical	30K	60K	90K
Socials Cience	36K	61K	84K
Recreation	29K	50K	50K

RECENT COLLEGE GRADUATE   EXPERIENCED COLLEGE GRADUATE   GRADUATE DEGREE HOLDER

Median earnings of college graduates range fairly widely, but you can see that experience counts. (SOURCE: GEORGETOWN UNIVERSITY ON EDUCATION AND THE WORKFORCE, *HARD TIMES: COLLEGE MAJORS, UNEMPLOYMENT AND EARNINGS.*)

it comes with a smaller paycheck but a greater sense of fulfillment (and in many cases lots of other tangible benefits, like money to pay for college; see Chapter 13). The truth is, most of us are not going to become petroleum engineers, lawyers, or heart surgeons simply because of those occupations' earning potential. Making a living is about much more than earning money; it's about making a life. For a lot of people, that could mean making less money but having more time to be with family or to pursue interests that aren't work-related. If you ask people about their career satisfaction, you'll find that it often comes because the work matters to the people they're serving, the planet they're protecting, the stories they're telling, or the cause they're promoting.

Occupations that have a "Bright Outlook"

The Bureau of Labor Statistics labels over a hundred occupations "bright outlook" because they are either projected to grow much faster than average (employment increase of 22 percent or more) over the period 2012–2022 and/or are projected to have 100,000 or more job openings over the period 2012–2022. Nationwide for the next ten years, technology-related occupations and teaching will have the most openings for individuals with bachelor's degrees. Accountants, auditors, construction managers, and market research analysts also make the big-growth list, but there are dozens you may not have thought about. These include:

Cytogenetic Technologists Analyze chromosomes found in biological specimens

Environmental Restoration Planner Collaborate with field and biology staff to oversee restoration projects and develop new products

Intelligence Analyst Gather, analyze, and evaluate information

Interpreter or Translator Interpret oral or sign language, or translate written text from one language into another

Logistician May be responsible for the entire life cycle of a product

Mental Health Counselor Provides counseling with emphasis on prevention

Photonics Engineer Design technologies specializing in light energy

You get the idea! There are hundreds of "bright outlook" occupations that you don't see every day. Click on any occupation at mynextmove.org to see the minimum educational requirements, and click on the "check out my state" link to see the demand in your state.

| Occupation | 2010 Total jobs ('000) | Rank | 2020 Total jobs ('000) | Rank | Changes in employment 2010–2020 | | Rank | |
					Increase in jobs ('000)	Rate of growth (% change)	Largest growth	Fastest growth
Healthcare professional & technical	6,480	6	8,490	6	2,010	31	5	1
Healthcare support	3,660	9	4,610	9	950	26	9	2
Community services & arts	6,290	7	7,920	7	1,630	26	9	3
STEM	6,050	8	7,600	8	1,550	26	8	4
Education	8,160	5	10,120	5	1,960	24	6	5
Managerial & professional office	19,980	4	24,740	4	4,760	24	1	6
Social science	700	10	830	10	130	19	10	7
Food & personal services	23,220	3	27,380	3	4,160	18	3	8
Sales & office support	37,660	1	42,130	1	4,470	12	2	9
Blue collar	28,400	2	30,750	2	2,350	8	4	10
Total Jobs and rate of growth (% change)	**140,600**		**164,590**		**23,990**	**17**		

Some of the occupations that do the most good are among the fastest growing occupational clusters—opportunities for those who are prepared to take advantage of them. (SOURCE: GEORGETOWN UNIVERSITY ON EDUCATION AND THE WORKFORCE, *RECOVERY: JOB GROWTH AND EDUCATION REQUIREMENTS THROUGH 2020*.)

Step 6:
Put It All Together

Lots of people start college but don't finish. We began this chapter asking you to imagine a whole huge future and then connect that dream back to your interests, your personality, and careers that are likely to be a match for you. We don't want you to be among the non-finishers. If you have a purpose for your journey, you're starting off on the right foot. You should be ready to pack your metaphorical travel bag with a dream, several interests, a complex blend of personality types, and a few good reasons for going to college.

1. A dream: One day I will

_____

_____

_____

_____

2. I am interested in

_____

_____

_____

3. My personality is a complex mix of Realistic, Investigative, Artistic, Social, Entrepreneurial, and Conventional, but mostly I think I'm

_____

4. Some careers that I am interested in are

_____

_____

_____

5. The reason I'm going to college is

_____

_____

_____

3.

IF THE SCHOOL FITS, PICK IT

FINDING YOUR TYPE OF COLLEGE

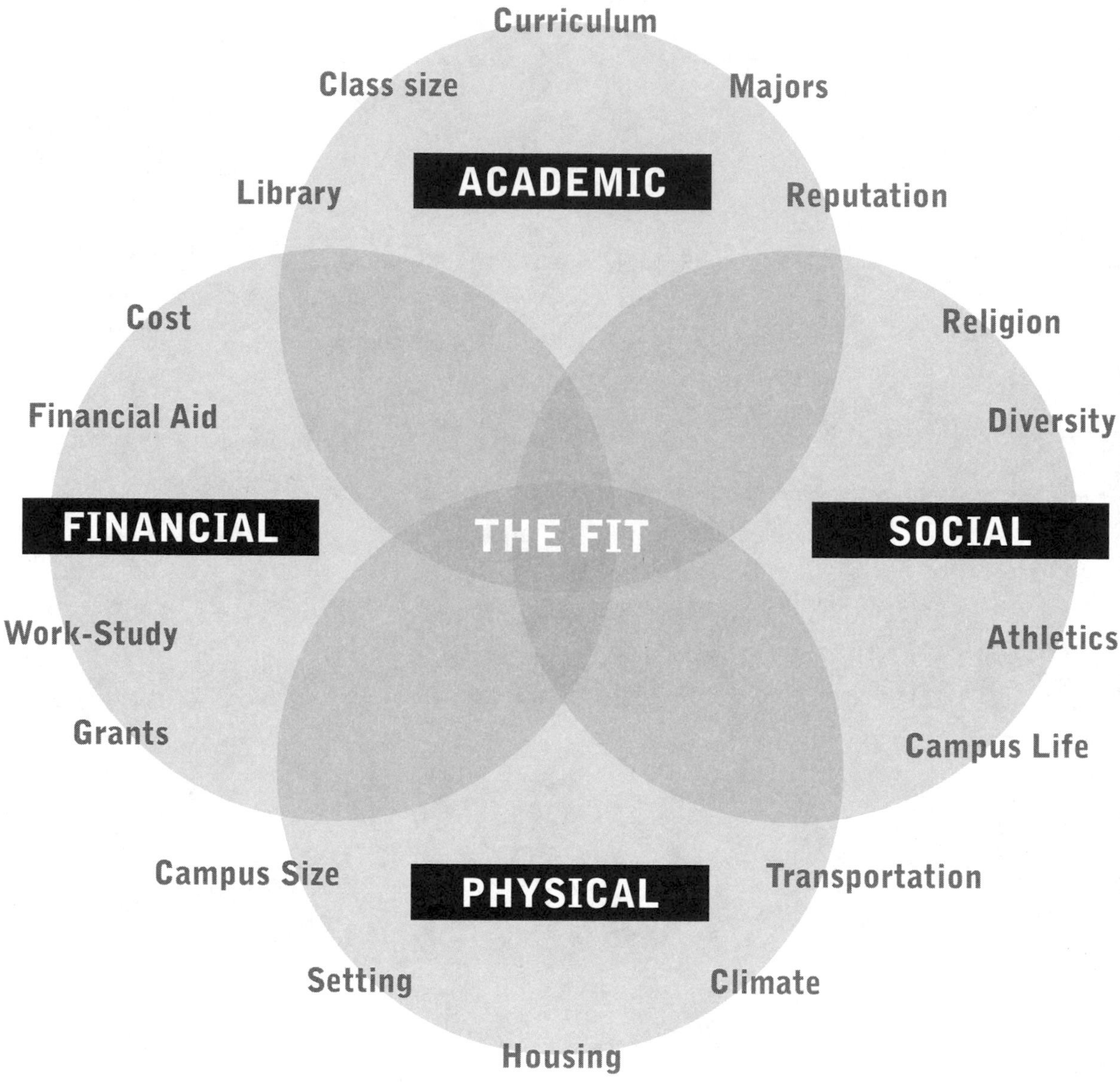

Curriculum

Class size

Majors

ACADEMIC

Library

Reputation

Cost

Religion

Financial Aid

Diversity

FINANCIAL

THE FIT

SOCIAL

Work-Study

Athletics

Grants

Campus Life

Campus Size

PHYSICAL

Transportation

Setting

Climate

Housing

When it comes to choosing a college, a lot of the advice you're going to hear is giddy and positive and encouraging: "Choose the college that feels right!" "Reach for the stars!" "All colleges are good for different people!" And while none of that's *bad* advice per se, it's also not that helpful. Our goal is to help you demystify the educational pipeline, because finding the right college for you is more than finding a place that matches your academic achievements. It's about finding an environment that is socially, culturally, academically, and physically a good fit, because completing college is both a goal in itself and a means to a future life.[11]

You can't ignore who you are or where you come from or what your family talked about at the dinner table. That's where this chapter comes in. This isn't a sunny pep talk about your grand future; it's a road map that will help you figure out how to tell apart the 3,900 accredited colleges that grant associate's degrees or higher in the United States. How are they the same? How are they different? What's accreditation and why should you care? (See the sidebar.) What kind of degrees do different colleges offer, and how will your experience differ at a public, private, or for-profit school? Can you transfer between them? (Hint: Sometimes, but not always.) We start this chapter with the whole bundle of colleges and sort them into two main groups: four-year and two-year. We touch on vocational schools because some of these are good options if your goal does not require a bachelor's degree. In this chapter, we focus on four-year colleges and universities; Chapter 5 is all about the possibilities (and pitfalls) of the two-year route if your actual goal is a bachelor's degree.

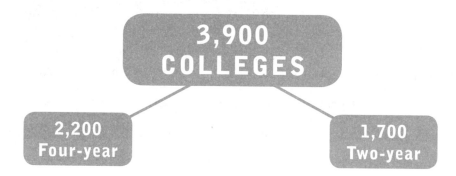

Types of Colleges

3,900 COLLEGES

2,200 Four-year

1,700 Two-year

Four-Year Colleges

There are 2,200 accredited four-year colleges, and they all award bachelor's or baccalaureate degrees, which are the same thing.[12] You can earn a bachelor's degree in the arts (BA) or a bachelor's degree in science (BS), depending on your major.

What's Accreditation and Why Should You Care?

Most students don't know what accreditation is, much less think to ask whether their college is accredited or not. So why should you care? Two words: *caveat emptor*. That's Latin for "buyer beware," which is another way of saying, *Don't get screwed*.

Here's the scoop: Some schools post a shiny gold seal from an accrediting agency in their front hall or on the landing page of their website. This looks impressive and it would seem to indicate that they all belong to one giant, friendly group where credits and courses can flow from one to the other.

Not so.

Accreditation allows institutions to award federal financial aid. It does not necessarily mean that their courses are transferable to another institution, or even that they serve their students well.

Within this large category of colleges, there are subcategories that are more or less self-explanatory. For example, you can go to an engineering school, or to a seminary or rabbinical college. Another large grouping is liberal arts colleges, which are schools whose curricula are rooted in a classical tradition of education, emphasizing history, literature, fine arts, and the development of character.[13] Every liberal arts college has a unique curriculum, but in general, they focus on teaching and undergraduate education and most of their degrees are awarded in a broad range of subjects spanning the arts, humanities, social sciences, and hard sciences.

Universities are in the four-year category, but in addition to the bachelor's degree they offer master's and doctoral degrees and often include research as part of their school mission. Within a single university, you might find professional schools of law, medicine, and business as well as liberal arts colleges. If your long-term goal includes an advanced or professional degree, you can complete your undergraduate work at either a college or a university.

Public? Private? For-Profit? What's the Difference?

All four-year colleges award bachelor's degrees. Depending on your family income and how much need-based financial aid you receive, the net price for you (what you actually need to pay) could be as little as $1,000 a year or as much as $65,000 a year. To understand this huge disparity, it's useful to understand where the colleges' funding is coming from.

Public colleges get some of their financing from tuition, but they also get some of it from state or local taxes. That's why state colleges have lower tuition for in-state students, because state residents are supporting the college with their tax dollars. If you are coming from out of state, tuition at a state school could be as high as (or higher than) a private nonprofit college. On the other hand, states in some regions have reciprocal agreements to offer reduced tuition to students from other states in that region, benefiting students from the region by increasing their choices and reducing tuition.[14] Public colleges vary widely in size, cost, quality, and the kind of degrees they award. Most community colleges are public, for example, and so are the big state flagships, which are often the oldest and most well-known universities in the state. Flagships are public, supported in part by taxpayer dollars, but not all colleges with a state or city in their name are either public or flagships. University of Washington, Indiana University at Bloomington, University of Texas at Austin, and University of Maine are examples of state flagships.

Private, nonprofit colleges don't get tax dollars, which is why the sticker price is usually higher, though private funding sometimes means there's more financial aid (either need-based or merit-based) available. Private nonprofit colleges also vary widely in size, cost, and quality. Almost all the Ivy League schools that you probably know by name—Harvard, Yale, Princeton, Dartmouth, the University of Pennsylvania—are in this category, but there are many other excellent, private nonprofit schools that may be an affordable fit for you.

How Much Education Do I Need?

The simple answer is: It depends on the career you want. The U.S. Department of Labor's website www.mynextmove.org is a place to start, but our experts warn that the education level posted there is often the minimum required. Sometimes you can get in with an associate's degree, but to advance, you need a bachelor's.

For-profit colleges are privately run companies offering a range of degrees; the National Association for College Admission Counseling points out that they're called for-profit because they're in business to earn money for their owners.[15] One question an informed consumer should ask a representative of a for-profit college: Will the credits I earn at your college transfer to a public university or a private college? Knowing the answer to that question in advance will help you understand your options for transferring, or for earning a master's or professional degree later.

Public two-year colleges vary, but all of them offer associate's degrees (in sciences, AS, and in arts, AA) and certificates of completion that meet requirements for some occupations (like culinary or hospitality management, fire technology, real estate appraisal, or tax preparation). Many degree paths at community colleges include "general education" requirements, and while the specific curriculum is unique to the campus, general education courses are generally designed to prepare students to transfer to four-year colleges. In general, most community colleges have an open-access, open-door philosophy: almost anyone, regardless of their grades or career goals, is welcome.[17] Our list of America's fifty best community colleges and information on how to research community colleges in your area can be found in Chapter 4.

Should You Go to a Two-Year College, *Then* Transfer?

Whew. That's a loaded question. Some people say yes: *It's a much cheaper option! And it's closer to home!* And some say hell no: 75 *percent of the students who go to a community college intending to transfer never do!*[16] Our answer is a little more nuanced, because the truth is, it depends on the degree you're going for and on your financial situation—lots of folks have no alternative. If your long-term goal is to end up with an associate's degree or a vocational certificate, or to prepare for a specific licensing exam, then the answer is yes, go to a community college. But if your goal is to end up with a bachelor's degree, then the answer is no. (Or, at the very least, a highly qualified maybe, but for now think of it as not-if-you-can-help-it.)

That may be contrary to the advice you've been given in the past. After all, millions of people—and probably lots of people you know— start their quest for a bachelor's degree at a community college. But if you're considering that path yourself, find some rubber boots, slap on a little mosquito repellent, and pack a flashlight, because navigating the community college transfer system can be a little bit like taking a walk in a swamp after dark, and you need a strategy. (See Chapter 5.)

Vocational Schools

Vocational schools, also called "career schools," generally do not lead to either associate's or bachelor's degrees, but they do train for a variety of jobs, so they can be a good choice if they're reputable and if the training they offer is your end goal. Some vocational schools partner with colleges to provide opportunities to earn college credit while learning a skill. Students at Pennsylvania's Lehigh Career and Technical Institute, for example, receive both college credit and a professional certification in metalworking for learning to use high-tech computer-controlled machining equipment such as a precision lathe.[18] One of our experts warned that some vocational schools will prepare you for a job that doesn't really exist, so do your homework before you pay for something that won't get you anywhere.[19]

Never assume that credit from a vocational school (or, for that matter, many private for-profit colleges) will transfer to a public college or university. Admission staff at state universities will acknowledge that it's hard to tell people who may have spent thousands of dollars already that they have to start over. The Federal Trade Commission is pretty straightforward, warning, "Not all these schools are reputable. Research any school you hope to attend, its training program, its record of job placement for graduates, and its fees before you commit. Look into alternatives, like community colleges. The tuition may be less than at private schools," even for the same or a similar course of study.[20]

Graduation Time by Program or Degree and Type of School.

Source: http://studentaid.ed.gov/prepare-for-college/choosing-schools/types

Program or Degree Graduate	Schools Where Offered	Typical to Graduation Time
Career, technical, trade, or vocational courses	Career, technical, vocational, and trade schools Community and junior colleges	1–2 years
Associate's degree	Community and junior colleges	2 years
Bachelor's degree	Four-year colleges and universities	4 years

Which Four-Year Colleges Are Right for You?

You know when you go to the supermarket and there are about a million choices on every aisle? Take bread, for example. Some loaves are sliced, some aren't; some have nuts and seeds, many don't; some are gluten-free, and others are sugar coated. They're all called bread, but the crunchy, nutty harvest loaf isn't anything like the sliced white bread. Which ones are good for you? Which ones are *better* for you? Which ones have the most attractive packaging?

There's the same abundance of choice when it comes to colleges. There are private colleges, public universities, and for-profit academies; big state flagships and tiny liberal arts schools.[21] They're all on the same shelf, but they are not all the same. So before you come home with a choice based on the most eye-catching packaging (without realizing what you bought), look critically at each college through a four-way lens: academic, financial, social, and physical.

Academic. Is it the right type of college for your career goal? Have you met the requirements for admission? How likely are you to be admitted? If you've worked really hard to get where you are, will this college be the right academic challenge for you? Does it have the resources to support you academically?

Financial. Is it affordable *for you*? How do you know what you are likely to have to pay? (Hint: Don't necessarily be discouraged by a high sticker price. Depending on your grades and financial situation, an expensive private school could end up being way cheaper for you than the state school nearby.)

Social. When you're choosing a college, you're also choosing to hang around with a group of people. Some of them will become

47

your friends, some will join your professional network, and some will connect you to their network, which may extend far beyond the boundaries of the college or even the country. We're going to talk more about the importance of networking in Chapter 12, but as you think about choosing a college, you should also think about college as an opportunity to meet new people. Is this a campus where you will connect with people who share your interests and goals? Will you be comfortable being you? Will you have an opportunity to meet leaders? Is it important for you to be around people who are like you, or do you want to be around people from different places and with different experiences? What will you be doing when you're not in class? Will you have opportunities to become a leader yourself? Is this campus likely to have other students who share your interests?

Anthony Antonio, professor of education at Stanford University, does research that focuses on racial and cultural diversity in colleges. His advice is that if you will be among a numerical minority on campus, see if the college has a multicultural center, because this is often the way that institutions codify their support for a group. More important, the role that these centers play is to create supportive, smaller subcommunities by making it easy to come together, meet, and support one another through challenges that might be different for students who are not in a majority population.[22]

Physical. Where is it, how big is it, and what does it look like? Is it close to art galleries, cow pastures, or both? Is it the right distance from home? Will you be living on campus or off? How do people get around? How will you get back and forth from home? What's the weather like?

There are several interactive websites that will guide you through the sorting process we're outlining. The U.S. Department of Education's College Navigator, the White House's College Scorecard, the College Board's Big Future, the Ed Trust's College Results, and The Institute for College Access and Success's College Insight are trustworthy and

Do Not Let Application Fees Stop You!

Application fee waivers are available from the colleges and from the National Association for College Admission Counseling (NACAC) to families that qualify.

You are eligible to use the form if:

✦ You have received or are eligible to receive an ACT or SAT testing fee waiver. (The testing fee waiver forms are available from your high school.)

✦ You are enrolled in or eligible for free or reduced-price lunches through the National School Lunch Program.

✦ Your annual family income falls within the income eligibility guidelines set by the USDA Food and Nutrition Service.

✦ You are enrolled in a federal, state, or local program that aids students from low-income families (For example, TRIO programs such as Upward Bound.)

✦ Your family receives public assistance. (For example, does your family use an EBT card to buy groceries or other household needs?)

✦ You live in federally subsidized public housing (Section 8 or a city-based housing development), a foster home, or are homeless.

✦ You are a ward of the state or an orphan.

Go to www.nacacnet.org and download the waiver, or copy it from page 50.

Request for Admission Application Fee Waiver

National Association for College Admission Counseling
Guiding the way to higher education

SEND THIS FORM DIRECTLY TO THE POSTSECONDARY INSTITUTION/ORGANIZATION

TO: DEAN/DIRECTOR OF ADMISSION AT _____

NAME OF COLLEGE OR UNIVERSITY

STUDENT: Print or type the information requested below. You must **personally** sign the Certification Statement.

CERTIFICATION STATEMENT: *I certify that I understand and meet all eligibility requirements to request an admission application fee waiver.*

STUDENT'S NAME   STUDENT'S SIGNATURE

STUDENT'S ADDRESS   CITY   STATE   ZIP

AUTHORIZED OFFICIAL: Print or type the information requested below, and check the indicator(s) of economic need. You must **personally** sign the Certification Statement.

CERTIFICATION STATEMENT: *I certify that the student named on this form is currently enrolled in the 11th or 12th grade at this school and meets the indicator(s) of economic need checked below.*

AUTHORIZED OFFICIAL'S NAME   AUTHORIZED OFFICIAL'S SIGNATURE

AUTHORIZED OFFICIAL'S TITLE   AUTHORIZED OFFICIAL'S EMAIL

NAME OF SECONDARY EDUCATIONAL INSTITUTION OR ORGANIZATION   CEEB# OR PROGRAM #

ADDRESS   PHONE

ECONOMIC NEED: The student must meet at least one of the following indicators of economic need. If no item is checked, the request will be denied.

☐ Student has received or is eligible to receive an ACT or SAT testing fee waiver.

☐ Student is enrolled in or eligible to participate in the Federal Free or Reduced Price Lunch program (FRPL).

☐ Student's annual family income falls within the income Eligibility Guidelines* set by the USDA Food and Nutrition Service.

☐ Student is enrolled in a federal, state or local program that aids students from low-income families (e.g., TRIO programs such as Upward Bound).

☐ Student's family receives public assistance.

☐ Student lives in federally subsidized public housing, a foster home or is homeless.

☐ Student is a ward of the state or an orphan.

☐ Other request from high school principal, high school counselor, financial aid officer, or community leader:

> Given my knowledge of this student's family circumstances and after reviewing the eligibility guidelines, I believe that providing the application fee would present a hardship. Explanation:
>
> _____
>
> _____
>
> _____

SCHOOL SEAL/STAMP

*To view USDA Income Eligibility Guidelines for the Free or Reduced Price Lunch Program or review FAQs related to this form visit http://bit.ly/NACACfeewaiver.

THE *OTHER* HELPFUL TOOL
COLLEGE GUIDE

Sharing Your Profile

When you check a box that says it's okay if colleges contact you, or you register on a website, you are entering the world of "active matching." That is, you are college shopping, and many schools are student hunting. This matching process can lead you to schools you never thought about, but it also can be overwhelming and misleading because it is not necessarily a guarantee that you will be admitted to a school that contacts you. If you get this kind of invitation and the school looks like it's a fit for you, follow up with your questions—including what your financial aid package will be. On the other hand, don't be pressured by a recruiter.[23] "Using high-pressure sales tactics to shame or intimidate millions of vulnerable students to enroll, these companies have abused the trust of American taxpayers and have potentially ruined the financial well-being of those they purport to assist," says NACAC's David Hawkins.[24]

have a lot of great information, and you can go through them without registering, changing your choices as many times as you want.

As you research colleges, think about what you're doing as the mirror of what an admission office does in selecting students. They start with thousands of applications and, using test scores, GPA, personal statements, and recommendations, put each one through a process measuring it against their criteria. The process includes weighting some parts of your application more heavily than others, evaluating the whole package, and "grading" it. You can kind of imagine all the applications on a scattergram—the college scoops up the ones that meet their criteria.*

Just as a college begins with more applicants than it will admit or enroll, your process may begin with a long list of possibilities. But as

---

* This process sounds pretty mechanical, and at some level it is. If you haven't taken required classes, or don't meet the minimum GPA requirement, a computer could deny your admission. If a school has a comprehensive application process (essays, portfolios, letters of recommendation) more human judgment is involved throughout the evaluation process. In all cases, however, there are humans behind the machines. If you have a story to tell, get to a human.

you think through the four-way fit process, some of the colleges will drop off your list because they aren't affordable, or won't challenge you, or don't have the type of courses you're interested in taking. By the time you get to your short list, you'll know that you will be happy on any of the campuses you've chosen.

The Four-Way Fit

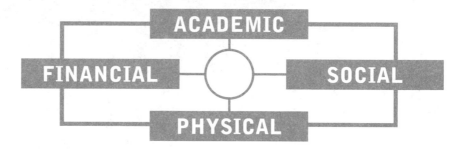

This section will help you think about ways to evaluate colleges by how well they match you academically, financially, socially, and physically.

Academic Fit

There are two parts of the academic fit: the college's side and your side. On the college's side, there are degrees of selectivity. On your side, it's what you bring to the table—do you have the academic credentials to be admitted?

SELECTIVITY

This is the news that gets lots of attention at admission time, but don't let it stress you or your parents out. You can't push this river! Selectivity is simply the ratio of admitted applicants to total applicants written as a percentage. The College Board uses the following categories:

- ✛ *Open admission (all or most admitted)*
- ✛ *Less selective (75 percent admitted)*
- ✛ *Somewhat selective (50–75 percent admitted)*
- ✛ *Very selective (25–50 percent admitted)*
- ✛ *Most selective (< 25 percent admitted)*

Some schools are so selective they admit less than 10 percent of their applicants even though nearly all of the people who apply are fully qualified. They're brilliant, harp-playing star soccer players, and many are also valedictorians, and they don't all get in. You get the picture. If you're applying to a "most selective" school, keep in mind it's a reach no matter how many amazing accomplishments you've racked up. It's a reach for *everyone*.

You should know about the level of selectivity for the colleges you're applying to because it will give you an opportunity to give it your best shot, but you cannot be in the room with the admission committee. They are looking at what you gave them. If they invite you to an interview, be yourself. Try to think of the whole journey as an extraordinary opportunity to learn at every stage. Knowing the selectivity of the colleges you're applying to will allow you to think logically about the next step.

WHAT YOU BRING TO THE TABLE

The question here is: Will you be admitted? That depends in part on the college's selectivity, but you *can* know if you've fulfilled their admission requirements and how your test scores and GPA stack up against those earned by students admitted in previous years. While test scores are not predictors of college success, you can use our rankings (Chapter 4) to quickly scan the test score range of colleges you're interested in to see where your score falls in (or outside of) that range. Keep in mind that what you're looking at is last year's data. While those data don't necessarily reflect or predict this year's average scores, they'll give you part of the fit picture.

In general, the National Association for College Admission Counseling reports, smaller schools pay more attention to all of the facets of your application, while for large colleges GPA and test scores usually play a major role. Only official personnel see essays, letters of recommendations, transcripts, and all the personal pieces that go into your application, so when you write those essays, remember that there's a real person (a group of people, or a committee) reading them. What do you want them to know about you?

SAFETY, MATCH, OR REACH

Once you know how you stack up against the admission requirements, you're ready to sort colleges into three groups: safety, match, or reach. As the College Board notes, whichever group they fall into, they should all be colleges that you would be happy to attend.

Safety. Open-access schools are, by definition, safeties because there are few (or no) barriers to admission. A regional college that guarantees admission to local students who qualify is a safety for you if you qualify and you make all their deadlines. Making deadlines is important because regional colleges sometimes cannot accommodate all the students in the area who qualify, so missing a deadline could keep you out even if you're academically qualified. A third way a school can be a safe bet is because your academic profile is better than that of the average student at the college, but there's something tricky going on here. If it appears that you are overqualified, the school might deny you admission. Why? Because to place well in some rankings (not ours, though), the college needs to enroll most of the students it admits, and if its admission staff thinks you're using them as a safety, they figure they probably won't be able to count you in. (If you really want to go there, let it be known that you will attend if the financial package they offer you is competitive. More on that in Chapter 10.)

Match. You have met all of their requirements, you have a good chance of being accepted, and you would be in a comfortable position among your academic peers. Remember that no college in the most selective group can be considered a match, because their acceptance rates are so low.

Reach. The College Board defines a reach as any school that's a challenge to get into. Remember, some schools admit and enroll such a small portion of their applicant pool that they really are reaches for *everyone*. Finally, often people will use the word "selective" or "best," but really what they're talking about is status. You know the status colleges—people mention them in movies or on sitcoms—and there are still others that have the same status but aren't as talked about. Everybody knows the logo, the colors. Brand recognition is high and they have a very, very cool collection of sweatshirts and in some cases maybe even a winning team. It's true that some of the so-called best schools have reasons to brag: they've got world-class professors doing cutting-edge research and they attract extremely bright and hardworking students. But do students actually learn more at these schools than at others? Hard to say (there is surprisingly little data on that), but probably not. A lot of the professors at the "best" schools are more focused on their research than on their students, whereas professors who can actually teach can be found in colleges all over the country.

What makes your education valuable is not the prestige of the institution but what you will have in your head when you graduate. In a 2013 Gallup/Lumina poll, business leaders rated the "amount of knowledge the candidate has in the field" as much more important than what college that candidate went to.[25] So when choosing a school, think less about whether the school has "status" and more about whether it's a good fit *for you*. Will it challenge you academically? Is it strong in the fields you want to study? Will it charge you a fair price? Is it filled with students you want to be around?

WHAT SCHOOLS BRING TO THE TABLE

The evaluation process is a two-way street. Just as the college evaluates you for fit, you need to evaluate the college. What are your academic fitness criteria? The Four-Way Fit questions (beginning on page 61) give you a detailed list of thirteen academic criteria to research about each college you're considering. What majors does it offer? If you have a passion for science and a school seems focused on business, it's probably not a fit. You may have been a top student in high school, but college is hard and presents new challenges, so you need to know what kind of tutoring, advising, or other academic supports are in place. Does the school offer opportunities to do research or to study abroad? Use these questions (and some of your own) to guide your research and focus your college visit on what will be important in the long run. Does this school have what it takes to be an academic fit for you?

Financial Fit

The cost of a college education is high. You know that. But the cost of not going to college is higher over the long term. The cost question itself is complicated, which is why we dedicate a whole chapter to paying for college. But we'll begin with this advice from the experts: research what the college will cost *you*. As college financial expert Sandy Baum told us, "Colleges would rather say they cost $30,000 and give everyone a $10,000 'scholarship' than lower their published price."[26] It's because we're kind of a wacky consumer society: we figure that if the advertised price of something is high, it must be good, and if it's cheap, it's probably low-quality. So the sticker price is in some cases a bit of a mind trick.

That is, of course, totally nuts. In the real world, the most expensive option is often a *very bad* choice, and the most affordable option is often a very good one. Take a look at our Best-Bang-for-the-Buck rankings, where you can see the average net price, broken out into three income levels. For a more personal comparison that takes into account your answers to a series of questions, go to College Abacus.

Affordability is a key factor, but it's difficult for families to talk about, particularly if money is tight. Take time to research your options and check to see what kind of financial aid might be available to you at the different institutions. We recommend you do this early on in your process so you keep it real for everyone.

Social Fit

A college that is a match for you should be academically challenging, and a place where there are support services (like free tutoring) and opportunities (like internships) that will get you all the way to graduation and set you up for your next move. It should also be a community where you can thrive, living, studying, and growing with your peers. That depends a great deal on you, but it also depends on the college itself.

Finding a social fit isn't about knowing where the good parties are. It's about finding people you connect with. Visit campuses if you possibly can, so that you can get a firsthand impression of the culture. Try to go mid-week because for the most part, campuses are very different places on the weekends and in the summer. Virtual tours are okay, but if you have time and can swing it, there's nothing that can beat walking around a campus mid-week, when all the students are there. The exception might be the one or two colleges that fall into your "reach" category. For those, you might want to wait to see if the reach is within your grasp before making plans to visit the campus.

When you do visit, plan to have a meal on campus, go to the student union, and hang out on the quad or in the library. Are there students like you? Ethnic diversity? Gender diversity? Are most students living on campus, near campus, or commuting? Visiting local colleges (even the ones you don't plan to attend) will give you a glimpse of college life.

Be aware of the overall population, and of how many of them are undergraduates. Size is critical because the bigger the school, the more anonymous you can be. It's not that it has to happen that way. With more people, after all, there should be more ways to connect. But there's a paradox: people who live in big cities often have a smaller social group than people who live in small towns where everyone knows one another. Many big schools balance this phenomenon by having colleges within colleges, or having students who share interests live or study or participate in linked classes together. Even so, a school with 1,500 students can feel very different from one with 30,000.

Part of finding out about the campus culture is seeing how students connect with one another. What do they do when they're not in class? Outside of class, what is important to you? What clubs, teams, or organizations could you imagine yourself joining? What about fraternities and sororities? Theater? Dance? What sports are available? Are they intramural? NCAA? How does the campus show its support for students like you? You can find out what the college wants you to know by reading their promotional material. You can find out what it looks like on the ground by visiting, talking to students, being there during the week, and checking out the notices on bulletin boards or chalked on sidewalks. Follow the campus on social media and participate in chat rooms to get a kind of mosaic of a lot of different people's experiences. Then ask yourself, *Where could I fit into this mix?*

Physical Fit

Location. For many students, finances and family obligations often decide the location question. For others, going away is an option, but the question is, how far? Our Best-Bang-for-the-Buck rankings are sorted by region because many students have a general idea of how far they want to travel from home. The online version of our rankings are also sortable by state, if you want to limit your search just to in-state schools. Many other college match sites, like College Navigator, allow you to input your preferences by state, region, or distance from home, so play with that and see what comes up.

Urban? Suburban? Rural? Setting can be an important part of the fit picture. Some students need the noise of a city, while others prefer crickets at night. For others, where the college is doesn't matter so much. We talked to several students who applied to a range—some colleges in the middle of big cities and others surrounded by farmland. If setting isn't a big deal to you, your list could range, too.

Climate. If you're considering going to a new region or state for college, think about weather and the surrounding geography. Mountains, shore, desert, and latitude all have an impact on weather. Everywhere has climactic challenges—you just need to be aware of them and how the climate impacts getting around. You can't bike to class in six feet of snow, and you can't go downhill skiing without a mountain nearby. Have you ever been through a long, cold winter? What about a seemingly endless series of hot days? You get the idea. If you're planning to leave familiar territory, do your research and think about what you're used to and what you prefer.

A Final Note

So what kind of school is right for you? That depends on your goals, your interests, and your personality, things you considered in Chapter 2. It also depends on your academic preparation and your family's financial situation, how you connect socially with others, and where you want to be on the planet. The four-way fit worksheets are designed to help you bring these decisions into focus. Think carefully about which is the most important element of your decision: Academics? Cost? A social fit? A place you want to spend the next four years? Focus heavily on what matters most to you and see how the colleges stack up.

Finally, we began organizing this chapter around the type of school that will help you achieve your career goals. This is not because your college experience is all about job training. The truth is, if you graduate from college, you are not only statistically much more likely to get a job, you're much more likely to get a job that brings you greater satisfaction, better pay, and more opportunities for advancement. Some of the most important work you will do while you're in college is becoming a more informed, thoughtful global citizen in a world where information—good tidings, revolutionary ideas, and cyber-threats—travels at lightning speed. It's a world where people must have the ability to think clearly, critically, and creatively to solve problems of global proportions. Learning how to navigate this vast, unpredictable world means making the most of your time in college. In many ways it's job prep, but it's also life prep. It's about gaining new knowledge, and it's also about building relationships and developing a stronger sense of yourself and the world around you.

The Four-Way Fit

Questions to Ask Yourself When You're Thinking About Fit

ACADEMICS

Rigor

Does the college offer opportunities that will challenge me academically?

Curriculum

Am I interested in the courses of study available?

Majors

Are there majors I'm interested in exploring?
Which ones?

Majors & Goals

How do possible majors connect to my goals?
Will the major I choose set me up for a career or graduate school?

Majors & Rules

Do I have to be admitted to a major separately?
How many apply? How many are admitted? Are there prerequisites to be admitted to the major?

Class size

How much instructor interaction would I like?
Lectures? Small group discussions? Labs? Seminars?

Departments

When I read the faculty bios, what interests me?
Would I be interacting mostly with teaching assistants or with professors?

Office Hours

What do current students say about instructors' availability?

Distance Learning

What do students say about the online classes?

(Online) Classes

Would online classes make my schedule easier or more difficult?

Tutors, Counselors, Advisors

How easy is it to see a counselor/advisor for guidance?
Are there tutors available for additional academic assistance when needed?

Research & Internships

Are there undergraduate research opportunities available?
Does the school partner with major companies in the area?
Outside of academics, what is important to me?

THE *OTHER* HELPFUL TOOL COLLEGE GUIDE

The Four-Way Fit

Library   Does the library have the hours/equipment/facilities I need?

Reputation   What is the school's reputation among other students and
                       employers?

Service Learning   Are any classes linked to opportunities in the community to apply
                       what I'm learning in the classroom?

Graduation Rates   What percentage of students graduate in six years? (See Chapter
                       4.) Is there a different graduation rate for certain racial or ethnic
                       groups? (See College Results website and compare.)

Career Services   What services do they provide? Résumé writing? Interview
                       practice? Will they help to connect me with internships, alumni
                       in my field, summer jobs, employment after graduation?

FINANCIAL

Net Price of   Start with net price in the rankings for your income group.
Attendance   Is the college likely to be within range? (For a more personal
                       estimate, go to College Abacus and each individual college's
                       net price calculator.)

Budget   Build a detailed budget using Financial Aid U's cost comparison
                       worksheet (Chapter 10). What costs are fixed? Which costs are
                       variable? Where do I have room for choice?

Work-Study   Are there several work-study jobs on campus or just a few?

SOCIAL

Campus Life   Outside of academics, what is important to me?

Clubs & Organizations   What campus activities are available? Service, professional,
                             academic, fraternities/sororities, student government?

The Four-Way Fit

Arts & Culture Are there opportunities to enjoy the arts (theater, dance, museums)? Do guest speakers come to campus?

Religious Affiliations Is the campus denominational?

Ethnic Diversity & Cultural Groups Will I be part of a majority? A minority? Is there racial, ethnic, religious diversity on campus? Are there student cultural centers, faith-based groups, or communities to join?

Athletics Division 1, 2, 3? Campus opportunities for sports? Gym facilities?

On-Campus Dining Nutritious? How is the meal plan structured? (By meal? By cost?)

Campus Visits Impressions? (The place, the students, the vibe.)

Campus Presence Online What do social media and the campus website add to my impression? Is the website easy or difficult to navigate?

PHYSICAL

Campus Size *Large campus?* Usually more activities, athletics, and academic programs, but also larger class sizes.

Small campus? More intimate setting, ability to get to know more people in your class, but not as many activities or programs.

Urban, Suburban, Rural Do I like it? Is it comfortable? New and exciting? Isolated? Peaceful? Crowded? Built into a city?

Climate What's it like during the school year? Is it very different from what I know? Am I ready for it?

THE *OTHER* HELPFUL TOOL COLLEGE GUIDE

The Four-Way Fit

Surrounding Geography Country roads? Mountains? Ocean? Big city?

Transportation How will I get around? Is there good public transportation (bus, train, etc.)? Do I need a bicycle? A car? What's the parking situation? Are there affordable ways to travel home occasionally? Bus? Train? Plane?

Housing *On-campus:* Availability? Cost?

Off-campus: Availability? Cost? Ease of access to campus? Safety? Whom will I be living with? Are there rules about living on/off campus freshman year?

Living at home: How far is the commute? What will it cost monthly? Will I need to contribute to rent, bills, groceries?

THE FOUR-WAY FIT WORKSHEET

On the next two pages, list the schools that you are interested in attending across the top. Rate each section using a scale of 1 through 5 (1 = Poor and 5 = Excellent). After totaling each section and all of your ratings, you will be able to see which schools rank higher than others in each category and overall.

If you're considering a lot of schools, you might want to make copies of this worksheet before filling it in. Seriously, it's really helpful!

The Four-Way Fit Worksheet:
Build Your Own Rankings

SCHOOLS >>>	1.	2.	3.	4.
ACADEMICS				
Do I like the curriculum?				
Does it have my major?				
Class sizes overall				
Department size				
Can I get into my major easily or is it competitive?				
Availability of professors				
Availability of tutors, counselors, advisors				
Research opportunities				
Library				
Reputation				
Graduation rates				
Service learning seminars				
Distance learning (online) classes				
TOTAL FOR ACADEMIC FIT:				
FINANCIAL				
Financial aid—federal*				
Financial aid—private*				
Financial aid—school*				
Additional expenses				
*Use Cost Comparison Worksheet in Chapter 10				
TOTAL FOR FINANCIAL FIT:				

THE
OTHER
HELPFUL
TOOL
COLLEGE
GUIDE

The Four-Way Fit Worksheet

SCHOOLS >>>

SOCIAL								
Campus life—how do I like to spend my free time?								
Clubs and organizations								
Speakers, presentations, arts, culture								
Spiritual affiliations and offerings								
Ethnic/racial/religious/cultural affiliations and offerings								
Campus diversity: racial, religious, economic, in student interests								
Athletics								
On-campus dining facilities								
Campus visit								
Campus online presence								
TOTAL FOR SOCIAL FIT:								
PHYSICAL								
Campus size								
Urban, suburban, rural								
Climate								
Surrounding geography								
Transportation and Housing								
TOTAL FOR PHYSICAL FIT:								
TOTAL:								

THE
OTHER
HELPFUL
TOOL
COLLEGE
GUIDE

4.
THE
OTHER
COLLEGE
RANKINGS

**MAKING A LIST
OF THE RIGHT SCHOOLS
FOR YOU**

OMG! How do you even figure out where to apply???

Is a college degree worth it? You've probably seen that headline, and it's not a bad question to ask. After all, college prices and debt loads keep rising. And we've all heard stories of college graduates tending bar or unable to get jobs at all.

Well, here's the truth: a college degree is definitely worth it. Study after study shows that young people with four-year college degrees are much less likely—in fact, one-third as likely—to be unemployed as those with only high school degrees.[27] They make on average twice as much per hour.[28] Young people with two-year degrees are nearly half as likely to be unemployed as those with only high school degrees and earn around $10,000 a year more.[29] Even bartenders

Earnings and unemployment rates by educational attainment

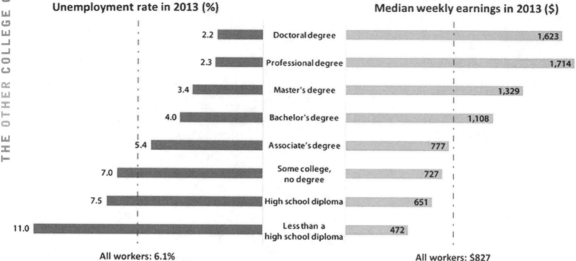

Unemployment rate in 2013 (%) **Median weekly earnings in 2013 ($)**

	Unemployment rate	Degree	Median weekly earnings
	2.2	Doctoral degree	1,623
	2.3	Professional degree	1,714
	3.4	Master's degree	1,329
	4.0	Bachelor's degree	1,108
	5.4	Associate's degree	777
	7.0	Some college, no degree	727
	7.5	High school diploma	651
	11.0	Less than a high school diploma	472

All workers: 6.1% **All workers: $827**

These education categories reflect only the highest level of education attained. They do not take into account completion of training programs in the form of apprenticeships and other on-the-job training, which may also influence earnings and unemployment rates.

SOURCE: CURRENT POPULATION SURVEY, U.S. BUREAU OF LABOR STATISTICS, U.S. DEPARTMENT OF LABOR. DATA ARE FOR PERSONS AGE TWENTY-FIVE AND OVER. EARNINGS ARE FOR FULL-TIME WAGE AND SALARY WORKERS.

and others whose jobs don't necessarily require a college degree tend to make more if they have one.[30] In fact, according to research cited in the *New York Times*, "the true cost of a college degree is about *negative* $500,000. That's right: Over the long run, college is cheaper than free. *Not* going to college will cost you about half a million dollars."[31]

But there are a couple of caveats. First, college is not worth it for those who start, rack up a load of debt, and drop out without a degree to show for it. To get the benefits, you need to get the degree. Second, how "worth it" a college degree is depends on how much you paid to get it and where you got it. In other words, you want to pick a college that is a good fit for you, that will help you graduate, and that will not overcharge you and leave you with a mountain of debt.

This chapter is all about giving you tools to help you decide which schools are right for you. Using our lists and the guidance on how to make sense of them, you'll be able to sort through the thousands of colleges and universities out there to choose a much smaller group of schools that suit your general preferences, will charge a fair price, and will help you walk away with a degree that's actually worth something in the job market. You'll then be able to take this shorter list of schools that are good prospects for you, do some deeper research about them, and ultimately get your list down to the four to eight colleges that you'll actually want to apply to.

- **The Best-Bang-for-the-Buck Colleges** list allows you to review colleges by region and quickly see the price tag, if you can get in, and if you're likely to graduate.

- **The Affordable Elite** list is where to look if you're basically an A student, you score well on standardized tests, and you want to go to one of the country's more selective colleges.

- **America's Best Community Colleges** is a list for those interested in going to a community college, either to earn a two-year certificate or an associate's degree or as a first step toward a bachelor's degree from a four-year college.

- **Best-Bang-for-the-Buck HBCUs** are provided for students who are considering historically black colleges and universities (HBCUs), to help you pick a school that's a good fit.

HOW TO USE THE BEST-BANG-FOR-THE-BUCK RANKINGS TO FIND THE RIGHT SCHOOL AT THE RIGHT PRICE

The Best-Bang-for-the-Buck lists 1,540 schools, divided into five regions: Midwest, Northeast, South, Southeast, and West.[32] This sorting allows you to narrow down your options based on one of your physical fit criteria: where the college is.

> Step 1

Start your search by selecting a region that meets one of your physical fit requirements: where is it located?

Let's say you want to go to college in Illinois. Start with the Midwest list and select only those colleges in Illinois. With one quick scan, you've gone from more thsan 1,500 colleges to 400 in the Midwest to 59 in Illinois (this is easiest if done online). If this is your personal copy of *The Other College Guide*, mark it up with a highlighter or notes to keep track of your sorting process.

Topping the Illinois list on the "best" end are Illinois State, Eastern Illinois University, and University of Illinois; bottoming out on the "worst" end, you'll see East-West, Columbia College–Chicago, and Shimer. In the middle, there are lots of colleges, some of which may be worth considering. Remember, the ultimate aim of this exercise is to whittle your list of colleges down to a handful that fit your needs and that you'll apply to. So right off the bat you might want to lop off, say, the bottom quarter of those sixty Illinois schools. (In our example, we reduced the list by eliminating all schools with overall scores less than 7.) The next steps will tell you how these colleges earned their place in our rankings and why an easy way to shrink your list is to cut the schools at the bottom of our rankings from consideration.

> Step 2

Next determine which of the forty-four schools left on your list will be academic fits by taking a look at two data points: Are you likely to be admitted? And are you likely to graduate? While test scores are not a definitive indicator of whether or not you'll be admitted, they do give you an idea of how your scores compare with those of currently enrolled students. Categorize them in one of these groups: matches (your score is in range), reach (your score is below range), or safety (your score is above range).

Say your ACT score is 20, which is about the median score nationally. Based on this measure alone (without taking into account your GPA), which schools are a match, a reach, a safety?

59
Illinois Colleges

44
Overall Score +7

20
Matches

School	Overall Score	School	Overall Score
Illinois State University	12	Saint Xavier University	7
University of Illinois at Chicago	11	Aurora University	7
Eastern Illinois University	11	Benedictine University	7
University of Illinois–Springfield	10	Olivet Nazarene University	7
Western Illinois University	10	Amer. InterCont. University–Online	7
Dominican University	10	Illinois Institute of Technology	7
Concordia University–Chicago	10	Trinity Christian College	7
National Louis University	10	Westwood College–O'Hare Airport	7
Robert Morris University Illinois	10	Westwood College–River Oaks	7
Elmhurst College	10	Augustana College	7
Know College	10	Lake Forest College	7
University of IL–Urbana-Champaign	9	DeVry University–Illinois	7
McKendree University	9	Illinois Wesleyan University	7
Trinity International University–Illinois	9	University of Chicago	7
Greenville College	9	North Park University	6
Millikin University	9	North Central College	6
Bradley University	9	Judson University	6
Wheaton College	9	Westwood College–Chicago Loop	6
DePaul University	9	Roosevelt University	6
Blackburn College	8	Northwestern University	6
University of St. Francis	8	Chicago State University	5
Monmouth College	8	Northeastern Illinois University	5
Northern Illinois University	8	MacMurray College	5
Illinois College	8	Loyola University–Chicago	5
Eureka College	8	Rockford College	4
Lewis University	8	Westwood College–Dupage	4
Kendall College	8	East-West University	4
Southern IL University–Carbondale	7	Columbia College–Chicago	4
Southern IL University–Edwardsville	7	Shimer College	3
Quincy University	7		

Fifty-nine colleges located in Illinois sorted by overall scores. Schools that scored less than seven overall are in gray.

Match Schools	ACT / SAT Range
Western Illinois University	18 – 23
Eastern Illinois University (IL)*	19 – 23
University of Illinois– Springfield (IL)*	20 – 26
Dominican University (IL)	20 – 24
Concordia University–Chicago (IL)	19 – 24
Millikin University (IL)	20 – 25
McKendree University (IL)	19 – 25
Trinity International University –Illinois (IL)	19 – 26
Greenville College (IL)	19 – 25
Illinois College (IL)	20 – 26
Lewis University (IL)	20 – 25
Monmouth College (IL)	19 – 24
Northern Illinois University (IL)*	19 – 24
Eureka College (IL)	19 – 26
Southern IL Univ.– Edwardsville (IL)*	20 – 25
Saint Xavier University (IL)	20 – 25
Aurora University (IL)	20 – 24
Olivet Nazarene University (IL)	20 – 27
Quincy University (IL)	19 – 24
Benedictine University (IL)	19 – 25
Trinity Christian College (IL)	19 – 26

From forty-four colleges on the big list to twenty that fit your test score range.

Safety Schools	ACT / SAT Range
Western Illinois University	18 – 23
National Louis University	15 – 17
Blackburn College	18 – 24
Southern Illinois University–Carbondale	18 – 24
Roosevelt University	19 – 25

Reach Schools	ACT / SAT Range
Bradley University	22 – 28
DePaul University	22 – 27
Illinois State University	22 – 26
University of Illinois at Chicago	21 – 26
Elmhurst College	21 – 26
University of St. Francis	21 – 25

Matches. With an ACT score of 20, you're a possible match for about twenty schools where the ranges begin at 19 or 20 at the low end (25th percentile). Are these all really a match? The whole picture depends on other parts of your academic profile. If your GPA is 2.9, for example, some of these "matches" might, in fact, be reaches. If your GPA is 3.9, some "matches" are likely to be safety schools for you.

In Chapter 3 we explained why you need to apply to schools both above and below your test scores. It might be helpful to review that, since there are many steps to determining if a school is actually a reach or a safety.

Safeties. A safety is a school that is likely to admit you based on your academic profile. Depending on your GPA and whether or not you've met all their requirements and deadlines, five schools are likely safety schools. (But remember, depending on your whole academic profile, there may be more safety schools in your match list!)

Reaches. By definition, reaches are a challenge to get into. Sometimes they're a challenge for everyone—like the University of Chicago, which admits only 16.1 percent of its applicants. Others are reaches because their average student's academic profile exceeds yours. A reasonable reach school exceeds your score by a little, not a lot.

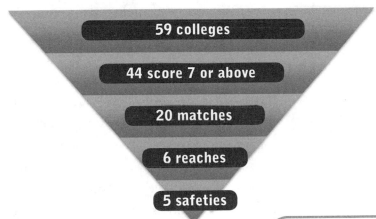

- 59 colleges
- 44 score 7 or above
- 20 matches
- 6 reaches
- 5 safeties

Schools	ACT / SAT Range
University of Chicago	1400 – 1567
Wheaton College	27 – 32
University of Illinois–Urbana-Champaign	26 – 31
Illinois Wesleyan University	25 – 30

Four schools that are likely beyond reach.

There's tons of research that says that the more you challenge yourself, the better you'll do (both in school and in life), so we strongly recommend that you reach! At the same time, be realistic. Four schools from that list of forty-four colleges are likely out of reach.

What about schools that don't report scores? Good question. You can't determine an academic fit by test score alone, and this is, of course, absolutely true for schools that don't report them at all. Nine schools that don't report scores remain on your list, and you will eliminate some of these later for other reasons. The next round of elimination (and the first for the no-score schools) will happen with the next step: graduation rates.

The other part of the academic fit is whether you're likely to graduate. Schools that top our Best Bang list do so in part because they tend to do a good job helping students who aren't endlessly wealthy graduate. This shows up in two of our scores: the graduation rate and the graduation performance rate. The graduation rate shows what percentage of the students graduate in six years. The graduation performance rate shows how well the school is doing to help students from lower-income families graduate. For many reasons, students in this category may come to college less prepared to suc-

Match Schools	Graduation Rate
Knox College	78.3
Augustana College	77.0
Lake Forest College	69.3
Dominican University	64.7
Eastern Illinois University	60.3
Illinois College	60.0
Millikin University	59.7
Lewis University	59.7
Trinity Christian College	59.7
University of Illinois–Springfield	58.7
Olivet Nazarene University	58.7
Trinity International University–Illinois	56.3
Monmouth College	56.3
Concordia University–Chicago	56.0
Northern Illinois University	55.3
Greenville College	55.0
Saint Xavier University	54.0
Eureka College	53.3
McKendree University	52.0
Southern Illinois University–Edwardsville	51.7
Kendall College	51.3
Benedictine University	51.3
Aurora University	50.0
Quincy University	50.0
Robert Morris University Illinois	47.3
~~Westwood College–O'Hare Airport~~	~~41.0~~
~~Westwood College–River Oaks~~	~~33.7~~
~~DeVry University–Illinois~~	~~32.3~~
~~Amer. InterCont. Univ.–Online~~	~~29.0~~

Graduation rates of your possible match schools. The top three schools on this list (Knox, Augustana, and Lake Forest) don't report test scores and neither do Kendall in the middle or the bottom four (Westwood-O'Hare, Westwood–River Oaks, DeVry-Illinois, and American InterContinental Online).

ceed. A positive number indicates that more such students are graduating than statistics would predict, which probably means the school is devoting resources and attention to making sure *all* its students succeed. A negative score tells you the opposite is true—that for whatever reason, the school isn't doing right by students who need a little extra guidance and support. You'll notice that schools at the bottom of the list (which you've already eliminated) are not graduating *most* of the students they admit.

Let's take a look at the graduation rate of your twenty match schools plus the nine schools that don't report test score ranges. For illustration purposes, we reordered the list to make it easier to see the range. Remember, this is just our example to guide you through refining your own list.

Keep whittling your list down! You can probably eliminate the four at the bottom without too much pain. For some in the middle, take a look at the graduation performance rate, which takes into account the student population at the school. Positive territory means that they're graduating students at a rate higher than predicted; negative means they aren't doing as well as they should be given who goes to school there.

Now we'll put these twenty-five schools (remember we crossed out the four at the bottom) through their next fitness test.

> Step 3

Which of these twenty-five academic matches are a financial fit as well? There are two ways you can look at this question: (1) What's the average price for a family like yours? (2) Do a lot of students fail to repay their loans (that's called the default rate)? Since the actual price schools will charge you has a lot to do with your family income, our rankings show the net price of attendance for each college broken down by three annual family income categories: $0–$30,000, $30,000–$75,000, and more than $75,000. Keep in mind that these are *average* net prices, since there is no way to account for every factor—but they do give a good sense of how affordable a school is likely to be for you or your family. The price of any school will vary with individual circumstances, such as how much your family has in savings.

The default rate adds another dimension because it tells you what percentage of the students graduating aren't paying off their loans. Students who can't repay loans are in that predicament because they (1) may have borrowed too much, (2) couldn't get a job, or (3) took out private loans before exhausting the federal loans available (federal loans have more flexible repayment plans and often have lower interest rates). In any case, a high default rate is not a positive indicator and is worth paying attention to.

Let's presume your family earned $52,000 last year, which is about the median household income in the United States. This puts your family in the $30,000–$75,000 category. The list here shows all twenty-five of the possible match schools, but this time we've reordered the list so you can easily see the range in prices. Try doing the same with your own list. And we're imagining that

Match Schools	Avg. Net Price
University of Illinois–Springfield	11,110
McKendree University	13,045
Monmouth College	13,977
Dominican University	13,992
Aurora University	14,017
Illinois College	14,342
Quincy University	14,418
Eastern Illinois University	15,118
Lewis University	15,556
Eureka College	15,728
Concordia University–Chicago	15,995
Millikin University	16,247
Trinity International University–Illinois	16,526
Greenville College	16,577
Saint Xavier University	17,182
Southern Illinois University–Edwardsville	17,253
Olivet Nazarene University	17,326
Northern Illinois University	17,332
Knox College	17,491
Robert Morris University Illinois	17,982
Elmhurst College	18,053
Benedictine University	19,543
Trinity Christian College	21,352
Kendall College	28,225

Match Schools	Default Rate
University of Illinois–Springfield	5.4
McKendree University	5.9
Monmouth College	6.3
Dominican University	5.0
Aurora University	4.6
Illinois College	3.7
Quincy University	6.8
Eastern Illinois University	4.1
Lewis University	4.7
Eureka College	4.9
Concordia University–Chicago	2.9

Safety Schools	Price
Blackburn College	14,037
Western Illinois University	16,014
Southern Illinois University–Carbondale	15,739
~~National Louis University~~	~~18,813~~
~~Robert Morris University Illinois~~	~~17,982~~

With a $16,000 budget at least two of these colleges may be out of your range.

Reach Schools	Price
~~Bradley University~~	~~17,479~~
~~DePaul University~~	~~26,685~~
Illinois State University	16,068
University of Illinois at Chicago	11,138
~~Elmhurst College~~	~~18,053~~
University of St. Francis	13,072

Budget considerations eliminate three, but you still have three possible reaches that fit your budget.

you've had that much-dreaded money talk with your parents (see Chapter 8) and you know that your family can afford only up to $16,000. The ones that aren't affordable are not a good financial fit for you, so we've crossed them out.

Your list of match schools is now down to eleven. Next, take a quick look at the default rates of that group. The default rates for the schools that made it through your winnowing process are all below 10 percent, which isn't so bad. You can see that they range from a high at Quincy (6.8 percent) to a low at Concordia (2.9 percent), so default rate may not bear much weight in your decision.

Now do the same financial fit calculations for the safety and reach schools on your academic fit list. You'll wind up with a list of schools to take with you to the next step of the search process.

> Step 4

You now have a total of seventeen schools on your list: eleven matches, three safeties, and three reaches. Of course there are nuances here—and trade-offs! To help you compare schools to one another, use the worksheet on page 94. You'll see that some schools are a little high here, a little low there. When you have choices, trade-offs are inevitable, but the wisest choices are based on a sound foundation: Is it the best academic match, and can you afford it?

> Step 5

The rankings give you a great head start and an easy way to eliminate some schools based on their own data. They also provide you with a lot of top schools that you may not have considered. After you've looked through these *quantitative* measures (those aspects that can be measured by numbers), there's lots of *qualitative* research you need to do on the seventeen schools still on your list. (That involves elements that may be measured by quality and may require your own opinion and judgment.) But now the number of schools to consider isn't so overwhelming. Getting more info on seventeen schools certainly beats trying to do the same for fifty or sixty, which just isn't reasonable. With a more tailored list, you can use the four-way fit questions we provided in Chapter 3 to add these qualitative dimensions to your list-making process.

For more information, go to the school's website. Find out where exactly each school is located: In a small town? In a suburb? In downtown Chicago? How far away are they from home? Find out if they have sports teams or fraternities and sororities, if those things are important to you. Read the postings by students on College Confidential, College Prowler, or Unigo, to name a few websites where individual students post thoughts about their experience. And most important of all, find out as much as you can about whether the school has strong programs in the areas you generally want to study in college: Engineering? Business? General arts and sciences?

Once you do that, you may find that a number of the schools you picked as Best-Bang-for-the-Buck schools aren't for you. If so, expand your search to some of the other schools on your academic fit list, or consider widening your geographic search by looking at schools in nearby states.

AFFORDABLE ELITE SCHOOLS

If you're academically gifted and you've spent your high school years proving to yourself that you could master another language, another skill, and whatever other challenge came your way, our Affordable Elite list is designed with you in mind. It's a list of the most selective colleges and universities in the country, ranked by the same criteria as our Best-Bang-for-the-Buck rankings. The Affordable Elites ranking begins on page 165.

You can use the Affordable Elites list to see the average ACT/SAT scores and admit rates of over two hundred highly selective colleges. This list also breaks out the average net price of attendance for each college for students from families in three different annual income categories: those making $0–$30,000, $30,000–$75,000, and more than $75,000. This information will help you decide which schools you have the best shot at getting into and which will charge you the least. (Keep in mind that test scores are indicators, not predictors, and these are *average net prices*; your actual cost will vary based on criteria such as family assets or savings.)

Now, let's be clear: selectivity isn't the be-all/end-all measure of college quality. It doesn't tell you, for instance, how much learning actually goes on in the classrooms. Selectivity is a measure of input (how smart and academically prepared the incoming class is), not outcome (how much you actually learn). There are great professors and lousy ones in every college.

While the teaching may or may not be better at selective colleges, there are valid reasons you (and every student) should want to apply to the most selective schools you can reasonably expect to get into. The opportunities for networking, internships and study abroad programs tend to be better at more selective schools. Because of peer pressure, among other things, students at many highly selective schools challenge one another to work harder.

Many researchers have shown that academically gifted students from middle- and low-income families tend to "undermatch" when choosing colleges. That is, they go to significantly *less* selective schools than they could have gotten into, often out of fear that they can't afford the more elite institutions. As a result, they graduate from college at lower rates and make lower lifetime incomes than they otherwise could have. So if you're a top student, whether your family is affluent, middle-class, or low-income (but *especially* if it's low-income), you should thoughtfully consider highly selective, elite schools. Some of them are looking for students just like you.

> General Rules of Thumb About the Affordable Elite List

When you look at the Affordable Elite list, you will notice a few interesting patterns emerge that might help you in your search for the right school.

THE PUBLICS

The first thing to notice is that the very top school on the list isn't a fancy private college but a public institution: the University of California, Los Angeles. UCLA scored 13 out of a possible 15 points by enrolling large numbers of students at every income level, graduating 91 percent of students within six years, and charging an average price of just over $10,000 for in-state students after taking grants into account. In fact, seven of the top twenty colleges on the list are public universities, including three other University of California campuses (Berkeley, Irvine, and San Diego) as well as flagship universities in Florida, Texas, and Virginia. And there are many other public institutions in the top one hundred, in states ranging from New York and Connecticut to Georgia, Texas, and Wisconsin.

The net prices listed for public universities are for students residing in those states (out-of-state students typically pay more, though not always). What this means is that if you live in one of these states (or a state with a reciprocal tuition agreement) and have high grades and test scores, you might not have to go far to attend an Affordable Elite school.

Keep in mind, though, that not all public universities are so affordable and accessible. Some near the bottom of the list either aren't letting in many lower-income students, are charging them very high prices, or both. The University of Pittsburgh (#201), Colorado School of Mines (#208), and Miami University of Ohio (#211) all charge at least $15,000 per year to middle-income students—more than some private colleges.

THE IVIES

Many of the Ivy League schools that perennially show up on other lists of top colleges also do well on our Affordable Elite rankings. That includes Harvard, which earns its number two ranking by charging an astonishingly low net price of $1,533 to students from families making $30,000 a year or less and $3,774 to those earning $30,000 to $75,000. Harvard doesn't admit many low-income students (11 percent of its students receive Pell Grants), but the ones it does let in get a great deal. Dartmouth, Columbia, Brown, and the Ivy-equivalent Stanford also make it into our top twenty. But a number of Ivies don't do as well, including Princeton (#30) and Yale (#33). Why? Mostly because they're charging non-wealthy students higher prices—three or four times as much as Harvard. (It's not that they can't afford it. If you look in the category titled "Endowment Funds per Full-Time Student" you'll see that Princeton and Yale both have more money in the bank per student than Harvard.)

THE STRIVERS

Other national universities and liberal arts colleges that rank in, say, the top fifty on the *U.S. News & World Report* list place much lower on our Affordable Elites list. These include Barnard (#65), Brandeis (#77), Northwestern (#78), Bryn Mawr (#110), Boston University (#169), George Washington (#178), Carnegie Mellon (#186), Reed (#197), and Northeastern (#215). One thing a lot of these schools have in common is that they have raised their admission standards in recent decades to ascend the prestige ladder, but they don't have as many super-rich alumni to hit up for donations as, say, old Ivy League schools do. (George Washington University's endowment, for instance, amounts to only $69,758 per student, one-eighteenth the size of Harvard's.) So instead of giving moderate-income students a break in price, they charge prices that break their bank accounts. Unless your family can afford the cost or you don't mind going deep into debt—a move we strongly discourage—you might want to avoid these schools.

> Navigating the Affordable Elite List

STEP 1

Start with the academic fit; that is, are you likely to be admitted and graduate? How do your test scores compare? Are your scores within the range of these selective colleges? Close to the range? Is their graduation rate excellent (it should be), and if it's not, why?

These schools are highly selective, many use holistic admission criteria, and tests are only one of many metrics they use to evaluate applicants, but filtering by test score is a useful first step in reducing your list to a manageable number of schools you have the best shot at getting into. Scores range from a low of 21 (ACT score, College of the Ozarks) and 1,190 (SAT score, University of California, Santa Barbara) to a high of 1,463 (SAT score, California Institute of Technology) or 32 (ACT score, Washington University in St. Louis). We've given you all the data points so you can be realistic. If their range is substantially higher than your score, it's probably out of reach, but you might also discover a few that could provide you with just the right academic peer group and just the right challenge.

STEP 2

Financial fit is dependent on your income, so pick the column that suits your situation and scan through the prices. For our example, we'll use the $30,000–$75,000 category.

There's quite a price range, and it will likely surprise you that Berea College is an outlier because their students pay nothing and earn as they go. But other colleges are doing well reducing the price for students, with Harvard leading ($3,774) and Amherst not far behind ($4,912). The University of Florida ($5,290) and California

Institute of Technology ($5,462) also do well, to name a few. In fact, there are twenty-four elite schools that charge less than $10,000 for families making less than $75,000. An additional sixty-eight schools charge less than $15,000.

STEP 3

This list might be full of surprises for you, so if you find a college that looks like an academic and financial fit, dig into the social and physical characteristics. Are there other students like you, and how much does that matter to you? If it's geographically distant, how often will you see your family? Can you handle the weather? Use the four-way fit questions at the end of Chapter 3 to help guide your research. Contact the school. Arrange a visit if you can swing it. Don't be shy.

BEST COMMUNITY COLLEGES

For many students, community college is the most direct, efficient, and cost-effective path to a life-changing career or certificate program. Other students attend community college as a first step, with the idea of transferring to a four-year institution. For students in the latter camp, we have more to say to you in Chapter 5. But whether community college is the beginning or the end of your goal, you can learn something by taking a look at our list of the top fifty community colleges.

The colleges on this list have extraordinarily high graduation rates for community colleges and follow the best educational practices, often more so than many of the top-100 four-year schools on the *U.S. News* ranking. Of the eight measures we provide, five are from research conducted by the respected Community College Survey of Student Engagement (CCSSE), which tracks the number of books and papers students are assigned, the number of interactions with faculty, the hours spent preparing for class, and the quality of support services—all practices that research shows lead to more learning. If you're aiming to go to community college and are lucky enough to live near one of these fifty schools, you're in great shape.

If your local community college isn't on our rather short list of top schools but you want some information on it, you can go to the website of the Community College Survey of Student Engagement: www.ccsse.org. Once at the site, look under "National Findings," then click "College Profiles" and then "All Years of Current Cohort." There you'll see a list of 716 community colleges. If your school is on that list, you can click on its name and you'll see how that institution scored on several measures.

WHAT ABOUT HBCUs?
THE RACIAL (AND CULTURAL)
LANDSCAPE OF COLLEGE CHOICE

>>>>>>

As we've shown and as we'll continue to discuss, everyone searching for the right school has several factors to consider. And if you identify as a minority (religious, racial, ethnic, or otherwise) or a person of color, or if you are not from the United States—and perhaps even if none of these describe you—you may be thinking about an additional factor when choosing a college: *Should I go to a school that, for one reason or another, has a history of service to people like me? Should I consider schools where I might be in the minority?*

Throughout American history, hundreds of schools have been founded for the benefit of various minority groups—groups that often have a history of being discriminated against and barred from many institutions of higher learning. Some of these schools serve particular religious affiliations—Jewish Americans, Catholics, evangelicals. Others serve racial and ethnic minorities and include many well-known historically black colleges and universities (HBCUs), Hispanic-serving institutions (HSIs), and tribal colleges and universities, which serve Native American students.[33] Because the sense of having to make this choice, as well as the ongoing discrimination and racial disparities that exist, tends to be keenest for African

Facts About HBCUs

Historically black colleges and universities (HBCUs) have the principal mission of educating black Americans. They were founded and developed in an environment of legal segregation and, by providing access to higher education, contributed substantially to the progress blacks have made on measures of social status. Today, there are a hundred HBCUs located in nineteen states, the District of Columbia, and the U.S. Virgin Islands. Of those, fifty-one are public institutions and forty-nine are private not-for-profit institutions. Although HBCUs were originally founded to educate black students, they have historically enrolled students other than black Americans, and this diversity has increased over time. In 2011, non-black students made up 19 percent of enrollment at HBCUs. As opportunities for African American students have expanded, the share of bachelor's and master's degrees awarded to blacks by HBCUs have decreased. In 1976–77, 35 percent of the bachelor's degrees blacks earned were awarded by HBCUs; by 2010–11, that number had shrunk to 16 percent.

Source: National Center for Education Statistics

Americans, that's whom we'll be focusing on here, though much of our advice and discussion may be helpful to other minority students, too.

HBCUs in particular are somewhat analogous to colleges that were once exclusively for women—both were born out of necessity. Case in point: unjust as it is, even high-achieving women such as Michelle Obama could not have gone to Princeton (her alma mater) prior to 1969, not because of their race but because of their gender. HBCUs were founded because prior to the Civil War, African Americans were denied many civil rights, education among them. While there are only about one hundred HBCUs, representing just 3 percent of the nation's colleges, and they do not exclusively serve African American students, they graduate close to 20 percent of all African American students who earn undergraduate degrees and close to half of African American professionals and public school teachers.[34]

Dr. Anthony Antonio of Stanford University conducts research on the question of how race impacts our educational experience and our decisions. He told us: "HBCUs were originally formed out of segregation, but in building the institutions, they focused on creating a social environment that allowed the students to achieve . . . to flourish academically. In many cases, expectations in the larger society for African Americans were low, and this led to fewer opportunities to achieve. HBCUs sought to change that, giving students powerful leadership opportunities that they would not have had. Of course, there is huge variation in the landscape of HBCUs, so students have to be aware of that. They have to ask themselves: *What social and academic environment is most conducive to my best performance?*"

Whether an HBCU might be right for you is ultimately a personal choice, even if, for example, you have a parent or mentor with strong opinions about whether or not you should attend an HBCU. (And, bear in mind that many schools where blacks are not the majority have vibrant African American communities built around clubs, fraternities, and student associations that in their own way mirror the support and camaraderie cherished by so many HBCU alumni.) If you're interested in an HBCU or other minority-serving institution, approach your search with the same eye for fit and value as you would with any other type of school. Just as there are better and worse Catholic or Jewish colleges, or better and worse public or private colleges, there are better and worse HBCUs.

The procedure for sorting through the HBCU list is the same as for the Best-Bang-for-the-Buck list, so follow the steps outlined above. Note that seven HBCUs earn an overall score of 10 points, placing them in the top twenty-five on the Best-Bang-for-the-Buck regional lists. These include three outstanding North Carolina HBCUs at the top of our list: Elizabeth City State University, Fayetteville State University, and North Carolina Central University. Each of these schools admits most students who apply. About three-quarters of those students are on Pell Grants, meaning they come from moderate- to low-income homes. And given their backgrounds on paper, students at these schools graduate at higher-than-average rates. Plus, the net prices these schools charge are very reasonable. Lower-income students at Elizabeth City pay almost nothing—now that's bang for your buck! Several quite selective HBCUs score well, too, including Howard, Fisk, and Spelman.

But it's also worth noting the schools that don't do so well. Paul Quinn College in Texas has a 5 percent graduation rate. The University of the District of Columbia is barely better, with a graduation rate under 15 percent and a net price for low- and middle-income students of nearly $15,000. Oakwood University in Alabama charges many students nearly $25,000 while underperforming on the graduation front.

In other words, it's important to do your homework.

If you're one of the majority of black students who will not go to an HBCU, you've also got homework to do. In addition to applying all the same tests for fit and value you've learned so far, you need to find out how African American students in particular do at the schools you're considering. This is important because at many schools the graduation rates for African American college students are lower than average, due both to historic discrimination and to the impact of possibly having gone to K–12 schools with fewer resources or opportunities. But it is also true that African American students tend to do better at some colleges. One way to find out the skinny on different graduation rates (at any school) is by going to the College Results Online website (www.collegeresults.org), run by a nonprofit research group, the Education Trust.

On the College Results website, click on the tab that says "Compare Colleges." Then put in as many colleges as you would like to compare. For this illustration, we'll input all seventeen Illinois schools (matches, reaches, safeties) that made it through the academic and financial fit tests we discussed in the Best-Bang-for-the-Buck section. Some of the schools on your list might not be in the College Results database—for instance, in this example, the University of St. Francis is one of the few colleges that is not in the database, so only sixteen schools are included in this comparison. In

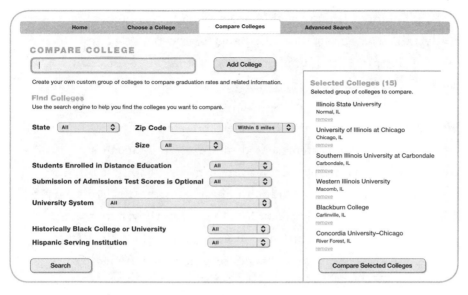

the screen shot here you can see that each of these seventeen colleges now appear on the "Selected Colleges" list on the right.

Once you've entered all your schools, click "Compare Selected Colleges" below that box on the right. That will take you to this page:

College	2012 6-Year Grad Rate	Underrepresented Minority 6-Year Grad Rate	% Pell Recipients Among Freshman	% Underrepresented Minority	Average High School GPA Among Collge Freshman	Estimated Median SAT/ACT	Total Price for In-State, On-Campus Students	Average Net Price After Grants
Illinois State University	71.2%	49.6%	25%	12.1%	3.33	1,110	$24,816	$16,293
Dominican University	66.0%	63.0%	60%	40.8%	3.47	1,030	$37,170	$17,124
Illinois College	61.8%	58.8%	38%	11%	3.33	N/A	$35,120	$17,438
Eastern Illinois University	60.4%	47.8%	41%	18.9%	3.10	990	$22,128	$15,528
Lewis University	59%	45.7%	36%	22.6%	3.31	1,050	$36,645	$17,638
Monmouth College	57.9%	39.6%	47%	16.5%	3.20	1,030	$38,600	$17,996
University of Illinois at Chicago	57.7%	46.9%	55%	30.1%	3.13	1,090	$27,878	$11,932
Eureka College	56.2%	38.5%	45%	7.0%	N/A	1,050	$28,690	$17,055
Quincy University	55.9%	47.1%	47%	13.2%	3.26	1,010	$36,960	$16,519
Western Illinois University	54.4%	44.9%	46%	20.5%	2.99	970	$23,420	$15,088
Aurora University	51.7%	46.9%	40%	25.8%	3.34	1,030	$31,476	$17,406
McKendree University	49.3%	43.2%	41%	17.6%	3.40	1,030	$36,010	$16,450
Concordia University–Chicago	48.8%	29.3%	47%	31.9%	2.98	1,030	$36,306	$18,014
Southern Illinois Univ.-Carbondale	47.6%	31.3%	51%	27.5%	N/A	990	$23,467	$13,513
Univ. of Illinois at Springfield	47.2%	23.3%	33%	17.0%	3.38	1,070	$21,351	$13,513
Blackburn College	44.6%	23.8%	47%	9.6%	3.21	970	$23,000	$13,444

The first two columns make it easy to compare the underrepresented minority graduation rate with the college's overall graduation rate.

There is lots of data on this page, including things we've already talked about in our Best-Bang-for-the-Buck section, like average net price (the numbers may be somewhat different because in this book we average the three most recent years of data and CollegeResults.org looks at only the most recent year). Focus instead on the column labeled "Underrepresented Minority 6-Year Grad Rate." By "underrepresented minority" they mean students who are black, Hispanic, or Native American. The first thing to notice is that the minority graduation rates for these schools vary widely, from a high of 63 percent for Dominican University to a low of 23.8 percent for Blackburn University. You're likely better off picking a school where your chances of graduating are highest. By this measure, it's not looking good for Blackburn.

The second thing to notice is how these numbers compare to those in the column immediately to the left, labeled "6-Year Grad Rate." This is the grad rate for all students at that school, including white students. See how at some schools (Dominican, Illinois College) the gap between the overall grad rate and the minority grad rate is small, only a few points? At other schools (Concordia,

College	2012 6-Year Grad Rate	Underrepresented Minority Female	Underrepresented Minority Male	Non-Underrepresented Minority Female	Non-Underrepresented Minority Male	Black Female	Black Male	Latino Female
Illinois State University	71.2%	52.7%	42.7%	77.5%	69.1%	44.7%	34.5%	64.5%
Dominican University	66.0%	66.7%	55.0%	67.5%	68.5%	64.3%	N/A	67.1%
Illinois College	61.8%	N/A	58.3%	71.2%	52.5%	N/A	N/A	N/A
Eastern Illinois University	60.4%	49.4%	44.8%	57.4%	56.3%	50.8%	44.1%	37.0%
Lewis University	59.0%	50.0%	38.8%	61.2%	65.0%	56.8%	56.3%	44.2%
Monmouth College	57.2%	40.0%	38.9%	65.7%	56.7%	30.8%	46.2%	46.7%
University of Illinois at Chicago	57.7%	48.0%	43.0%	60.5%	62.4%	43.4%	23.8%	52.5%
Eureka College	56.2%	N/A	N/A	56.9%	61.4%	N/A	N/A	N/A
Quincy University	55.9%	N/A	33.3%	62.0%	52.8%	N/A	N/A	N/A
Western Illinois University	54.4%	40.9%	48.4%	56.7%	54.5%	38.8%	41.1%	41.2%
Aurora University	51.7%	44.6%	51.5%	61.6%	43%	35.3%	37.5%	54.8%
McKendree University	48.3%	46.2%	41.9%	62.5%	40.2%	50.0%	37.5%	N/A
Concordia University–Chicago	48.8%	36.0%	24.2%	66.7%	54.5%	18.2%	16.7%	50.0%
Southern Illinois Univ.-Carbondale	47.6%	36.1%	25.4%	60.1%	50.1%	34.1%	25.1%	53.1%
University of Illinois at Springfield	47.2%	37.5%	5.3%	59.0%	47.5%	33.3%	6.3%	N/A
Blackburn College	44.6%	36.4%	10.0%	51.0%	41.5%	N/A	N/A	N/A

Grad rates by race and gender

University of Illinois–Springfield), the gap is large, close to twenty points. Colleges in the former group are clearly doing a better job of serving *all* their students than those in the latter.

Let's drill down a little more. On that webpage just above the tables, click on the button that says "Grad Rate by Race and Gender." That will take you to this page, which breaks the "Underrepresented Minorities" category into specific minority groups.

Under the columns "Black Female" and "Black Male" you can see again big differences in graduation rates among the colleges (and in some cases between genders). They range from a high of 64.3 percent for black females at Dominican University to a low of 6.3 percent for black males at the University of Illinois–Springfield. (If a box says "N/A," that means there are very few students in that category at that school.) You'll notice there are columns for other groups as well.

These numbers give you a pretty clear idea which schools from this list deserve a deeper look and which you might want to scratch off your list. You can get more detail on each college by clicking on the name of that college in the column on the left. For instance, try Dominican University, the school that has the smallest gap between white and minority graduation rates and the highest grad rate for black females— and, you may have noticed, high rates for Latino students, too.

There's all kinds of relevant information on that page, including its location (River Forest, a tony suburb north of Chicago) and the average GPA of incoming freshmen, which is 3.47. That means Dominican is probably a reach unless your grades are quite good.

Let's say they are good. Here's one more test you can do to get an even better sense of the school's quality. Click on the tab that says "Similar Colleges." That'll take you to a page that compares Dominican to schools all over the country that are similar in size, selectivity, and other dimensions.

As you can see, Dominican comes out on top. Its graduation rates for underrepresented minorities are the highest of the bunch. That's especially impressive because, as you can see elsewhere on that chart, Dominican has the second-highest percentage of students

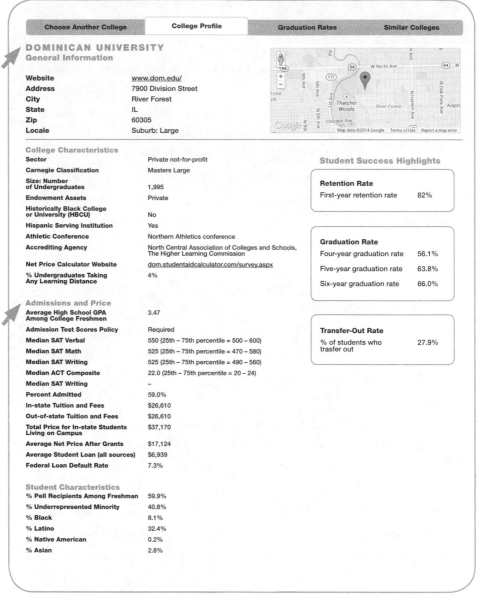

DOMINICAN UNIVERSITY
General Information

Website	www.dom.edu/
Address	7900 Division Street
City	River Forest
State	IL
Zip	60305
Locale	Suburb: Large

College Characteristics

Sector	Private not-for-profit
Carnegie Classification	Masters Large
Size: Number of Undergraduates	1,995
Endowment Assets	Private
Historically Black College or University (HBCU)	No
Hispanic Serving Institution	Yes
Athletic Conference	Northern Athletics conference
Accrediting Agency	North Central Association of Colleges and Schools, The Higher Learning Commission
Net Price Calculator Website	dom.studentaidcalculator.com/survey.aspx
% Undergraduates Taking Any Learning Distance	4%

Admissions and Price

Average High School GPA Among College Freshmen	3.47
Admission Test Scores Policy	Required
Median SAT Verbal	550 (25th – 75th percentile = 500 – 600)
Median SAT Math	525 (25th – 75th percentile = 470 – 580)
Median SAT Writing	525 (25th – 75th percentile = 490 – 560)
Median ACT Composite	22.0 (25th – 75th percentile = 20 – 24)
Median SAT Writing	–
Percent Admitted	59.0%
In-state Tuition and Fees	$26,610
Out-of-state Tuition and Fees	$26,610
Total Price for In-state Students Living on Campus	$37,170
Average Net Price After Grants	$17,124
Average Student Loan (all sources)	$6,939
Federal Loan Default Rate	7.3%

Student Characteristics

% Pell Recipients Among Freshman	59.9%
% Underrepresented Minority	40.8%
% Black	8.1%
% Latino	32.4%
% Native American	0.2%
% Asian	2.8%

Student Success Highlights

Retention Rate

First-year retention rate	82%

Graduation Rate

Four-year graduation rate	56.1%
Five-year graduation rate	63.8%
Six-year graduation rate	66.0%

Transfer-Out Rate

% of students who trasfer out	27.9%

When you click on the college name, you will see details about the college.

who are minorities (32 percent Latino and 8 percent black) and is the second-highest on Pell Grants as well. That means Dominican is doing an outstanding job of getting students over the finish line. So if you're a black or Latino student (with a strong academic record) looking for a school in this area that's right for you, you may have found a great option.

College	2012 6-Year Grad Rate	Underrepresented Minority 6-Year Grad Rate	% Pell Recipients Among Freshman	% Under-represented Minority	Average High School GPA Among Collge Freshman	Estimated Median SAT/ACT	Total Price for In-State, On-Campus Students	Average Net Price After Grants
Dominican University	66.0%	63.0%	60%	40.8%	3.47	1,030	$37,170	$17,124
Geneva College	62.4%	60.0%	40%	12.1%	3.55	1,075	$33,940	$19,711
BethelCollege–Indiana	61.5%	38.1%	55%	15.9%	3.43	1,015	$33,700	$18,333
Millikin University	55.3%	50.8%	43%	17.6%	3.34	1,070	$40,242	$19,765
Greenville College	54.2%	46.7%	47%	13.1%	3.24	1,030	$32,360	$18,661
Saint Xavier University	53.7%	39.5%	55%	34.2%	3.40	1,050	$38,830	$16,111
Aurora University	51.7%	46.9%	40%	25.8%	3.34	1,030	$31,476	$17,406
Piedmont College	51.7%	42.4%	40%	12.9%	3.45	1,020	$30,874	$15,,788
Lenoir-Rhyne University	49.0%	34.1%	50%	17.3%	3.59	1,000	$39,904	$17,799
Concordia University–Chicago	48.8%	29.3%	47%	31.9%	2.98	1,030	$36,306	$18,014
Hardin-Simmons University	46.8%	23.2%	34%	20.1%	3.56	1,040	$32,638	$21,227
Houston Baptist University	44.7%	31.6%	56%	45.4%	N/A	1,090	$37,195	$18,064
D'Youville College	40.1%	24.5%	43%	15.9%	N/A	1,030	$35,660	$18,070
Charleston Southern University	37.8%	27.7%	49%	33.1%	3.39	989	$33,240	$15,885
Judson College	37.3%	52.9%	64%	17.3%	3.39	1,030	$26,925	$17,310
Cumberland University	30.7%	9.4%	43%	13.9%	3.40	1,030	$31,760	$16,395

Click the "Similar Colleges" tab to see how your selection compares to other colleges like it.

Now it's time to go through this exercise for yourself. To help, we've designed "The Four-Way Fit + Rankings Worksheet." Use the various rankings in this chapter and online, and the four-way fit strategy. Find four schools that interest you and use the worksheet to see how the schools compare to one another in each category. Go to the campus website to learn more about region, setting, and campus life and check the profiles at the end of the book to see if your college is among them.

The Four-Way Fit + Rankings Worksheet

SCHOOLS >>>	1.	2.	3.	4.
Washington Monthly ranking				
My Four-Way Fit ranking (page 65)				
ACADEMIC				
Test score range				
Admit rate				
Match, reach, safety?*				
Graduation rate				
Graduation rate minority students				
FINANCIAL				
Net price for my family income				
Default rate				
PHYSICAL FIT				
Region				
Setting				
Distance away				
SOCIAL FIT				
Campus visit				
Campus life				
OTHER FACTORS >>>				

THE
OTHER
HELPFUL
TOOL
COLLEGE
GUIDE

BEST-BANG-FOR-the-BUCK COLLEGES (by region)

RANK	NAME	OVERALL SCORE	STUDENT LOAN DEFAULT RATE	GRADUATION RATE	GRADUATION RATE PERFORMANCE
MIDWESTERN SCHOOLS					
1.	Michigan Jewish Institute (MI)	14	4.7	72.3	35.4
2.	College of the Ozarks (MO)	13	0.0	61.3	25.4
3.	Grace Bible College (MI)	13	0.7	50.3	6.3
4.	Martin Luther College (MN)	12	1.2	72.3	10.1
5.	Illinois State University (IL)*	12	2.8	71.0	6.2
6.	Northland International University (WI)	12	0.7	66.0	25.0
7.	University of Michigan–Dearborn (MI)*	11	4.5	51.0	0.4
8.	Wayne State College (NE)*	11	5.9	50.3	1.7
9.	University of Illinois at Chicago (IL)*	11	2.9	55.0	-1.4
10.	Pittsburg State University (KS)*	11	7.0	52.3	9.8
11.	Michigan State University (MI)*	11	3.7	77.7	8.7
12.	Eastern Illinois University (IL)*	11	4.1	60.3	8.6
13.	Western Michigan University (MI)*	11	4.6	54.7	5.4
14.	Huntington University (IN)	11	2.1	61.0	9.4
15.	Maharishi Univ. of Mgmt. (IA)	11	3.8	60.0	9.3
16.	Bethel College–Mishawaka (IN)	11	5.8	58.0	8.6
17.	Hanover College (IN)	11	2.0	67.3	11.0
18.	Ripon College (WI)	11	2.9	71.0	6.1
19.	Univ. of Wisconsin–Green Bay (WI)*	10	2.7	52.3	-1.9
20.	Univ. of Wisconsin–Stevens Point (WI)*	10	2.6	60.3	1.1
21.	Indiana University–Bloomington (IN)*	10	3.6	72.7	6.1
22.	Univ. of Wisconsin–Eau Claire (WI)*	10	2.4	65.0	0.4
23.	Univ. of Wisconsin–La Crosse (WI)*	10	1.4	69.3	1.2
24.	Marygrove College (MI)	10	5.1	25.0	5.0
25.	University of Illinois–Springfield (IL)*	10	5.4	58.7	6.5
26.	South Dakota State University (SD)*	10	2.9	56.0	1.7
27.	Graceland University–Lamoni (IA)	10	5.6	50.0	1.8
28.	University of Northern Iowa (IA)*	10	3.2	66.7	5.0
29.	University of Iowa (IA)*	10	2.5	70.3	1.3
30.	Western Illinois University (IL)*	10	6.1	55.0	5.7
31.	University of Michigan–Ann Arbor (MI)*	10	1.5	90.3	4.9
32.	Grand Valley State University (MI)*	10	3.0	63.3	1.4
33.	Hannibal-LaGrange University (MO)	10	3.9	50.0	0.1
34.	University of Wisconsin–Madison (WI)*	10	1.1	82.3	5.0
35.	Baker Coll. Ctr. Graduate Studies (MI)	10	0.0	30.0	4.9
36.	Ursuline College (OH)	10	3.7	50.0	5.8
37.	Saint Mary-of-the-Woods College (IN)	10	4.6	56.7	17.5
38.	Dominican University (IL)	10	5.0	64.7	5.2
39.	Maranatha Baptist Bible College (WI)	10	0.6	51.3	4.2
40.	Grace College & Theological Seminary (IN)	10	2.5	58.0	8.6
41.	Univ. of St. Francis–Fort Wayne (IN)	10	4.7	53.7	7.7
42.	Concordia University–Chicago (IL)	10	2.9	56.0	0.0
43.	National Louis University (IL)	10	3.4	30.0	7.9
44.	Robert Morris University Illinois (IL)	10	4.5	47.3	7.7
45.	Marian University (IN)	10	3.7	57.7	5.8

STUDENTS RECEIVING PELL GRANTS	NET PRICE (all students)	NET PRICE (annual family income, $0–$30K)	NET PRICE (annual family income, $30–75K)	NET PRICE (annual family income above $75k)	PERCENT OF APPLICANTS ADMITTED	ACT/SAT 25TH PERCENTILE SCORE	ACT/SAT 75TH PERCENTILE SCORE
75.3	8,900	8,487	9,523		73.6		
61.0	10,393	10,078	11,079		9.5	21	25
59.3	14,194	12,882	13,942	17,178	76.2		
34.3	13,845	11,533	12,241	17,166	96.1	22	28
23.7	14,591	9,635	16,068	22,939	70.6	22	26
57.3	15,991	12,461	14,531	19,398	97.7		
40.7	8,284	5,318	8,320	12,519	60.4	21	26
40.0	9,197	6,767	9,117	12,795	75.6		
46.3	9,600	7,600	11,138	21,469	63.3	21	26
40.7	9,904	9,542	10,849	12,655	80.6	19	24
24.7	13,641	5,922	14,098	20,330	71.2	23	28
35.3	13,966	10,504	15,118	20,042	66.0	19	23
36.0	14,663	11,351	16,149	19,334	83.6	20	25
36.3	17,094	15,252	18,311	23,192	90.1	904	1139
64.0	17,364	15,915	15,878		47.2		
52.3	17,880	13,354	16,819	20,997	71.5	897	1140
44.3	18,230	11,585	14,697	20,999	66.2	1007	1233
34.3	19,321	12,000	16,361	21,056	76.7	21	27
31.0	9,005	6,254	11,015	14,507	87.2	21	25
32.3	10,108	6,880	11,722	15,264	77.9	21	25
19.0	10,481	4,094	10,693	18,509	71.9	1053	1253
26.0	10,872	7,129	11,483	16,068	74.8	22	26
21.7	11,344	7,647	12,815	16,573	75.1	23	27
72.3	12,517	11,900	13,531		46.5	14	19
34.7	12,701	7,986	11,110	16,395	58.6	20	26
28.3	12,933	10,438	13,427	15,681	91.8	20	25
37.7	13,227	10,331	12,228	15,696	45.8	18	24
26.0	13,700	9,687	13,725	16,289	79.4	21	25
18.3	14,004	8,902	13,718	18,071	80.7	23	28
36.3	14,233	11,826	16,014	21,114	64.3	18	23
15.7	14,306	5,171	10,592	20,689	42.6	28	32
33.7	14,323	9,317	13,622	18,673	81.8	21	26
36.0	14,342	12,705	13,118	14,419	62.5	19	25
15.7	14,773	6,721	13,242	19,920	67.2	26	30
52.0	15,816	15,439	16,916		82.4		
49.7	16,104	13,542	14,294	19,323	67.4	18	23
45.3	16,167	11,714	16,251	20,764	61.1	830	1120
40.0	16,410	12,856	13,992		59.1	20	24
46.0	16,783	15,200	17,082	20,422	65.7	20	25
31.3	16,900	13,554	16,940	20,781	86.7	907	1153
42.0	16,987	11,423	14,545	19,652	53.5	873	1053
40.3	17,558	15,465	15,995	20,499	53.6	19	24
52.3	17,991	18,813			76.0	15	17
65.0	17,994	18,104	17,982	19,965	47.1		
39.7	18,554	14,419	17,041	21,229	53.9	913	1,107

RANK	NAME	OVERALL SCORE	STUDENT LOAN DEFAULT RATE	GRADUATION RATE	GRADUATION RATE PERFORMANCE
46.	Simpson College (IA)	10	2.7	68.0	6.5
47.	Ohio State University–Main (OH)*	10	3.8	80.0	9.1
48.	Goshen College (IN)	10	3.9	70.7	7.4
49.	Baldwin Wallace University (OH)	10	2.1	69.7	5.5
50.	Elmhurst College (IL)	10	1.5	71.3	6.9
51.	Earlham College (IN)	10	2.6	70.3	6.7
52.	Saint Norbert College (WI)	10	1.9	74.0	6.2
53.	Mount Mercy University (IA)	10	2.9	58.7	7.9
54.	John Carroll University (OH)	10	2.6	73.0	8.5
55.	Knox College (IL)	10	2.6	78.3	7.1
56.	Calvin College (MI)	10	2.2	77.0	6.3
57.	University of St. Thomas (MN)	10	2.5	75.0	7.2
58.	Univ. of Wisconsin–Whitewater (WI)*	9	4.5	56.0	-3.3
59.	Park University (MO)	9	6.7	39.0	5.2
60.	Univ. of Wisconsin–River Falls (WI)*	9	2.3	53.3	-2.2
61.	Fort Hays State University (KS)*	9	4.5	42.0	7.3
62.	Univ. of Wisconsin–Platteville (WI)*	9	2.9	52.7	-2.6
63.	Indiana State University (IN)*	9	7.4	43.7	5.5
64.	University of Wisconsin–Stout (WI)*	9	2.6	52.7	-1.3
65.	Truman State University (MO)*	9	2.6	71.0	-4.4
66.	Univ. of Nebraska–Kearney (NE)*	9	3.7	58.3	2.8
67.	Purdue University–Main (IN)*	9	3.2	68.3	2.4
68.	Ohio State University–Lima (OH)*	9	3.8	40.3	1.0
69.	Iowa State University (IA)*	9	3.2	69.7	3.8
70.	University of North Dakota (ND)*	9	2.8	53.0	-4.8
71.	Wilberforce University (OH)	9	9.7	46.7	13.6
72.	University of Minnesota–Morris (MN)*	9	3.5	62.0	2.1
73.	Silver Lake Coll. of the Holy Family (WI)	9	4.2	40.0	13.8
74.	University of Minnesota–Twin Cities (MN)*	9	2.4	71.0	-0.6
75.	Saint Josephs College (IN)	9	5.2	55.0	8.3
76.	University of IL–Urbana-Champaign (IL)*	9	2.1	83.3	0.8
77.	McKendree University (IL)	9	5.9	52.0	0.6
78.	Central Christian College of Kansas (KS)	9	7.1	51.0	8.7
79.	Kuyper College (MI)	9	5.2	50.3	0.2
80.	College of Mount St. Joseph (OH)	9	5.4	57.7	10.6
81.	Malone University (OH)	9	3.3	59.7	3.0
82.	Mount Marty College (SD)	9	4.5	52.7	7.2
83.	Stevens Inst. of Bus. & Arts (MO)°	9	9.7	57.0	22.2
84.	Walsh University (OH)	9	4.4	60.0	4.3
85.	Marian University (WI)	9	3.9	51.7	3.5
86.	Trinity International University–Illinois (IL)	9	4.9	56.3	0.2
87.	Greenville College (IL)	9	4.7	55.0	0.1
88.	Union College (NE)	9	2.5	52.7	-0.4
89.	Millikin University (IL)	9	5.7	59.7	1.4
90.	Franklin College (IN)	9	3.6	56.7	4.2
91.	Rockhurst University (MO)	9	4.0	72.3	6.1

STUDENTS RECEIVING PELL GRANTS	NET PRICE (all students)	NET PRICE (annual family income, $0–$30K)	NET PRICE (annual family income, $30–75K)	NET PRICE (annual family income above $75k)	PERCENT OF APPLICANTS ADMITTED	ACT/SAT 25TH PERCENTILE SCORE	ACT/SAT 75TH PERCENTILE SCORE
30.0	18,879	14,881	16,584	20,817	86.6	21	26
24.3	19,111	11,825	17,274	23,127	63.1	26	30
32.7	19,146	14,820	15,712	21,165	58.2	990	1227
30.3	19,835	14,825	18,174	22,295	64.2	21	26
31.7	20,245	15,138	18,053	22,137	71.3	21	26
26.7	20,381	14,141	17,227	27,947	72.4	1017	1340
22.0	20,843	15,466	16,445	23,746	80.5	22	27
43.0	21,285	17,510	19,618	21,416	70.0	20	24
30.7	22,398	13,324	17,907	25,673	82.2	22	27
25.0	22,409	14,594	17,491	26,077	75.0		
24.7	24,018	16,717	20,186	26,362	81.0	23	29
20.3	28,292	19,143	23,702	30,233	85.4	23	28
28.0	9,596	6,491	11,206	14,902	81.6	20	25
25.3	9,781	10,013	10,479	13,060	71.8	18	24
30.7	10,314	8,118	11,801	15,538	88.9	20	24
25.0	10,593	7,440	10,480	12,735	80.0	18	24
31.7	10,836	7,053	11,240	14,988	95.9	20	25
40.3	11,307	7,753	12,061	16,822	80.4	813	1020
29.3	11,726	8,881	13,146	16,851	87.5	20	24
19.7	11,872	7,434	10,834	13,426	74.2	25	30
34.7	12,154	7,978	10,670	13,036	85.7	20	25
21.0	12,544	6,803	12,078	19,453	65.0	1047	1227
46.3	13,015	10,220	12,911	15,460	76.4		
23.7	13,483	8,608	11,718	15,509	83.9	22	28
22.0	13,818	9,946	12,930	15,821	71.3	21	26
75.0	13,941	12,887	16,301	20,696	54.1		
30.7	13,975	6,981	10,362	18,122	62.1	23	28
30.3	14,490	11,914	13,656		61.7	16	22
22.7	15,175	7,652	11,118	19,761	48.0	25	30
30.0	15,576	11,489	14,454	20,956	61.0	860	1047
19.3	15,710	7,392	14,855	24,410	66.0	26	31
37.3	15,965	10,314	13,045	20,027	67.2	19	25
46.3	16,534	14,799	15,784	18,658	60.9		
49.3	17,189	15,592	17,789	21,212	64.4	19	25
34.7	17,521	12,609	14,734	18,078	65.9	20	24
40.3	17,598	14,358	16,737	20,401	73.7	20	26
34.7	18,184	22,727	25,519	28,102	68.6	19	24
69.0	18,263	17,155	19,107		48.8		
37.3	18,323	13,564	17,331	21,078	78.2	20	24
39.3	18,339	14,641	17,310	21,699	79.8	17	23
36.7	18,382	14,316	16,526	21,372	94.5	19	26
43.3	18,526	14,833	16,577	21,707	71.1	19	25
39.7	18,643	16,098	16,452	17,887	54.5	19	26
38.0	18,939	13,370	16,247	23,067	56.7	20	25
37.0	19,232	12,282	16,918	22,088	61.2	920	1100
16.0	19,374	16,875	17,613	20,169	77.4	22	28

BEST-BANG-FOR-THE-BUCK COLLEGES

MIDWEST

RANK	NAME	OVERALL SCORE	STUDENT LOAN DEFAULT RATE	GRADUATION RATE	GRADUATION RATE PERFORMANCE
92.	Clarke University (IA)	9	4.6	62.3	4.2
93.	University of Indianapolis (IN)	9	3.7	52.3	2.3
94.	Bluffton University (OH)	9	4.3	57.7	5.6
95.	Hamline University (MN)	9	3.0	67.7	5.2
96.	Saint Mary's University of Minnesota (MN)	9	2.0	61.0	7.1
97.	Hiram College (OH)	9	5.4	65.7	10.8
98.	University of Mount Union (OH)	9	4.4	64.3	5.3
99.	Albion College (MI)	9	2.7	71.3	3.3
100.	Northwestern College (MN)	9	2.9	66.3	7.9
101.	Dordt College (IA)	9	1.1	67.7	6.3
102.	Grinnell College (IA)	9	1.1	88.7	4.6
103.	Gustavus Adolphus College (MN)	9	1.9	80.7	0.1
104.	Franciscan Univ.–Steubenville (OH)	9	2.3	74.3	1.4
105.	Saint Johns University (MN)	9	1.4	77.0	11.4
106.	Bradley University (IL)	9	2.1	75.3	4.7
107.	Hope College (MI)	9	2.5	78.0	3.1
108.	Wheaton College (IL)	9	1.2	88.3	3.6
109.	College of Saint Benedict (MN)	9	1.0	80.3	1.6
110.	DePauw University (IN)	9	2.0	82.7	10.5
111.	Taylor University (IN)	9	2.3	78.3	10.4
112.	Bethel University (MN)	9	1.9	70.7	4.1
113.	DePaul University (IL)	9	3.2	67.3	5.8
114.	Saint Mary's College (IN)	9	1.3	79.7	3.5
115.	Xavier University (OH)	9	2.4	78.0	8.7
116.	Lawrence University (WI)	9	1.7	74.3	0.3
117.	Missouri Southern State Univ. (MO)*	8	10.5	34.0	-4.6
118.	Chadron State College (NE)*	8	6.7	44.7	-0.5
119.	Calumet College of Saint Joseph (IN)	8	10.8	29.3	8.2
120.	NW Missouri State University (MO)*	8	5.9	51.3	-3.4
121.	Univ. of Wisconsin–Superior (WI)*	8	5.8	40.7	-0.8
122.	Univ. of Wisconsin–Oshkosh (WI)*	8	3.1	50.7	-2.8
123.	University of Central Missouri (MO)*	8	5.8	49.3	-0.4
124.	Emporia State University (KS)*	8	5.6	41.7	-4.4
125.	MN State University–Mankato (MN)*	8	3.9	50.7	-3.0
126.	Youngstown State University (OH)*	8	11.4	34.0	1.1
127.	Saint Cloud State University (MN)*	8	4.6	48.7	4.4
128.	Missouri State Univ–Springfield (MO)*	8	5.2	54.7	-3.2
129.	Bemidji State University (MN)*	8	5.7	47.7	0.1
130.	Ball State University (IN)*	8	5.0	56.7	-1.4
131.	Blackburn College (IL)	8	7.3	45.7	-5.0
132.	Metropolitan State University (MN)*	8	5.1	30.0	-0.2
133.	Ferris State University (MI)*	8	5.4	44.0	-4.4
134.	Central Michigan University (MI)*	8	3.7	55.0	-1.9
135.	University of Nebraska–Lincoln (NE)*	8	3.1	65.3	-0.6
136.	North Dakota State University–Main (ND)*	8	2.3	52.7	-7.2
137.	Columbia College (MO)	8	7.5	41.7	0.7

STUDENTS RECEIVING PELL GRANTS	NET PRICE (all students)	NET PRICE (annual family income, $0–$30K)	NET PRICE (annual family income, $30–75K)	NET PRICE (annual family income above $75k)	PERCENT OF APPLICANTS ADMITTED	ACT/SAT 25TH PERCENTILE SCORE	ACT/SAT 75TH PERCENTILE SCORE
37.7	19,638	15,513	17,740	22,744	76.4	20	25
37.3	19,769	14,017	17,644	23,711	69.9	903	1107
40.0	20,282	17,482	18,779	23,520	61.2	19	24
34.0	20,316	15,639	17,608	23,729	72.9	21	27
25.7	20,521	15,393	17,183	22,885	74.1	20	25
43.7	21,214	16,031	19,977	25,136	70.9	20	26
35.0	21,259	18,934	20,921	23,374	73.3	20	25
24.3	21,331	14,740	16,953	23,316	69.3	23	28
30.0	21,476	16,278	17,927	22,953	68.5	21	27
32.7	21,566	18,576	19,524	23,420	80.7	21	27
20.3	21,928	8,660	12,897	26,937	40.0	1240	1487
23.0	22,199	12,035	16,818	25,408	65.9	25	30
28.3	22,614	18,712	19,556	24,792	75.8	23	29
18.7	22,902	13,623	17,164	24,894	76.5	23	29
26.3	23,174	13,567	17,479	25,437	68.4	22	28
21.0	23,362	13,559	17,833	26,915	82.4	24	29
20.0	23,371	12,147	14,544	27,651	66.5	27	32
22.7	23,891	13,566	18,193	26,717	77.0	23	29
18.7	24,065	13,017	17,400	25,933	58.6	24	29
18.7	24,135	16,386	20,261	27,489	83.6	24	30
27.3	24,169	15,541	19,219	26,672	82.6	22	28
36.3	24,833	23,250	26,685	33,321	66.9	22	27
21.7	25,866	14,848	20,493	29,355	83.1	22	28
19.3	26,500	23,753	25,945	28,472	69.0	22	28
21.0	26,899	15,366	19,780	27,948	65.0		
55.0	7,971	7,402	9,171		95.7	18	24
36.3	9,132	7,010	9,211	11,387	67.5		
44.3	9,987	9,819	11,825	14,911	34.0	643	980
33.7	10,344	6,763	10,015	13,920	70.5	20	25
44.0	10,407	8,278	12,004	16,093	88.7	20	24
27.3	10,695	8,335	12,568	16,280	84.4	20	24
35.0	10,915	9,035	12,195	14,564	81.3	19	24
38.0	10,973	8,724	11,381	13,967	80.8	19	25
28.3	11,437	8,807	11,737	15,555	80.8	20	24
52.0	11,522	10,389	12,885	15,624	84.8		
27.7	11,522	9,622	12,306	16,206	88.4	19	24
30.3	11,873	11,237	13,866		81.2	21	27
34.7	11,928	9,159	11,830	16,466	70.3	19	24
30.0	12,200	8,007	13,273	18,548	64.4	963	1160
50.0	12,397	11,304	14,037		62.0	18	24
35.3	12,592	11,806	13,293		98.7		
40.7	12,961	9,573	14,607	17,844	67.4	19	24
34.0	13,066	10,776	12,810	17,844	76.5	20	25
21.3	13,124	9,184	12,458	17,159	62.0	22	28
23.0	13,402	9,709	12,829	15,872	82.2	21	26
46.7	13,469	12,616	13,979	14,885	70.9		

RANK	NAME	OVERALL SCORE	STUDENT LOAN DEFAULT RATE	GRADUATION RATE	GRADUATION RATE PERFORMANCE
138.	Mount Mary College (WI)	8	4.1	39.3	-3.9
139.	Kansas State University (KS)*	8	4.6	57.7	-3.1
140.	Alverno College (WI)	8	6.2	38.7	-2.4
141.	Lourdes University (OH)	8	8.4	37.0	2.8
142.	University of St. Francis (IL)	8	2.4	59.3	-3.1
143.	University of Kansas (KS)*	8	3.8	62.0	3.7
144.	Southwest Baptist University (MO)	8	7.0	51.3	1.2
145.	Bowling Green State Univ.–Main (OH)*	8	7.2	58.7	4.1
146.	Spring Arbor University (MI)	8	3.9	55.3	-0.2
147.	Monmouth College (IL)	8	6.3	56.3	2.6
148.	Davenport University (MI)	8	7.7	28.0	6.1
149.	Northern Illinois University (IL)*	8	6.3	55.3	0.5
150.	Illinois College (IL)	8	3.7	60.0	0.7
151.	Muskingum University (OH)	8	3.9	52.0	-1.4
152.	Finlandia University (MI)	8	8.1	40.7	2.6
153.	Eureka College (IL)	8	4.9	53.3	-3.2
154.	National Amer. Univ.–Rapid City (SD)°	8	14.9	30.7	8.3
155.	Buena Vista University (IA)	8	5.0	54.7	-1.8
156.	Concordia University Nebraska (NE)	8	2.6	58.7	-0.4
157.	Lewis University (IL)	8	4.7	59.7	0.2
158.	Wisconsin Lutheran College (WI)	8	2.4	59.7	-2.4
159.	Manchester College (IN)	8	6.7	53.7	1.4
160.	Doane College–Crete (NE)	8	3.3	60.7	-0.5
161.	Morningside College (IA)	8	3.8	55.3	-4.3
162.	William Woods University (MO)	8	3.0	50.0	-4.5
163.	Westminster College (MO)	8	4.7	65.3	1.7
164.	University of Evansville (IN)	8	3.7	66.0	0.6
165.	Presentation College (SD)	8	6.7	41.0	8.8
166.	Southwestern College (KS)	8	6.1	53.3	17.1
167.	Hastings College (NE)	8	3.3	58.7	0.2
168.	Mt. Vernon Nazarene Univ. (OH)	8	4.5	57.0	-1.9
169.	Andrews University (MI)	8	4.8	58.0	1.0
170.	University of Findlay (OH)	8	2.7	56.0	-2.2
171.	Lake Erie College (OH)	8	5.5	49.3	2.3
172.	Wartburg College (IA)	8	2.9	63.7	0.8
173.	Augsburg College (MN)	8	3.3	61.7	4.8
174.	Valparaiso University (IN)	8	3.5	71.7	0.6
175.	Brown College–Mendota Heights (MN)°	8	11.3	50.0	17.8
176.	Maryville University of Saint Louis (MO)	8	3.8	66.7	7.8
177.	Anderson University (IN)	8	3.5	59.0	3.9
178.	Webster University (MO)	8	4.6	63.3	9.6
179.	Wabash College (IN)	8	7.4	75.0	13.8
180.	Beloit College (WI)	8	1.6	77.0	-1.4
181.	Ohio Christian University (OH)	8	8.6	43.0	6.5
182.	Drake University (IA)	8	2.1	75.7	0.2
183.	Ohio Northern University (OH)	8	0.8	70.0	-2.5

STUDENTS RECEIVING PELL GRANTS	NET PRICE (all students)	NET PRICE (annual family income, $0–$30K)	NET PRICE (annual family income, $30–75K)	NET PRICE (annual family income above $75k)	PERCENT OF APPLICANTS ADMITTED	ACT/SAT 25TH PERCENTILE SCORE	ACT/SAT 75TH PERCENTILE SCORE
45.0	13,892	9,850	12,975	19,856	52.0	17	23
25.0	14,161	11,364	13,065	16,707	98.8		
57.7	14,946	13,497	14,067	19,296	75.1	17	22
54.0	15,141	13,828	15,123	19,808	77.1		
30.3	15,223	10,174	13,072	18,079	47.2	21	25
21.0	15,257	11,613	15,287	18,902	92.2	22	28
43.7	15,734	13,891	13,934	17,627	89.7	20	26
35.3	15,858	12,824	15,961	18,722	76.4	19	24
43.7	16,083	13,199	15,482	19,491	73.0	20	26
38.0	16,261	9,546	13,977	20,668	64.2	19	24
58.0	16,452	17,057	19,629		93.7		
38.3	16,504	14,161	17,332	22,846	54.4	19	24
33.0	16,520	11,865	14,342	20,040	58.6	20	26
41.7	16,525	11,973	14,744	19,598	77.2	19	24
63.0	16,585	14,214	15,608	19,753	57.4		
37.7	16,960	12,566	15,728	20,206	71.9	19	26
57.0	17,036	16,807	17,943		73.4		
49.7	17,215	15,444	15,593	19,431	68.6	20	25
26.3	17,248	14,259	16,374	19,298	72.4	21	27
29.3	17,402	13,323	15,556	20,579	62.2	20	25
32.0	17,420	11,918	14,702	20,481	68.6	21	26
39.0	17,765	14,228	15,957	20,980	64.5	887	1103
36.0	18,182	12,512	16,880	20,589	80.5	20	26
37.3	18,682	15,059	17,419	20,624	60.7	20	25
32.7	18,874	15,469	17,581	20,875	79.8	20	25
28.7	18,933	14,753	17,070	20,249	73.3	22	27
27.0	19,134	13,517	17,233	21,729	82.1	1023	1240
48.7	19,193	18,955	19,580	22,173	63.6	17	22
31.7	19,302	15,986	18,014	21,521	88.9	19	24
32.7	19,318	15,611	17,866	20,693	71.4	20	26
39.7	19,613	16,856	18,070	22,323	73.5	20	26
34.0	19,682	14,665	16,453	21,828	43.2	20	26
22.3	19,784	15,056	18,217	22,072	68.2	21	26
42.0	19,992	15,785	18,402	22,442	70.8	18	24
27.0	20,142	14,092	18,318	22,852	72.8	21	26
36.7	20,689	15,630	22,032	27,150	52.0	21	25
27.0	20,940	15,302	17,231	22,770	79.5	23	29
58.0	21,213	20,952	23,189	26,542	70.3		
32.3	21,678	16,756	19,669	22,990	70.4	23	27
36.0	21,883	18,405	20,403	22,694	63.2	913	1133
31.7	22,664	19,327	23,172		68.5	21	27
26.3	22,844	15,614	19,902	26,986	62.1	1046	1230
20.0	23,011	9,645	16,251	26,698	69.8	24	30
71.3	24,149	24,217	23,850	24,939	68.0	17	23
18.3	24,329	18,852	20,743	26,007	64.7	24	29
25.0	24,459	18,430	22,003	25,478	81.2	24	29

RANK	NAME	OVERALL SCORE	STUDENT LOAN DEFAULT RATE	GRADUATION RATE	GRADUATION RATE PERFORMANCE
184.	Kalamazoo College (MI)	8	0.6	80.7	0.9
185.	Denison University (OH)	8	1.0	82.7	0.2
186.	University of Dayton (OH)	8	1.6	76.0	2.2
187.	Kendall College (IL)°	8	6.3	51.3	13.1
188.	Marquette University (WI)	8	2.3	80.7	3.8
189.	Wichita State University (KS)*	7	4.6	42.3	-7.2
190.	Peru State College (NE)*	7	8.4	32.7	-0.1
191.	Central State University (OH)*	7	20.2	23.3	-1.0
192.	University of Michigan–Flint (MI)*	7	6.5	37.7	-6.9
193.	Dickinson State University (ND)*	7	4.5	37.7	-6.5
194.	Harris-Stowe State University (MO)*	7	18.8	9.7	-3.5
195.	University of Nebraska–Omaha (NE)*	7	4.7	44.7	-3.6
196.	Northern Michigan University (MI)*	7	7.0	45.0	-4.5
197.	Valley City State University (ND)*	7	4.9	41.0	-1.0
198.	Saginaw Valley State University (MI)*	7	5.8	40.0	-8.0
199.	Univ. of Minnesota–Crookston (MN)*	7	5.3	44.0	-1.6
200.	MN State Univ. Moorhead (MN)*	7	4.1	44.7	-3.6
201.	Dakota State University (SD)*	7	5.9	41.3	-3.4
202.	Washburn University (KS)*	7	8.8	38.0	-2.3
203.	Eastern Michigan University (MI)*	7	7.3	38.3	-3.7
204.	Black Hills State University (SD)*	7	6.1	32.0	-4.9
205.	University of Mary (ND)	7	2.9	49.7	-7.1
206.	University of Toledo (OH)*	7	8.3	44.3	-0.7
207.	Madonna University (MI)	7	4.3	43.3	-2.1
208.	Chancellor University (OH)°	7	9.8	6.3	1.9
209.	Southern IL University–Carbondale (IL)*	7	6.3	46.7	-1.1
210.	MO Univ. of Science & Technology (MO)*	7	3.7	66.0	-6.8
211.	University of Akron–Main (OH)*	7	8.6	39.3	-0.8
212.	Upper Iowa University (IA)	7	6.4	41.3	-4.7
213.	Grace University (NE)	7	4.3	39.7	-7.8
214.	Aquinas College (MI)	7	4.5	55.3	-5.9
215.	Winona State University (MN)*	7	2.6	54.0	-6.7
216.	Southern IL Univ.–Edwardsville (IL)*	7	4.9	51.7	-2.5
217.	Michigan Technological University (MI)*	7	3.3	65.3	-1.1
218.	Quincy University (IL)	7	6.8	50.0	-0.3
219.	University of Missouri–Columbia (MO)*	7	3.8	69.7	-0.7
220.	Siena Heights University (MI)	7	4.4	41.7	-1.0
221.	Univ. of Minnesota–Duluth (MN)*	7	2.8	54.3	-7.5
222.	Saint Xavier University (IL)	7	5.0	54.0	-5.5
223.	Wright State University–Main (OH)*	7	5.3	42.0	-3.7
224.	Aurora University (IL)	7	4.6	50.0	-6.3
225.	Oakland City University (IN)	7	6.8	64.0	29.8
226.	Briar Cliff University (IA)	7	5.8	48.0	-1.1
227.	Olivet College (MI)	7	8.9	43.3	-0.9
228.	Bethel College–North Newton (KS)	7	4.9	54.7	-5.5
229.	Midland University (NE)	7	5.5	47.7	-4.6

STUDENTS RECEIVING PELL GRANTS	NET PRICE (all students)	NET PRICE (annual family income, $0–$30K)	NET PRICE (annual family income, $30–75K)	NET PRICE (annual family income above $75k)	PERCENT OF APPLICANTS ADMITTED	ACT/SAT 25TH PERCENTILE SCORE	ACT/SAT 75TH PERCENTILE SCORE
16.0	26,512	12,159	19,634	28,625	70.8	26	30
16.0	26,862	32,822	36,495		49.0	27	30
14.3	27,191	21,587	25,660	30,369	69.3	24	28
43.0	29,108	28,077	28,225	33,269	96.5		
17.7	29,149	17,305	22,894	30,867	58.1	24	29
34.0	7,754	11,141	11,644		93.0	21	26
32.0	8,987	7,175	9,814	12,051	77.1		
79.7	9,020	8,944	10,586	14,270	30.5	14	18
44.0	9,423	6,943	10,864	14,149	72.3	19	25
24.0	9,433	7,367	9,283	11,841	76.5	18	24
74.7	9,602	9,163	10,305	11,965	64.1		
29.0	10,058	8,587	11,185	14,381	77.1	20	26
38.3	10,962	7,785	11,891	15,113	70.7	19	25
26.3	11,214	7,883	10,211	12,822	84.6	18	22
38.7	11,322	9,846	12,253	14,686	87.9	18	24
20.7	11,677	7,191	9,045	16,578	74.8	19	24
31.7	11,709	8,884	11,819	15,816	73.3	20	24
23.7	11,959	10,110	12,118	14,758	90.0	19	25
36.7	12,615	10,766	14,263	15,610	98.5	19	24
42.3	12,901	11,075	12,861	15,853	59.6	18	24
36.3	12,968	11,319	14,121	16,082	91.5	18	23
28.3	13,287	9,773	11,639	15,202	81.6	20	25
39.3	13,372	11,193	13,125	16,124	80.0		
34.7	13,425	11,175	13,289	15,710	69.6	20	24
72.3	13,617	13,994			88.3		
41.3	13,949	12,241	15,739	20,615	51.6	18	24
27.0	14,639	11,101	14,042	16,987	90.0	25	31
40.7	14,705	14,197	16,568	18,908	96.7	18	24
56.0	15,017	15,290	15,945	17,177	62.0	19	24
58.0	15,049	11,604	12,977		58.9	19	26
37.0	15,109	10,212	11,689		78.9	21	26
25.0	15,538	10,631	14,215	18,608	65.6	21	25
32.7	15,538	12,463	17,253	21,977	81.6	20	25
26.0	15,659	9,770	12,749	18,774	74.1	23	29
42.3	15,783	13,842	14,418	18,511	91.0	19	24
21.3	15,822	11,760	14,437	19,019	81.2	23	28
44.3	16,041	12,572	15,236	18,936	61.8	18	23
23.7	16,092	8,075	11,247	19,787	76.8	22	26
46.3	16,227	15,243	17,182	21,516	61.8	20	25
40.0	16,268	14,423	17,267	20,631	76.6		
37.0	16,410	12,132	14,017	19,622	73.9	20	24
13.0	16,527	14,203	17,137		60.7	838	1040
42.0	16,757	18,697	17,011		58.3	18	23
53.7	17,073	13,651	16,228	19,794	60.1	18	22
36.0	17,345	14,996	16,146	19,084	70.2	20	26
43.0	17,377	15,641	16,511	18,651	73.6	19	25

RANK	NAME	OVERALL SCORE	STUDENT LOAN DEFAULT RATE	GRADUATION RATE	GRADUATION RATE PERFORMANCE
230.	Waldorf College (IA)°	7	6.5	41.3	-0.6
231.	Benedictine University (IL)	7	4.4	51.3	-3.2
232.	Lakeland College (WI)	7	4.8	44.0	4.6
233.	Augustana College (SD)	7	2.2	66.0	-6.0
234.	Ohio University–Main (OH)*	7	7.9	64.7	3.5
235.	Northland College (WI)	7	4.1	52.0	-5.8
236.	Adrian College (MI)	7	4.1	50.7	-5.5
237.	Olivet Nazarene University (IL)	7	3.6	58.7	-4.8
238.	Amer. InterCont. Univ.–Online (IL)°	7	18.7	29.0	8.8
239.	Wilmington College (OH)	7	5.1	45.7	-2.0
240.	Alma College (MI)	7	4.7	65.7	-0.9
241.	Kaplan University–Davenport (IA)°	7	16.4	23.3	20.9
242.	Illinois Institute of Technology (IL)	7	2.3	65.3	-5.6
243.	Union Institute & University (OH)	7	4.0	20.3	-1.8
244.	Concordia Univ.–Saint Paul (MN)	7	4.5	49.3	2.5
245.	Heidelberg University (OH)	7	5.2	53.3	-1.6
246.	Concordia University–Wisconsin (WI)	7	4.4	59.0	3.9
247.	Baker University (KS)	7	3.7	59.7	4.4
248.	Edgewood College (WI)	7	2.7	53.7	-3.7
249.	Northwestern College (IA)	7	1.3	65.0	-2.0
250.	Concordia College–Moorhead (MN)	7	1.4	68.0	-1.0
251.	Defiance College (OH)	7	5.3	48.7	1.7
252.	Crown College (MN)	7	4.3	52.0	-0.5
253.	Cornell College (IA)	7	2.4	69.0	-4.7
254.	Central College (IA)	7	3.1	65.3	0.3
255.	Cedarville University (OH)	7	0.7	69.0	-1.8
256.	Ashland University (OH)	7	3.4	60.7	3.7
257.	Trinity Christian College (IL)	7	3.4	59.7	-0.2
258.	Nebraska Wesleyan University (NE)	7	2.1	64.7	-4.3
259.	College of Saint Scholastica (MN)	7	3.3	63.3	3.9
260.	Saint Ambrose University (IA)	7	3.9	62.3	0.8
261.	Westwood College–O'Hare Airport (IL)°	7	14.1	41.0	10.0
262.	Otterbein University (OH)	7	3.4	60.0	-0.3
263.	St. Catherine University (MN)	7	3.8	61.3	-3.7
264.	Stephens College (MO)	7	5.5	55.3	-2.3
265.	Macalester College (MN)	7	1.3	88.3	-1.5
266.	Indiana Wesleyan University (IN)	7	4.4	64.7	1.8
267.	Westwood College–River Oaks (IL)°	7	13.2	33.7	11.8
268.	Miami University–Oxford (OH)*	7	6.4	80.3	6.5
269.	Augustana College (IL)	7	3.2	77.0	4.4
270.	Lake Forest College (IL)	7	3.1	69.3	1.6
271.	Luther College (IA)	7	2.0	73.3	-4.0
272.	DeVry University–Ohio (OH)°	7	14.6	35.0	11.3
273.	MN School of Business–Richfield (MN)°	7	8.7	33.3	4.2
274.	College of Wooster (OH)	7	3.2	76.0	0.4
275.	University of Rio Grande (OH)	7	11.8	41.0	5.4

STUDENTS RECEIVING PELL GRANTS	NET PRICE (all students)	NET PRICE (annual family income, $0–$30K)	NET PRICE (annual family income, $30–75K)	NET PRICE (annual family income above $75k)	PERCENT OF APPLICANTS ADMITTED	ACT/SAT 25TH PERCENTILE SCORE	ACT/SAT 75TH PERCENTILE SCORE
56.0	17,572	17,917	17,678	20,143	50.4	17	23
31.3	17,784	16,423	19,543	23,043	76.5	19	25
31.7	17,828	14,567	16,432	21,066	75.5	19	24
26.0	18,061	13,604	15,754	19,917	79.4	23	28
22.0	18,067	14,143	17,920	21,650	83.0	21	26
38.0	18,201	14,382	16,394	20,792	72.5	20	27
40.7	18,266	15,611	19,458	25,498	60.7	19	25
32.0	18,718	16,477	17,326	20,356	79.9	20	27
70.7	18,871	18,853	20,264	23,136	93.5		
40.7	18,895	15,284	18,071	21,974	90.1	18	23
33.0	19,124	15,020	16,243	24,060	54.7	22	27
58.3	19,246	19,110	20,647		125.4		
30.0	19,302	10,751	14,974	22,881	60.8	24	31
65.7	19,382	19,560			71.7		
32.0	19,822	17,128	18,746	24,324	96.9	18	24
42.7	20,017	16,855	19,006	22,193	61.9	19	25
32.7	20,023	16,186	17,836	22,108	66.6	20	26
33.3	20,055	18,043	19,383	21,009	89.4	21	26
34.3	20,118	14,725	16,113	23,044	73.6	20	24
32.0	20,236	22,317	22,752	26,073	72.8	22	27
25.3	20,498	12,759	16,807	23,819	88.9	22	28
46.7	20,632	17,818	19,335	23,711	65.6	18	23
43.7	20,662	16,976	19,088	23,794	70.2	20	25
31.0	20,796	12,411	14,096	21,970	47.1	24	30
28.0	20,960	14,710	16,667	22,957	70.6	21	26
23.3	21,036	15,751	18,284	23,057	75.2	24	29
30.0	21,637	18,033	19,929	24,267	72.7	20	25
35.7	21,818	20,079	21,352	25,811	84.1	19	26
24.7	21,988	17,145	20,120	23,396	79.7	23	28
31.3	22,135	20,857	22,914	26,051	79.9	20	26
25.3	22,248	17,706	20,810	21,937	80.4	20	25
75.0	22,421	22,836	23,335		50.0		
38.0	22,458	19,874	23,047	27,307	78.8	21	26
41.0	22,640	20,765	20,752	25,782	59.3	21	26
37.3	22,655	19,343	21,124	20,655	77.0	20	26
15.3	22,719	11,715	14,401	28,631	38.1	1270	1480
33.0	22,948	24,381	24,034	24,742	72.7	21	27
84.3	22,973	22,906	24,398		48.0		
16.0	23,062	16,465	21,442	25,372	75.0	24	29
19.0	23,299	16,862	19,817	25,304	72.2		
34.3	23,307	15,334	18,352	27,344	57.0		
19.7	23,524	16,870	19,572	25,784	71.3	24	29
65.0	23,680	23,203	24,037	26,472	79.5		
52.0	23,830	22,607	24,916		78.5		
18.7	24,193	10,177	15,629	26,170	62.0	24	30
62.7	24,425	23,953	25,549	25,676	73.4		

RANK	NAME	OVERALL SCORE	STUDENT LOAN DEFAULT RATE	GRADUATION RATE	GRADUATION RATE PERFORMANCE
276.	DeVry University–Illinois (IL)°	7	14.6	32.3	13.4
277.	Creighton University (NE)	7	1.5	76.3	-0.5
278.	Wittenberg University (OH)	7	2.9	67.3	-1.9
279.	St. Olaf College (MN)	7	1.2	85.3	-0.2
280.	Case Western Reserve University (OH)	7	0.6	79.3	-10.3
281.	Illinois Wesleyan University (IL)	7	2.4	81.7	-1.9
282.	Carleton College (MN)	7	0.8	93.3	-1.1
283.	University of Chicago (IL)	7	1.4	92.3	-4.6
284.	Kenyon College (OH)	7	1.6	87.7	-0.6
285.	Saint Louis University–Main (MO)	7	2.7	71.0	-1.1
286.	Oberlin College (OH)	7	0.8	86.7	-2.9
287.	Purdue University Calumet (IN)*	6	8.6	27.7	-8.2
288.	Lincoln University (MO)*	6	17.7	23.7	-6.1
289.	Missouri Western State University (MO)*	6	13.1	29.7	-3.1
290.	University of Wisconsin–Parkside (WI)*	6	8.0	30.0	-9.5
291.	Mayville State University (ND)*	6	6.3	31.7	-3.0
292.	Bellevue University (NE)	6	4.5	31.3	-11.0
293.	Lake Superior State University (MI)*	6	6.7	36.3	-7.3
294.	Northern State University (SD)*	6	7.1	39.7	-4.7
295.	University of Southern Indiana (IN)*	6	6.7	38.0	-5.6
296.	Minot State University (ND)*	6	3.7	35.0	-13.4
297.	IN Univ./Purdue Univ.–Indianapolis (IN)*	6	5.5	35.3	-6.4
298.	Southwest MN State Univ. (MN)*	6	6.0	40.0	-0.0
299.	University of Wisconsin–Milwaukee (WI)*	6	4.1	42.0	-6.3
300.	University of South Dakota (SD)*	6	4.7	49.0	-6.8
301.	Oakland University (MI)*	6	4.1	41.0	-9.2
302.	Cleveland State University (OH)*	6	6.8	31.3	-9.0
303.	Capella University (MN)°	6	8.9	0.0	-25.5
304.	Shawnee State University (OH)*	6	14.2	27.7	-4.7
305.	Ctrl. Methodist U.–Lib. Arts & Sciences (MO)	6	6.8	46.0	-4.6
306.	Rochester College (MI)	6	6.7	38.0	-1.0
307.	Ottawa University–Ottawa (KS)	6	6.2	43.7	-3.8
308.	Martin University (IN)	6	16.9	12.7	3.3
309.	University of Missouri–St. Louis (MO)*	6	5.7	47.0	-3.6
310.	Viterbo University (WI)	6	3.5	49.3	-9.2
311.	University of Saint Mary (KS)	6	4.7	38.0	-10.3
312.	Bethany Lutheran College (MN)	6	3.7	49.3	-10.2
313.	Cornerstone University (MI)	6	4.1	46.3	-10.2
314.	Culver-Stockton College (MO)	6	7.3	48.0	-0.4
315.	University of Dubuque (IA)	6	8.1	41.0	-6.1
316.	Concordia University–Ann Arbor (MI)	6	4.5	44.7	-7.3
317.	Kent State University–Kent (OH)*	6	8.4	50.7	-6.0
318.	University of Cincinnati–Main (OH)*	6	6.0	51.3	-8.4
319.	University of Sioux Falls (SD)	6	4.1	52.7	-8.1
320.	North Central University (MN)	6	3.9	43.0	-9.0
321.	Ohio Dominican University (OH)	6	5.0	44.7	-5.4

STUDENTS RECEIVING PELL GRANTS	NET PRICE (all students)	NET PRICE (annual family income, $0–$30K)	NET PRICE (annual family income, $30–75K)	NET PRICE (annual family income above $75k)	PERCENT OF APPLICANTS ADMITTED	ACT/SAT 25TH PERCENTILE SCORE	ACT/SAT 75TH PERCENTILE SCORE
63.0	25,160	25,011	25,641	28,462	74.2		
19.0	25,485	18,769	20,000	25,100	78.1	24	29
23.0	25,626	21,679	22,493	28,565	78.7	22	28
15.7	26,385	10,594	15,687	29,090	56.9	26	31
22.0	26,909	18,075	23,144	31,556	57.4	1250	1413
18.3	27,130	17,274	20,483	29,503	60.7	25	30
12.7	28,592	11,594	16,311	32,867	29.1	1320	1507
17.0	28,721	11,198	13,784	35,793	16.1	1400	1567
10.0	30,310	10,789	14,486	36,549	36.3	1247	1473
13.7	32,654	23,952	25,389	32,885	66.0	25	30
12.7	34,385	11,022	15,558	33,300	30.5	1273	1480
38.0	8,600	7,396	10,399	13,597	47.2	863	1060
59.0	8,725	9,960	10,437	11,647	78.9		
41.7	9,566	8,584	9,975	12,656	73.6		
41.3	10,625	8,987	12,578	16,760	82.7	18	23
31.3	10,995	7,195	9,919	12,560	74.3		
22.7	11,150	9,642			63.1		
40.0	11,479	7,530	11,674	15,705	85.5	20	25
27.3	11,591	9,324	11,934	14,066	92.1	19	24
43.0	11,891	8,777	13,620	16,395	72.3	877	1080
26.7	11,995	9,382	11,646	14,852	61.8	19	24
33.7	12,028	8,593	13,745	18,710	66.6	887	1100
15.7	12,285	9,559	11,887	16,057	74.6	19	24
32.7	12,978	11,156	15,666	19,616	90.0	19	24
29.7	13,598	10,972	13,541	16,027	74.3	20	26
28.3	13,703	13,073	12,406	14,374	65.6	20	25
46.0	13,730	12,263	14,779	17,732	58.0	18	24
52.3	14,215	14,014			100.0		
55.7	14,467	13,557	15,398	17,683	89.0		
44.3	15,513	13,184	16,267		65.1	20	24
46.3	15,530	13,618	14,603	18,273	69.9	18	23
43.3	15,912	13,349	15,284	18,404	84.0	18	24
83.3	16,053	16,180			53.1		
29.3	16,054	13,973	16,186	20,623	70.1	21	26
38.3	16,262	11,855	13,693	18,927	77.1	21	25
44.7	16,415	14,920	15,163	17,194	56.4	18	24
40.7	16,823	10,537	13,891	21,637	81.9	20	27
42.0	16,936	14,686	15,196	18,920	67.6	20	26
48.3	16,979	14,248	16,579	20,039	62.6	18	24
50.0	17,009	14,484	16,710	18,985	77.6	18	23
41.0	17,467	16,415	17,218	21,387	69.0	19	24
36.0	17,496	14,542	17,927	21,192	82.7	20	25
26.7	18,273	15,310	19,110	23,288	66.3	22	27
28.7	18,420	16,737	18,334	19,662	74.2	20	25
38.7	18,587	15,129	17,365	20,971	78.9	19	25
36.7	18,741	18,310	19,347	26,035	62.0	19	24

RANK	NAME	OVERALL SCORE	STUDENT LOAN DEFAULT RATE	GRADUATION RATE	GRADUATION RATE PERFORMANCE
322.	McPherson College (KS)	6	8.0	48.0	-2.0
323.	CO Technical Univ.–Sioux Falls (SD)°	6	17.1	28.0	4.9
324.	Notre Dame College (OH)	6	5.7	42.0	-4.6
325.	North Park University (IL)	6	6.6	55.3	-3.3
326.	Tabor College (KS)	6	5.0	48.3	-3.9
327.	Loras College (IA)	6	3.3	62.7	-2.5
328.	Carroll University (WI)	6	2.4	58.0	-5.4
329.	Tiffin University (OH)	6	6.6	41.7	-0.0
330.	Cardinal Stritch University (WI)	6	5.1	45.3	-4.8
331.	Drury University (MO)	6	11.5	55.0	-4.7
332.	University of Detroit Mercy (MI)	6	4.1	55.0	-3.9
333.	North Central College (IL)	6	3.7	66.7	-2.7
334.	William Jewell College (MO)	6	3.7	65.7	-3.0
335.	Marietta College (OH)	6	4.4	57.7	-4.1
336.	Argosy University–Twin Cities (MN)°	6	9.2	41.3	8.5
337.	Judson University (IL)	6	3.8	53.3	-6.6
338.	Westwood College–Chicago Loop (IL)°	6	13.2	23.0	5.0
339.	University of Notre Dame (IN)	6	0.6	95.7	-6.2
340.	DeVry University–Missouri (MO)°	6	14.6	28.0	5.7
341.	Milwaukee School of Engineering (WI)	6	2.7	58.0	-14.9
342.	Ohio Wesleyan University (OH)	6	2.7	64.0	-5.6
343.	Roosevelt University (IL)	6	5.0	45.3	-4.7
344.	Northwestern University (IL)	6	1.1	93.7	-6.0
345.	Kettering University (MI)	6	2.7	57.7	-11.6
346.	Butler University (IN)	6	1.0	73.0	-5.0
347.	Washington University in St Louis (MO)	6	1.9	93.7	-5.0
348.	Indiana University–East (IN)*	5	13.1	22.3	-6.6
349.	Indiana University–Kokomo (IN)*	5	8.3	23.7	-9.6
350.	Wayne State University (MI)*	5	8.1	28.3	-12.3
351.	Southeast MO State University (MO)*	5	8.4	46.7	-5.9
352.	IN U.–Purdue U.–Ft. Wayne (IN)*	5	6.9	25.3	-10.1
353.	Chicago State University (IL)*	5	9.9	18.7	-7.5
354.	Northeastern Illinois University (IL)*	5	7.0	21.3	-7.8
355.	Trine Univ.–Regional/Non-Traditional (IN)	5	6.2	0.0	-21.8
356.	Jamestown College (ND)	5	3.1	48.0	-9.6
357.	MacMurray College (IL)	5	10.4	37.0	-5.5
358.	Newman University (KS)	5	4.4	35.7	-15.5
359.	York College (NE)	5	7.4	39.0	-8.6
360.	MidAmerica Nazarene University (KS)	5	4.4	48.7	-6.6
361.	Grand View University (IA)	5	6.3	44.7	-5.2
362.	Urbana University (OH)	5	8.8	30.7	-8.4
363.	Dakota Wesleyan University (SD)	5	8.5	41.3	-9.1
364.	Avila University (MO)	5	6.1	45.0	-6.4
365.	Fontbonne University (MO)	5	6.8	40.7	-7.6
366.	College of Saint Mary (NE)	5	6.7	41.3	-10.4
367.	Kansas Wesleyan University (KS)	5	8.8	39.0	-16.9

STUDENTS RECEIVING PELL GRANTS	NET PRICE (all students)	NET PRICE (annual family income, $0–$30K)	NET PRICE (annual family income, $30–75K)	NET PRICE (annual family income above $75k)	PERCENT OF APPLICANTS ADMITTED	ACT/SAT 25TH PERCENTILE SCORE	ACT/SAT 75TH PERCENTILE SCORE
41.7	19,117	15,253	17,527	22,260	67.3	19	24
62.7	19,464	18,479	20,511		87.7		
32.0	19,824	16,169	18,481	22,495	73.6	18	22
32.7	19,977	15,651	17,418	24,007	41.0	19	25
39.0	20,264	18,278	19,046	22,714	89.8	19	25
26.0	20,302	18,607	19,115	23,168	69.4	21	26
27.0	20,322	15,808	17,674	21,595	79.6	20	26
60.3	20,432	24,049	21,990		53.9	18	23
41.3	20,591	23,642	21,478	23,928	42.9	19	24
55.0	20,663	16,683	20,304	24,821	80.1	21	30
32.0	20,755	20,369	20,256	21,161	59.3	22	27
25.3	21,136	13,921	16,255	21,897	64.4	22	27
26.7	21,141	17,557	18,857	22,882	55.2	23	28
30.0	21,409	14,348	18,216	24,826	69.1	21	26
46.0	21,540	19,663	21,742	24,015	83.2		
41.3	21,683	15,253	20,593		65.0	21	26
84.7	22,875	22,691	22,876		48.9		
12.0	24,344	12,042	13,161	34,884	25.4	31	34
61.0	24,396	23,815	25,303	27,351	71.8		
28.0	24,537	20,245	20,778	26,076	63.9	24	29
22.0	25,049	18,564	22,164	26,876	71.0	23	29
41.3	25,571	24,691	27,782		66.6	19	25
12.7	27,967	15,794	18,232	36,915	22.8	1373	1500
22.7	28,085	21,140	25,712	29,698	63.5	24	29
17.3	28,819	22,347	22,718	28,538	66.6	25	30
6.7	32,330	4,668	13,381	37,677	18.6	32	34
38.3	8,319	5,609	9,564	13,437	61.3	817	1027
31.7	9,104	6,341	10,807	14,831	72.2	850	1047
47.3	10,434	8,779	11,566	15,511	80.8	18	25
34.3	10,516	8,012	10,416	14,223	97.2	20	25
37.0	12,359	13,936	14,877	18,492	89.3	867	1073
78.0	12,635	11,233	12,466		42.6	16	19
45.3	12,862	14,195	14,094	18,128	64.1	16	21
47.7	14,368	14,306			56.8		
29.0	15,744	13,863	15,265	16,778	60.9	20	25
56.3	16,018	13,443	15,669	23,049	71.4	17	21
25.0	16,180	16,356	15,201	17,157	44.4	21	27
49.7	16,236	15,126	15,091	17,885	68.3	18	24
33.3	16,388	13,793	15,026	16,192	87.8	20	25
43.7	16,917	13,344	15,554	19,223	92.5	18	23
35.0	17,131	15,481	17,278	21,309	69.6		
47.0	17,143	14,849	16,412	18,387	75.9	18	26
36.0	18,028	16,506	15,798	19,837	54.3	20	25
41.0	18,677	17,287	17,479	19,245	72.0	20	25
48.0	18,785	17,703	17,866	22,151	48.3	19	24
42.7	18,902	17,549	17,619	20,337	52.5	20	24

RANK	NAME	OVERALL SCORE	STUDENT LOAN DEFAULT RATE	GRADUATION RATE	GRADUATION RATE PERFORMANCE
368.	Coe College (IA)	5	3.7	69.0	-5.1
369.	Evangel University (MO)	5	4.0	49.7	-6.5
370.	Capital University (OH)	5	3.3	59.7	-5.6
371.	Benedictine College (KS)	5	3.3	55.3	-7.1
372.	ITT Tech. Institute–Indianapolis (IN)°	5	17.8	16.7	2.9
373.	Lindenwood University (MO)	5	2.9	43.7	-11.5
374.	Carthage College (WI)	5	4.1	59.0	-10.4
375.	Loyola University–Chicago (IL)	5	3.6	69.0	-9.1
376.	Purdue Univ.–North Central (IN)*	4	9.6	23.0	-10.0
377.	Indiana University–South Bend (IN)*	4	9.8	24.0	-8.1
378.	Indiana University–Southeast (IN)*	4	7.6	27.7	-5.7
379.	Indiana University–Northwest (IN)*	4	9.1	23.7	-7.6
380.	Missouri Valley College (MO)	4	10.1	28.7	-9.2
381.	William Penn University (IA)	4	10.7	33.3	-6.3
382.	Sterling College (KS)	4	9.3	41.0	-10.0
383.	Bethany College (KS)	4	9.6	37.7	-14.7
384.	Friends University (KS)	4	6.3	28.7	-15.8
385.	Ashford University (IA)°	4	11.9	26.7	-15.8
386.	Iowa Wesleyan College (IA)	4	11.3	30.7	-9.7
387.	University of Missouri–Kansas City (MO)*	4	7.3	45.7	-7.0
388.	Missouri Baptist University (MO)	4	5.7	34.3	-2.7
389.	Rockford College (IL)	4	6.4	42.0	-7.9
390.	Westwood College–Dupage (IL)°	4	12.8	24.3	-2.2
391.	Trine University (IN)	4	6.2	48.7	-5.4
392.	East-West University (IL)	4	14.0	25.0	-1.7
393.	Columbia College–Chicago (IL)	4	8.7	41.3	-1.9
394.	Holy Cross College (IN)	3	7.3	25.0	-19.5
395.	Univ. of Phoenix–West Michigan (MI)°	3	17.0	10.7	-7.7
396.	University of Phoenix–Wichita (KS)°	3	17.0	7.3	-10.4
397.	Univ. of Phoenix–Kansas City (MO)°	3	17.0	13.0	-11.4
398.	U. of Phoenix–Minn./St. Paul (MN)°	3	17.0	9.3	-14.7
399.	Univ. of Phoenix–Metro Detroit (MI)°	3	17.0	11.0	-8.3
400.	Lawrence Technological Univ. (MI)	3	5.4	47.3	-6.8
401.	Univ. of Phoenix–Cleveland (OH)°	3	17.0	10.7	-8.7
402.	Shimer College (IL)	3	12.3	34.0	-16.3
403.	Grantham University (MO)°	2		23.7	-16.6

NORTHEASTERN SCHOOLS

RANK	NAME	OVERALL SCORE	STUDENT LOAN DEFAULT RATE	GRADUATION RATE	GRADUATION RATE PERFORMANCE
1.	CUNY Bernard M. Baruch College (NY)*	12	2.9	62.3	2.6
2.	Rutgers University-Camden (NJ)*	12	3.8	63.0	12.3
3.	CUNY Lehman College (NY)*	11	5.4	36.7	0.9
4.	CUNY John Jay Col. of Crim. Just. (NY)*	11	5.1	31.3	0.8
5.	CUNY Queens College (NY)*	11	3.7	53.0	2.6
6.	Rhode Island College (RI)*	11	4.8	44.3	7.1
7.	New Jersey City University (NJ)*	11	6.3	36.7	8.8
8.	Fashion Institute of Technology (NY)*	11	5.3	67.0	7.5

STUDENTS RECEIVING PELL GRANTS	NET PRICE (all students)	NET PRICE (annual family income, $0–$30K)	NET PRICE (annual family income, $30–75K)	NET PRICE (annual family income above $75k)	PERCENT OF APPLICANTS ADMITTED	ACT/SAT 25TH PERCENTILE SCORE	ACT/SAT 75TH PERCENTILE SCORE
26.0	20,270	15,330	16,991	21,698	64.1	23	28
44.0	20,822	17,894	20,674	24,483	68.1	19	25
28.7	21,215	18,920	21,147	23,084	75.3	21	27
21.0	21,839	17,361	19,406	22,820	60.0	21	27
64.3	22,715	22,734	23,845	26,474	70.0		
34.7	25,104	23,988	24,430	26,356	58.3	20	25
27.7	26,245	21,177	24,141	28,082	69.7	22	27
31.3	29,046	21,791	24,478	32,724	57.5	25	29
34.3	8,277	5,227	9,826	13,073	79.5	847	1060
34.3	9,792	7,630	12,004	15,698	70.5	843	1047
33.3	10,156	7,714	11,839	15,763	78.7	840	1060
35.7	12,163	10,068	13,551	17,184	74.1	780	1013
44.7	14,224	12,264	13,791	16,799	50.1	17	21
49.7	16,527	15,658	16,001	18,645	58.7	16	21
43.7	16,682	13,669	16,126	19,098	48.6	19	25
41.7	17,753	15,251	17,084	18,664	60.5	19	25
43.3	18,052	16,385	16,073	19,000	61.0	18	25
56.7	18,150	19,081	18,605	16,105	84.6	18	22
49.0	19,296	18,075	18,911	21,013	61.4	18	22
31.7	19,427	16,725	19,025	21,946	58.5	20	27
19.7	20,456	17,921	20,113	22,154	59.9	19	23
49.0	20,680	19,779	18,876	22,289	42.4	18	23
67.3	20,901	21,580	22,661	24,995	49.1		
35.7	23,173	18,305	22,796		72.6	21	24
86.3	25,050	24,649	25,225		53.8		
32.3	27,278	25,624	28,500	33,601	75.9		
39.0	20,888	15,962	18,746	24,298	81.8	867	1100
74.7	22,770	22,831	23,743		70.1		
60.3	22,905	22,497			76.9		
64.7	22,976	22,829	24,142	26,815	71.8		
53.0	23,220	23,103			72.9		
67.0	23,454	23,459	25,269		65.4		
19.7	23,511	22,263	23,639	24,761	49.3	21	27
64.3	23,775	23,707			72.3		
47.0	25,416	24,983	27,361	27,834	50.4		
1.0	14,925				60.9		
42.7	6,072	2,876	6,552	12,607	22.6	1103	1227
39.7	9,953	6,797	11,122	15,796	57.3	957	1148
54.3	3,955	1,729	5,772	11,272	21.5	913	1067
53.3	4,804	2,288	6,082	11,454	51.2	853	1013
35.7	5,815	2,228	6,024	11,879	31.2	1007	1153
35.7	8,133	5,560	8,618	13,143	75.0	837	1040
54.0	8,277	6,869	10,315	16,590	44.1	755	947
22.0	9,636	7,110	11,352	15,422	42.4		

RANK	NAME	OVERALL SCORE	STUDENT LOAN DEFAULT RATE	GRADUATION RATE	GRADUATION RATE PERFORMANCE
9.	Rutgers University–Newark (NJ)*	11	3.8	64.0	12.5
10.	Penn State Fayette–Eberly (PA)*	11	5.3	43.3	12.1
11.	Penn State–Wilkes-Barre (PA)*	11	5.3	51.3	14.7
12.	SUNY College at Brockport (NY)*	11	3.6	66.0	7.8
13.	Ramapo College of New Jersey (NJ)*	11	3.8	73.7	7.5
14.	University of Maine–Farmington (ME)*	11	4.9	58.3	7.2
15.	University of Vermont (VT)*	11	1.6	75.0	5.3
16.	Penn State–Shenango (PA)*	11	5.3	35.7	8.8
17.	Holy Family University (PA)	11	3.8	59.7	20.1
18.	Univ. of Pittsburgh–Greensburg (PA)*	11	2.7	52.7	0.2
19.	Saint Peter's University (NJ)	11	6.0	51.7	6.4
20.	Maine Maritime Academy (ME)*	11	2.2	71.0	19.6
21.	Georgian Court University (NJ)	11	2.7	53.0	12.2
22.	Amherst College (MA)	11	2.7	95.3	7.3
23.	University of New Hampshire–Main (NH)*	11	1.9	75.7	9.2
24.	Saint Vincent College (PA)	11	2.3	74.3	13.8
25.	Philad. Biblical Univ.–Langhorne (PA)	11	2.9	61.3	7.2
26.	CUNY Brooklyn College (NY)*	10	4.0	49.7	2.8
27.	CUNY City College (NY)*	10	5.0	40.3	-3.3
28.	Buffalo State College (NY)*	10	7.0	47.3	5.4
29.	Penn State–Abington (PA)*	10	5.3	46.7	8.9
30.	E. Stroudsburg University of PA (PA)*	10	3.7	58.0	8.3
31.	Saint Joseph's College–New York (NY)	10	4.0	66.7	16.5
32.	Westfield State University (MA)*	10	3.2	59.3	6.2
33.	Keystone College (PA)	10	7.7	43.0	12.7
34.	Shippensburg University of PA (PA)*	10	3.6	59.0	7.4
35.	Towson University (MD)*	10	3.8	66.0	6.9
36.	Penn. State Univ.–New Kensington (PA)*	10	5.3	41.0	5.8
37.	Montclair State University (NJ)*	10	3.1	62.3	9.8
38.	University of Delaware (DE)*	10	2.5	77.3	3.4
39.	Monroe College–Main (NY)°	10	8.3	49.3	20.5
40.	SUNY–Binghamton (NY)*	10	2.3	78.0	-2.4
41.	Bloomsburg University of PA (PA)*	10	3.7	62.7	10.3
42.	Slippery Rock University of PA (PA)*	10	3.7	60.7	6.6
43.	Plymouth State University (NH)*	10	3.5	57.0	7.2
44.	Waynesburg University (PA)	10	3.0	56.3	2.6
45.	Carlow University (PA)	10	3.8	53.3	16.7
46.	Penn State–Schuylkill (PA)*	10	5.3	41.3	8.6
47.	University of Pittsburgh–Johnstown (PA)*	10	2.7	57.0	5.3
48.	College of the Atlantic (ME)	10	1.3	68.0	5.2
49.	Williams College (MA)	10	0.9	95.3	6.3
50.	Central Penn College (PA)°	10	8.8	51.7	10.5
51.	College of Mount Saint Vincent (NY)	10	5.2	60.0	13.7
52.	La Roche College (PA)	10	4.7	50.3	6.7
53.	Mount Aloysius College (PA)	10	5.9	50.7	11.2
54.	Geneva College (PA)	10	3.7	64.0	5.5

STUDENTS RECEIVING PELL GRANTS	NET PRICE (all students)	NET PRICE (annual family income, $0–$30K)	NET PRICE (annual family income, $30–75K)	NET PRICE (annual family income above $75k)	PERCENT OF APPLICANTS ADMITTED	ACT/SAT 25TH PERCENTILE SCORE	ACT/SAT 75TH PERCENTILE SCORE
42.3	10,063	9,461	13,198	18,247	54.9	957	1113
50.3	12,606	10,073	12,631	17,242	90.4	800	1000
36.0	12,789	8,975	12,685	17,413	90.4	860	1060
40.0	12,958	6,881	12,723	17,039	43.3	967	1140
24.3	13,314	7,639	15,758	24,446	48.3	1008	1200
43.0	13,388	13,156	15,869	18,905	83.2		
19.3	13,797	7,568	11,223	20,550	74.2	1088	1280
57.7	13,865	12,208	13,925	18,736	75.0	783	993
44.7	13,941	14,424	14,847	15,860	69.8	860	1020
35.7	14,364	12,502	14,567	19,127	81.3	927	1100
50.0	15,963	12,401	14,879	20,905	57.4	838	1033
32.3	16,629	13,379	16,540	19,800	61.6	917	1093
40.0	17,283	11,172	16,156	23,638	65.5	760	1000
21.3	17,800	1,745	4,912	29,790	14.0	1327	1527
20.7	19,032	12,194	18,273	25,198	75.2	997	1180
27.0	19,113	13,929	17,003	18,672	69.2	955	1147
41.3	19,974	17,750	18,639	23,191	73.6	923	1167
48.3	5,252	2,567	6,030	12,110	28.6	1003	1173
50.3	6,167	3,235	6,911	12,598	30.5	933	1127
50.3	11,042	8,664	12,293	15,899	44.1	873	1067
41.0	11,174	8,738	12,219	17,771	80.5	827	1040
27.7	11,669	9,422	13,013	17,172	70.9	893	1047
30.3	11,953	7,692	11,085	15,994	74.0	930	1140
26.7	12,386	9,738	13,347	17,619	62.8	913	1093
54.0	12,627	9,237	11,675	18,409	92.1	797	993
27.3	12,627	9,943	13,774	18,184	76.4	887	1067
22.7	13,059	7,827	12,505	18,911	54.5	990	1153
35.7	13,134	9,370	13,061	17,498	84.5	837	1047
34.0	13,270	15,812	18,811	21,687	53.6	907	1067
11.0	13,385	9,375	11,880	17,986	57.0	1080	1287
82.3	13,444	12,698	15,440	20,223	59.0		
27.0	13,930	8,426	14,286	19,476	38.0	1207	1347
29.0	14,395	11,462	15,250	19,828	66.3	910	1080
33.0	14,405	10,637	14,498	19,308	63.7	920	1087
25.3	14,859	8,977	15,639	20,829	75.6	877	1055
35.0	15,053	14,226	15,353	16,994	73.9	910	1100
37.0	15,380	11,115	13,674	20,449	58.6	853	1059
56.0	15,588	13,425	16,772	21,733	82.9	753	980
31.7	15,942	12,387	16,153	20,231	88.5	910	1080
33.0	16,358	13,485	16,943	27,180	70.9		
19.0	16,883	4,453	8,816	29,868	18.8	1310	1540
54.3	17,226	16,588	18,109	22,424	42.0		
48.3	18,040	14,898	17,313	21,846	77.6	817	1020
38.0	18,104	14,823	17,323	21,199	51.6	823	1047
46.3	18,172	15,839	17,821	22,305	76.0	820	1002
43.7	18,210	12,806	14,408	20,411	77.0	940	1200

RANK	NAME	OVERALL SCORE	STUDENT LOAN DEFAULT RATE	GRADUATION RATE	GRADUATION RATE PERFORMANCE
55.	Colby College (ME)	10	1.0	90.3	6.7
56.	College of New Jersey (NJ)*	10	1.5	86.7	7.1
57.	College of St. Joseph (VT)	10	6.5	59.3	28.3
58.	Vassar College (NY)	10	0.3	91.7	1.7
59.	Trinity College (CT)	10	2.4	85.0	11.6
60.	Rosemont College (PA)	10	8.0	60.0	15.4
61.	College of Our Lady of the Elms (MA)	10	5.2	64.0	20.1
62.	Westminster College (PA)	10	2.5	77.0	16.0
63.	McDaniel College (MD)	10	2.5	72.3	8.7
64.	Smith College (MA)	10	1.8	84.3	5.2
65.	Nazareth College (NY)	10	2.3	73.0	7.9
66.	Manhattan College (NY)	10	2.9	73.3	9.1
67.	Duquesne University (PA)	10	1.6	76.7	9.4
68.	Elizabethtown College (PA)	10	1.7	77.0	9.8
69.	Moravian Coll./Moravian Theo. Sem. (PA)	10	2.8	73.7	11.4
70.	Clark University (MA)	10	2.8	79.0	7.1
71.	Mount St. Mary's University (MD)	10	2.9	72.0	7.6
72.	Lebanon Valley College (PA)	10	1.9	73.0	10.1
73.	Susquehanna University (PA)	10	2.2	76.7	9.8
74.	CUNY Hunter College (NY)*	9	2.7	46.0	-8.6
75.	Massachusetts Coll. of Liberal Arts (MA)*	9	3.5	50.3	-1.4
76.	Lock Haven University (PA)*	9	5.3	48.7	0.4
77.	Penn State–Lehigh Valley (PA)*	9	5.3	48.3	7.8
78.	SUNY Plattsburgh (NY)*	9	3.7	59.7	4.9
79.	Clarion University of PA (PA)*	9	5.5	48.3	4.0
80.	University at Buffalo (NY)*	9	3.3	69.3	2.7
81.	St. Francis College (NY)	9	10.8	51.3	16.5
82.	SUNY Inst. of Tech–Utica-Rome (NY)*	9	2.7	45.7	-1.0
83.	SUNY Potsdam (NY)*	9	5.4	52.0	-0.9
84.	State Univ. of NY–New Paltz (NY)*	9	3.8	69.7	1.1
85.	Millersville University of PA (PA)*	9	3.6	63.0	3.1
86.	SUNY at Albany (NY)*	9	4.8	65.0	3.0
87.	SUNY Coll. of Envir. Science & Forestry (NY)*	9	2.4	65.7	-2.0
88.	Edinboro Univ. of Pennsylvania (PA)*	9	6.0	46.0	0.0
89.	Kutztown University of PA (PA)*	9	4.7	54.0	3.7
90.	SUNY College at Oneonta (NY)*	9	4.7	66.3	1.3
91.	New Jersey Institute of Technology (NJ)*	9	3.8	54.3	-4.5
92.	University of MD–College Park (MD)*	9	2.5	81.7	-0.8
93.	University of Maine (ME)*	9	4.6	58.7	4.0
94.	Bridgewater State University (MA)*	9	5.1	53.0	0.2
95.	Wilmington University (DE)	9	5.6	38.7	4.8
96.	SUNY Fredonia (NY)*	9	4.5	63.7	1.7
97.	Husson University (ME)	9	7.8	40.0	0.2
98.	Salisbury University (MD)*	9	3.5	68.0	0.9
99.	College of Saint Elizabeth (NJ)	9	4.6	59.3	25.3
100.	SUNY College at Cortland (NY)*	9	2.5	65.7	2.9

STUDENTS RECEIVING PELL GRANTS	NET PRICE (all students)	NET PRICE (annual family income, $0–$30K)	NET PRICE (annual family income, $30–75K)	NET PRICE (annual family income above $75k)	PERCENT OF APPLICANTS ADMITTED	ACT/SAT 25TH PERCENTILE SCORE	ACT/SAT 75TH PERCENTILE SCORE
9.7	18,513	7,524	12,777	30,533	30.9	1247	1420
17.3	18,612	6,684	16,598	24,758	46.6	1137	1313
51.0	18,664	15,252	20,082	24,674	74.1	820	953
20.0	18,871	5,078	9,552	31,091	23.0	1313	1487
13.7	19,303	8,516	12,102	34,843	35.8	1190	1367
60.0	19,368	14,550	17,566	25,528	51.7	851	1093
37.7	19,678	14,681	17,623	23,411	82.7	827	1033
31.3	20,582	16,198	18,958	22,665	59.0	960	1173
27.7	21,700	9,971	16,365	26,123	71.1	990	1220
24.7	22,522	14,445	17,363	33,849	45.0		
31.3	23,745	19,208	25,009	29,033	71.1		
24.7	24,039	16,050	21,270	28,085	63.2	1000	1160
21.0	24,390	16,559	20,766	27,265	73.9	1037	1193
23.0	24,620	15,797	19,799	27,462	70.0	1003	1207
29.0	24,713	17,814	20,586	27,331	79.0	950	1180
20.0	24,849	16,874	18,825	28,067	69.0	1070	1320
21.3	24,966	16,946	21,945	26,958	67.2	987	1187
21.3	25,184	18,208	21,783	27,551	67.3	990	1072
22.0	26,231	18,222	19,423	26,554	73.0	1020	1220
37.3	7,000	3,084	6,760	12,438	26.1	1040	1213
40.7	11,480	9,265	11,967	16,849	70.1	903	1140
37.3	11,510	8,720	12,824	17,129	68.2	850	1020
33.7	11,896	8,654	11,855	17,502	89.5	857	1080
33.7	12,457	6,320	11,931	16,453	46.3	940	1113
38.0	12,473	10,288	13,421	17,920	63.9	827	1033
29.7	12,764	9,483	13,462	17,520	53.2	1050	1213
39.3	12,764	9,506	12,817	16,760	71.6	837	1040
36.3	12,821	8,540	13,456	16,436	37.0	967	1133
40.7	12,862	8,245	13,276	17,384	63.6		
27.0	12,893	7,712	14,026	18,963	37.2	1043	1220
28.0	12,981	9,391	13,843	18,233	59.4	950	1133
34.7	13,112	8,528	14,059	19,115	48.5	1027	1173
21.7	13,264	8,863	14,244	19,438	47.9	1080	1253
45.7	13,368	11,228	14,346	18,436	64.6	837	1073
28.3	13,447	10,525	14,432	18,909	66.8	867	1053
29.7	13,476	7,820	13,250	18,114	42.7	1013	1153
36.0	13,579	10,046	14,657	21,075	66.4	1013	1180
18.7	13,770	6,376	12,860	19,766	45.5	1190	1367
32.7	13,923	12,920	16,320	19,920	78.5	950	1173
21.0	13,988	9,466	13,838	17,061	69.6	923	1100
35.7	14,031	14,310	15,109	16,638	70.9		
33.3	14,439	8,542	14,276	18,440	51.4	983	1173
53.7	14,867	11,762	14,459	19,451	77.7	840	1020
21.3	14,915	8,337	13,790	17,533	53.0	1063	1207
29.3	15,007	16,418	19,540	27,874	61.6	726	947
27.0	15,104	9,353	15,000	19,307	42.4	987	1153

RANK	NAME	OVERALL SCORE	STUDENT LOAN DEFAULT RATE	GRADUATION RATE	GRADUATION RATE PERFORMANC
101.	SUNY–Geneseo (NY)*	9	1.8	79.0	-2.0
102.	Indiana University of Penn.–Main (PA)*	9	5.3	52.0	0.2
103.	University of Connecticut (CT)*	9	2.5	81.3	4.4
104.	Keene State College (NH)*	9	2.8	57.7	2.4
105.	Rutgers University–New Brunswick (NJ)*	9	3.8	77.7	2.3
106.	Penn State–Beaver (PA)*	9	5.3	44.0	7.9
107.	Rowan University (NJ)*	9	3.8	69.3	8.2
108.	CA University of Pennsylvania (PA)*	9	5.2	51.0	4.0
109.	Penn State–Greater Allegheny (PA)*	9	5.3	44.7	10.5
110.	Cooper Un. Advance. of Science & Art (NY)	9	1.7	81.3	4.3
111.	Harvard University (MA)	9	1.1	97.0	3.4
112.	Caldwell College (NJ)	9	7.0	53.7	10.3
113.	Massachusetts Maritime Academy (MA)*	9	2.9	64.3	7.4
114.	Niagara University (NY)	9	5.2	66.7	10.2
115.	Penn State–Harrisburg (PA)*	9	5.3	62.7	17.0
116.	Penn State–Berks (PA)*	9	5.3	55.0	5.4
117.	Canisius College (NY)	9	4.4	68.3	8.9
118.	Notre Dame of MD University (MD)	9	4.9	53.3	6.4
119.	Temple University (PA)*	9	3.9	66.7	8.0
120.	Colgate University (NY)	9	2.0	90.0	3.5
121.	Penn State–Altoona (PA)*	9	5.3	65.7	20.3
122.	Gannon University (PA)	9	3.2	67.7	13.0
123.	Molloy College (NY)	9	3.4	63.0	5.0
124.	Valley Forge Christian College (PA)	9	7.5	51.0	8.6
125.	St. Mary's College of Maryland (MD)*	9	2.6	79.0	4.4
126.	Saint Bonaventure University (NY)	9	4.2	65.0	6.6
127.	Penn State Erie–Behrend Coll. (PA)*	9	5.3	67.7	13.0
128.	Bates College (ME)	9	1.0	89.3	7.0
129.	Bay Path College (MA)	9	6.1	62.0	9.8
130.	Houghton College (NY)	9	2.2	68.0	1.6
131.	Robert Morris University (PA)	9	2.9	58.0	6.7
132.	Saint John Fisher College (NY)	9	3.4	73.3	10.2
133.	Saint Francis University (PA)	9	3.3	66.0	12.6
134.	Albertus Magnus College (CT)	9	5.3	52.0	11.5
135.	Eastern University (PA)	9	5.1	64.3	6.9
136.	Le Moyne College (NY)	9	4.3	71.7	13.8
137.	College of the Holy Cross (MA)	9	2.1	92.3	10.5
138.	La Salle University (PA)	9	2.4	67.0	14.8
139.	Skidmore College (NY)	9	1.9	85.3	9.7
140.	Juniata College (PA)	9	1.2	74.0	2.3
141.	Yeshiva University (NY)	9	1.8	83.3	15.1
142.	Lafayette College (PA)	9	1.3	89.3	8.3
143.	Clarkson University (NY)	9	1.9	70.3	3.8
144.	Neumann University (PA)	9	5.7	52.7	14.7
145.	Mount Holyoke College (MA)	9	2.5	82.7	1.7
146.	Messiah College (PA)	9	1.4	75.0	4.3

STUDENTS RECEIVING PELL GRANTS	NET PRICE (all students)	NET PRICE (annual family income, $0–$30K)	NET PRICE (annual family income, $30–75K)	NET PRICE (annual family income above $75k)	PERCENT OF APPLICANTS ADMITTED	ACT/SAT 25TH PERCENTILE SCORE	ACT/SAT 75TH PERCENTILE SCORE
21.7	15,171	9,110	14,964	19,033	41.3	1200	1380
37.3	15,195	12,133	15,915	20,533	59.6	897	1067
19.7	15,237	7,633	12,854	21,265	48.7	1130	1287
21.3	15,470	11,253	15,885	20,133	74.6	893	1093
29.0	15,534	13,337	17,833	23,722	60.4	1080	1260
36.3	15,706	11,810	15,461	20,670	90.4	833	1053
28.7	15,833	20,473	20,480		65.3	1000	1180
37.7	15,872	13,384	16,346	20,302	59.7	873	1040
49.0	15,970	12,826	16,441	22,452	83.3	763	1007
19.3	16,350	9,829	10,910	15,423	7.9	1247	1447
10.7	16,394	1,533	3,774	25,378	6.4	1397	1593
37.0	16,936	14,140	16,453	22,552	64.3	817	1013
17.3	16,970	9,636	16,202	21,252	61.9	953	1120
26.3	17,399	12,084	15,313	21,153	73.6	943	1160
32.3	17,443	14,341	18,581	22,921	82.8	907	1100
31.7	18,170	15,022	19,457	24,312	82.3	877	1067
30.0	18,346	13,101	16,310	22,198	75.5	977	1193
26.7	18,828	14,105	18,759	22,038	56.5	913	1127
33.7	18,981	15,505	17,685	22,363	64.9	1010	1200
10.7	19,006	10,361	11,715	23,547	30.6	1267	1447
33.7	19,158	16,673	20,188	25,393	83.1	900	1073
34.0	19,282	15,209	18,730	26,696	82.9	917	1127
31.7	19,397	15,042	17,784	22,150	65.4	957	1133
42.7	19,700	17,746	19,525	22,780	73.7	826	1113
14.3	19,873	7,691	15,803	24,028	61.3	1116	1367
32.3	19,899	11,313	18,236	23,396	79.1	933	1150
32.7	19,911	16,351	20,387	25,580	84.3	940	1113
11.7	20,419	8,162	11,535	33,114	28.4		
50.7	20,535	18,224	19,902	23,075	61.3	860	1073
38.3	21,022	15,882	19,466	24,231	76.0	1027	1280
32.0	21,558	17,197	18,793	23,837	83.3	907	1107
33.3	21,772	13,680	18,583	24,426	65.3	983	1140
39.7	21,779	18,033	20,455	24,741	74.1	910	1120
43.7	22,447	20,641	23,824	25,321	82.3	837	940
36.7	22,681	19,573	20,771	24,552	70.7	943	1180
32.7	22,719	14,557	20,629	25,100	65.1	955	1153
16.0	23,130	10,528	16,768	36,972	34.0		
33.0	23,373	19,043	20,949	26,617	72.8	887	1093
15.7	23,416	12,324	18,850	35,747	43.6	1137	1353
21.0	23,565	14,686	17,618	25,224	70.0	1063	1273
16.3	23,671	16,937	17,288	25,797	75.0	1088	1353
10.3	24,033	11,609	16,709	35,823	38.8	1193	1353
28.7	24,037	13,074	19,058	28,166	77.7	1053	1220
45.0	24,302	20,122	24,018	25,713	87.2	767	947
21.7	24,355	11,467	15,951	30,548	48.4		
20.7	24,744	19,339	20,897	26,114	65.3	1030	1253

RANK	NAME	OVERALL SCORE	STUDENT LOAN DEFAULT RATE	GRADUATION RATE	GRADUATION RATE PERFORMANCE
147.	Allegheny College (PA)	9	2.6	78.7	4.7
148.	Siena College (NY)	9	2.6	75.7	4.8
149.	Washington & Jefferson College (PA)	9	1.7	73.0	1.4
150.	Alvernia University (PA)	9	5.2	52.3	5.9
151.	Bard College (NY)	9	2.8	78.3	5.9
152.	Merrimack College (MA)	9	2.9	66.0	5.3
153.	Gordon College (MA)	9	0.7	73.0	0.8
154.	DeSales University (PA)	9	2.7	67.0	6.7
155.	Syracuse University (NY)	9	3.2	81.3	13.0
156.	Saint Michael's College (VT)	9	1.2	80.3	8.8
157.	Salve Regina University (RI)	9	2.7	71.0	3.3
158.	Bucknell University (PA)	9	0.7	91.0	7.1
159.	Ursinus College (PA)	9	1.7	78.3	3.4
160.	Loyola University Maryland (MD)	9	1.5	83.0	8.0
161.	Bentley University (MA)	9	0.7	86.7	13.8
162.	Fairfield University (CT)	9	0.9	82.0	15.7
163.	University of Scranton (PA)	9	2.7	79.0	10.9
164.	Drew University (NJ)	9	2.7	69.3	5.1
165.	Providence College (RI)	9	1.4	86.0	16.3
166.	Stonehill College (MA)	9	0.6	82.0	8.0
167.	Ithaca College (NY)	9	1.8	76.0	4.5
168.	Bryant University (RI)	9	1.9	77.7	10.3
169.	Marist College (NY)	9	1.3	80.0	9.9
170.	Muhlenberg College (PA)	9	1.3	86.3	9.7
171.	Quinnipiac University (CT)	9	1.1	76.7	8.4
172.	Saint Joseph's University (PA)	9	2.8	77.7	13.8
173.	CUNY York College (NY)*	8	6.9	22.0	-2.0
174.	University of Maine–Machias (ME)*	8	10.7	34.0	4.8
175.	University of Maine–Presque Isle (ME)*	8	11.1	33.3	0.6
176.	Touro College (NY)	8	6.8	30.3	-2.7
177.	Fitchburg State University (MA)*	8	5.7	50.0	-2.2
178.	University of Maine–Fort Kent (ME)*	8	8.4	38.7	11.4
179.	Univ. of Massachusetts–Boston (MA)*	8	5.7	39.3	-4.0
180.	SUNY Empire State College (NY)*	8	6.9	30.7	5.6
181.	William Paterson Univ. of NJ (NJ)*	8	6.9	47.7	0.6
182.	Stony Brook University (NY)*	8	4.0	67.3	-7.0
183.	Lincoln Univ. of Pennsylvania (PA)*	8	16.6	38.0	3.9
184.	Worcester State University (MA)*	8	5.2	47.7	3.3
185.	Penn State–York (PA)*	8	5.3	44.0	4.9
186.	Delaware State University (DE)*	8	8.6	35.7	-2.6
187.	Mansfield University of PA (PA)*	8	6.2	49.0	3.4
188.	Central Connecticut State Univ. (CT)*	8	4.8	49.0	3.8
189.	SUNY Oswego (NY)*	8	4.8	58.3	-8.3
190.	Mercy College (NY)	8	5.3	28.7	-2.5
191.	University of Pittsburgh–Bradford (PA)*	8	2.7	45.7	-1.5
192.	West Chester University of PA (PA)*	8	3.1	67.3	4.5

STUDENTS RECEIVING PELL GRANTS	NET PRICE (all students)	NET PRICE (annual family income, $0–$30K)	NET PRICE (annual family income, $30–75K)	NET PRICE (annual family income above $75k)	PERCENT OF APPLICANTS ADMITTED	ACT/SAT 25TH PERCENTILE SCORE	ACT/SAT 75TH PERCENTILE SCORE
25.7	25,468	15,400	19,129	28,471	59.9	1097	1320
21.3	25,782	13,741	22,060	29,012	57.2	1040	1233
24.0	25,853	19,050	20,815	28,177	40.9		
36.0	26,065	21,263	23,732	30,614	79.0	862	1053
16.7	26,379	19,500	26,979	37,463	35.0		
20.3	26,555	22,624	26,333	32,043	81.1		
23.3	26,647	20,854	22,795	25,857	50.2	1032	1307
21.7	26,695	18,456	23,283	28,941	72.6	967	1187
26.3	26,906	17,160	21,032	34,775	53.5	1053	1240
16.0	27,963	17,351	21,970	29,785	79.5	1043	1260
22.7	28,174	19,175	22,125	31,414	69.6	1023	1193
11.0	28,269	16,664	21,027	37,366	28.6	1217	1360
21.0	28,491	16,403	21,206	31,829	65.1	1107	1313
13.3	28,587	20,673	20,757	32,205	61.1	1092	1273
15.3	29,006	18,341	20,680	33,810	44.9	1111	1257
15.0	29,756	17,068	23,374	35,830	68.5	1050	1220
19.7	29,859	21,135	23,851	31,884	78.5	1033	1200
26.7	29,947	16,796	22,509	33,653	83.2	990	1253
12.0	30,551	23,549	25,880	37,416	62.9	1050	1253
13.3	30,836	20,061	24,331	33,595	69.6	1090	1280
20.3	30,971	19,921	26,386	34,940	67.3	1050	1260
16.7	31,039	24,692	28,873	34,119	68.9	1043	1180
16.0	31,056	18,148	24,109	32,550	34.9	1070	1240
10.7	31,981	17,620	19,687	31,668	45.8	1120	1353
13.3	32,946	28,118	30,571	35,636	67.9	990	1160
13.7	35,053	28,279	29,658	35,805	78.8	1027	1200
51.0	5,202	3,247	6,358	12,006	37.9	819	950
38.0	8,868	9,214	11,894	15,669	80.6	797	1047
36.7	9,806	9,161	11,516	14,501	70.1		
59.0	10,371	9,778	13,130	20,985	60.2		
29.0	10,869	7,429	10,011	15,118	67.5	913	1113
28.7	11,105	9,409	11,764	15,681	69.3	810	1000
35.7	11,290	8,329	11,563	16,755	62.3	890	1100
33.0	11,513	11,184	12,848	16,493	78.0		
36.3	11,579	10,167	15,443	20,182	62.0	907	1087
35.3	11,759	7,189	11,935	17,607	40.1	1123	1273
65.0	12,111	9,941			28.9	783	953
24.3	12,138	8,848	11,558	15,474	66.1	913	1080
30.7	12,554	9,639	12,728	17,167	83.6	858	1070
53.0	12,910	13,137	14,774	16,443	42.3	800	940
45.3	13,635	11,256	14,515	18,901	72.9	843	1060
28.3	14,208	11,145	13,408	17,930	62.4	920	1087
37.3	14,228	8,325	14,102	18,679	48.0	1060	1200
58.0	14,262	12,201	15,494	22,305	61.3		
44.0	15,167	12,537	15,280	17,604	78.1	870	1073
22.7	15,294	11,616	15,483	19,748	46.0	990	1153

RANK	NAME	OVERALL SCORE	STUDENT LOAN DEFAULT RATE	GRADUATION RATE	GRADUATION RATE PERFORMANCE
193.	University of Rhode Island (RI)*	8	4.7	63.0	4.2
194.	Peirce College (PA)	8	10.9	44.0	13.6
195.	Kean University (NJ)*	8	6.4	48.7	10.3
196.	Medaille College (NY)	8	6.8	48.7	11.6
197.	Richard Stockton Coll. of NJ (NJ)*	8	4.2	64.7	4.6
198.	Pine Manor College (MA)	8	17.1	32.7	7.3
199.	Nyack College (NY)	8	9.0	42.0	0.4
200.	Yale University (CT)	8	0.9	96.3	-0.1
201.	Wellesley College (MA)	8	1.1	91.3	-3.1
202.	Princeton University (NJ)	8	1.9	96.0	-1.2
203.	American International College (MA)	8	4.2	37.3	-4.0
204.	Cazenovia College (NY)	8	4.0	47.0	1.2
205.	Concordia College–New York (NY)	8	5.7	48.0	4.2
206.	Cedar Crest College (PA)	8	6.0	56.7	2.4
207.	Columbia Univ. in the City of NY (NY)	8	2.0	93.3	-0.4
208.	York College Pennsylvania (PA)	8	2.7	60.7	-1.4
209.	Hood College (MD)	8	3.9	68.3	8.9
210.	Dartmouth College (NH)	8	1.0	95.3	1.2
211.	Roberts Wesleyan College (NY)	8	4.8	61.0	1.6
212.	Eastern Nazarene College (MA)	8	4.3	50.7	1.7
213.	Marywood University (PA)	8	4.0	64.3	4.9
214.	Haverford College (PA)	8	2.2	92.7	3.9
215.	Saint Thomas Aquinas College (NY)	8	5.4	52.0	8.4
216.	Wells College (NY)	8	4.5	59.3	1.7
217.	Gwynedd-Mercy College (PA)	8	4.5	68.0	15.1
218.	Penn State–Main (PA)*	8	5.3	86.0	13.0
219.	Wesleyan University (CT)	8	0.9	92.3	3.9
220.	Keuka College (NY)	8	4.2	51.7	1.1
221.	Mercyhurst College (PA)	8	8.1	65.0	8.2
222.	Misericordia University (PA)	8	3.8	66.3	6.3
223.	Manhattanville College (NY)	8	4.3	59.0	6.4
224.	Lycoming College (PA)	8	4.5	68.3	9.4
225.	Stevenson University (MD)	8	4.5	62.7	11.7
226.	Alfred University (NY)	8	4.4	62.3	1.8
227.	Chatham University (PA)	8	1.9	59.7	1.9
228.	Middlebury College (VT)	8	1.3	92.7	4.9
229.	Brown University (RI)	8	1.0	95.3	4.5
230.	Bowdoin College (ME)	8	1.1	93.3	4.4
231.	Newbury College–Brookline (MA)	8	8.1	45.3	5.1
232.	Southern NH University (NH)	8	4.9	53.7	7.7
233.	Connecticut College (CT)	8	1.6	85.3	3.2
234.	Franklin and Marshall College (PA)	8	1.4	85.0	3.1
235.	Boston College (MA)	8	1.6	91.7	2.5
236.	Adelphi University (NY)	8	3.2	66.7	6.5
237.	Saint Joseph's College of Maine (ME)	8	3.6	53.7	10.8
238.	Brandeis University (MA)	8	1.3	90.7	0.9

STUDENTS RECEIVING PELL GRANTS	NET PRICE (all students)	NET PRICE (annual family income, $0–$30K)	NET PRICE (annual family income, $30–75K)	NET PRICE (annual family income above $75k)	PERCENT OF APPLICANTS ADMITTED	ACT/SAT 25TH PERCENTILE SCORE	ACT/SAT 75TH PERCENTILE SCORE
26.7	15,326	10,201	15,150	21,073	86.3	950	1140
50.7	15,558	14,464	16,841		52.0		
39.0	16,126	13,717	18,196	23,142	66.8	837	1000
42.7	16,164	13,949	16,269	22,806	65.7	797	980
32.7	17,033	14,046	19,438	25,044	63.6	960	1140
74.7	17,337	16,029	17,333	24,716	69.5	683	920
55.7	18,058	14,177	19,264	22,382	96.2	777	1025
13.7	18,349	6,819	9,393	28,575	7.7	1403	1593
18.3	18,727	8,502	11,867	33,071	31.2	1283	1480
11.7	18,807	6,954	7,445	25,674	8.4	1407	1580
51.0	18,843	17,264	18,130	21,360	72.9	827	1007
43.0	19,001	10,605	18,089	23,647	70.4	853	1080
35.7	19,211	15,884	16,526	21,166	70.8	817	987
41.7	19,389	14,351	16,293	25,178	55.1	903	1113
18.0	19,533	8,259	7,203	30,164	8.8	1387	1553
22.7	19,920	15,170	18,093	21,957	64.9	987	1153
31.7	20,163	12,434	18,900	24,100	80.8	947	1207
15.7	20,219	6,783	7,369	32,549	11.5	1353	1553
45.7	20,436	15,151	18,591	24,020	52.1	943	1220
39.7	20,563	20,109	20,071	22,206	63.4	843	1140
35.3	20,661	17,001	18,072	22,444	69.9	950	1127
15.0	20,813	6,217	10,805	33,875	24.6	1303	1500
21.3	20,821	15,207	21,254	25,506	79.3	840	1045
44.0	21,171	15,966	19,236	25,217	65.2	937	1187
31.0	21,237	16,184	17,928	23,772	53.6	883	1067
18.3	21,239	16,638	21,302	28,070	52.9	1090	1260
16.7	21,340	7,654	13,304	35,258	22.3	1295	1487
45.7	21,407	18,008	19,535	24,112	71.8		
37.3	21,880	20,038	20,473	22,904	75.5	947	1167
25.7	21,961	15,907	19,457	23,865	60.9	957	1133
30.7	22,295	12,523	16,083	23,728	60.7	987	1227
32.3	22,306	16,352	20,024	24,901	68.4	935	1160
27.3	22,384	16,167	20,704	26,005	60.2	867	1080
37.0	22,506	13,928	19,353	26,965	70.7	980	1167
31.3	22,588	19,002	20,315	25,624	61.2		
10.3	22,927	6,617	12,599	34,362	17.6	1290	1480
14.3	22,982	5,410	9,165	34,967	9.3	1310	1507
14.7	23,091	6,138	10,391	26,585	17.2	1327	1507
50.3	23,805	24,465	28,277		62.1	780	960
29.0	23,825	20,234	22,151	27,339	83.2	883	1067
12.0	23,906	7,724	15,934	38,061	34.2		
11.0	24,165	11,576	16,328	37,580	42.9		
13.0	24,179	14,299	19,896	39,138	29.3	1257	1413
29.0	24,711	21,324	24,214	27,246	68.4	990	1173
20.3	24,834	17,986	21,074	28,221	86.9	857	1047
18.7	24,854	14,856	18,500	35,463	39.8	1240	1433

RANK	NAME	OVERALL SCORE	STUDENT LOAN DEFAULT RATE	GRADUATION RATE	GRADUATION RATE PERFORMANCE
239.	Lehigh University (PA)	8	1.0	87.7	4.4
240.	Iona College (NY)	8	4.2	61.7	7.8
241.	Seton Hall University (NJ)	8	2.3	66.0	3.9
242.	Assumption College (MA)	8	2.3	71.3	4.0
243.	St. Lawrence University (NY)	8	1.3	81.0	1.4
244.	Goucher College (MD)	8	2.9	67.3	0.4
245.	Springfield College (MA)	8	5.5	66.0	9.5
246.	Sarah Lawrence College (NY)	8	2.0	74.3	1.0
247.	Suffolk University (MA)	8	3.7	56.0	7.0
248.	Union College (NY)	8	1.7	84.0	4.1
249.	Wheaton College (MA)	8	3.4	78.3	1.4
250.	Saint Anselm College (NH)	8	1.4	73.7	5.0
251.	Dickinson College (PA)	8	1.7	83.7	3.8
252.	Gettysburg College (PA)	8	1.3	84.7	0.4
253.	Marlboro College (VT)	8	2.6	61.0	4.3
254.	Villanova University (PA)	8	1.2	89.3	4.6
255.	Rider University (NJ)	8	4.5	64.7	5.6
256.	Stevens Institute of Technology (NJ)	8	2.5	76.3	-2.7
257.	Emerson College (MA)	8	1.6	81.0	2.3
258.	Hobart and William Smith Colleges (NY)	8	1.4	75.3	2.6
259.	Endicott College (MA)	8	2.5	69.3	6.1
260.	Champlain College (VT)	8	3.5	67.0	6.2
261.	Boston University (MA)	8	1.5	84.0	2.7
262.	Worcester Polytechnic Institute (MA)	8	2.0	80.0	1.8
263.	Sacred Heart University (CT)	8	2.5	66.0	14.7
264.	New York University (NY)	8	1.9	86.0	-4.9
265.	University of Maine–Augusta (ME)*	7	14.8	15.3	-1.4
266.	Coppin State University (MD)*	7	14.1	16.0	-3.9
267.	Granite State College (NH)*	7	7.7	27.0	-3.0
268.	Southern CT State University (CT)*	7	4.4	43.3	-2.4
269.	Bowie State University (MD)*	7	8.2	37.7	-0.6
270.	Univ. of MD Eastern Shore (MD)*	7	14.2	31.7	-1.7
271.	Penn State–Brandywine (PA)*	7	5.3	36.7	-1.8
272.	Univ. of NH–Manchester (NH)*	7	1.9	38.0	-5.9
273.	University of MD–Baltimore County (MD)*	7	4.6	58.3	-13.7
274.	Johnson State College (VT)*	7	6.8	32.7	-7.7
275.	Castleton State College (VT)*	7	4.1	45.3	-2.6
276.	University of Massachusetts–Lowell (MA)*	7	5.1	51.7	-7.5
277.	Framingham State University (MA)*	7	4.3	51.7	-4.9
278.	Hilbert College (NY)	7	8.3	43.0	2.0
279.	SUNY–Purchase College (NY)*	7	5.2	56.7	-4.8
280.	Bloomfield College (NJ)	7	9.6	32.7	4.0
281.	Eastern CT State University (CT)*	7	3.8	51.3	-1.2
282.	University of MA–Amherst (MA)*	7	3.7	68.3	-2.4
283.	Fairleigh Dickinson U.–Metro. (NJ)	7	3.7	46.0	4.3
284.	Thomas College (ME)	7	9.2	42.0	8.2

STUDENTS RECEIVING PELL GRANTS	NET PRICE (all students)	NET PRICE (annual family income, $0–$30K)	NET PRICE (annual family income, $30–75K)	NET PRICE (annual family income above $75k)	PERCENT OF APPLICANTS ADMITTED	ACT/SAT 25TH PERCENTILE SCORE	ACT/SAT 75TH PERCENTILE SCORE
14.0	25,088	17,008	16,791	34,689	34.6	1213	1347
26.0	25,368	18,829	22,952	28,290	80.5	900	1093
28.7	26,233	21,292	25,149	30,497	82.7	980	1167
18.3	26,392	21,760	25,872	31,540	75.5		
18.7	26,595	11,347	18,405	30,637	43.4		
21.3	27,035	16,408	24,136	32,794	73.1	1030	1300
27.7	27,544	20,839	22,644	29,886	68.0	903	1107
19.0	27,580	17,487	24,493	35,142	60.4		
25.7	27,725	23,326	25,923	32,667	80.6	907	1127
17.0	27,869	9,684	18,249	34,912	41.1		
21.3	27,952	15,683	21,001	33,421	61.1		
18.0	28,151	19,160	21,268	30,507	74.4	997	1187
11.7	28,167	13,624	16,865	32,763	43.2	1193	1373
13.3	28,172	10,854	14,782	28,659	40.1	1217	1380
30.3	28,384	17,494	21,477	31,539	84.7		
11.3	28,579	16,003	22,247	38,559	44.9	1207	1360
25.0	28,729	18,156	25,185	31,963	72.0	940	1133
23.7	28,738	17,271	21,865	31,856	43.0	1193	1313
15.7	28,836	24,274	27,731	34,606	48.0	1143	1360
19.7	30,177	13,524	20,365	32,695	58.5		
14.7	30,233	23,274	27,054	33,177	58.6	987	1160
23.7	30,502	22,699	27,517	33,676	81.0	990	1213
14.3	30,524	23,630	25,889	39,081	55.3	1177	1333
15.7	33,768	21,651	27,809	35,751	56.1		
18.0	34,260	26,798	29,746	36,436	61.3	851	1046
20.7	35,925	24,266	31,573	44,112	35.3	1250	1427
54.0	7,834	8,557	10,597	13,353	86.2		
67.3	8,560	6,819	9,974	9,320	47.2	793	927
39.0	9,519	10,044			82.0		
30.0	10,880	9,160	10,962	15,258	72.8	840	1040
47.3	11,468	9,134	13,885	17,872	49.9	813	967
55.7	12,183	9,933	14,679	18,300	52.5	777	940
32.0	12,509	8,228	12,403	17,152	83.3	857	1060
30.7	13,099	12,499	15,366	17,826	71.1	913	1133
25.7	13,433	8,995	14,054	15,499	62.3	1113	1287
50.3	13,485	10,667	13,227	17,170	91.2	840	1087
32.0	13,594	11,493	14,462	17,826	82.7	870	1053
28.3	13,673	8,476	12,295	18,025	67.9	1000	1180
23.7	15,164	10,710	13,947	18,205	63.1	927	1107
47.0	15,290	11,948	14,957	19,693	74.0		
30.0	15,527	11,234	16,938	20,272	32.6	983	1233
64.0	15,920	14,161	15,674	24,307	51.4	767	907
24.7	16,180	13,978	16,639	21,243	67.4	930	1107
25.7	16,988	8,776	12,555	20,791	65.3	1080	1253
23.3	17,981	14,556	16,795	23,094	60.8	890	1060
44.3	18,264	16,667	16,034	22,252	77.4	760	1000

RANK	NAME	OVERALL SCORE	STUDENT LOAN DEFAULT RATE	GRADUATION RATE	GRADUATION RATE PERFORMANC
285.	Sojourner-Douglass College (MD)	7	9.6	26.0	6.7
286.	Wilson College (PA)	7	4.4	49.0	1.4
287.	MA Institute of Technology (MA)	7	0.8	93.0	-6.5
288.	Seton Hill University (PA)	7	4.9	52.7	-0.4
289.	Swarthmore College (PA)	7	0.2	93.3	-0.5
290.	University of Pittsburgh–Pittsburgh (PA)*	7	2.7	78.7	-2.5
291.	DeVry University–New Jersey (NJ)°	7	14.6	34.3	8.4
292.	New York Institute of Technology (NY)	7	5.3	47.3	3.9
293.	Hamilton College (NY)	7	2.7	89.3	-0.0
294.	University of Pennsylvania (PA)	7	1.0	96.0	-1.5
295.	King's College (PA)	7	4.2	66.0	2.5
296.	Centenary College (NJ)	7	4.7	49.0	5.1
297.	Chestnut Hill College (PA)	7	5.7	44.7	-1.3
298.	Wilkes University (PA)	7	3.9	61.0	3.8
299.	College of Saint Rose (NY)	7	3.3	66.3	3.0
300.	University of Saint Joseph (CT)	7	3.5	52.0	-3.7
301.	Burlington College (VT)	7	9.3	45.7	8.9
302.	Utica College (NY)	7	5.5	46.0	0.2
303.	Elmira College (NY)	7	3.4	60.0	1.1
304.	Mount Saint Mary College (NY)	7	3.9	54.7	0.5
305.	Barnard College (NY)	7	1.7	90.3	-3.2
306.	Cornell University (NY)	7	1.2	93.0	-1.2
307.	Anna Maria College (MA)	7	6.1	47.3	6.5
308.	Arcadia University (PA)	7	3.3	63.0	-3.8
309.	Colby-Sawyer College (NH)	7	3.5	59.0	0.1
310.	Delaware Valley College (PA)	7	4.6	54.7	1.7
311.	Monmouth University (NJ)	7	4.1	63.3	0.4
312.	Wheelock College (MA)	7	3.7	58.7	3.3
313.	Bryn Mawr College (PA)	7	1.2	85.3	-3.1
314.	Fairleigh Dick. U.–Coll. Florham (NJ)	7	3.7	57.0	1.0
315.	Tufts University (MA)	7	1.1	91.0	-2.5
316.	DeVry University–Pennsylvania (PA)°	7	14.6	31.3	10.6
317.	Philadelphia University (PA)	7	2.7	60.0	-3.5
318.	Immaculata University (PA)	7	4.3	56.0	19.3
319.	Cabrini College (PA)	7	4.3	51.0	3.8
320.	Western New England University (MA)	7	2.9	59.7	-1.6
321.	Wentworth Institute of Technology (MA)	7	4.2	61.7	4.8
322.	University of New England (ME)	7	2.8	57.0	-2.0
323.	Washington College (MD)	7	1.2	71.7	-0.4
324.	University of Rochester (NY)	7	1.5	84.0	-2.5
325.	Fordham University (NY)	7	3.5	79.7	-1.0
326.	CUNY College of Staten Island (NY)*	6	7.9	26.3	-8.7
327.	Farmingdale State College (NY)*	6	6.5	32.0	-10.6
328.	SUNY College–Old Westbury (NY)*	6	9.7	36.3	-10.5
329.	Bryn Athyn Coll. of the New Church (PA)	6	3.2	43.7	-12.4
330.	Frostburg State University (MD)*	6	7.5	45.7	-1.0

STUDENTS RECEIVING PELL GRANTS	NET PRICE (all students)	NET PRICE (annual family income, $0–$30K)	NET PRICE (annual family income, $30–75K)	NET PRICE (annual family income above $75k)	PERCENT OF APPLICANTS ADMITTED	ACT/SAT 25TH PERCENTILE SCORE	ACT/SAT 75TH PERCENTILE SCORE
80.7	18,825	18,444	19,349		47.0		
31.3	19,155	14,044	16,813	23,942	44.2	873	1127
19.7	19,978	4,402	6,581	32,262	9.6	1410	1533
35.3	20,167	16,857	17,874	22,293	66.4	907	1120
14.7	20,173	8,263	10,720	31,553	15.1	1347	1540
18.0	20,217	17,626	22,112	26,822	58.1	1167	1367
50.7	20,855	19,420	22,300	25,871	81.5		
35.7	21,066	16,132	18,245		69.8	910	1073
13.0	21,305	7,051	11,807	32,210	28.0	1303	1480
12.7	21,381	6,801	11,061	31,948	13.1	1350	1507
27.0	21,813	15,560	19,086	23,958	72.1		
24.3	21,951	25,361	23,480	28,209	88.5	810	1007
50.3	21,981	16,748	19,975	24,281	89.1	867	1087
31.7	22,659	17,652	19,917	26,105	75.8	947	1140
34.0	22,712	24,315	25,447	30,026	70.7		
35.7	22,716	17,559	19,400	25,613	80.4	897	1100
55.7	22,920	19,466	21,366	29,814	83.6		
41.3	23,192	17,775	23,146	27,178	79.5	853	1033
32.7	23,259	21,398	21,068	25,965	82.0	970	1200
33.0	23,370	15,740	22,515	26,583	79.6	897	1080
19.7	23,458	11,412	14,884	37,581	25.1	1249	1460
16.3	23,490	9,278	11,560	33,339	17.6	1303	1467
37.3	23,845	19,337	21,947	27,291	63.6	795	977
35.0	24,571	19,968	22,509	24,475	58.3	1010	1213
31.3	24,722	19,461	22,660	29,213	81.6		
25.7	24,992	20,600	21,754	26,540	71.7	897	1107
23.7	25,165	13,834	21,448	28,689	64.8	977	1127
33.0	25,170	19,445	23,513	27,693	70.1	870	1087
19.3	25,349	12,052	15,279	34,945	45.4	1187	1427
28.3	25,697	14,930	21,900	30,066	66.3	917	1107
12.7	26,184	11,392	16,371	38,097	22.5	1353	1493
63.0	26,331	25,956	26,786	29,179	72.2		
25.0	26,846	19,890	21,718	29,417	72.0	973	1140
18.3	27,161	22,500	25,076	30,355	79.3	833	1033
23.3	27,200	20,775	22,639	29,683	71.7	820	1020
23.0	27,613	22,831	24,540	29,976	79.8	963	1160
26.3	28,088	23,195	26,855	30,231	60.3	977	1140
24.7	28,519	23,384	25,366	30,709	84.2	950	1133
14.7	28,593	15,041	21,130	30,761	65.8	1077	1260
19.0	29,910	13,552	18,144	32,595	35.8	1233	1393
21.3	33,124	21,382	28,203	36,026	45.3	1157	1340
41.0	6,652	4,099	7,481	12,495	96.3	907	1080
23.0	7,206	2,866	7,376	12,188	42.6	950	1040
46.0	8,552	4,880	9,717	15,167	48.7	910	1053
28.0	10,917	5,416	9,365	14,662	51.3	893	1200
33.7	11,448	12,808			57.6	877	1067

RANK	NAME	OVERALL SCORE	STUDENT LOAN DEFAULT RATE	GRADUATION RATE	GRADUATION RATE PERFORMANC
331.	Cheyney University of PA (PA)*	6	17.4	23.7	-1.1
332.	Lyndon State College (VT)*	6	6.3	34.0	-6.0
333.	Salem State University (MA)*	6	6.8	43.0	-0.9
334.	Western CT State University (CT)*	6	4.9	42.7	-7.6
335.	SUNY Maritime College (NY)*	6	5.5	47.0	-8.5
336.	Goddard College (VT)	6	4.3	27.3	-9.7
337.	Felician College (NJ)	6	6.4	38.7	0.6
338.	Five Towns College (NY)°	6	9.5	39.3	7.0
339.	Polytechnic Inst. of New York Univ. (NY)	6	4.5	57.0	-19.0
340.	Dowling College (NY)	6	5.6	38.3	1.2
341.	Long Island University–Brooklyn (NY)	6	6.1	32.0	-2.0
342.	Rivier College (NH)	6	3.4	46.7	0.3
343.	Pace University–New York (NY)	6	3.7	55.0	-2.8
344.	Norwich University (VT)	6	3.1	53.7	-2.2
345.	Franklin Pierce University (NH)	6	5.0	49.3	2.0
346.	Albright College (PA)	6	4.7	58.0	-3.7
347.	St. John's College (MD)	6	0.6	69.7	-9.5
348.	Paul Smiths College of Arts & Science (NY)	6	7.6	46.0	0.9
349.	Johns Hopkins University (MD)	6	1.3	91.0	-5.3
350.	Johnson & Wales U.–Providence (RI)	6	7.9	54.3	0.4
351.	Rochester Institute of Technology (NY)	6	2.6	63.0	-7.4
352.	Widener University–Main (PA)	6	3.4	52.3	-0.8
353.	University of Hartford (CT)	6	4.1	58.0	-4.9
354.	Emmanuel College (MA)	6	3.1	61.0	-2.3
355.	Hampshire College (MA)	6	1.6	64.7	-11.9
356.	Curry College (MA)	6	5.8	46.0	2.3
357.	Bennington College (VT)	6	2.0	63.7	-5.3
358.	Carnegie Mellon University (PA)	6	0.7	86.7	-9.5
359.	Simmons College (MA)	6	1.6	68.0	-6.0
360.	Rensselaer Polytechnic Institute (NY)	6	1.7	83.3	-8.4
361.	Drexel University (PA)	6	2.4	67.0	-7.9
362.	The New School (NY)	6	4.5	62.7	-2.2
363.	Univ. of MD–University College (MD)*	5	5.5	8.3	-24.3
364.	Morgan State University (MD)*	5	14.7	29.7	-7.3
365.	University of Mass.–Dartmouth (MA)*	5	6.0	48.7	-6.3
366.	Daemen College (NY)	5	4.4	43.3	-9.7
367.	Washington Adventist University (MD)	5	8.5	29.3	-6.6
368.	D'Youville College (NY)	5	6.5	40.3	-8.6
369.	Unity College (ME)	5	3.9	45.0	-6.0
370.	Metropolitan College of NY (NY)	5	10.4	26.3	1.3
371.	Point Park University (PA)	5	7.0	49.3	-1.8
372.	DeVry College of New York (NY)°	5	14.6	21.0	1.5
373.	Hartwick College (NY)	5	3.9	56.0	-6.7
374.	St. John's University–New York (NY)	5	7.5	57.7	-4.3
375.	New England College (NH)	5	6.5	40.0	-1.4
376.	Mount Ida College (MA)	5	6.2	40.0	-2.9

STUDENTS RECEIVING PELL GRANTS	NET PRICE (all students)	NET PRICE (annual family income, $0–$30K)	NET PRICE (annual family income, $30–75K)	NET PRICE (annual family income above $75k)	PERCENT OF APPLICANTS ADMITTED	ACT/SAT 25TH PERCENTILE SCORE	ACT/SAT 75TH PERCENTILE SCORE
74.0	12,532	12,170	13,586	17,868	58.2		
42.7	12,910	10,142	12,872	16,804	98.1	820	1033
31.0	13,311	10,108	13,718	18,005	60.4	893	1100
25.0	14,429	16,403			61.6	893	1080
25.7	14,751	12,280	15,329	19,070	60.4	1007	1127
54.7	19,210	21,129			100.0		
43.7	20,436	17,641	19,893	26,568	86.3	747	953
41.0	21,030	17,501	22,521	26,630	60.2	787	1033
46.7	21,062	14,775	19,199	25,211	66.5	1198	1307
29.3	21,623	21,913	23,956	26,797	82.2		
56.7	22,267	19,347	23,940	28,408	79.8	773	947
28.7	22,714	16,589	20,131	25,675	80.6	830	1013
33.7	22,726	15,605	18,856	26,292	80.3	953	1153
26.7	23,857	16,416	18,133	25,439	65.4	960	1160
24.3	24,212	21,042	23,047	27,039	90.4	867	1060
34.7	24,883	16,787	24,071	30,275	47.5	960	1140
25.0	25,019	20,116	19,400	36,034	80.4	1210	1467
40.7	25,264	21,183	23,650	26,984	77.0	840	1060
13.3	25,410	13,591	14,361	37,283	20.0	1297	1467
32.7	25,507	21,862	23,244	27,361	75.1		
32.0	25,863	20,051	23,167	29,648	58.7	1100	1293
27.7	26,137	22,013	24,070	29,198	68.8	897	1067
24.3	26,637	21,940	24,300	28,599	54.9	917	1233
25.0	28,432	21,661	24,974	30,363	53.8	987	1193
20.0	29,163	16,780	21,316	31,561	66.0	1130	1407
23.3	29,181	23,364	26,659	31,879	71.5	827	1000
22.3	30,366	17,559	24,022	35,222	66.8		
14.3	31,830	21,314	23,862	37,052	30.5	1310	1453
23.7	32,658	25,378	28,302	35,955	49.6	1020	1233
17.0	33,858	21,523	26,972	34,943	41.1	1277	1407
21.0	34,701	26,541	31,304	36,472	62.5	1110	1273
26.0	38,031	23,960	31,421	36,452	65.9	985	1240
21.0	12,033	11,357			66.4		
64.7	12,203	10,873	14,450	17,606	46.7	820	973
33.7	15,169	11,303	14,980	20,626	69.8	948	1133
33.0	15,947	11,445	14,578	19,833	57.1		
57.3	16,667	13,633	16,579	19,637	43.2	740	980
36.7	17,110	12,229	15,983	19,683	85.7	920	1127
44.0	20,473	14,935	18,558	25,309	75.7		
77.7	20,934	20,334	21,342		46.8		
38.7	21,315	17,142	19,441	23,818	75.0	910	1153
68.3	22,596	22,110	23,832	27,768	81.0		
31.3	22,985	17,389	21,357	26,958	79.1	1010	1207
34.7	25,236	21,207	23,786	29,705	45.9	970	1173
35.0	25,921	19,875	23,103	28,292	76.3	800	1020
35.0	26,340	21,206	24,037	29,352	69.3	770	953

RANK	NAME	OVERALL SCORE	STUDENT LOAN DEFAULT RATE	GRADUATION RATE	GRADUATION RATE PERFORMANCE
377.	University of New Haven (CT)	5	3.3	53.7	-5.5
378.	King's College (NY)	5	4.9	53.0	-15.2
379.	Hofstra University (NY)	5	4.6	59.7	-10.8
380.	Lesley University (MA)	5	2.7	49.0	-12.5
381.	Northeastern University (MA)	5	3.0	77.7	-8.8
382.	Roger Williams University (RI)	5	3.0	60.7	-1.8
383.	Harrisburg Univ. of Science and Tech. (PA)	4	15.0	18.0	-14.5
384.	University of Southern Maine (ME)*	4	6.1	32.7	-6.0
385.	Dominican College of Blauvelt (NY)	4	7.3	38.0	-7.1
386.	Thiel College (PA)	4	9.6	37.0	-4.2
387.	University of Bridgeport (CT)	4	9.6	30.7	-9.2
388.	Post University (CT)°	4	10.6	29.7	3.0
389.	Green Mountain College (VT)	4	7.3	44.3	-13.1
390.	Lasell College (MA)	4	3.6	47.3	-9.0
391.	Daniel Webster College (NH)°	4	6.2	43.0	-2.3
392.	Wesley College (DE)	4	12.1	32.0	-2.4
393.	Wagner College (NY)	4	3.3	66.3	-6.1
394.	Southern Vermont College (VT)	3	10.3	33.3	-8.7
395.	University of Phoenix–Jersey City (NJ)°	3	17.0	12.7	-9.0
396.	Nichols College (MA)	3	9.6	45.0	-1.4
397.	Cambridge College (MA)	3	6.8	2.7	-13.6
398.	Long Island Univ.–C. W. Post (NY)	3	6.1	43.0	-3.1
399.	Becker College (MA)	3	10.7	30.7	-12.7
400.	College of New Rochelle (NY)	3	12.8	29.0	-10.6
401.	Marymount Manhattan College (NY)	3	8.6	43.0	-21.5
402.	Mitchell College (CT)	2	10.2	40.7	-8.5

SOUTHERN SCHOOLS

RANK	NAME	OVERALL SCORE	STUDENT LOAN DEFAULT RATE	GRADUATION RATE	GRADUATION RATE PERFORMANCE
1.	Berea College (KY)	12	7.4	64.0	25.7
2.	Texas A&M University–College Station (TX)*	11	3.7	80.3	14.0
3.	University of Texas–Austin (TX)*	11	3.7	80.0	5.8
4.	Texas A&M International Univ. (TX)*	10	9.9	40.3	5.0
5.	Univ. of Texas–Pan American (TX)*	10	8.4	38.7	4.2
6.	University of Texas–El Paso (TX)*	10	7.6	36.7	3.5
7.	East Central University (OK)*	10	12.6	32.7	11.8
8.	Sam Houston State University (TX)*	10	8.0	49.0	5.4
9.	Texas Woman's University (TX)*	10	5.8	44.0	4.3
10.	Tougaloo College (MS)	10	9.6	46.3	13.1
11.	Lane College (TN)	10	13.2	34.0	12.0
12.	Jackson State University (MS)*	10	11.7	41.7	10.3
13.	Alice Lloyd College (KY)	10	5.7	39.7	1.0
14.	Oklahoma State University–Main (OK)*	10	5.6	61.0	6.6
15.	William Carey University (MS)	10	6.0	50.3	-1.6
16.	Midway College (KY)	10	7.5	55.0	13.8
17.	Asbury University (KY)	10	4.5	70.0	7.3
18.	Tennessee State University (TN)*	9	9.3	35.0	0.4

STUDENTS RECEIVING PELL GRANTS	NET PRICE (all students)	NET PRICE (annual family income, $0–$30K)	NET PRICE (annual family income, $30–75K)	NET PRICE (annual family income above $75k)	PERCENT OF APPLICANTS ADMITTED	ACT/SAT 25TH PERCENTILE SCORE	ACT/SAT 75TH PERCENTILE SCORE
27.3	27,634	21,635	24,726	30,026	69.6	957	1140
29.3	28,047	25,344	25,422	30,075	68.0	1065	1340
21.7	29,187	25,843	29,163	31,582	58.1	1083	1247
28.3	30,007	24,932	27,311	32,358	66.1	954	1193
14.0	32,399	20,065	26,244	36,486	34.8	1253	1400
13.7	33,442	27,079	30,852	34,443	77.9	1000	1167
51.7	15,851	14,195	16,401	20,208	75.2		
34.0	17,757	16,328	19,151	22,152	78.8	880	1113
40.0	20,152	21,437	21,369	24,530	70.6	786	973
45.7	20,874	19,194	19,281	24,408	65.9	837	1033
51.7	23,054	22,826	24,263	28,445	59.2	823	993
42.0	23,733	26,275	23,334	27,318	63.8	730	933
36.3	24,427	18,569	23,120	28,904	76.9	943	1222
32.3	25,785	20,574	26,054		70.5	893	1073
32.3	25,914	24,312	26,008	28,637	68.3	837	1053
38.0	26,756	27,122	27,758		48.6	740	940
16.7	27,115	18,740	25,607	29,772	69.4	1050	1273
46.3	20,640	21,053	23,605		79.3	797	993
56.3	22,496	22,418	24,115		71.8		
32.0	23,551	19,605	24,110	28,644	74.5	782	1020
44.7	23,864	24,530			79.8		
15.0	24,089	20,188	23,562	27,527	80.6	883	1073
41.3	26,051	21,941	25,878	27,920	70.5	823	1047
79.7	30,148	30,781	30,559	28,669	66.3	880	1080
25.0	30,354	24,656	28,142	33,004	73.6	980	1227
32.7	26,333	19,043	22,980	30,135	77.5		
85.3	1,225	-22,045	-19,294		20.5	22	27
21.0	11,925	4,403	10,236	18,075	66.3	1093	1293
26.3	14,636	7,421	14,017	22,079	46.8	1117	1333
60.3	1,820	1,373	2,013	6,556	49.1	810	960
64.3	2,268	826	3,659	10,630	68.6	17	21
59.3	3,258	2,287	5,887	13,653	99.3	807	1000
51.7	7,726	7,560			93.2	18	23
35.7	8,411	8,354	10,233	13,729	66.3	907	1080
43.3	8,732	7,069	9,710	13,635	88.5	814	1020
89.3	8,804	8,660	12,932	17,276	35.5	15	22
90.0	8,815	8,532	10,117		34.1	14	17
74.7	9,783	11,402	13,589		36.4	17	20
57.3	10,444	8,999	10,433		26.2	19	22
30.3	13,213	8,684	11,894	17,371	80.2	22	28
67.3	13,359	15,129	16,232	7,418	67.5	20	26
59.7	17,803	19,126	19,595	20,322	61.1	18	24
29.0	18,870	17,128	20,547	26,182	64.3	21	27
64.7	7,011	6,669	8,890	12,746	56.3		

RANK	NAME	OVERALL SCORE	STUDENT LOAN DEFAULT RATE	GRADUATION RATE	GRADUATION RATE PERFORMANCE
19.	Rust College (MS)	9	19.2	30.3	5.0
20.	Middle Tennessee State University (TN)*	9	8.5	45.3	1.2
21.	Prairie View A&M University (TX)*	9	15.4	34.0	1.2
22.	Texas A&M University–Commerce (TX)*	9	8.0	36.7	1.0
23.	Texas State Univ.–San Marcos (TX)*	9	6.2	55.3	3.5
24.	Williams Baptist College (AR)	9	4.5	41.3	-4.7
25.	Texas Tech University (TX)*	9	5.7	62.0	0.7
26.	Tennessee Technological Univ. (TN)*	9	4.8	50.0	-1.1
27.	Mississippi State University (MS)*	9	6.0	58.7	1.4
28.	Mississippi College (MS)	9	4.8	56.0	-2.4
29.	Martin Methodist College (TN)	9	17.2	55.7	7.4
30.	Transylvania University (KY)	9	1.8	73.3	-1.1
31.	Fisk University (TN)	9	11.9	52.7	10.0
32.	Belhaven University (MS)	9	4.7	50.3	-1.3
33.	Vanderbilt University (TN)	9	1.7	91.7	0.2
34.	Saint Edward's University (TX)	9	4.8	68.7	5.2
35.	Sewanee–University of the South (TN)	9	2.0	81.7	7.3
36.	Northwestern OK State Univ. (OK)*	8	12.8	33.0	3.4
37.	Northeastern State University (OK)*	8	12.8	28.0	14.9
38.	Nicholls State University (LA)*	8	6.6	35.3	-4.9
39.	University of Texas at Dallas (TX)*	8	5.3	62.7	-11.0
40.	Texas A&M University–Kingsville (TX)*	8	11.1	37.7	-4.7
41.	Mississippi Univ. for Women (MS)*	8	7.5	38.0	-10.7
42.	Southeastern OK State Univ. (OK)*	8	13.3	29.3	17.3
43.	Southern Univ. and A&M College (LA)*	8	7.1	29.0	-1.0
44.	Murray State University (KY)*	8	6.4	53.7	4.7
45.	Alcorn State University (MS)*	8	11.2	34.3	1.5
46.	Wayland Baptist University (TX)	8	7.9	38.3	9.3
47.	Blue Mountain College (MS)	8	10.5	44.3	0.6
48.	Christian Brothers University (TN)	8	6.9	55.7	-3.4
49.	Lincoln Memorial University (TN)	8	4.8	45.7	-8.4
50.	University of Mississippi (MS)*	8	5.9	59.0	-0.3
51.	Oklahoma Baptist University (OK)	8	6.1	52.0	0.1
52.	Carson-Newman College (TN)	8	7.5	51.0	-4.1
53.	University of Oklahoma–Norman (OK)*	8	4.2	66.0	4.4
54.	Bryan College–Dayton (TN)	8	4.6	53.3	-0.0
55.	Milligan College (TN)	8	3.5	60.3	0.5
56.	Maryville College (TN)	8	5.0	55.7	-4.7
57.	Trevecca Nazarene University (TN)	8	4.8	51.7	-1.7
58.	Spalding University (KY)	8	6.2	43.3	9.3
59.	John Brown University (AR)	8	3.3	65.0	4.5
60.	Georgetown College (KY)	8	3.5	62.3	0.8
61.	St. Mary's University (TX)	8	5.4	58.3	-2.0
62.	Southern Nazarene University (OK)	8	4.3	43.3	-1.9
63.	Rice University (TX)	8	1.5	92.0	-2.3
64.	Southern Adventist University (TN)	8	4.0	53.7	-1.9

STUDENTS RECEIVING PELL GRANTS	NET PRICE (all students)	NET PRICE (annual family income, $0–$30K)	NET PRICE (annual family income, $30–75K)	NET PRICE (annual family income above $75k)	PERCENT OF APPLICANTS ADMITTED	ACT/SAT 25TH PERCENTILE SCORE	ACT/SAT 75TH PERCENTILE SCORE
84.7	7,897	7,849	8,738	12,175	37.4	15	19
40.0	8,762	5,377	9,221	12,627	69.5	19	24
65.7	8,996	11,073	12,571	14,015	40.1	757	907
48.7	9,407	8,393	10,802	14,715	47.6	863	1060
34.7	9,698	10,369	10,558	16,789	73.1	953	1133
50.3	10,861	8,977	10,746	13,039	62.6	19	24
27.3	11,369	11,037	14,309	17,591	67.4	1010	1173
37.7	11,836	7,451	11,621	14,245	94.7	20	26
34.0	13,451	11,104	14,448	18,082	60.1	20	27
37.7	14,101	11,393	13,669	15,305	55.2	20	27
52.3	16,928	16,396	17,774		60.9		
25.7	19,006	13,885	15,440	21,362	84.2	24	30
56.3	19,161	18,961			56.5	17	23
62.0	19,262	20,462	19,267	21,733	46.2	20	25
14.3	19,447	6,236	7,597	26,644	16.2	31	34
32.3	19,905	13,428	16,345	24,787	63.1	1017	1240
10.7	23,441	8,335	10,263	21,762	60.8	1157	1373
42.0	6,518	4,301	6,157	9,260	77.5	17	22
48.7	6,640	5,168	7,478		68.1	18	23
36.0	6,869	5,067	7,584	11,119	84.6	20	24
33.3	7,528	6,451	10,039	15,325	51.7	1143	1340
51.0	7,536	5,258	8,618	14,330	70.3	15	20
55.3	7,687	6,784	8,729	10,432	43.4	18	24
46.3	8,273	6,830	8,853	12,114	78.6	18	23
67.3	9,950	9,234	8,302	11,721	40.6	17	20
34.7	10,009	7,443	9,347	10,461	79.4	19	25
80.3	10,760	10,396	11,869	12,773	39.2	16	19
25.3	10,976	9,089	12,057		97.8	17	22
62.7	11,005	8,907	10,177	10,966	49.1	18	24
44.0	11,348	5,324	8,528	11,249	47.8	21	26
51.0	11,852	11,671	14,110	16,661	74.4	20	25
29.3	12,703	9,408	12,839	16,118	72.6	20	27
31.7	14,160	10,413	12,142	16,916	64.8	21	27
38.0	14,827	11,837	14,882	18,361	67.2	20	25
25.0	15,064	12,262	14,658	18,469	82.0	23	29
36.0	15,341	11,422	13,807	18,778	53.9	20	26
34.0	15,495	9,388	14,508	18,626	68.4	21	27
39.7	15,881	10,769	14,332	18,709	51.0	21	27
35.7	16,457	15,869	16,448	18,646	73.3	19	25
48.0	16,760	15,153	17,309	20,463	39.7	16	21
33.0	16,920	12,704	14,819	18,275	69.3	22	28
32.3	17,014	12,020	15,362	19,223	83.1	21	27
49.0	17,370	13,603	16,395	21,659	59.1	930	1107
52.3	18,084	13,665	16,502		69.5		
16.3	19,129	6,159	8,160	29,782	18.9	1343	1500
35.3	19,190	15,529	17,313	21,885	58.3	19	25

RANK	NAME	OVERALL SCORE	STUDENT LOAN DEFAULT RATE	GRADUATION RATE	GRADUATION RATE PERFORMANCE
65.	Oral Roberts University (OK)	8	6.9	55.0	1.4
66.	Austin College (TX)	8	2.1	77.0	-1.1
67.	Centre College (KY)	8	1.9	85.0	3.4
68.	Trinity University (TX)	8	1.9	79.3	1.0
69.	University of Dallas (TX)	8	2.8	72.0	-0.3
70.	University of Louisiana at Lafayette (LA)*	7	7.4	41.7	-2.8
71.	Univ. of Science & Arts of Okla. (OK)*	7	13.5	37.3	-3.6
72.	University of Texas–Brownsville (TX)*	7	10.8	21.3	-3.4
73.	McNeese State University (LA)*	7	11.6	36.7	-3.7
74.	Arkansas Tech University (AR)*	7	13.8	41.0	-2.2
75.	So. Arkansas Univ.–Campus (AR)*	7	12.6	33.0	-9.1
76.	University of Tennessee–Martin (TN)*	7	10.9	47.3	-0.3
77.	Midwestern State University (TX)*	7	6.5	33.7	-10.7
78.	Louisiana Tech University (LA)*	7	4.7	47.7	-7.2
79.	University of Arkansas–Pine Bluff (AR)*	7	21.4	25.0	-3.5
80.	Univ. of Arkansas–Monticello (AR)*	7	19.3	27.3	-0.6
81.	Henderson State University (AR)*	7	11.7	33.3	-9.8
82.	University of Texas–Arlington (TX)*	7	6.5	40.0	-11.4
83.	Texas A&M University–Corpus Christi (TX)*	7	9.5	39.0	-2.4
84.	University of Central Arkansas (AR)*	7	8.7	41.0	-12.0
85.	University of Arkansas (AR)*	7	5.2	59.0	-6.6
86.	LA State Univ./Agri. & Mech.l Coll. (LA)*	7	3.0	63.3	-4.0
87.	Western Kentucky University (KY)*	7	8.9	42.3	-2.5
88.	University of Southern Mississippi (MS)*	7	8.5	48.0	-1.4
89.	University of the Ozarks (AR)	7	10.3	49.0	0.7
90.	Tennessee Wesleyan College (TN)	7	8.3	46.7	-1.7
91.	University of Louisville (KY)*	7	6.9	50.7	-3.2
92.	Campbellsville University (KY)	7	9.6	44.7	4.1
93.	University of Kentucky (KY)*	7	4.2	59.0	-6.7
94.	Lyon College (AR)	7	5.8	49.7	-13.0
95.	University of Tennessee (TN)*	7	5.2	63.0	-6.9
96.	Free Will Baptist Bible College (TN)	7	11.4	49.7	2.7
97.	University of the Cumberlands (KY)	7	7.4	42.0	-3.7
98.	Tarleton State University (TX)*	7	7.7	38.7	-1.6
99.	Harding University (AR)	7	3.3	63.7	-0.7
100.	Freed-Hardeman University (TN)	7	7.1	53.7	-3.9
101.	Texas Wesleyan University (TX)	7	5.8	36.7	-7.6
102.	Xavier University of Louisiana (LA)	7	8.0	48.3	-3.9
103.	Oklahoma Wesleyan University (OK)	7	7.3	45.0	0.8
104.	Millsaps College (MS)	7	4.8	68.7	-2.4
105.	Southwestern University (TX)	7	4.2	74.0	-0.7
106.	Sullivan University (KY)°	7	17.5	51.0	9.9
107.	Rhodes College (TN)	7	1.8	78.7	-1.8
108.	Mid-Continent University (KY)	7	9.0	33.7	9.2
109.	Baylor University (TX)	7	4.4	72.7	-4.4
110.	Texas Christian University (TX)	7	3.9	74.3	0.7

STUDENTS RECEIVING PELL GRANTS	NET PRICE (all students)	NET PRICE (annual family income, $0–$30K)	NET PRICE (annual family income, $30–75K)	NET PRICE (annual family income above $75k)	PERCENT OF APPLICANTS ADMITTED	ACT/SAT 25TH PERCENTILE SCORE	ACT/SAT 75TH PERCENTILE SCORE
45.0	19,555	15,598	19,105	22,320	61.8	20	25
27.3	21,183	14,702	16,988	24,666	64.9	23	29
17.7	22,940	14,706	17,425	24,130	71.1	26	31
12.7	24,621	13,894	17,113	27,336	62.7	1160	1360
22.7	26,466	21,110	21,181	26,609	88.7	1080	1373
32.0	5,418	3,058	5,597	8,743	64.4	20	24
44.3	5,579	2,808	5,348	8,762	40.5	20	26
55.3	6,363	5,144	7,599	11,798	70.6		
35.7	6,976	5,190	7,256	10,879	68.3	20	24
44.7	7,509	7,601	8,353	11,008	89.7	19	25
54.7	7,643	7,866	8,218	11,598	66.0	18	24
42.3	8,030	4,811	8,638	11,560	74.2	20	24
38.7	8,247	4,827	8,040	13,484	63.6	917	1230
22.7	8,355	5,506	8,160	10,938	64.6	21	26
73.3	8,406	8,287	8,861	10,378	30.8	14	19
58.3	8,570	8,406	9,085	10,872	68.5		
52.0	8,873	7,821	8,189		61.0	18	24
40.3	9,478	7,995	10,530	17,095	70.9	950	1160
41.0	9,602	11,303	12,734		86.3	853	1060
37.0	9,776	8,632	10,519	13,809	92.6	20	26
24.0	10,379	7,538	10,730	14,146	61.6	23	28
19.3	10820	2,643	8,747	12,958	73.6	23	28
40.3	11,213	10,842	14,723		92.9	18	24
47.3	11,309	10,821	12,208	13,865	63.2	19	24
39.0	11,565	17,449	18,991	22,455	90.4	20	25
49.3	11,766	7,908	11,254	13,495	82.1	19	24
29.0	12,060	6,762	11,022	15,460	73.4	21	28
42.7	13,496	11,628	12,157	13,935	64.9	18	23
23.0	13,538	7,886	12,666	16,535	70.1	22	28
46.0	13,930	9,471	11,936	14,887	64.8	23	28
28.3	14,275	8,376	12,600	16,443	70.5	24	29
43.3	14,542	14,586	13,012	17,965	63.8		
44.7	14,928	12,854	14,327	17,278	69.1	19	24
46.0	14,967	11,280	13,383		60.2	870	1060
27.3	15,072	11,210	13,768	17,655	73.2	22	28
37.7	16,171	14,126	15,361	17,186	80.9	20	26
53.7	16,206	14,451	16,796	18,219	50.2	913	1067
61.0	17,266	19,082	20,216	19,421	65.5	19	24
40.7	18,194	15,311	17,579	19,276	58.2	18	25
21.7	19,172	13,885	15,789	20,817	64.0	23	29
25.0	23,783	16,074	19,976	26,859	64.0	1100	1347
47.3	23,925	22,368	24,153	26,461	70.3		
15.3	26,151	16,923	18,421	27,516	48.9	26	31
61.0	26,977	28,879	29,817	31,343	88.7	17	21
23.3	27,061	20,529	23,407	29,657	49.4	24	29
15.0	27,851	19,818	23,590	33,153	43.8	24	29

RANK	NAME	OVERALL SCORE	STUDENT LOAN DEFAULT RATE	GRADUATION RATE	GRADUATION RATE PERFORMANCE
111.	Southern Methodist University (TX)	7	4.1	76.3	0.8
112.	University of TX Permian Basin (TX)*	6	10.0	34.3	-6.4
113.	University of New Orleans (LA)*	6	6.6	30.7	-13.1
114.	University of Louisiana–Monroe (LA)*	6	9.1	35.3	-8.6
115.	Northwestern State Univ. of LA (LA)*	6	10.3	32.0	-7.8
116.	Northern Kentucky University (KY)*	6	7.1	36.0	-8.0
117.	Southeastern Louisiana Univ. (LA)*	6	6.5	33.3	-10.1
118.	Sul Ross State University (TX)*	6	11.9	24.7	-7.5
119.	AR State Univ.–Main (AR)*	6	12.7	37.3	-5.6
120.	Kentucky State University (KY)*	6	16.0	20.0	-9.7
121.	Southern Univ. New Orleans (LA)*	6	11.4	17.0	-5.2
122.	Morehead State University (KY)*	6	9.2	35.7	-10.2
123.	Texas Southern University (TX)*	6	15.2	12.3	-9.9
124.	Langston University (OK)*	6	20.6	15.0	-7.9
125.	Southwestern OK State Univ. (OK)*	6	12.7	36.0	-6.0
126.	Mississippi Valley State Univ. (MS)*	6	10.6	24.3	-6.9
127.	Paul Quinn College (TX)	6	14.6	5.0	-21.7
128.	Texas A&M University–Galveston (TX)*	6	3.7	30.0	-27.6
129.	University of Memphis (TN)*	6	7.6	38.0	-5.6
130.	West Texas A&M University (TX)*	6	7.9	42.0	-8.1
131.	Wiley College (TX)	6	14.8	21.3	-4.6
132.	Austin Peay State University (TN)*	6	10.0	34.0	-2.4
133.	University of Texas–Tyler (TX)*	6	7.2	39.7	-5.4
134.	Central Baptist College (AR)	6	10.5	33.3	-4.6
135.	Delta State University (MS)*	6	9.1	38.3	-4.4
136.	Eastern Kentucky University (KY)*	6	9.0	37.0	-9.7
137.	University of Houston (TX)*	6	6.1	46.0	-11.4
138.	Our Lady of the Lake U.–San Antonio (TX)	6	7.0	31.7	-13.5
139.	Lee University (TN)	6	7.9	48.7	-10.2
140.	Grambling State University (LA)*	6	12.8	29.0	-3.8
141.	Univ. of Tennessee–Chattanooga (TN)*	6	7.4	38.3	-13.7
142.	Stephen F. Austin State Univ. (TX)*	6	10.5	44.3	-1.8
143.	Texas College (TX)	6	22.8	16.0	-3.7
144.	Our Lady of Holy Cross College (LA)	6	5.0	24.0	-13.8
145.	East Tennessee State University (TN)*	6	10.0	41.3	-0.2
146.	Louisiana College (LA)	6	6.2	38.7	-10.1
147.	Lamar University (TX)*	6	11.1	30.7	-4.7
148.	Dillard University (LA)	6	7.0	27.7	-8.4
149.	Jarvis Christian College (TX)	6	28.0	18.7	-4.7
150.	Bethel University (TN)	6	9.1	31.0	-6.2
151.	Kentucky Wesleyan College (KY)	6	10.2	43.3	-7.5
152.	Centenary College of Louisiana (LA)	6	5.6	58.0	-5.3
153.	Ouachita Baptist University (AR)	6	6.4	59.7	-1.7
154.	King College (TN)	6	5.6	49.0	-6.7
155.	Texas Lutheran University (TX)	6	5.9	46.7	-7.7
156.	University of the Incarnate Word (TX)	6	7.6	42.7	-1.8

STUDENTS RECEIVING PELL GRANTS	NET PRICE (all students)	NET PRICE (annual family income, $0–$30K)	NET PRICE (annual family income, $30–75K)	NET PRICE (annual family income above $75k)	PERCENT OF APPLICANTS ADMITTED	ACT/SAT 25TH PERCENTILE SCORE	ACT/SAT 75TH PERCENTILE SCORE
16.7	29,148	15,763	20,294	34,058	54.1	1170	1353
39.0	6,383	2,414	4,670	9,534	82.2	896	1073
31.7	7,542	6,193	8,498	11,899	53.5	20	24
38.0	7,750	5,764	9,277	12,043	85.4	20	24
38.7	7,766	6,152	8,768	11,325	83.5	19	24
32.3	7,952	3,908	7,643	11,447	65.6	19	24
34.3	8,009	5,890	8,563	11,527	43.7	20	24
62.0	8,868	7,370	10,234	14,499	85.1	15	21
48.0	8,921	8,408	10,054	12,784	67.1	20	25
58.7	8,986	8,343	11,430	14,634	33.5	15	19
75.7	9,057	7,212	8,270		28.8	16	19
43.7	9,168	7,290	9,594	12,729	86.8	19	24
72.0	9,211	13,397	18,395		42.8	727	900
71.7	9,474	9,281	10,913		59.3		
41.0	9,528	7,287	9,304	12,676	91.5	18	24
69.3	9,896	10,062			22.8	15	19
80.0	9,990	9,241			57.5	850	880
23.3	10,185	6,589	11,981	15,441	65.3	1030	1165
48.3	10,249	7,914	11,396	14,452	65.1	19	25
35.3	10,280	6,523	9,564	15,351	70.2	18	24
81.3	10,391	11,665	12,161	13,927	45.1		
49.7	10,491	8,185	11,615	14,104	87.0	19	23
37.7	10,723	5,221	9,823	15,878	65.6	943	1140
45.7	11,016	9,001	10,862		61.3	19	23
46.3	11,300	8,386	11,736	13,428	73.4	18	22
41.3	11,367	6,841	10,193	14,323	67.0	19	23
37.7	11,559	8,416	12,012	18,159	63.3	1000	1180
44.3	11,667	21,886	23,108		56.3	803	993
35.0	11,750	10,482	13,338	15,714	71.5	21	27
69.3	11,754	10,675	12,834	15,405	42.8	15	20
36.0	12,217	6,770	11,097	14,112	72.4	21	25
43.3	12,473	14,772	17,150	18,808	56.0	883	1053
89.0	12,523	12,885	14,400	16,619	48.4		
48.7	13,004	12,163	15,180	15,653	63.3	19	20
42.0	13,197	10,558	13,244	16,626	84.6	19	24
49.0	13,200	12,246	10,755	14,160	67.0	17	24
40.7	13,327	12,486	15,366	19,152	60.3	830	1027
76.0	13,600	13,487	14,554	14,875	41.6	16	20
83.0	13,688	15,202	14,485		48.0		
57.3	13,803	14,680	16,355	16,546	52.0	17	23
50.0	14,102	11,432	13,127	16,444	42.8	19	24
32.0	15,847	12,276	15,261	22,598	62.4	22	28
27.7	15,851	13,061	14,971	18,816	65.2	21	28
36.3	16,762	14,026	17,064	19,565	68.6	19	25
39.7	17,166	13,050	15,818	17,927	60.7	900	1107
41.7	17,369	15,121	16,294	19,833	85.6	863	1060

RANK	NAME	OVERALL SCORE	STUDENT LOAN DEFAULT RATE	GRADUATION RATE	GRADUATION RATE PERFORMANCE
157.	Southwestern Adventist University (TX)	6	8.9	40.0	-3.6
158.	Dallas Baptist University (TX)	6	5.0	52.3	-7.3
159.	Thomas More College (KY)	6	5.3	49.0	-1.3
160.	LeTourneau University (TX)	6	5.0	53.7	-10.5
161.	Union University (TN)	6	4.5	62.3	-3.3
162.	Bellarmine University (KY)	6	3.9	65.7	-0.8
163.	LA State University–Shreveport (LA)*	5	7.5	27.0	-13.9
164.	Univ. of Arkansas–Fort Smith (AR)*	5	16.5	20.0	-15.1
165.	Louisiana State Univ.–Alexandria (LA)*	5	9.6	10.7	-22.1
166.	Cameron University (OK)*	5	13.5	17.0	-8.3
167.	University of Arkansas at Little Rock (AR)*	5	9.9	21.0	-17.3
168.	Univ. of Houston–Downtown (TX)*	5	9.6	13.0	-12.2
169.	University of North Texas (TX)*	5	7.9	48.3	-8.3
170.	Rogers State University (OK)*	5	12.8	13.3	-4.0
171.	University of Texas–San Antonio (TX)*	5	7.7	27.3	-21.4
172.	Philander Smith College (AR)	5	12.5	26.0	-5.9
173.	Brescia University (KY)	5	9.1	41.0	-7.2
174.	University of Central Oklahoma (OK)*	5	9.3	34.7	-2.5
175.	Le Moyne-Owen College (TN)	5	14.6	13.3	-6.3
176.	Angelo State University (TX)*	5	11.4	31.7	-14.4
177.	Lindsey Wilson College (KY)	5	11.3	29.3	-7.1
178.	Mid-America Christian University (OK)	5	9.7	20.3	-1.8
179.	Cumberland University (TN)	5	7.8	32.3	-18.5
180.	University of Pikeville (KY)	5	9.5	30.0	-10.8
181.	East Texas Baptist University (TX)	5	8.8	37.0	-8.7
182.	Union College (KY)	5	9.8	33.0	-9.1
183.	Huston-Tillotson University (TX)	5	20.5	23.0	-3.1
184.	Victory University (TN)°	5	10.8	13.0	-4.3
185.	Kentucky Christian University (KY)	5	9.9	40.7	-6.7
186.	Tusculum College (TN)	5	9.1	34.3	-12.7
187.	Howard Payne University (TX)	5	10.6	42.7	-2.8
188.	Oklahoma Christian University (OK)	5	5.5	46.3	-14.6
189.	Houston Baptist University (TX)	5	6.1	44.3	-16.6
190.	Lubbock Christian University (TX)	5	8.3	46.3	-9.9
191.	Schreiner University (TX)	5	6.7	40.3	-12.8
192.	Lipscomb University (TN)	5	4.0	58.0	-8.6
193.	Southwestern Assemb. of God U. (TX)	5	8.7	38.0	-11.1
194.	Loyola University–New Orleans (LA)	5	3.1	59.0	-10.2
195.	Oklahoma City University (OK)	5	5.9	56.0	-6.8
196.	University of Tulsa (OK)	5	5.0	66.3	-4.8
197.	Abilene Christian University (TX)	5	5.3	58.7	-6.2
198.	DeVry University–Texas (TX)°	5	14.6	24.3	2.9
199.	Belmont University (TN)	5	2.4	67.3	-6.8
200.	Tulane University of Louisiana (LA)	5	3.6	75.0	-7.3
201.	Oklahoma Panhandle State Univ. (OK)*	4	11.6	21.7	-10.9
202.	Southwestern Christian University (OK)	4	11.0	26.0	-9.4

STUDENTS RECEIVING PELL GRANTS	NET PRICE (all students)	NET PRICE (annual family income, $0–$30K)	NET PRICE (annual family income, $30–75K)	NET PRICE (annual family income above $75k)	PERCENT OF APPLICANTS ADMITTED	ACT/SAT 25TH PERCENTILE SCORE	ACT/SAT 75TH PERCENTILE SCORE
44.3	18,000	16,380	17,303	22,146	99.0	830	1080
30.0	18,197	14,370	16,488	20,046	42.7	19	28
23.3	19,304	16,559	18,314	21,470	87.0	20	25
42.3	21,629	16,696	18,791	23,859	52.7	1047	1300
23.3	22,094	15,465	20,282	25,407	76.7	22	29
21.7	22,539	16,174	19,742	23,390	63.1	22	27
32.0	6,972	5,550	7,774	11,369	72.3	20	24
49.0	7,082	6,783	7,862	10,617	56.3	19	24
41.0	7,099	5,831	7,852	11,348	65.3	19	22
43.0	7,742	6,184	8,410	12,310	70.0		
39.3	8,618	8,418	9,579	13,196	94.3	18	25
49.7	9,019	7,862	9,441	16,575	56.8		
33.3	10,116	1,779	7,813	15,991	64.5	980	1200
44.3	10,152	8,005	9,933	11,489	53.1	17	23
43.0	10,253	6,257	10,106	16,797	82.8	923	1120
82.3	10,718	10,303	11,833	12,350	69.0	16	20
46.3	10,813	9,412	10,697	11,482	44.5	19	24
33.0	11,068	9,215	11,130		79.0	19	24
76.3	11,267	11,369	11,663		33.9	14	17
44.3	11,579	8,742	11,890	15,604	92.8	18	23
65.0	14,894	14,273	14,560	16,751	72.5		
51.3	15,057	16,019	17,127	20,139	75.2		
38.3	15,467	13,463	15,980		50.7	20	24
54.7	15,584	14,244	15,649		77.7		
44.3	15,714	12,497	13,873	18,746	55.7	18	22
60.0	16,048	14,784	16,363	19,721	58.4	18	23
68.0	16,147	16,466	17,008		80.1	703	900
76.0	16,285	16,570			25.4	14	18
52.0	16,495	15,117	16,130	18,579	41.7	19	24
58.0	16,673	15,038	17,850	22,052	70.6	18	24
39.3	16,949	13,112	15,648	19,773	60.6	870	1067
28.7	17,482	14,680	15,313	19,632	50.4	20	28
45.7	17,993	17,044	18,790	21,436	37.1	977	1173
40.0	18,283	15,844	17,795	20,770	71.3	19	24
41.0	18,661	14,439	16,109	20,814	61.5	890	1107
28.0	20,095	16,826	19,857	22,634	54.6	22	28
50.7	20,300	18,676	20,145	23,468	35.7		
28.3	22,360	17,534	20,227	24,186	62.4	23	28
21.3	22,784	17,904	21,193	26,835	73.3	23	28
17.3	23,774	18,469	22,114	26,386	40.3	25	31
24.3	24,220	20,563	22,153	26,084	54.1	22	28
63.7	24,533	24,096	25,487	28,052	82.0		
17.0	27,218	22,267	25,366	31,149	82.3	24	29
17.3	28,630	18,607	20,396	30,744	26.1	1237	1413
34.7	5,882	3,636	5,750	7,853	83.5	16	20
64.7	16,297	15,923	16,007		70.7	17	23

RANK	NAME	OVERALL SCORE	STUDENT LOAN DEFAULT RATE	GRADUATION RATE	GRADUATION RATE PERFORMANCE
203.	McMurry University (TX)	4	11.6	37.0	-5.6
204.	Concordia University–Texas (TX)	4	6.1	34.0	-14.4
205.	Hardin-Simmons University (TX)	4	6.6	47.3	-11.1
206.	Hendrix College (AR)	4	4.5	68.3	-15.9
207.	University of St. Thomas (TX)	4	5.4	46.3	-11.5
208.	Univ. of Mary Hardin–Baylor (TX)	4	6.0	46.3	-8.2
209.	Saint Gregorys University (OK)	3	15.0	29.7	-7.2
210.	Univ. of Phoenix–Oklahoma City (OK)°	3	17.0	12.7	-7.0
211.	University of Phoenix–Tulsa (OK)°	3	17.0	14.0	-7.5
212.	University of Phoenix–Louisville (KY)°	3	17.0	9.7	-8.3
213.	University of Phoenix–Memphis (TN)°	3	17.0	15.3	-6.0
214.	University of Phoenix–Chattanooga (TN)°	3	17.0	14.0	-5.3

SOUTHEASTERN SCHOOLS

RANK	NAME	OVERALL SCORE	STUDENT LOAN DEFAULT RATE	GRADUATION RATE	GRADUATION RATE PERFORMANCE
1.	East Carolina University (NC)*	12	3.0	57.7	8.8
2.	North Carolina State Univ.–Raleigh (NC)*	12	2.4	71.7	4.4
3.	University of Georgia (GA)*	12	2.6	82.3	8.7
4.	University of Florida (FL)*	12	2.4	84.3	8.9
5.	Coker College (SC)	12	4.9	53.0	7.2
6.	Columbia International University (SC)	12	3.2	64.0	9.9
7.	Univ. of NC–Pembroke (NC)*	11	7.1	35.3	10.6
8.	University of NC–Greensboro (NC)*	11	3.7	53.3	1.3
9.	Appalachian State University (NC)*	11	2.5	65.7	1.4
10.	Univ. of North Carolina–Charlotte (NC)*	11	3.0	53.7	-1.1
11.	University of NC–Chapel Hill (NC)*	11	0.9	88.7	8.0
12.	Radford University (VA)*	11	3.0	57.7	6.3
13.	University of Virginia–Main (VA)*	11	1.8	93.3	6.7
14.	James Madison University (VA)*	11	1.9	81.0	11.3
15.	Florida State University (FL)*	11	4.5	74.3	8.5
16.	University of Mary Washington (VA)*	11	1.5	74.0	7.8
17.	Elizabeth City State University (NC)*	10	14.0	43.0	16.4
18.	Fayetteville State University (NC)*	10	11.6	32.0	5.2
19.	North Carolina Central Univ. (NC)*	10	12.0	39.7	6.3
20.	Georgia Institute of Technology–Main (GA)*	10	1.8	79.3	-3.9
21.	Voorhees College (SC)	10	11.5	30.3	6.3
22.	Albany State University (GA)*	10	11.4	41.7	10.5
23.	Gallaudet University (DC)	10	5.7	36.3	7.7
24.	Claflin University (SC)	10	7.8	43.3	8.7
25.	College of William and Mary (VA)*	10	0.8	90.3	4.6
26.	Virginia Military Institute (VA)*	10	3.5	70.0	6.5
27.	Citadel: The Military College of SC (SC)*	10	3.2	69.3	17.1
28.	Presbyterian College (SC)	10	1.8	67.3	8.4
29.	Salem College (NC)	10	4.8	57.7	3.5
30.	Mount Olive College (NC)	10	4.7	40.7	9.6
31.	Univ. of South Carolina–Columbia (SC)*	10	2.3	70.0	0.5
32.	Erskine College and Seminary (SC)	10	2.0	61.0	8.6

STUDENTS RECEIVING PELL GRANTS	NET PRICE (all students)	NET PRICE (annual family income, $0–$30K)	NET PRICE (annual family income, $30–75K)	NET PRICE (annual family income above $75k)	PERCENT OF APPLICANTS ADMITTED	ACT/SAT 25TH PERCENTILE SCORE	ACT/SAT 75TH PERCENTILE SCORE
47.7	18,316	16,613	18,220	22,198	56.6	843	1033
33.7	19,108	15,422	17,939	21,639	68.1	900	1107
33.3	19,656	21,126	23,117	23,474	48.3	20	25
19.7	20,162	14,649	17,050	23,377	82.8	27	32
32.3	20,471	17,311	18,942	24,584	79.8	1027	1229
40.7	21,902	19,309	19,800	23,914	45.6	923	1120
44.3	15,023	9,674	16,695	20,950	55.7	18	23
65.7	21,413	21,552			68.8		
68.7	21,558	21,627	23,711		72.9		
64.0	21,865	21,911			76.8		
72.7	22,341	22,434	23,807		57.5		
74.7	22,415	22,483	22,997		70.0		
31.0	9,609	6,601	10,221	16,739	65.7	963	1107
22.0	9,957	4,846	8,748	16,304	53.9	1087	1240
22.7	10,561	5,376	9,079	11,956	58.7	1123	1313
30.0	11,891	4,710	5,290	12,215	43.5	1167	1340
61.0	12,907	12,705			54.1	883	1080
50.7	14,291	10,262	11,727	15,711	63.7	1000	1267
53.3	7,424	5,646	8,020	13,396	74.5	837	987
39.0	7,868	5,154	8,672	15,169	65.5	923	1120
24.7	8,681	5,339	8,571	14,768	64.2	1053	1227
38.0	9,325	6,615	9,446	15,459	72.5	973	1120
19.7	10,378	4,247	8,762	17,673	32.8	1203	1400
26.0	10,753	8,393	11,906	18,012	77.2	920	1100
12.0	12,005	4,195	11,862	21,600	31.8	1240	1433
13.3	13,030	9,057	13,024	19,551	60.9	1063	1247
28.7	13,090	8,938	12,958	16,311	57.2	25	28
14.3	13,289	9,135	13,476	19,064	75.6	1040	1280
70.0	1,225	416	1,874	6,990	66.8	760	907
64.7	4,985	3,837	5,453	11,188	64.8	767	900
62.7	7,123	6,114	8,433	14,614	64.4	773	920
17.7	8,643	2,149	7,758	11,006	53.9	1243	1373
81.7	9,687	8,945	10,486	15,031	65.3		
76.7	9,715	9,381	11,141	13,901	41.8	793	927
48.7	11,032	7,647	8,358	14,907	61.7	15	20
77.7	11,682	12,905	12,489	12,306	36.1	778	987
12.0	12,356	4,207	10,826	21,618	32.8	1250	1467
17.0	12,409	5,153	9,830	18,216	49.6	1047	1233
22.7	13,800	8,926	14,015	17,948	71.1	977	1160
22.0	15,047	9,488	11,926	16,749	64.2	988	1189
58.3	15,348	23,848	24,640	23,643	62.4	940	1213
50.0	15,663	14,808	13,837	16,717	55.3	827	987
23.0	15,691	9,438	14,385	18,035	65.5	1093	1273
30.0	16,402	11,874	13,440	15,092	69.1	913	1157

RANK	NAME	OVERALL SCORE	STUDENT LOAN DEFAULT RATE	GRADUATION RATE	GRADUATION RATE PERFORMANCE
33.	Clemson University (SC)*	10	1.9	79.3	6.4
34.	VA Polytechnic Inst. & State Univ. (VA)*	10	1.7	81.7	6.9
35.	Saint Thomas University (FL)	10	5.8	37.0	5.1
36.	Howard University (DC)	10	6.8	72.3	10.2
37.	Carlos Albizu University–Miami (FL)	10	0.0	43.7	12.9
38.	North Carolina A&T State University (NC)*	9	11.4	40.7	4.7
39.	Winston-Salem State University (NC)*	9	10.0	39.0	2.9
40.	Savannah State University (GA)*	9	14.3	32.3	1.1
41.	Univ. of North Carolina–Asheville (NC)*	9	4.5	57.0	-4.7
42.	Univ. of NC–Wilmington (NC)*	9	3.9	67.3	0.7
43.	Univ. of Virginia's College–Wise (VA)*	9	8.9	43.0	6.8
44.	Florida Memorial University (FL)	9	14.5	40.7	9.4
45.	Virginia State University (VA)*	9	12.4	40.3	6.5
46.	University of South Carolina–Upstate (SC)*	9	4.7	38.7	0.7
47.	George Mason University (VA)*	9	1.5	64.3	-1.1
48.	University of Central Florida (FL)*	9	4.6	64.0	2.3
49.	Southern Wesleyan University (SC)	9	7.9	44.7	7.4
50.	Longwood University (VA)*	9	2.9	60.0	4.6
51.	Toccoa Falls College (GA)	9	3.4	49.3	3.6
52.	Converse College (SC)	9	3.0	57.0	-1.5
53.	Everglades University (FL)	9	9.7	67.0	24.4
54.	Catawba College (NC)	9	6.2	53.7	8.3
55.	Averett U.–Non-Traditional Progs. (VA)	9	8.0	71.0	30.0
56.	Emory and Henry College (VA)	9	6.7	51.7	5.2
57.	Bethany College (WV)	9	8.3	51.3	10.7
58.	Washington and Lee University (VA)	9	1.3	91.3	4.0
59.	Digital Media Arts College (FL)°	9	6.4	44.7	16.5
60.	Agnes Scott College (GA)	9	5.3	65.7	1.7
61.	University of Richmond (VA)	9	1.7	84.3	4.6
62.	Meredith College (NC)	9	2.6	59.3	2.1
63.	Wofford College (SC)	9	0.5	82.0	13.2
64.	Davidson College (NC)	9	1.5	91.7	9.1
65.	Roanoke College (VA)	9	2.8	68.3	6.7
66.	Furman University (SC)	9	0.7	84.7	9.7
67.	Spelman College (GA)	9	8.6	74.3	16.0
68.	Elon University (NC)	9	1.3	82.0	6.4
69.	Beacon College (FL)	9	1.4	78.0	7.0
70.	West Virginia University (WV)*	8	6.6	57.7	-1.3
71.	Alabama A&M University (AL)*	8	9.9	32.3	-1.5
72.	North GA College & State Univ. (GA)*	8	4.4	51.0	-6.3
73.	Western Carolina University (NC)*	8	5.1	49.7	-0.6
74.	University of West Florida (FL)*	8	6.6	46.7	-1.8
75.	FL Agricultural & Mechanical Univ. (FL)*	8	12.3	40.3	-1.1
76.	Columbus State University (GA)*	8	8.2	32.7	-3.8
77.	Norfolk State University (VA)*	8	13.4	34.0	0.6
78.	Emmanuel College (GA)	8	11.0	41.0	3.2

STUDENTS RECEIVING PELL GRANTS	NET PRICE (all students)	NET PRICE (annual family income, $0–$30K)	NET PRICE (annual family income, $30–75K)	NET PRICE (annual family income above $75k)	PERCENT OF APPLICANTS ADMITTED	ACT/SAT 25TH PERCENTILE SCORE	ACT/SAT 75TH PERCENTILE SCORE
17.0	16,929	9,931	13,552	15,753	61.2	1137	1293
17.0	16,981	9,765	15,028	21,303	68.0	1113	1280
52.3	17,426	11,933	17,271	19,396	53.8	784	958
43.0	19,125	17,628	22,922	24,249	54.1	940	1213
62.0	23,195	22,919			57.6		
57.3	6,139	4,940	7,210	13,125	64.4	803	960
58.0	6,977	6,056	8,340	13,885	58.4	817	947
74.0	8,504	7,930	9,770	13,056	79.5	800	940
29.3	9,187	6,207	8,554	14,351	73.9	1067	1287
26.0	10,053	5,565	9,549	15,540	55.9	1087	1240
40.3	10,411	8,485	11,070	14,564	79.1	833	1053
83.3	11,522	14,921	15,170	15,750	54.9		
66.3	11,745	10,027	12,034	15,518	69.4	783	933
43.0	12,078	9,268	12,476	15,264	67.7	877	1047
26.7	12,543	9,484	12,754	18,040	53.1	1050	1240
31.0	12,691	7,323	10,952	14,815	45.9	1083	1260
47.7	14,797	13,386	14,885	16,744	95.8	857	1040
21.0	16,299	11,908	15,377	20,293	75.0	943	1120
54.0	16,482	14,760	15,675	18,757	48.6	863	1153
42.3	16,556	14,986	16,409	18,418	60.4	937	1187
64.7	17,587	16,596	19,729	20,076	83.9		
43.7	17,942	15,625	19,833	27,251	47.1	850	1073
28.7	18,551	18,717	19,972		81.3		
43.0	18,638	13,907	16,593	21,970	71.1	886	1102
47.7	18,817	19,544	18,733	24,705	56.2	773	1007
7.7	19,401	14,177	16,696	31,255	18.9	1307	1473
64.3	19,419	18,899			64.1		
40.0	19,616	14,792	15,807	22,995	51.3		
17.3	19,751	7,432	11,522	29,505	32.0	1190	1380
33.0	19,951	16,434	18,522	23,983	62.7	913	1127
19.3	20,161	20,525	22,556	28,174	63.2	1087	1300
11.7	24,113	8,204	11,135	27,707	26.6	1263	1447
23.0	25,472	18,036	20,415	25,316	68.4	980	1187
14.0	27,394	19,486	19,356	30,514	71.6	1150	1353
47.7	27,871	25,570	29,736	33,516	38.1	945	1132
9.7	28,406	19,012	23,265	32,481	52.7	1123	1313
19.3	33,298	30,675			56.3		
26.7	8,304	6,229	8,871	11,380	86.6	21	26
67.3	8,698	8,471	10,710	13,660	51.9	16	19
29.3	9,119	5,506	8,123	10,937	55.2	1010	1193
34.7	9,359	5,637	9,138	14,775	40.5	945	1113
37.3	9,376	5,552	8,560	11,466	65.3	21	26
66.7	9,393	8,368	11,298	14,341	52.7	18	22
42.7	9,458	8,364	10,450	13,372	54.2	860	1100
64.0	10,442	10,356	11,354	14,099	65.4	793	947
56.0	11,182	9,608	11,143	13,502	51.6	840	1027

RANK	NAME	OVERALL SCORE	STUDENT LOAN DEFAULT RATE	GRADUATION RATE	GRADUATION RATE PERFORMANCE
79.	Fort Valley State University (GA)*	8	14.4	31.7	2.1
80.	Georgia State University (GA)*	8	5.1	48.7	-3.9
81.	Warner University (FL)	8	11.2	43.7	4.5
82.	Auburn University (AL)*	8	4.6	66.7	0.1
83.	Livingstone College (NC)	8	19.6	28.7	11.3
84.	Shorter University (GA)	8	8.9	48.3	4.3
85.	Brenau University (GA)	8	4.1	45.0	-1.4
86.	Winthrop University (SC)*	8	6.1	55.0	-1.8
87.	Columbia College (SC)	8	6.2	50.0	-1.5
88.	Piedmont College (GA)	8	3.3	46.7	-3.8
89.	Trinity Washington University (DC)	8	9.4	36.7	9.2
90.	Francis Marion University (SC)*	8	5.1	41.7	-1.8
91.	Wingate University (NC)	8	4.2	50.3	-1.7
92.	South Carolina State University (SC)*	8	13.7	36.0	7.6
93.	West Virginia Wesleyan College (WV)	8	7.2	57.0	5.6
94.	Bethune-Cookman University (FL)	8	13.5	38.0	8.7
95.	Johnson C. Smith University (NC)	8	17.9	39.3	6.1
96.	Mid-Atlantic Christian University (NC)	8	9.6	46.7	9.0
97.	Saint Leo University (FL)	8	6.8	44.7	2.3
98.	Wheeling Jesuit University (WV)	8	4.1	61.0	2.2
99.	Mary Baldwin College (VA)	8	3.4	48.3	2.4
100.	Polytech. Univ. Puerto Rico–Orlando (FL)	8	0.0	12.7	-0.8
101.	Spring Hill College (AL)	8	5.3	62.3	-1.1
102.	Barry University (FL)	8	3.8	37.0	-2.4
103.	Life University (GA)	8	6.3	42.3	9.6
104.	Eastern Mennonite University (VA)	8	1.9	60.7	2.8
105.	Herzing University–Atlanta (GA)°	8	0.0	20.0	4.7
106.	Samford University (AL)	8	1.2	71.3	1.7
107.	Everest University–Brandon (FL)°	8	0.0	22.0	1.5
108.	Clark Atlanta University (GA)	8	8.4	41.0	5.1
109.	Sweet Briar College (VA)	8	2.8	63.7	1.1
110.	Emory University (GA)	8	1.4	88.3	-3.8
111.	Shorter U. Coll. Adult/Prof. Progs. (GA)	8	8.9	40.7	5.9
112.	Georgetown University (DC)	8	0.6	93.7	2.6
113.	Rollins College (FL)	8	3.1	70.3	0.8
114.	University of Miami (FL)	8	1.8	79.7	-2.3
115.	Full Sail University (FL)°	8	10.6	79.7	33.4
116.	Columbia Southern University (AL)°	7	5.0	46.0	-0.9
117.	Marshall University (WV)*	7	9.1	45.0	-4.2
118.	University of South Alabama (AL)*	7	4.8	37.0	-8.1
119.	Fairmont State University (WV)*	7	11.3	34.7	-4.4
120.	Southern Polytechnic State Univ. (GA)*	7	6.1	33.0	-13.9
121.	West Liberty University (WV)*	7	11.9	42.3	-3.3
122.	Alabama State University (AL)*	7	13.1	25.3	-0.5
123.	University of West Georgia (GA)*	7	6.1	37.0	-7.1
124.	University of South Carolina–Aiken (SC)*	7	3.7	40.7	-6.3

STUDENTS RECEIVING PELL GRANTS	NET PRICE (all students)	NET PRICE (annual family income, $0–$30K)	NET PRICE (annual family income, $30–75K)	NET PRICE (annual family income above $75k)	PERCENT OF APPLICANTS ADMITTED	ACT/SAT 25TH PERCENTILE SCORE	ACT/SAT 75TH PERCENTILE SCORE
74.7	12,160	11,689	13,788	17,170	41.0	741	941
46.3	12,729	10,319	12,722	16,676	51.6	997	1180
59.7	13,877	14,342	16,541	19,169	50.5	16	22
17.0	14,074	9,701	14,454	17,945	75.3	24	30
89.3	14,283	14,508	14,769	17,176	53.0	658	813
42.7	14,690	12,702	14,726	17,879	63.9	850	1093
47.0	14,762	11,123	15,514	16,631	28.4	883	1100
38.0	14,803	10,968	14,183	16,956	68.1	943	1160
62.7	15,380	15,067	13,350	13,623	70.1	907	1140
52.0	15,408	13,582	15,104	16,514	60.7	917	1133
64.7	15,551	13,571	16,132	21,893	69.7		
50.3	15,615	11,684	13,882		59.0	846	1067
36.3	15,697	12,159	14,036	18,524	83.0	903	1087
72.0	16,109	15,655		21,017	90.4	758	913
34.3	16,425	13,950	15,415	19,290	77.8	20	25
78.3	16,554	16,066	17,444	19,462	69.7	15	19
70.7	16,866	16,808	20,161	21,260	30.7	757	940
61.3	17,012	15,824	17,737	19,057	41.5	817	1083
50.3	17,451	16,191	19,161	21,640	85.1	873	1053
28.0	18,090	15,177	16,873	20,994	69.8	20	25
49.7	18,292	15,102	16,671	20,297	50.3	837	1113
64.3	19,093	18,483			100.0		
35.7	19,268	13,368	16,328	21,916	49.7	21	26
50.0	19,444	14,967			58.1	837	1027
45.0	19,994	18,258	21,338	24,035	66.7	800	955
28.3	20,457	18,263	17,974	20,969	69.7	903	1193
72.7	21,508	21,263	23,845		86.7		
15.7	22,955	15,640	21,419	25,873	81.6	23	29
79.3	24,050	24,254	24,564	28,085	31.8		
69.7	24,076	25,242	28,220	30,822	69.8	790	953
21.7	25,085	19,345	20,389	27,836	81.6	940	1227
21.3	25,461	14,715	19,274	36,338	28.4	1283	1427
57.7	25,877	14,769	15,299		90.0		
12.7	26,531	9,966	15,148	36,580	19.3	1293	1493
28.7	27,673	18,704	21,575	32,337	55.1	1102	1287
20.3	27,836	20,953	24,249	34,710	39.1	1223	1380
47.7	34,951	35,323	36,823	39,054	77.0		
16.7	7,744	6,267	8,161	11,726	52.3		
42.0	7,952	5,749	7,800	11,874	81.3	19	24
34.3	8,790	7,580	10,079	12,152	87.0	19	25
48.3	8,895	7,716	9,764	12,856	57.7	18	23
37.3	9,002	6,930	9,345	12,562	75.8	1033	1190
42.3	9,131	6,789	9,620	11,521	73.8	18	23
75.0	9,395	6,169	8,111	10,213	46.9	14	18
45.0	9,901	8,246	10,820	13,836	55.0	883	1060
39.3	10,038	7,083	10,757	13,754	50.9	883	1087

RANK	NAME	OVERALL SCORE	STUDENT LOAN DEFAULT RATE	GRADUATION RATE	GRADUATION RATE PERFORMANCE
125.	Amridge University (AL)	7	6.8	16.0	-0.7
126.	Glenville State College (WV)*	7	12.9	33.7	0.5
127.	Florida International University (FL)*	7	6.6	46.0	-6.2
128.	New College of Florida (FL)*	7	3.4	68.3	-9.9
129.	Old Dominion University (VA)*	7	4.1	49.7	-3.2
130.	University of West Alabama (AL)*	7	7.0	31.7	-10.3
131.	Morris College (SC)	7	19.8	29.7	3.2
132.	Thomas University (GA)	7	6.0	15.0	-5.1
133.	University of South Florida–Main (FL)*	7	6.2	53.3	-5.4
134.	Lander University (SC)*	7	4.3	39.7	-6.5
135.	Wesleyan College (GA)	7	7.7	49.7	-1.9
136.	Georgia College & State Univ. (GA)*	7	3.5	57.0	-8.0
137.	Georgia Southern University (GA)*	7	6.0	47.3	-12.6
138.	Coastal Carolina University (SC)*	7	5.0	45.3	-5.2
139.	Alderson Broaddus College (WV)	7	7.6	48.0	-4.4
140.	Paine College (GA)	7	14.4	25.0	0.8
141.	College of Charleston (SC)*	7	4.2	66.0	-3.2
142.	Ohio Valley University (WV)	7	4.3	42.3	-6.8
143.	Davis & Elkins College (WV)	7	10.5	48.7	7.6
144.	Virginia Commonwealth University (VA)*	7	3.8	53.0	-3.3
145.	Pfeiffer University (NC)	7	5.5	42.0	-0.9
146.	University of Alabama (AL)*	7	5.0	66.7	-1.1
147.	University of Mobile (AL)	7	3.4	42.3	-12.0
148.	Clearwater Christian College (FL)	7	3.6	47.0	-0.5
149.	Mercer University (GA)	7	3.5	61.0	-8.2
150.	Virginia Union University (VA)	7	15.9	30.3	3.9
151.	Amer. InterCont. Univ.–Atlanta (GA)°	7	18.7	18.3	13.2
152.	LaGrange College (GA)	7	6.5	50.7	-0.8
153.	Mars Hill College (NC)	7	12.6	39.7	0.1
154.	Flagler College–St. Augustine (FL)	7	3.3	63.0	-0.1
155.	Bennett College for Women (NC)	7	10.2	41.0	1.4
156.	Gardner-Webb University (NC)	7	6.6	50.3	2.3
157.	Amer. InterContinental Univ.–Florida (FL)°	7	18.7	24.3	5.5
158.	Stetson University (FL)	7	3.5	63.0	-1.7
159.	Bridgewater College (VA)	7	3.7	60.0	1.5
160.	Virginia College–Birmingham (AL)°	7	14.9	32.7	16.5
161.	Marymount University (VA)	7	2.2	51.7	-3.4
162.	Westwood College–Atlanta Midtown (GA)°	7	12.8	30.3	9.9
163.	Palm Bch. Atl. Univ.–W. Palm Bch. (FL)	7	6.2	54.0	2.2
164.	Tuskegee University (AL)	7	8.7	45.0	4.6
165.	Johns. & Wales Univ.–N. Miami (FL)	7	7.9	41.3	0.4
166.	Westwood College–Northlake (GA)°	7	14.1	39.7	16.4
167.	Hollins University (VA)	7	3.9	60.7	-3.9
168.	Duke University (NC)	7	0.7	94.3	-4.6
169.	Lynchburg College (VA)	7	3.6	55.3	2.6
170.	Guilford College (NC)	7	6.4	58.3	2.9

STUDENTS RECEIVING PELL GRANTS	NET PRICE (all students)	NET PRICE (annual family income, $0–$30K)	NET PRICE (annual family income, $30–75K)	NET PRICE (annual family income above $75k)	PERCENT OF APPLICANTS ADMITTED	ACT/SAT 25TH PERCENTILE SCORE	ACT/SAT 75TH PERCENTILE SCORE
70.0	10,231				71.4		
42.7	10,527	10,384	11,834	14,694	81.3	16	22
52.0	10,627	9,563	13,081	16,202	47.4	1010	1180
28.0	10,766	5,616	8,989	12,379	56.3	1203	1480
31.3	11,197	8,251	11,522	16,396	72.8	937	1120
61.3	11,457	10,177	11,796	13,367	52.2	18	23
89.3	11,788	11,545	13,158	16,546	44.3		
57.7	11,988	10,704	13,433	15,906	66.5		
38.3	12,533	6,580	10,693	16,062	41.9	1053	1240
48.0	12,859	10,203	12,863	13,694	45.8	850	1053
36.3	12,914	9,531	11,520	16,493	53.4	873	1223
22.7	13,057	8,882	12,019	14,661	71.7	1053	1227
36.0	13,269	10,793	13,511	16,501	53.8	1023	1167
35.0	13,317	10,832	13,805	17,022	74.3	917	1080
49.0	14,168	11,952	13,643	14,696	60.4	19	24
78.0	14,752	14,510	15,624	16,582	60.0	670	853
21.0	15,412	10,287	14,316	17,492	71.0	1107	1293
50.7	15,445	15,677	15,455	18,004	47.8	18	26
44.3	15,574	11,660	13,710	17,033	65.2	17	23
26.7	15,696	12,609	16,317	21,350	68.8	983	1213
47.3	17,008	18,950	21,041	23,404	58.4	853	973
22.3	17,095	13,960	16,452	18,116	50.1	22	29
52.3	17,144	15,278	16,568	19,604	78.5	20	26
48.0	17,348	13,732	15,426	21,290	73.1	19	25
37.7	17,937	15,884	17,581	19,732	69.9	1070	1267
66.7	17,993	17,482	20,294	22,410	92.8	690	860
81.0	18,017	17,983	19,264		96.4		
41.7	18,526	14,844	17,314	20,527	55.3	907	1113
60.0	18,698	17,521	17,895		64.9	837	1040
28.7	18,770	13,996	16,986	22,453	45.9	1040	1193
67.3	18,994	17,650	20,288	25,305	63.6		
24.7	19,032	18,004	20,174	24,829	67.0	883	1140
65.0	19,705	19,109	21,789		78.9		
34.0	19,933	15,957	18,433	22,688	59.1	1018	1247
27.3	20,124	16,773	18,629	21,445	53.3	930	1147
70.0	21,159	21,348			76.9		
24.3	21,358	18,417	21,281	22,552	80.3	884	1120
78.7	21,436	22,007	22,711		45.1		
36.3	21,552	17,188	19,472	24,200	86.3	922	1162
56.7	21,558	22,728	23,934		62.8	17	22
56.0	22,265	19,762	21,390	25,482	61.9		
80.3	22,311	22,308	23,690	26,356	56.1		
40.3	22,383	18,635	21,122	24,820	79.2	957	1280
13.3	22,619	6,486	9,657	35,495	16.4	1347	1500
29.0	22,845	16,804	18,756	24,547	67.4	897	1109
45.3	23,467	14,604	18,408	26,846	65.8	953	1240

RANK	NAME	OVERALL SCORE	STUDENT LOAN DEFAULT RATE	GRADUATION RATE	GRADUATION RATE PERFORMANCE
171.	Westwood Coll.–Arlington Ballston (VA)°	7	14.0	33.0	11.6
172.	Hampden-Sydney College (VA)	7	3.7	67.7	11.5
173.	DeVry University–Florida (FL)°	7	14.6	33.7	12.1
174.	Morehouse College (GA)	7	19.9	55.7	7.6
175.	Stratford University (VA)°	7	10.2	37.3	12.0
176.	George Washington University (DC)	7	1.0	80.7	-3.5
177.	Eckerd College (FL)	7	6.0	64.0	1.1
178.	American University (DC)	7	2.4	77.7	-3.3
179.	Wake Forest University (NC)	7	0.7	88.0	-1.6
180.	Catholic University of America (DC)	7	1.3	68.0	1.5
181.	West Virginia Univ. Inst. of Tech. (WV)*	6	6.6	28.7	-6.1
182.	University of North Alabama (AL)*	6	10.2	30.7	-11.4
183.	Troy University (AL)*	6	9.6	33.0	-10.1
184.	Clayton State University (GA)*	6	7.3	25.3	-9.4
185.	University of North Florida (FL)*	6	5.8	48.3	-5.4
186.	Florida Atlantic University (FL)*	6	5.2	42.0	-5.9
187.	University of Montevallo (AL)*	6	8.2	43.7	-11.0
188.	Jacksonville State University (AL)*	6	8.4	31.3	-14.1
189.	Florida Gulf Coast University (FL)*	6	4.7	45.7	-5.9
190.	Bluefield State College (WV)*	6	16.0	27.0	-4.3
191.	Armstrong Atlantic State Univ. (GA)*	6	6.8	31.3	-7.5
192.	Kennesaw State University (GA)*	6	6.6	41.3	-7.6
193.	University of Alabama–Huntsville (AL)*	6	5.5	45.3	-11.9
194.	Valdosta State University (GA)*	6	6.4	41.7	-7.2
195.	University of Alabama at Birmingham (AL)*	6	4.5	44.7	-8.3
196.	Miles College (AL)	6	16.6	19.7	-2.9
197.	University of Charleston (WV)	6	8.9	45.0	-11.0
198.	Edward Waters College (FL)	6	15.3	18.7	-3.4
199.	Charleston Southern University (SC)	6	4.6	36.7	-10.7
200.	Saint Pauls College (VA)	6		16.3	0.3
201.	Anderson University (SC)	6	5.1	46.7	-8.6
202.	Chowan University (NC)	6	11.6	27.7	0.3
203.	Shaw University (NC)	6	16.3	28.0	1.3
204.	Benedict College (SC)	6	21.5	27.3	1.3
205.	North Greenville University (SC)	6	3.6	49.0	-6.7
206.	Stillman College (AL)	6	8.2	27.7	-1.2
207.	Southeastern University (FL)	6	6.0	42.7	-5.2
208.	Huntingdon College (AL)	6	9.6	48.7	0.3
209.	Lenoir-Rhyne University (NC)	6	6.3	47.0	-4.4
210.	Ferrum College (VA)	6	11.5	31.7	-4.4
211.	Florida Southern College (FL)	6	7.7	54.0	-2.3
212.	Ave Maria University (FL)	6	9.6	64.0	4.4
213.	Southern Virginia University (VA)	6	3.8	27.3	-22.3
214.	Bluefield College (VA)	6	5.8	34.7	-6.0
215.	Averett University (VA)	6	8.0	38.3	-3.2
216.	Montreat College (NC)	6	5.8	38.3	-8.4

STUDENTS RECEIVING PELL GRANTS	NET PRICE (all students)	NET PRICE (annual family income, $0–$30K)	NET PRICE (annual family income, $30–75K)	NET PRICE (annual family income above $75k)	PERCENT OF APPLICANTS ADMITTED	ACT/SAT 25TH PERCENTILE SCORE	ACT/SAT 75TH PERCENTILE SCORE
73.7	23,528	23,520	24,787		61.9		
18.0	23,761	14,742	17,784	24,684	54.8	1003	1220
62.7	24,193	23,811	24,493	27,781	76.4		
47.7	24,280	24,387	28,246	30,298	64.2	923	1160
59.7	26,005	25,756			63.7		
13.0	28,777	16,249	15,874	32,885	33.8	1207	1380
24.0	28,875	20,906	24,084	31,081	69.5	1008	1240
14.3	30,810	23,377	26,183	36,601	43.1	1167	1400
11.7	31,313	21,521	28,086	36,318	38.0		
13.0	34,471	31,178	32,538	35,226	78.6	1007	1220
41.3	7,987	6,496	9,074	11,111	52.2	18	23
37.0	8,233	8,978	9,450	9,733	87.7	18	24
45.7	9,673	10,542	12,002		67.8	18	24
56.3	10,523	9,712	11,629	14,961	38.7	870	1040
30.7	10,955	4,123	8,710	14,074	50.8	1063	1240
34.7	11,164	6,383	9,736		42.6	980	1140
38.3	11,291	9,314	12,387	14,700	75.2	20	26
45.0	11,355	12,235	15,598	17,594	83.3	18	25
28.3	11,416	8,545	12,180	15,920	68.5	937	1100
69.3	11,912	10,960	11,186	11,595	62.6	17	21
44.0	12,014	10,416	12,776	15,599	62.1	907	1107
35.0	12,666	10,434	12,809	15,920	63.3	993	1160
31.0	12,849	6,721	10,039	11,975	69.2	22	29
42.7	13,091	11,167	14,082	16,662	62.8	937	1100
33.3	13,113	11,151	14,366	17,427	75.6	21	27
82.7	13,687	13,326	14,550	17,922	48.9		
38.0	13,922	11,981	13,252	15,615	56.0	20	26
84.3	14,112	13,724	15,030	18,563	24.7	14	18
46.0	15,151	14,637	16,303	20,079	68.4	867	1107
80.7	15,628	14,672	17,075	17,151	99.8	617	807
35.7	15,955	14,331	16,005	18,449	71.6	937	1172
64.3	16,011	15,530	16,345	17,926	58.8	717	887
77.0	16,148	16,551	18,390	21,907	46.6		
89.3	16,325	15,579	18,647		44.5		
40.0	17,299	18,205	17,516	18,138	59.3	913	1347
81.0	17,424	17,070	19,910	21,153	45.3	16	19
40.0	17,450	15,100	16,229	19,483	68.3		
39.3	17,463	14,044	17,420	19,391	61.6	19	24
42.0	17,528	15,226	15,761	20,714	71.2	887	1080
57.0	17,597	14,122	17,434	26,172	76.8	797	1000
30.0	17,735	21,361	23,532	22,419	62.7	977	1167
34.0	17,902	14,004	16,159	21,439	52.4	21	27
51.7	17,940	14,499	15,735	19,527	98.8	20	26
46.0	18,401	16,840	17,870	19,855	49.6	817	1047
46.0	18,428	15,087	17,235	19,110	66.0	843	1033
44.7	18,438	17,902	16,168		51.5	863	1093

RANK	NAME	OVERALL SCORE	STUDENT LOAN DEFAULT RATE	GRADUATION RATE	GRADUATION RATE PERFORMANCE
217.	Christopher Newport Univ. (VA)*	6	2.3	63.3	-6.1
218.	Oglethorpe University (GA)	6	6.4	53.7	-11.0
219.	Barton College (NC)	6	7.0	44.0	-0.0
220.	Brevard College (NC)	6	5.5	33.7	-7.8
221.	Faulkner University (AL)	6	9.0	34.3	-6.3
222.	William Peace University (NC)	6	4.5	34.0	-7.5
223.	Everest Univ.–Pompano Beach (FL)°	6	12.9	25.3	9.2
224.	Point University (GA)	6	5.1	33.0	-5.3
225.	Hampton University (VA)	6	8.4	56.0	-2.5
226.	Campbell University (NC)	6	3.3	51.3	-4.9
227.	Queens University of Charlotte (NC)	6	4.6	54.7	-0.7
228.	Limestone College (SC)	6	9.0	41.3	2.9
229.	Nova Southeastern University (FL)	6	2.3	42.0	-8.9
230.	Randolph College (VA)	6	3.6	60.0	-4.7
231.	Randolph-Macon College (VA)	6	4.6	60.0	-4.6
232.	University of Tampa (FL)	6	4.9	57.7	-1.8
233.	DeVry University–Georgia (GA)°	6	14.6	26.3	9.6
234.	Embry-Riddle Aero. U.–Dayt. Beach (FL)	6	4.5	55.7	-0.2
235.	Macon State College (GA)*	5		12.0	-13.4
236.	West Virginia State University (WV)*	5	9.8	25.7	-10.1
237.	Augusta State University (GA)*?	5		23.0	-14.5
238.	Auburn Univ. at Montgomery (AL)*	5	9.2	29.3	-12.5
239.	GA Southwestern State Univ. (GA)*	5	6.1	29.7	-12.6
240.	Shepherd University (WV)*	5	6.6	43.3	-8.0
241.	Concord University (WV)*	5	12.5	37.0	-11.6
242.	Univ. of S. Florida–St. Petersburg (FL)*	5	6.2	30.7	-16.5
243.	Talladega College (AL)	5	22.2	21.3	-5.7
244.	Allen University (SC)	5	18.4	12.7	-9.0
245.	Univ. of South Carolina–Beaufort (SC)*	5	6.5	21.3	-12.2
246.	Univ. of the District of Columbia (DC)*	5	9.8	14.7	-4.1
247.	Judson College (AL)	5	8.0	38.0	-14.9
248.	Newberry College (SC)	5	8.3	41.0	-5.2
249.	Hodges University (FL)	5	8.6	19.3	-25.5
250.	Webber International University (FL)	5	11.7	34.7	-1.1
251.	Berry College (GA)	5	3.5	59.7	-8.5
252.	Covenant College (GA)	5	3.6	55.7	-11.1
253.	Regent University (VA)	5	4.0	36.0	-8.8
254.	Liberty University (VA)	5	4.7	47.7	-5.7
255.	Saint Augustines College (NC)	5	22.9	27.0	3.4
256.	Westwood College–Annandale (VA)°	5	14.0	27.0	0.1
257.	Warren Wilson College (NC)	5	3.5	50.3	-14.0
258.	Methodist University (NC)	5	7.3	39.7	-3.6
259.	Florida Institute of Technology (FL)	5	7.7	56.0	-2.7
260.	American Public Univ. System (WV)°	4	6.8	19.0	-22.7
261.	Brewton-Parker College (GA)	4	11.4	22.0	-9.7
262.	Salem International University (WV)°	4	16.4	26.3	-5.1

STUDENTS RECEIVING PELL GRANTS	NET PRICE (all students)	NET PRICE (annual family income, $0–$30K)	NET PRICE (annual family income, $30–75K)	NET PRICE (annual family income above $75k)	PERCENT OF APPLICANTS ADMITTED	ACT/SAT 25TH PERCENTILE SCORE	ACT/SAT 75TH PERCENTILE SCORE
16.3	18,569	13,410	16,643	21,155	61.1	1077	1267
40.3	18,901	14,951	16,376	21,583	71.3	1047	1260
49.7	19,073	19,093	20,303	24,925	48.5	833	1080
39.0	19,131	15,845	17,492	21,707	54.2	840	1027
70.7	19,529	18,062	17,962	19,222	55.7	17	26
45.3	19,931	16,435	17,268	25,149	57.6	857	1020
75.3	20,097	20,116			96.8		
77.0	20,108	20,955	22,185	22,633	49.7	833	1053
38.0	20,383	21,060	23,628		36.8	963	1097
34.0	20,739	20,416	24,139	23,998	52.8	848	1311
32.7	21,050	18,172	18,546	23,400	60.3	933	1167
53.0	21,151	20,521	20,365	22,785	50.2	830	1000
42.0	22,844	21,259	22,531	26,049	55.5	933	1147
31.7	23,104	17,809	20,356	24,339	76.4	978	1220
23.7	23,809	18,567	20,771	25,493	55.1	987	1180
24.0	24,213	19,058	21,727	25,848	51.0	977	1140
70.0	25,469	25,128	26,363	28,490	83.4		
28.0	34,398	29,409	32,121	35,496	79.0	977	1173
49.7	2,864	1,941	3,552	7,235	46.9	823	1053
43.7	7,951	6,918	9,221	9,517	89.6	17	22
43.3	8,130	7,016	9,416	12,985	59.1	873	1087
39.3	9,550	9,145	10,673	12,275	82.6	19	23
47.0	10,086	8,586	10,664	13,820	67.6	890	1073
31.7	10,276	9,059	10,914	14,451	89.6	19	24
46.7	11,355	7,764	9,789	12,884	53.6	17	26
34.7	11,473	5,965	10,350	14,168	49.8	987	1153
82.3	12,367	12,359	14,042		51.9		
90.3	12,561	12,959	14,001		54.1		
36.0	13,278	11,183	14,299	16,768	73.6	840	1020
45.3	14,760	14,629	16,387		58.0		
44.3	16,019	13,597	15,523	17,893	79.1	19	24
45.7	17,067	13,312	19,284	20,100	51.9	863	1053
65.7	17,931	17,788	18,886	20,300	70.0	19	25
43.0	18,954	16,143	19,170	20,082	58.2	17	22
28.3	20,430	15,160	17,208	22,026	64.1	1053	1273
30.7	20,948	15,819	17,528	22,610	59.2	1060	1327
48.7	21,100	17,959	21,130	24,548	82.4	947	1220
46.0	21,270	20,700	20,523	22,734	74.9		
71.7	23,165	22,997	23,645	26,370	47.9	670	860
63.7	24,247	24,344	26,022	27,601	56.9		
28.0	25,078	16,203	21,240	29,251	87.9	1023	1320
40.0	25,936	28,499	31,289		62.5	877	1060
34.3	29,302	22,113	25,706	31,365	58.4	1040	1213
19.0	8,988	9,214	10,476	13,252	66.1		
45.0	12,775	15,565	16,662		79.0	801	1007
73.0	16,136	17,318	18,070	20,256	65.3		

RANK	NAME	OVERALL SCORE	STUDENT LOAN DEFAULT RATE	GRADUATION RATE	GRADUATION RATE PERFORMANC
263.	Lees-McRae College (NC)	4	6.6	27.0	-14.7
264.	North Carolina Wesleyan College (NC)	4	13.1	21.3	-8.4
265.	Reinhardt University (GA)	4	6.6	38.0	-6.5
266.	Greensboro College (NC)	4	9.1	39.3	-3.4
267.	Birmingham Southern College (AL)	4	6.1	64.0	-7.2
268.	Univ. of Phoenix–Columbus Georgia (GA)°	4	17.0	13.7	-3.9
269.	Virginia Wesleyan College (VA)	4	7.8	47.0	-3.0
270.	South University–West Palm Beach (FL)°	4	14.3	22.3	-1.1
271.	South University–Columbia (SC)°	4	14.3	17.3	-2.9
272.	DeVry University–Virginia (VA)°	4	14.6	21.0	0.6
273.	South University–Savannah (GA)°	4	14.3	20.3	-1.6
274.	Shenandoah University (VA)	4	4.6	43.3	-10.6
275.	High Point University (NC)	4	7.0	59.3	-4.2
276.	Strayer University–DC (DC)°	4	9.7	28.7	2.7
277.	Lynn University (FL)	4	5.1	41.7	-16.4
278.	Truett-McConnell College (GA)	3	10.1	25.3	-9.9
279.	Jacksonville University (FL)	3	7.3	40.3	-12.4
280.	Univ. of Phoenix–Atlanta (GA)°	3	17.0	13.7	-9.6
281.	Belmont Abbey College (NC)	3	9.7	39.3	-8.4
282.	Univ. of Phoenix–South Florida (FL)°	3	17.0	18.7	-11.1
283.	Univ. of Phoenix–Central Florida (FL)°	3	17.0	17.3	-8.5
284.	St. Andrews University (NC)	3	11.7	42.3	-8.5
285.	South University–Tampa (FL)°	3	14.3	0.0	-21.9
286.	Oakwood University (AL)	3	12.4	37.7	-7.2
287.	Univ. of Phoenix–North Florida (FL)°	2	17.0	15.3	-13.6
288.	Univ. of Phoenix–West Florida (FL)°	2	17.0	17.0	-11.8

WESTERN SCHOOLS

RANK	NAME	OVERALL SCORE	STUDENT LOAN DEFAULT RATE	GRADUATION RATE	GRADUATION RATE PERFORMANC
1.	University of Washington–Seattle (WA)*	13	2.2	80.3	12.0
2.	Brigham Young University–Idaho (ID)	13	1.7	62.7	21.8
3.	University of California–Irvine (CA)*	13	2.0	84.7	8.2
4.	University of California–Davis (CA)*	13	2.5	81.7	5.1
5.	University of California–Los Angeles (CA)*	13	1.7	90.7	7.0
6.	CA State University–Los Angeles (CA)*	12	3.8	36.7	7.0
7.	California State Univ.–Fullerton (CA)*	12	4.6	50.7	5.9
8.	CA State University–Bakersfield (CA)*	12	5.1	41.0	9.7
9.	CA State Univ.–San Bernardino (CA)*	12	5.1	44.3	8.5
10.	CA State University–Stanislaus (CA)*	12	4.9	49.0	14.8
11.	CA State University–Long Beach (CA)*	12	3.9	55.0	6.2
12.	CA State Poly. Univ.–Pomona (CA)*	12	3.0	52.7	1.2
13.	University of WA Bothell (WA)*	12	2.2	64.0	16.7
14.	San Diego State University (CA)*	12	3.3	66.0	15.0
15.	Brigham Young University–Provo (UT)	12	0.9	77.7	16.1
16.	University of California–San Diego (CA)*	12	2.1	85.7	4.9
17.	University of CA–Santa Barbara (CA)*	12	2.2	79.7	7.6
18.	University of California–Santa Cruz (CA)*	12	2.9	73.7	5.0

SOUTHEAST

BEST-BANG-FOR-THE-BUCK COLLEGES

STUDENTS RECEIVING PELL GRANTS	NET PRICE (all students)	NET PRICE (annual family income, $0–$30K)	NET PRICE (annual family income, $30–75K)	NET PRICE (annual family income above $75k)	PERCENT OF APPLICANTS ADMITTED	ACT/SAT 25TH PERCENTILE SCORE	ACT/SAT 75TH PERCENTILE SCORE
47.3	19,563	14,135	18,796	19,915	64.8	781	1132
64.7	19,895	23,916	22,088	24,426	59.6	777	953
35.3	20,361	17,852	19,011	15,885	56.3	842	1106
35.7	20,409	20,098	21,514	26,173	46.4	807	1096
22.3	20,905	17,492	18,495	22,629	65.3	23	29
76.3	22,111	22,083	22,907		61.2		
33.3	22,559	18,696	19,944	24,633	82.1	880	1100
70.3	22,705	23,281	24,879		76.7		
74.7	24,642	24,464	27,269		56.3		
47.3	25,119	23,998	26,112	27,204	80.1		
72.7	25,157	25,710	27,303		72.6		
24.3	25,680	21,474	23,220	27,133	80.9	893	1133
18.0	29,121	23,366	27,381	31,746	64.6	991	1173
37.7	29,589	28,252			51.2		
20.0	30,996	24,402	27,192	35,166	60.6		
36.3	15,532	13,734	14,747	17,552	82.1	827	1080
34.3	20,178	20,412	20,969	24,480	42.8	933	1113
62.0	21,596	21,542			60.6		
48.0	21,812	21,492	20,435	23,036	66.7	880	1120
52.0	22,300	22,043	24,175		66.8		
57.3	22,487	22,504	23,877		69.5		
37.7	23,141	17,100	20,541	23,883	60.9		
62.0	24,920	25,194	26,531		63.3		
47.3	25,184	24,478	24,853	26,828	42.1	17	22
48.3	22,304	22,109	24,176		69.9		
48.0	22,316	22,266			68.2		
23.3	9,018	6,788	9,706	20,230	58.2	1093	1300
44.0	9,773	6,836	9,070	10,789	98.7	20	26
35.7	12,960	8,316	11,856	23,592	45.6	1057	1233
40.0	13,914	8,775	11,947	23,655	47.3	1083	1287
35.3	14,356	8,466	11,774	23,997	24.8	1167	1367
58.7	3,480	2,122	5,419	12,347	64.6	767	967
35.3	5,252	2,220	6,545	13,738	49.0	897	1087
58.3	5,727	3,892	6,874	14,022	68.2	793	1007
54.3	6,674	4,662	7,553	14,910	33.5	807	1000
53.0	6,950	3,614	7,422	14,102	48.9	817	1027
40.7	7,119	4,450	8,418	15,224	32.2	900	1120
40.7	7,544	4,184	8,135	15,288	53.7	937	1133
29.3	7,777	5,008	7,390	16,807	74.7	910	1133
35.3	8,519	4,969	10,360	17,238	33.1	957	1153
34.3	11,515	8,239	10,762	14,897	60.7	26	30
44.0	12,726	8,706	11,905	22,918	36.5	1137	1320
34.7	13,761	8,591	12,062	26,104	46.6	1090	1300
36.7	14,481	9,687	13,355	26,451	64.9	1017	1253

RANK	NAME	OVERALL SCORE	STUDENT LOAN DEFAULT RATE	GRADUATION RATE	GRADUATION RATE PERFORMANC
19.	CA State University–Fresno (CA)*	11	5.4	49.3	13.0
20.	CA State University–Northridge (CA)*	11	5.9	47.3	14.5
21.	CA State University–San Marcos (CA)*	11	3.2	46.0	7.0
22.	University of WA–Tacoma (WA)*	11	2.2	43.0	1.3
23.	CA State University–East Bay (CA)*	11	5.0	43.0	6.5
24.	Arizona State University (AZ)*	11	5.2	57.7	6.3
25.	Utah State University (UT)*	11	3.6	52.3	8.7
26.	University of Utah (UT)*	11	2.3	56.7	9.0
27.	University of California–Riverside (CA)*	11	3.1	67.0	4.0
28.	CA State University–Chico (CA)*	11	5.0	59.3	16.0
29.	Evergreen State College (WA)*	11	5.9	53.3	6.7
30.	Western Washington University (WA)*	11	2.0	69.7	9.2
31.	Oregon State University (OR)*	11	2.9	60.7	9.8
32.	Fresno Pacific University (CA)	11	4.6	59.7	9.5
33.	Northwest Christian University (OR)	11	2.2	50.7	2.6
34.	University of La Verne (CA)	11	2.9	62.3	10.7
35.	University of Hawaii–Hilo (HI)*	10	5.5	36.3	4.1
36.	CA State University–Sacramento (CA)*	10	5.5	41.7	4.2
37.	Eastern Washington University (WA)*	10	4.6	46.7	10.1
38.	Montana State University–Northern (MT)*	10	7.6	30.7	10.0
39.	CA State Univ.–Channel Islands (CA)*	10	4.5	54.3	14.1
40.	Brigham Young University–Hawaii (HI)	10	5.3	51.7	7.0
41.	University of Arizona (AZ)*	10	4.8	60.7	8.8
42.	Sonoma State University (CA)*	10	3.2	56.3	5.6
43.	University of Idaho (ID)*	10	4.9	54.0	1.5
44.	Central Washington University (WA)*	10	5.0	55.0	8.1
45.	Lincoln University (CA)	10	10.8	94.7	32.9
46.	University of Oregon (OR)*	10	3.2	67.0	13.8
47.	Trinity Lutheran College (WA)	10	4.5	66.3	26.7
48.	University of California–Berkeley (CA)*	10	2.1	90.7	0.3
49.	Soka University of America (CA)	10	5.1	89.0	23.5
50.	Humphreys Coll.–Stockton & Modesto (CA)	10	11.7	86.0	35.2
51.	Woodbury University (CA)	10	5.1	54.7	6.8
52.	Whitworth University (WA)	10	2.1	78.3	6.6
53.	Seattle Pacific University (WA)	10	1.3	72.3	5.1
54.	Point Loma Nazarene University (CA)	10	2.2	77.0	6.1
55.	CA State Univ.–Dominguez Hills (CA)*	9	6.1	27.7	2.5
56.	University of Wyoming (WY)*	9	3.4	53.3	1.0
57.	University of Hawaii–Manoa (HI)*	9	3.1	53.7	2.9
58.	Montana State Univ.–Billings (MT)*	9	6.3	43.7	5.2
59.	San Francisco State University (CA)*	9	5.1	47.0	2.1
60.	Southern Utah University (UT)*	9	4.3	43.3	0.1
61.	San Jose State University (CA)*	9	3.6	47.0	0.4
62.	Colorado State Univ.–Fort Collins (CO)*	9	3.0	63.7	-0.2
63.	Oregon Institute of Technology (OR)*	9	3.2	44.7	7.3
64.	California Maritime Academy (CA)*	9	7.2	60.3	10.5

STUDENTS RECEIVING PELL GRANTS	NET PRICE (all students)	NET PRICE (annual family income, $0–$30K)	NET PRICE (annual family income, $30–75K)	NET PRICE (annual family income above $75k)	PERCENT OF APPLICANTS ADMITTED	ACT/SAT 25TH PERCENTILE SCORE	ACT/SAT 75TH PERCENTILE SCORE
48.3	5,763	3,070	6,622	14,020	62.8	820	1033
44.7	9,469	8,194	11,995	19,141	69.4	810	1033
35.0	9,499	6,014	9,943	16,990	56.9	863	1060
40.3	9,599	5,002	7,767	16,594	78.6	897	1113
37.7	9,686	7,225	12,071	18,374	43.7	803	1007
36.7	10,584	6,958	9,672	15,052	88.7	963	1200
36.0	10,734	8,492	9,884	12,481	97.4	20	27
29.0	10,764	10,879	12,509	15,423	82.9	21	27
53.0	11,406	8,248	10,402	21,654	75.9	937	1140
35.0	11,438	8,149	12,657	20,007	72.5	917	1113
41.0	11,685	7,382	11,818	17,555	96.2	970	1280
23.7	13,201	8,021	12,535	18,805	77.3	1010	1240
32.0	14,638	13,362	14,711	17,693	80.4	960	1193
54.7	15,239	11,746	16,956		64.3	873	1100
51.3	18,502	13,559	16,785	20,084	60.7	890	1113
36.0	19,722	14,501	16,541	25,788	55.7	897	1093
43.0	8,492	6,742	8,778	12,907	65.3	843	1073
45.3	8,827	6,553	10,639	17,753	72.8	837	1053
37.0	10,830	7,131	10,863	16,431	81.1	853	1067
52.3	11,064	11,238	13,304	16,180	69.6	17	22
34.0	11,329	8,841	12,948	19,756	59.8	873	1080
30.7	12,220	10,391	11,992	13,438	37.8	22	26
31.0	12,785	9,036	12,232	17,553	74.0	963	1213
26.0	13,116	8,555	14,202	21,233	81.0	913	1120
38.7	13,616	10,242	12,768	16,666	66.8	20	26
32.7	13,852	8,688	13,906	18,243	80.0	890	1107
40.3	13,951	13,987			69.5		
24.3	14,625	9,748	14,240	19,301	77.1	991	1218
40.3	15,099	7,537	15,276	17,145	57.2	780	1060
33.0	15,844	7,994	11,746	25,542	21.6	1237	1440
26.3	16,254	10,980	12,569	22,392	37.5	1042	1233
73.3	16,325	16,158	17,079	22,291	44.9		
53.7	22,488	20,053	20,402	28,813	62.4	880	1193
24.7	24,249	17,751	20,494	26,879	51.3	1060	1300
29.0	24,262	18,391	20,426	27,639	78.9	1023	1253
25.7	26,653	21,052	23,722	30,070	54.4	1037	1247
54.0	2,509	898	4,424	10,883	56.7	740	927
23.3	10,113	7,861	9,796	12,991	95.8	21	27
28.3	10,499	6,405	9,904	14,713	72.2	987	1160
39.0	10,532	10,544	12,789	15,398	99.1	19	24
37.7	10,826	8,395	13,117	20,002	66.3	890	1120
39.7	11,294	9,231	11,144	12,982	71.7	19	26
35.0	11,890	10,059	13,958	20,623	68.7	900	1093
23.7	11,925	7,439	11,824	18,323	77.0	22	27
31.3	12,437	8,951	12,948	16,692	73.7	900	1113
32.7	12,533	7,866	13,489	19,382	72.9	933	1163

RANK	NAME	OVERALL SCORE	STUDENT LOAN DEFAULT RATE	GRADUATION RATE	GRADUATION RATE PERFORMANCE
65.	University of Nevada–Reno (NV)*	9	4.4	51.3	4.5
66.	CA Poly. St. U.–San Luis Obispo (CA)*	9	2.0	73.3	1.0
67.	Vanguard University of So. California (CA)	9	3.4	56.0	7.1
68.	Washington State University (WA)*	9	3.5	67.7	12.8
69.	Pomona College (CA)	9	1.1	95.0	3.8
70.	Warner Pacific College (OR)	9	5.7	62.3	19.6
71.	Claremont McKenna College (CA)	9	0.8	92.0	7.5
72.	California Baptist University (CA)	9	5.5	56.0	5.4
73.	Pepperdine University (CA)	9	1.5	80.7	5.5
74.	Willamette University (OR)	9	2.0	77.3	4.0
75.	American Jewish University (CA)	9	2.5	65.3	20.4
76.	Gonzaga University (WA)	9	2.0	81.3	5.3
77.	Occidental College (CA)	9	1.8	84.0	1.2
78.	University of Portland (OR)	9	1.4	75.7	2.1
79.	Seattle University (WA)	9	1.8	74.3	2.5
80.	Westmont College (CA)	9	2.2	77.7	5.0
81.	University of Puget Sound (WA)	9	1.7	76.7	1.0
82.	Santa Clara University (CA)	9	1.5	86.0	7.3
83.	Weber State University (UT)*	8	4.9	33.7	-3.1
84.	University of Nevada–Las Vegas (NV)*	8	5.5	40.0	-3.1
85.	University of New Mexico–Main (NM)*	8	6.4	45.0	2.7
86.	Portland State University (OR)*	8	4.2	38.7	-4.4
87.	Eastern Oregon University (OR)*	8	6.5	32.0	1.3
88.	University of Montana (MT)*	8	5.8	46.0	-2.5
89.	University of the Southwest (NM)	8	11.3	34.7	2.9
90.	Northern Arizona University (AZ)*	8	6.5	50.0	-2.8
91.	Western Oregon University (OR)*	8	4.6	42.0	-1.0
92.	Rocky Mountain College (MT)	8	4.0	51.0	-4.1
93.	Northwest Nazarene University (ID)	8	4.0	53.7	-4.6
94.	University of Colorado–Boulder (CO)*	8	3.4	68.0	5.5
95.	Westwood College–Denver North (CO)°	8	13.3	42.3	16.2
96.	Thomas Aquinas College (CA)	8	0.4	72.7	-6.0
97.	Westwood College–Denv. South (CO)°	8	13.3	39.0	10.2
98.	Westwood College–Anaheim (CA)°	8	13.3	43.7	13.7
99.	Stanford University (CA)	8	0.8	95.3	2.6
100.	Linfield College–McMinnville (OR)	8	2.4	67.7	4.1
101.	Pacific Lutheran University (WA)	8	2.4	67.3	4.3
102.	Colorado College (CO)	8	1.3	88.3	4.3
103.	George Fox University (OR)	8	2.6	64.3	3.9
104.	Pitzer College (CA)	8	2.2	82.3	3.7
105.	Master's College and Seminary (CA)	8	2.1	60.7	3.4
106.	Argosy University–Denver (CO)°	8	9.2	63.0	22.4
107.	University of Redlands (CA)	8	2.1	68.7	3.8
108.	Mt. Sierra College (CA)°	8	6.0	28.0	5.3
109.	DigiPen Institute of Tech. (WA)°	8	2.0	61.0	0.4
110.	University of Denver (CO)	8	1.9	76.7	0.8

STUDENTS RECEIVING PELL GRANTS	NET PRICE (all students)	NET PRICE (annual family income, $0–$30K)	NET PRICE (annual family income, $30–75K)	NET PRICE (annual family income above $75k)	PERCENT OF APPLICANTS ADMITTED	ACT/SAT 25TH PERCENTILE SCORE	ACT/SAT 75TH PERCENTILE SCORE
23.3	14,028	10,634	12,687	16,312	86.4	940	1153
18.7	15,223	8,542	13,598	20,404	35.7	1120	1273
34.3	15,454	18,211	19,373	26,112	73.3	897	1087
30.0	15,969	9,975	14,656	22,178	76.4	953	1153
17.0	17,818	2,843	7,985	28,715	13.9	1370	1553
48.7	20,381	17,999	20,083	23,407	57.9	870	1140
14.0	22,443	11,629	10,696	26,516	14.9	1303	1473
43.3	22,469	21,133	23,296	29,176	72.7	843	1093
19.0	23,437	16,874	18,961	32,598	33.6	1110	1320
23.0	26,697	16,632	19,092	29,361	55.7	1127	1353
31.3	26,990	33,931	37,408		92.4	933	1137
19.3	27,136	17,282	22,060	28,116	68.2	1100	1360
22.7	29,148	12,625	16,836	34,622	40.0	1203	1393
21.0	29,582	27,478	24,715	32,759	65.1	1093	1313
22.0	29,816	21,422	24,800	31,653	71.0	1057	1273
20.0	30,285	20,786	24,586	29,084	67.6	1077	1300
21.7	31,268	21,558	25,495	33,837	52.6	1137	1365
14.3	34,433	30,019	32,203	41,952	57.2	1147	1333
27.3	8,619	8,086	9,504		75.1		
28.0	9,483	6,682	8,835	11,034	80.0	887	1113
37.0	10,392	6,984	10,045	13,087	64.0	19	25
38.7	12,175	10,526	14,138	17,945	71.4	923	1180
48.0	12,831	10,199	13,389	15,569	72.5	840	1080
37.3	13,329	12,588	14,406	17,149	94.1	21	26
62.3	13,543	10,924	14,026	17,654	66.8		
37.3	13,835	10,021	12,706	17,447	68.8	947	1167
40.3	14,190	12,656	15,488	19,190	88.0	840	1073
36.3	18,092	16,439	18,258		62.6	20	25
36.3	18,231	16,351	16,865	20,861	67.2	21	27
17.3	18,807	12,557	18,739	24,758	84.4	23	28
64.3	18,885	18,928	18,791	21,964	56.4		
31.7	19,039	15,521	17,567	23,552	79.4	1180	1427
69.0	19,562	19,404	21,688		75.6		
74.7	19,770	20,647	21,457		64.7		
17.3	20,337	4,776	6,540	31,198	7.0	1367	1540
24.7	22,937	16,942	19,336	25,689	78.7	983	1200
27.0	23,033	17,014	19,939	25,560	75.9	980	1240
10.3	23,161	12,249	14,761	32,298	27.4	28	32
34.7	23,190	19,413	22,491	28,245	74.9	983	1260
18.0	23,715	12,529	16,721	32,419	22.0	1197	1377
28.3	24,005	24,173	25,227	25,093	72.6	957	1240
60.0	25,097	23,744			60.5		
24.0	25,391	17,582	18,747	26,557	66.0	1030	1227
62.3	25,981	25,807			78.9		
33.7	28,704	28,790	28,685	29,310	44.4	1076	1290
18.3	30,810	22,265	24,629	33,455	69.1	25	30

RANK	NAME	OVERALL SCORE	STUDENT LOAN DEFAULT RATE	GRADUATION RATE	GRADUATION RATE PERFORMANCE
111.	Whitman College (WA)	8	1.1	86.3	3.2
112.	Loyola Marymount University (CA)	8	2.9	77.3	4.0
113.	CA State Univ.–Monterey Bay (CA)*	7	6.6	38.7	-9.0
114.	NM Inst. of Mining and Tech (NM)*	7	4.7	46.7	-16.3
115.	Utah Valley University (UT)*	7	5.3	24.7	-1.8
116.	New Mexico State University–Main (NM)*	7	12.7	45.0	4.5
117.	Humboldt State University (CA)*	7	7.0	39.0	-3.2
118.	University of Montana–Western (MT)*	7	6.9	32.0	-3.6
119.	Heritage University (WA)	7	13.0	19.3	3.4
120.	Idaho State University (ID)*	7	9.4	31.7	-3.9
121.	Southern Oregon University (OR)*	7	5.6	32.0	-5.2
122.	College of Idaho (ID)	7	4.4	61.7	-2.1
123.	Simpson University (CA)	7	4.2	42.3	-8.6
124.	Chaminade University of Honolulu (HI)	7	6.0	40.3	-0.2
125.	Northwest University (WA)	7	3.5	51.7	-5.1
126.	Reed College (OR)	7	2.9	77.7	-8.6
127.	Westwood College–Inland Empire (CA)°	7	13.3	33.3	8.0
128.	Saint Martin's University (WA)	7	5.0	50.0	3.1
129.	Cogswell College (CA)	7	5.0	50.7	4.3
130.	Carroll College (MT)	7	1.7	60.7	-3.2
131.	Westwood College–South Bay (CA)°	7	14.0	43.3	18.7
132.	St. John's College (NM)	7	2.2	56.0	-3.8
133.	Corban University (OR)	7	2.7	54.3	-4.0
134.	Westminster College (UT)	7	2.0	60.7	-4.3
135.	DeVry University–California (CA)°	7	14.6	31.7	8.4
136.	Colorado Christian University (CO)	7	3.9	42.3	0.9
137.	San Diego Christian College (CA)	7	4.9	44.3	3.8
138.	Mount St. Mary's College (CA)	7	3.9	52.0	-6.1
139.	DeVry University–Arizona (AZ)°	7	14.6	34.0	11.3
140.	Regis University (CO)	7	3.6	60.7	4.2
141.	Naropa University (CO)	7	3.6	39.3	0.1
142.	Pacific University (OR)	7	2.0	63.0	-3.5
143.	Notre Dame de Namur Univ. (CA)	7	5.2	48.7	3.2
144.	Lewis & Clark College (OR)	7	1.5	75.0	-1.1
145.	California Lutheran University (CA)	7	1.9	63.0	-2.8
146.	University of the Pacific (CA)	7	2.1	59.7	-14.2
147.	University of Southern California (CA)	7	1.4	89.7	-5.2
148.	Azusa Pacific University (CA)	7	2.5	62.7	-2.5
149.	University of San Francisco (CA)	7	3.5	69.0	1.4
150.	Biola University (CA)	7	1.7	66.0	-3.3
151.	Chapman University (CA)	7	2.6	71.3	-6.6
152.	University of San Diego (CA)	7	2.3	74.7	-0.4
153.	Embry-Riddle Aero. Univ.–Prescott (AZ)	7	4.5	57.3	1.3
154.	New Mexico Highlands Univ. (NM)*	6	8.0	18.7	-9.6
155.	University of the West (CA)	6	3.2	41.7	-22.6
156.	Montana Tech/Univ. of Montana (MT)*	6	7.9	45.3	-1.9

STUDENTS RECEIVING PELL GRANTS	NET PRICE (all students)	NET PRICE (annual family income, $0–$30K)	NET PRICE (annual family income, $30–75K)	NET PRICE (annual family income above $75k)	PERCENT OF APPLICANTS ADMITTED	ACT/SAT 25TH PERCENTILE SCORE	ACT/SAT 75TH PERCENTILE SCORE
12.7	31,229	16,073	24,016	36,447	49.6	1230	1453
19.3	34,930	25,554	27,448	39,113	52.5	1107	1273
42.3	8,918	5,060	10,704	18,024	60.3	857	1093
25.7	9,327	5,094	8,701	11,665	57.7	23	29
37.3	10,208	10,170	11,707	14,766	84.1		
43.0	10,441	8,352	10,534	12,991	85.0	18	24
44.7	10,935	8,019	12,299	19,115	82.6	913	1167
43.3	11,159	8,820	11,079	12,204	77.5		
76.3	11,384	11,385	11,529		73.9		
54.0	11,838	11,680	13,437	16,047	82.9		
37.7	13,221	9,680	13,209	16,505	70.7	890	1167
32.3	17,214	13,784	15,361	19,795	64.5	22	27
55.3	17,444	13,152	15,329	21,999	59.2	903	1133
38.7	18,115	15,278	18,158	21,196	89.2	865	1020
38.3	19,222	14,799	16,305	21,707	62.7	913	1193
18.7	19,521	11,871	18,339	37,079	39.5	1303	1513
78.0	20,226	21,067	21,943	25,368	63.2		
33.3	20,339	14,854	19,808	25,409	85.4	900	1147
31.7	21,398	20,045	21,905	27,112	82.0	960	1120
23.0	21,507	19,839	21,769	24,911	70.6	22	27
87.3	21,595	22,862	23,571		62.4		
31.7	21,872	17,461	22,301	35,092	85.4		
31.7	21,972	18,443	19,370	23,130	39.4	939	1199
30.0	22,678	19,962	20,960	23,833	71.8	22	27
62.3	23,073	22,538	23,211	27,047	79.4		
36.0	23,747	20,677	22,327	24,571	81.1		
47.0	24,016	23,435	20,556	26,136	43.3	822	1027
55.7	24,479	24,377	25,145	31,081	67.0	858	1047
59.7	24,535	23,712	24,884	26,885	80.5		
28.0	25,001	19,425	21,098	27,137	78.3	21	26
46.7	25,010	21,128	23,640	35,967	88.7		
32.3	25,291	18,335	20,824	28,745	68.4	997	1193
36.7	26,674	21,697	23,767	30,286	73.1	847	1047
18.7	26,976	17,654	21,550	30,861	64.2	1190	1420
25.0	27,319	21,323	24,548	32,792	46.1	1017	1193
38.3	27,524	17,700	21,946	34,314	37.2	1053	1273
21.0	27,751	15,923	20,313	40,648	22.4	1273	1440
28.0	27,800	22,968	25,533	29,947	52.9	980	1193
28.7	28,289	26,989	30,899	39,724	64.9	1023	1233
31.0	29,020	23,573	27,355	35,101	76.3	993	1240
20.7	30,167	28,052	31,246	39,098	46.6	1103	1293
16.0	31,363	18,320	21,787	37,391	47.1	1123	1293
30.0	32,185	28,148	30,921	33,353	82.2	1007	1200
51.7	10,399	8,401	10,150	13,304	67.2		
20.0	11,216				31.6		
31.7	11,735	10,055	11,432	15,064	89.3	21	26

RANK	NAME	OVERALL SCORE	STUDENT LOAN DEFAULT RATE	GRADUATION RATE	GRADUATION RATE PERFORMANCE
157.	Lewis-Clark State College (ID)*	6	10.1	30.3	-1.1
158.	University of Northern Colorado (CO)*	6	5.1	45.7	-10.3
159.	Montana State University (MT)*	6	3.3	49.0	-7.8
160.	Boise State University (ID)*	6	7.1	30.3	-15.5
161.	Univ. of CO–Colorado Springs (CO)*	6	3.9	44.3	-6.0
162.	Western Governors University (UT)	6	4.9	20.3	-17.5
163.	Colorado School of Mines (CO)*	6	2.3	67.0	-11.7
164.	Hawaii Pacific University (HI)	6	3.1	39.3	0.1
165.	Hope International University (CA)	6	5.9	33.3	-5.7
166.	Grand Canyon University (AZ)°	6	13.2	30.3	2.3
167.	La Sierra University (CA)	6	4.8	44.3	-3.4
168.	California Institute of Technology (CA)	6	1.0	89.7	-15.7
169.	Scripps College (CA)	6	0.8	87.0	-7.2
170.	Sierra Nevada College (NV)	6	4.0	40.0	-4.4
171.	Whittier College (CA)	6	3.8	62.7	-1.1
172.	Mills College (CA)	6	3.7	60.3	-9.5
173.	Alaska Pacific University (AK)	6	5.0	41.7	4.6
174.	Saint Mary's College of California (CA)	6	3.7	63.3	-1.3
175.	Harvey Mudd College (CA)	6	0.0	86.3	-16.7
176.	Platt College–Aurora (CO)°	6	8.7	39.7	-1.0
177.	University of Alaska Southeast (AK)*	5	8.4	19.3	-3.3
178.	Nevada State College (NV)*	5	6.8	18.3	-11.4
179.	Western NM University (NM)*	5	14.0	18.7	-6.4
180.	Eastern NM University–Main (NM)*	5	13.6	25.7	-12.0
181.	University of Alaska–Anchorage (AK)*	5	7.4	26.7	-8.0
182.	Metropolitan State Coll. of Denver (CO)*	5	10.9	22.0	-18.3
183.	CO State University–Pueblo (CO)*	5	11.1	32.3	-8.5
184.	Adams State College (CO)*	5	10.8	22.0	-20.1
185.	Trident University International (CA)°	5	1.2	11.0	-19.2
186.	Fort Lewis College (CO)*	5	9.2	37.7	-2.7
187.	Western State College of Colorado (CO)*	5	6.2	37.3	-9.4
188.	University of Colorado–Denver (CO)*	5	4.0	42.3	-5.9
189.	CO Tech. U.–Greenwood Village (CO)°	5	17.1	13.0	-3.3
190.	Nat. Amer. Univ.–Colorado Springs (CO)°	5	14.9	10.7	-1.7
191.	Arizona Christian University (AZ)	5	9.9	44.3	-1.9
192.	Concordia University–Portland (OR)	5	3.4	46.7	-6.9
193.	Marylhurst University (OR)	5	2.3	20.0	-6.1
194.	National University (CA)	5	4.5	37.3	-2.0
195.	Holy Names University (CA)	5	5.6	36.0	-9.5
196.	Walla Walla University (WA)	5	3.1	53.7	-6.4
197.	University of Phoenix–Hawaii (HI)°	5	17.0	18.3	7.7
198.	Pacific Union College (CA)	5	5.9	44.3	-12.3
199.	Concordia University–Irvine (CA)	5	3.1	51.7	-5.4
200.	Prescott College (AZ)	5	5.7	39.0	-12.0
201.	DeVry University–Washington (WA)°	5	14.6	26.3	2.5
202.	DeVry University–Colorado (CO)°	5	14.6	29.0	4.4

STUDENTS RECEIVING PELL GRANTS	NET PRICE (all students)	NET PRICE (annual family income, $0–$30K)	NET PRICE (annual family income, $30–75K)	NET PRICE (annual family income above $75k)	PERCENT OF APPLICANTS ADMITTED	ACT/SAT 25TH PERCENTILE SCORE	ACT/SAT 75TH PERCENTILE SCORE
38.0	12,838	11,442	13,185	15,959	98.7	17	23
29.7	12,883	11,373			76.9	20	25
31.3	12,986	11,809	14,716	17,643	60.9	21	27
40.7	12,987	9,108	11,264	14,456	78.1	20	25
32.3	13,674	11,498	14,459	17,489	64.0	21	26
51.7	15,877	15,748	17,369	19,494	87.5		
19.0	19,935	16,446	19,085	22,904	45.2	27	31
21.7	20,060	20,645	24,288	26,243	73.5	873	1093
51.0	20,921	16,562	20,445	26,712	52.6	808	1033
55.7	20,955	20,340	22,314	23,818	56.4		
41.3	23,176	18,438	20,803	27,302	49.5	823	1047
11.0	23,218	5,385	5,462	31,191	12.7	1463	1573
12.0	25,093	12,099	14,930	31,528	35.9	1270	1473
35.0	25,177	21,985	27,091		62.1	870	1120
34.3	26,102	19,466	22,213	30,151	68.5	943	1160
45.3	27,250	18,771	21,752	33,445	59.0	1033	1313
27.7	27,836	25,611	28,158	30,441	43.1	921	1187
32.3	29,076	21,582	23,389	34,652	70.0	997	1207
13.0	29,774	9,249	16,555	34,195	21.2	1420	1533
52.7	36,786				100.0		
15.0	8,876	9,737	12,061	13,784	73.0		
27.3	9,157	7,350	9,625	12,736	65.3		
48.0	9,195	9,514	10,323		69.8		
42.7	9,234	6,634	9,596	12,245	62.9	17	23
20.7	9,530	9,559	11,783	14,093	75.3		
35.3	9,622	7,427	9,624	13,013	68.2	18	23
41.3	10,130	8,750	11,376	14,862	94.0	18	23
59.0	10,639	8,853	10,688	14,378	59.8	17	22
7.0	12,494				68.0		
32.0	12,522	10,961	13,151	16,545	75.0	20	25
27.7	13,178	9,351	12,883	16,443	84.9	19	24
25.0	15,096	13,349	16,193	20,361	64.8	20	25
50.0	15,945	16,208			84.6		
54.0	18,280	18,440			80.7		
38.7	19,772	19,578	19,514	21,832	65.3	867	1140
40.7	20,199	17,595	18,481	22,006	56.3	903	1133
48.7	20,493	17,812			78.7		
27.0	20,974	21,856	22,908	23,288	63.1		
46.7	22,130	18,959	21,207	25,567	66.4	821	1005
33.7	22,507	17,606	20,479	23,460	84.7	20	27
43.3	23,324	23,228	24,473		103.6		
39.7	24,236	17,978	20,451	26,091	44.7	873	1160
26.3	24,257	18,622	20,237	27,884	69.7	913	1127
44.3	24,788	19,177	21,670	28,163	87.8	977	1300
55.3	25,927	25,444	27,361	29,624	69.4		
52.0	26,137	25,452	27,605	27,693	80.2		

RANK	NAME	OVERALL SCORE	STUDENT LOAN DEFAULT RATE	GRADUATION RATE	GRADUATION RATE PERFORMANCE
203.	Dominican University of CA (CA)	5	3.4	56.0	-8.3
204.	University of Alaska–Fairbanks (AK)*	4	8.7	29.3	-4.5
205.	Colorado Mesa University (CO)*	4	10.7	28.7	-8.7
206.	CO Technical Univ.–Colorado Springs (CO)°	4	17.1	10.0	-7.0
207.	Jones International University (CO)°	4	9.0	0.0	-16.6
208.	University of Phoenix–Online (AZ)°	4	17.0	14.0	-5.2
209.	Univ. of Phoenix–Albuquerque (NM)°	4	17.0	25.3	-1.7
210.	Westwood College–Los Angeles (CA)°	4	13.2	19.7	-0.8
211.	CO Technical University–Online (CO)°	3	17.1	11.3	-11.1
212.	University of Phoenix–Idaho (ID)°	3	17.0	11.0	-14.9
213.	U. of Phoenix–Southern Arizona (AZ)°	3	17.0	22.7	-6.2
214.	Univ. of Phoenix–Oregon (OR)°	3	17.0	20.0	-8.9
215.	University of Great Falls (MT)	3	7.7	23.7	-13.6
216.	Univ. of Phoenix–Central Valley (CA)°	3	17.0	20.7	-5.3
217.	Argosy University–Los Angeles (CA)°	3	9.2	0.0	-16.4
218.	U. of Phoenix–Sacramento Valley (CA)°	3	17.0	13.7	-11.6
219.	DeVry University–Nevada (NV)°	3	14.6	6.0	-7.9
220.	City University of Seattle (WA)	3	4.2	12.7	-16.1
221.	University of Phoenix–Colorado (CO)°	2	17.0	15.7	-20.0
222.	U. of Phoenix–Phoenix-Hohokam (AZ)°	2	17.0	17.3	-14.6
223.	University of Phoenix–Las Vegas (NV)°	2	17.0	20.7	-6.0
224.	Univ. of Phoenix–Southern CO (CO)°	2	17.0	17.7	-14.0
225.	U. of Phoenix–Northern Nevada (NV)°	2	17.0	23.0	-6.2
226.	Univ. of Phoenix–San Diego (CA)°	2	17.0	13.0	-14.1
227.	University of Phoenix–Utah (UT)°	2	17.0	22.0	-10.1
228.	U. of Phoenix–So. California (CA)°	2	17.0	15.7	-11.3
229.	University of Phoenix–Bay Area (CA)°	2	17.0	16.0	-7.8
230.	Western International University (AZ)°	2	8.2	6.7	-29.1
231.	Argosy University–Orange County (CA)°	2	9.2	0.0	-21.7
232.	Menlo College (CA)	2	9.3	34.7	-10.2
233.	University of Advancing Technology (AZ)°	2	9.7	29.7	-14.9

STUDENTS RECEIVING PELL GRANTS	NET PRICE (all students)	NET PRICE (annual family income, $0–$30K)	NET PRICE (annual family income, $30–75K)	NET PRICE (annual family income above $75k)	PERCENT OF APPLICANTS ADMITTED	ACT/SAT 25TH PERCENTILE SCORE	ACT/SAT 75TH PERCENTILE SCORE
32.3	31,404	25,853	27,247	34,165	55.1	943	1140
19.3	10,457	10,676	13,154	15,110	66.7		
38.3	13,415	13,121	15,306		80.7	17	23
45.3	14,658	16,054	17,682	20,624	83.8		
50.7	15,792	15,988	17,409		75.3		
55.0	17,078	17,083	18,674	21,321	136.1		
62.7	21,224	21,323	22,592		70.5		
64.0	22,280	23,388	24,166	26,274	57.1		
66.7	21,188	21,204	22,647	25,056	88.7		
62.0	22,270	22,379			81.9		
54.0	22,469	22,412			77.3		
54.3	22,590	22,455	23,893		79.3		
44.7	22,624	21,805	22,683	24,332	76.1		
61.7	22,875	22,753			70.8		
60.3	23,055	23,611			79.4		
52.0	23,352	23,270	24,834		76.7		
54.0	24,562	24,348			83.1		
29.3	26,581	29,852			77.1		
37.7	22,021	22,149	24,167		79.5		
45.0	22,069	22,231	22,899		72.8		
46.0	22,276	22,291	23,905		80.1		
37.7	22,301	22,503	23,311		77.1		
43.7	22,675	23,149	23,702		82.0		
43.3	22,824	22,930	23,834		76.9		
41.7	23,057	22,669	24,243		78.7		
49.7	23,870	23,893	24,762	27,920	77.5		
46.0	23,907	23,963	25,184		78.0		
32.3	24,038	23,374	25,411		75.1		
47.7	25,476				85.7		
30.3	28,312	21,212	22,307	29,039	67.0	882	1050
41.3	28,664	26,903	29,881	32,826	78.7	923	1180

AFFORDABLE ELITE COLLEGES

RANK	NAME	OVERALL SCORE	STUDENT LOAN DEFAULT RATE	GRADUATION RATE	GRADUATION RATE PERFORMANCE	STUDENTS RECEIVING PELL GRANTS
1.	University of California–Los Angeles (CA)*	13	2%	91%	6%	35%
2.	Harvard University (MA)	12	1%	97%	9%	11%
3.	Williams College (MA)	12	1%	95%	5%	19%
4.	Dartmouth College (NH)	12	1%	95%	8%	16%
5.	Vassar College (NY)	12	0%	92%	3%	20%
6.	University of California–Berkeley (CA)*	12	2%	91%	2%	33%
7.	University of California–Irvine (CA)*	12	2%	85%	6%	36%
8.	University of California–San Diego (CA)*	12	2%	86%	8%	44%
9.	Hanover College (IN)	12	2%	67%	6%	44%
10.	Amherst College (MA)	11	3%	95%	4%	21%
11.	University of Florida (FL)*	11	2%	84%	4%	30%
12.	Stanford University (CA)	11	1%	95%	3%	17%
13.	Pomona College (CA)	11	1%	95%	1%	17%
14.	Columbia Univ. in the City of NY (NY)	11	2%	93%	4%	18%
15.	Texas A&M University–College Station (TX)*	11	4%	80%	6%	21%
16.	Brown University (RI)	11	1%	95%	2%	14%
17.	College of William and Mary (VA)*	11	1%	90%	0%	12%
18.	University of Michigan–Ann Arbor (MI)*	11	2%	90%	1%	16%
19.	University of Virginia–Main (VA)*	11	2%	93%	1%	12%
20.	Bowdoin College (ME)	11	1%	93%	1%	15%
21.	Swarthmore College (PA)	11	0%	93%	1%	15%
22.	University of Pennsylvania (PA)	11	1%	96%	3%	13%
23.	Grinnell College (IA)	11	1%	89%	6%	20%
24.	Wheaton College (IL)	11	1%	88%	7%	20%
25.	Berea College (KY)	10	7%	64%	11%	85%
26.	CUNY Bernard M. Baruch College (NY)*	10	3%	62%	-3%	43%
27.	MA Institute of Technology (MA)	10	1%	93%	-1%	20%
28.	University of NC–Chapel Hill (NC)*	10	1%	89%	3%	20%
29.	Vanderbilt University (TN)	10	2%	92%	-4%	14%
30.	Princeton University (NJ)	10	2%	96%	-5%	12%
31.	Rice University (TX)	10	1%	92%	-1%	16%
32.	University of Georgia (GA)*	10	3%	82%	1%	23%
33.	Yale University (CT)	10	1%	96%	-2%	14%
34.	Duke University (NC)	10	1%	94%	-2%	13%
35.	Haverford College (PA)	10	2%	93%	2%	15%
36.	University of CA–Santa Barbara (CA)*	10	2%	80%	4%	35%
37.	Davidson College (NC)	10	1%	92%	3%	12%
38.	College of the Ozarks (MO)	10	0%	61%	-2%	61%
39.	Middlebury College (VT)	10	1%	93%	1%	10%
40.	Wesleyan University (CT)	10	1%	92%	2%	17%
41.	University of Notre Dame (IN)	10	1%	96%	2%	12%
42.	Georgetown University (DC)	10	1%	94%	1%	13%
43.	Beloit College (WI)	10	2%	77%	5%	20%
44.	College of the Holy Cross (MA)	10	2%	92%	9%	16%
45.	Carleton College (MN)	10	1%	93%	3%	13%
46.	Willamette University (OR)	10	2%	77%	5%	23%

NET PRICE (annual family income $0–$75K)	NET PRICE (annual family income, $0–$30K)	NET PRICE (annual family income, $30–75K)	NET PRICE (annual family income above $75k)	ENDOWMENT FUNDS PER FULL-TIME STUDENT	PERCENT OF APPLICANTS ADMITTED	ACT/SAT 25TH PERCENTILE SCORE	ACT/SAT 75TH PERCENTILE SCORE	MEDIAN ACT/SAT CONVERTED TO MEDIAN ACT*
10,125	8,466	11,774	23,997	31,495	25%	1167	1367	29
3,142	1,533	3,774	25,378	1,240,548	6%	1397	1593	34
6,998	4,453	8,816	29,868	770,511	19%	1310	1540	32
7,222	6,783	7,369	32,549	536,322	11%	1353	1553	33
8,325	5,078	9,552	31,091	315,668	23%	1313	1487	31
9,809	7,994	11,746	25,542	29,411	22%	1237	1440	31
10,108	8,316	11,856	23,592	7,686	46%	1057	1233	26
10,153	8,706	11,905	22,918	12,687	36%	1137	1320	28
13,700	11,585	14,697	20,999	128,092	66%	1007	1233	24
3,926	1,745	4,912	29,790	829,629	14%	1327	1527	32
5,092	4,710	5,290	12,215	22,620	44%	1167	1340	28
5,963	4,776	6,540	31,198	1,035,133	7%	1367	1540	33
6,102	2,843	7,985	28,715	1,040,939	14%	1370	1553	33
7,536	8,259	7,203	30,164	299,178	9%	1387	1553	33
7,692	4,403	10,236	18,075	101,410	66%	1093	1293	27
8,150	5,410	9,165	34,967	289,438	9%	1310	1507	32
8,704	4,207	10,826	21,618	75,073	33%	1250	1467	30
8,726	5,171	10,592	20,689	155,963	43%	28	32	30
9,009	4,195	11,862	21,600	181,416	32%	1240	1433	30
9,127	6,138	10,391	26,585	482,411	17%	1327	1507	32
9,887	8,263	10,720	31,553	913,107	15%	1347	1540	33
9,983	6,801	11,061	31,948	255,636	13%	1350	1507	33
11,371	8,660	12,897	26,937	850,454	40%	1240	1487	30
14,193	12,147	14,544	27,651	101,528	66%	27	32	30
-20,796	-22,045	-19,294		573,787	21%	22	27	25
3,925	2,876	6,552	12,607	6,853	23%	1103	1227	27
5,891	4,402	6,581	32,262	894,599	10%	1410	1533	34
6,975	4,247	8,762	17,673	74,043	33%	1203	1400	29
7,097	6,236	7,597	26,644	278,124	16%	31	34	33
7,239	6,954	7,445	25,674	2,063,464	8%	1407	1580	34
7,315	6,159	8,160	29,782	678,715	19%	1343	1500	33
7,566	5,376	9,079	11,956	1,843	59%	1123	1313	27
8,356	6,819	9,393	28,575	1,409,391	8%	1403	1593	34
8,533	6,486	9,657	35,495	342,168	16%	1347	1500	33
9,104	6,217	10,805	33,875	307,124	25%	1303	1500	32
10,295	8,591	12,062	26,104	5,108	47%	1090	1300	26
10,379	8,204	11,135	27,707	255,433	27%	1263	1447	30
10,722	10,078	11,079		200,452	10%	21	25	23
11,353	6,617	12,599	34,362	249,332	18%	1290	1480	31
11,469	7,654	13,304	35,258	179,087	22%	1295	1487	31
12,907	12,042	13,161	34,884	505,429	25%	31	34	33
13,188	9,966	15,148	36,580	69,319	19%	1293	1493	31
13,965	9,645	16,251	26,698	85,586	70%	24	30	27
14,318	10,528	16,768	36,972	183,600	34%			28
14,687	11,594	16,311	32,867	317,368	29%	1320	1507	32
18,309	16,632	19,092	29,361	74,349	56%	1127	1353	27

* (for sorting by test scores)

RANK	NAME	OVERALL SCORE	STUDENT LOAN DEFAULT RATE	GRADUATION RATE	GRADUATION RATE PERFORMANCE	STUDENTS RECEIVING PELL GRANTS
47.	Georgia Institute of Technology–Main (GA)*	9	2%	79%	-3%	18%
48.	Sewanee–University of the South (TN)	9	2%	82%	-0%	11%
49.	Bates College (ME)	9	1%	89%	2%	12%
50.	University of Richmond (VA)	9	2%	84%	3%	17%
51.	Wellesley College (MA)	9	1%	91%	-2%	18%
52.	Washington University in St Louis (MO)	9	2%	94%	-2%	7%
53.	Cornell University (NY)	9	1%	93%	-2%	16%
54.	Claremont McKenna College (CA)	9	1%	92%	-0%	14%
55.	University of Texas–Austin (TX)*	9	4%	80%	2%	26%
56.	Colby College (ME)	9	1%	90%	-1%	10%
57.	University of Wisconsin–Madison (WI)*	9	1%	82%	0%	16%
58.	SUNY–Geneseo (NY)*	9	2%	79%	-4%	22%
59.	College of New Jersey (NJ)*	9	2%	87%	4%	17%
60.	University of Chicago (IL)	9	1%	92%	-2%	17%
61.	VA Polytechnic Inst. & State Univ. (VA)*	9	2%	82%	0%	17%
62.	Kenyon College (OH)	9	2%	88%	2%	10%
63.	Cornell College (IA)	9	2%	69%	0%	31%
64.	Macalester College (MN)	9	1%	88%	2%	15%
65.	Barnard College (NY)	9	2%	90%	-4%	20%
66.	St. Olaf College (MN)	9	1%	85%	2%	16%
67.	Johns Hopkins University (MD)	9	1%	91%	-2%	13%
68.	Tufts University (MA)	9	1%	91%	-3%	13%
69.	Union College (NY)	9	2%	84%	4%	17%
70.	Occidental College (CA)	9	2%	84%	3%	23%
71.	Gustavus Adolphus College (MN)	9	2%	81%	4%	23%
72.	College of the Atlantic (ME)	9	1%	68%	4%	33%
73.	Austin College (TX)	9	2%	77%	6%	27%
74.	Smith College (MA)	9	2%	84%	1%	25%
75.	Knox College (IL)	9	3%	78%	8%	25%
76.	Thomas Aquinas College (CA)	9	0%	73%	4%	32%
77.	Brandeis University (MA)	9	1%	91%	4%	19%
78.	Northwestern University (IL)	9	1%	94%	0%	13%
79.	Boston College (MA)	9	2%	92%	1%	13%
80.	Allegheny College (PA)	9	3%	79%	5%	26%
81.	Pepperdine University (CA)	9	2%	81%	6%	19%
82.	Houghton College (NY)	9	2%	68%	6%	38%
83.	University of Southern California (CA)	9	1%	90%	0%	21%
84.	Susquehanna University (PA)	9	2%	77%	7%	22%
85.	Calvin College (MI)	9	2%	77%	5%	25%
86.	Syracuse University (NY)	9	3%	81%	8%	26%
87.	Ursinus College (PA)	9	2%	78%	5%	21%
88.	Bucknell University (PA)	9	1%	91%	2%	11%
89.	Bentley University (MA)	9	1%	87%	9%	15%
90.	California Institute of Technology (CA)	8	1%	90%	-7%	11%
91.	University of Texas at Dallas (TX)*	8	5%	63%	-1%	33%
92.	Stony Brook University (NY)*	8	4%	67%	-7%	35%

NET PRICE annual family income $0–$75K	NET PRICE (annual family income, $0–$30K)	NET PRICE (annual family income, $30–75K)	NET PRICE (annual family income above $75k)	ENDOWMENT FUNDS PER FULL-TIME STUDENT	PERCENT OF APPLICANTS ADMITTED	ACT/SAT 25TH PERCENTILE SCORE	ACT/SAT 75TH PERCENTILE SCORE	MEDIAN ACT/SAT CONVERTED TO MEDIAN ACT*
5,375	2,149	7,758	11,006	55,719	54%	1243	1373	30
9,628	8,335	10,263	21,762	177,225	61%	1157	1373	28
10,303	8,162	11,535	33,114	124,744	28%			29
10,315	7,432	11,522	29,505	421,057	32%	1190	1380	29
10,358	8,502	11,867	33,071	558,848	31%	1283	1480	31
10,786	4,668	13,381	37,677	435,226	19%	32	34	33
10,849	9,278	11,560	33,339	174,738	18%	1303	1467	32
11,016	11,629	10,696	26,516	398,379	15%	1303	1473	31
11,038	7,421	14,017	22,079	59,892	47%	1117	1333	28
11,529	7,524	12,777	30,533	294,470	31%	1247	1420	30
11,691	6,721	13,242	19,920	54,085	67%	26	30	28
12,336	9,110	14,964	19,033	2,596	41%	1200	1380	28
12,611	6,684	16,598	24,758	2,976	47%	1137	1313	27
12,843	11,198	13,784	35,793	416,329	16%	1400	1567	33
13,039	9,765	15,028	21,303	17,833	68%	1113	1280	27
13,392	10,789	14,486	36,549	94,087	36%	1247	1473	30
13,568	12,411	14,096	21,970	50,223	47%	24	30	27
13,594	11,715	14,401	28,631	299,330	38%	1270	1480	31
13,807	11,412	14,884	37,581	88,035	25%	1249	1460	30
14,080	10,594	15,687	29,090	102,177	57%	26	31	29
14,122	13,591	14,361	37,283	119,325	20%	1297	1467	32
14,551	11,392	16,371	38,097	128,911	23%	1353	1493	32
14,842	9,684	18,249	34,912	152,020	41%			28
15,254	12,625	16,836	34,622	151,843	40%	1203	1393	29
15,296	12,035	16,818	25,408	41,303	66%	25	30	28
15,578	13,485	16,943	27,180	89,926	71%			25
16,076	14,702	16,988	24,666	91,848	65%	23	29	27
16,256	14,445	17,363	33,849	428,890	45%			26
16,387	14,594	17,491	26,077	56,189	75%			26
16,988	15,521	17,567	23,552	30,626	79%	1180	1427	28
17,091	14,856	18,500	35,463	103,245	40%	1240	1433	30
17,413	15,794	18,232	36,915	279,935	23%	1373	1500	33
17,755	14,299	19,896	39,138	128,039	29%	1257	1413	30
17,992	15,400	19,129	28,471	70,039	60%	1097	1320	26
18,118	16,874	18,961	32,598	78,416	34%	1110	1320	27
18,319	15,882	19,466	24,231	28,592	76%	1027	1280	25
18,619	15,923	20,313	40,648	96,652	22%	1273	1440	31
19,103	18,222	19,423	26,554	43,977	73%	1020	1220	24
19,159	16,717	20,186	26,362	25,479	81%	23	29	26
19,446	17,160	21,032	34,775	41,608	53%	1053	1240	25
19,577	16,403	21,206	31,829	67,443	65%	1107	1313	26
19,615	16,664	21,027	37,366	94,283	29%	1217	1360	29
19,846	18,341	20,680	33,810	35,792	45%	1111	1257	26
5,436	5,385	5,462	31,191	762,956	13%	1463	1573	34
8,319	6,451	10,039	15,325	17,236	52%	1143	1340	28
9,186	7,189	11,935	17,607	4,864	40%	1123	1273	27

* (for sorting by test scores)

AFFORDABLE ELITE COLLEGES

RANK	NAME	OVERALL SCORE	STUDENT LOAN DEFAULT RATE	GRADUATION RATE	GRADUATION RATE PERFORMANCE	STUDENTS RECEIVING PELL GRANTS
93.	University of Central Florida (FL)*	8	5%	64%	-1%	31%
94.	University of Minnesota–Twin Cities (MN)*	8	2%	71%	-4%	23%
95.	Hamilton College (NY)	8	3%	89%	-0%	13%
96.	Cooper Un. Advance. of Science & Art (NY)	8	2%	81%	-1%	19%
97.	University of Connecticut (CT)*	8	3%	81%	0%	20%
98.	Trinity College (CT)	8	2%	85%	1%	14%
99.	SUNY–Binghamton (NY)*	8	2%	78%	-3%	27%
100.	Colgate University (NY)	8	2%	90%	-1%	11%
101.	George Mason University (VA)*	8	2%	64%	-3%	27%
102.	Clemson University (SC)*	8	2%	79%	-0%	17%
103.	Ramapo College of New Jersey (NJ)*	8	4%	74%	4%	24%
104.	Connecticut College (CT)	8	2%	85%	-1%	12%
105.	Illinois Institute of Technology (IL)	8	2%	65%	-2%	30%
106.	Gettysburg College (PA)	8	1%	85%	-1%	13%
107.	Colorado College (CO)	8	1%	88%	-1%	10%
108.	College of Wooster (OH)	8	3%	76%	0%	19%
109.	Harvey Mudd College (CA)	8	0%	86%	-5%	13%
110.	Bryn Mawr College (PA)	8	1%	85%	-3%	19%
111.	Oberlin College (OH)	8	1%	87%	-3%	13%
112.	Mount Holyoke College (MA)	8	3%	83%	-2%	22%
113.	Franklin and Marshall College (PA)	8	1%	85%	-0%	11%
114.	Lafayette College (PA)	8	1%	89%	4%	10%
115.	Ohio State University–Main (OH)*	8	4%	80%	4%	24%
116.	Skidmore College (NY)	8	2%	85%	2%	16%
117.	Washington and Lee University (VA)	8	1%	91%	-3%	8%
118.	St. Lawrence University (NY)	8	1%	81%	1%	19%
119.	Rutgers University–New Brunswick (NJ)*	8	4%	78%	1%	29%
120.	University of Rochester (NY)	8	1%	84%	0%	19%
121.	Hope College (MI)	8	2%	78%	3%	21%
122.	Centre College (KY)	8	2%	85%	4%	18%
123.	Lehigh University (PA)	8	1%	88%	2%	14%
124.	Kalamazoo College (MI)	8	1%	81%	3%	16%
125.	Lake Forest College (IL)	8	3%	69%	1%	34%
126.	Emory University (GA)	8	1%	88%	-2%	21%
127.	Clark University (MA)	8	3%	79%	5%	20%
128.	Lawrence University (WI)	8	2%	74%	1%	21%
129.	Taylor University (IN)	8	2%	78%	12%	19%
130.	Muhlenberg College (PA)	8	1%	86%	5%	11%
131.	Wheaton College (MA)	8	3%	78%	0%	21%
132.	Furman University (SC)	8	1%	85%	4%	14%
133.	Creighton University (NE)	8	1%	76%	1%	19%
134.	Stevens Institute of Technology (NJ)	8	3%	76%	9%	24%
135.	Wofford College (SC)	8	1%	82%	6%	19%
136.	Westmont College (CA)	8	2%	78%	6%	20%
137.	Providence College (RI)	8	1%	86%	11%	12%
138.	New College of Florida (FL)*	7	3%	68%	-9%	28%

NET PRICE (annual family income $0–$75K)	NET PRICE (annual family income, $0–$30K)	NET PRICE (annual family income, $30–75K)	NET PRICE (annual family income above $75k)	ENDOWMENT FUNDS PER FULL-TIME STUDENT	PERCENT OF APPLICANTS ADMITTED	ACT/SAT 25TH PERCENTILE SCORE	ACT/SAT 75TH PERCENTILE SCORE	MEDIAN ACT/SAT CONVERTED TO MEDIAN ACT*
9,331	7,323	10,952	14,815	2,353	46%	1083	1260	26
9,888	7,652	11,118	19,761	49,693	48%	25	30	28
9,969	7,051	11,807	32,210	367,350	28%	1303	1480	31
10,506	9,829	10,910	15,423	569,490	8%	1247	1447	31
11,110	7,633	12,854	21,265	12,070	49%	1130	1287	27
11,146	8,516	12,102	34,843	174,663	36%	1190	1367	28
11,325	8,426	14,286	19,476	4,346	38%	1207	1347	29
11,355	10,361	11,715	23,547	233,155	31%	1267	1447	31
11,499	9,484	12,754	18,040	1,914	53%	1050	1240	25
12,131	9,931	13,552	15,753	8,368	61%	1137	1293	27
12,447	7,639	15,758	24,446	1,345	48%	1008	1200	24
12,776	7,724	15,934	38,061	96,580	34%			29
13,142	10,751	14,974	22,881	27,084	61%	24	31	28
13,617	10,854	14,782	28,659	85,889	40%	1217	1380	29
13,928	12,249	14,761	32,298	211,980	27%	28	32	30
14,014	10,177	15,629	26,170	118,403	62%	24	30	27
14,255	9,249	16,555	34,195	290,896	21%	1420	1533	34
14,433	12,052	15,279	34,945	362,266	45%	1187	1427	29
14,481	11,022	15,558	33,300	246,819	31%	1273	1480	31
14,708	11,467	15,951	30,548	229,399	48%			28
14,838	11,576	16,328	37,580	114,639	43%			29
15,387	11,609	16,709	35,823	246,590	39%	1193	1353	29
15,518	11,825	17,274	23,127	33,516	63%	26	30	28
15,522	12,324	18,850	35,747	103,474	44%	1137	1353	27
15,739	14,177	16,696	31,255	540,070	19%	1307	1473	31
15,856	11,347	18,405	30,637	95,515	43%			28
15,904	13,337	17,833	23,722	13,224	60%	1080	1260	26
16,485	13,552	18,144	32,595	153,353	36%	1233	1393	30
16,550	13,559	17,833	26,915	43,321	82%	24	29	27
16,660	14,706	17,425	24,130	160,123	71%	26	31	29
16,864	17,008	16,791	34,689	158,036	35%	1213	1347	29
17,031	12,159	19,634	28,625	104,946	71%	26	30	28
17,121	15,334	18,352	27,344	44,849	57%			26
17,360	14,715	19,274	36,338	341,953	28%	1283	1427	31
18,217	16,874	18,825	28,067	80,248	69%	1070	1320	26
18,299	15,366	19,780	27,948	127,105	65%			27
18,943	16,386	20,261	27,489	27,957	84%	24	30	26
19,021	17,620	19,687	31,668	50,357	46%	1120	1353	27
19,038	15,683	21,001	33,421	93,487	61%			27
19,405	19,486	19,356	30,514	181,031	72%	1150	1353	28
19,632	18,769	20,000	25,100	34,296	78%	24	29	27
20,355	17,271	21,865	31,856	29,472	43%	1193	1313	28
21,727	20,525	22,556	28,174	91,992	63%	1087	1300	26
23,449	20,786	24,586	29,084	45,433	68%	1077	1300	26
25,154	23,549	25,880	37,416	35,206	63%	1050	1253	25
7,535	5,616	8,989	12,379	35,363	56%	1203	1480	29

* (for sorting by test scores)

RANK	NAME	OVERALL SCORE	STUDENT LOAN DEFAULT RATE	GRADUATION RATE	GRADUATION RATE PERFORMANCE	STUDENTS RECEIVING PELL GRANTS
139.	University of MD–College Park (MD)*	7	3%	82%	-3%	19%
140.	Florida International University (FL)*	7	7%	46%	2%	52%
141.	Florida State University (FL)*	7	5%	74%	3%	29%
142.	University at Buffalo (NY)*	7	3%	69%	-0%	30%
143.	University of IL–Urbana-Champaign (IL)*	7	2%	83%	-1%	19%
144.	St. Mary's College of Maryland (MD)*	7	3%	79%	-1%	14%
145.	MO Univ. of Science & Technology (MO)*	7	4%	66%	-0%	27%
146.	Scripps College (CA)	7	1%	87%	-8%	12%
147.	Pitzer College (CA)	7	2%	82%	1%	18%
148.	Agnes Scott College (GA)	7	5%	66%	-3%	40%
149.	Dickinson College (PA)	7	2%	84%	-1%	12%
150.	Earlham College (IN)	7	3%	70%	3%	27%
151.	Trinity University (TX)	7	2%	79%	-2%	13%
152.	Richard Stockton Coll. of NJ (NJ)*	7	4%	65%	2%	33%
153.	Cedarville University (OH)	7	1%	69%	-3%	23%
154.	Rhodes College (TN)	7	2%	79%	-4%	15%
155.	Augustana College (IL)	7	3%	77%	2%	19%
156.	Illinois Wesleyan University (IL)	7	2%	82%	2%	18%
157.	St. John's College (MD)	7	1%	70%	-1%	25%
158.	Villanova University (PA)	7	1%	89%	4%	11%
159.	Gonzaga University (WA)	7	2%	81%	4%	19%
160.	Loyola University Maryland (MD)	7	1%	83%	3%	13%
161.	Case Western Reserve University (OH)	7	1%	79%	-2%	22%
162.	Whitman College (WA)	7	1%	86%	3%	13%
163.	University of Miami (FL)	7	2%	80%	-2%	20%
164.	Stonehill College (MA)	7	1%	82%	5%	13%
165.	University of Denver (CO)	7	2%	77%	0%	18%
166.	University of Puget Sound (WA)	7	2%	77%	-0%	22%
167.	Salem College (NC)	7	5%	58%	10%	58%
168.	Fordham University (NY)	7	4%	80%	1%	21%
169.	Boston University (MA)	7	2%	84%	0%	14%
170.	Emerson College (MA)	7	2%	81%	1%	16%
171.	New York University (NY)	7	2%	86%	-3%	21%
172.	Quinnipiac University (CT)	7	1%	77%	1%	13%
173.	Santa Clara University (CA)	7	1%	86%	3%	14%
174.	Indiana University–Bloomington (IN)*	6	4%	73%	-5%	19%
175.	Truman State University (MO)*	6	3%	71%	-6%	20%
176.	Lyon College (AR)	6	6%	50%	-9%	46%
177.	Univ. of South Carolina–Columbia (SC)*	6	2%	70%	-6%	23%
178.	George Washington University (DC)	6	1%	81%	-6%	13%
179.	Southwestern University (TX)	6	4%	74%	2%	25%
180.	Hampshire College (MA)	6	2%	65%	-12%	20%
181.	Tulane University of Louisiana (LA)	6	4%	75%	-3%	17%
182.	Rollins College (FL)	6	3%	70%	0%	29%
183.	Marquette University (WI)	6	2%	81%	2%	18%
184.	University of Dallas (TX)	6	3%	72%	2%	23%

NET PRICE (annual family income $0–$75K)	NET PRICE (annual family income, $0–$30K)	NET PRICE (annual family income, $30–75K)	NET PRICE (annual family income above $75k)	ENDOWMENT FUNDS PER FULL-TIME STUDENT	PERCENT OF APPLICANTS ADMITTED	ACT/SAT 25TH PERCENTILE SCORE	ACT/SAT 75TH PERCENTILE SCORE	MEDIAN ACT/SAT CONVERTED TO MEDIAN ACT*
10,645	6,376	12,860	19,766	11,679	45%	1190	1367	29
11,123	9,563	13,081	16,202	4,697	47%	1010	1180	24
11,132	8,938	12,958	16,311	14,509	57%	25	28	27
11,367	9,483	13,462	17,520	16,919	53%	1050	1213	25
11,997	7,392	14,855	24,410	19,566	66%	26	31	29
12,611	7,691	15,803	24,028	12,597	61%	1116	1367	27
13,072	11,101	14,042	16,987	21,236	90%	25	31	28
13,842	12,099	14,930	31,528	257,236	36%	1270	1473	31
15,164	12,529	16,721	32,419	104,630	22%	1197	1377	28
15,400	14,792	15,807	22,995	268,620	51%			24
15,770	13,624	16,865	32,763	122,598	43%	1193	1373	28
16,004	14,141	17,227	27,947	275,430	72%	1017	1340	25
16,172	13,894	17,113	27,336	354,247	63%	1160	1360	28
17,410	14,046	19,438	25,044	2,072	64%	960	1140	23
17,678	15,751	18,284	23,057	5,767	75%	24	29	26
17,790	16,923	18,421	27,516	148,272	49%	26	31	29
19,072	16,862	19,817	25,304	44	72%			26
19,461	17,274	20,483	29,503	90,596	61%	25	30	28
19,726	20,116	19,400	36,034	126,715	80%	1210	1467	29
20,122	16,003	22,247	38,559	35,162	45%	1207	1360	29
20,216	17,282	22,060	28,116	18,445	68%	1100	1360	27
20,735	20,673	20,757	32,205	28,841	61%	1092	1273	26
21,575	18,075	23,144	31,556	191,367	57%	1250	1413	30
21,866	16,073	24,016	36,447	250,158	50%	1230	1453	29
22,814	20,953	24,249	34,710	42,672	39%	1223	1380	29
23,246	20,061	24,331	33,595	57,479	70%	1090	1280	25
23,672	22,265	24,629	33,455	32,023	69%	25	30	28
23,984	21,558	25,495	33,837	88,814	53%	1137	1365	27
24,249	23,848	24,640	23,643	47,643	62%	940	1213	23
24,720	21,382	28,203	36,026	30,186	45%	1157	1340	28
25,059	23,630	25,889	39,081	35,686	55%	1177	1333	28
26,667	24,274	27,731	34,606	26,182	48%	1143	1360	27
28,046	24,266	31,573	44,112	59,109	35%	1250	1427	30
29,885	28,118	30,571	35,636	31,852	68%	990	1160	24
31,391	30,019	32,203	41,952	73,854	57%	1147	1333	28
8,331	4,094	10,693	18,509	18,653	72%	1053	1253	25
9,788	7,434	10,834	13,426	4,434	74%	25	30	28
10,806	9,471	11,936	14,887	77,432	65%	23	28	26
12,277	9,438	14,385	18,035	13,496	66%	1093	1273	26
15,990	16,249	15,874	32,885	69,758	34%	1207	1380	29
18,457	16,074	19,976	26,859	187,095	64%	1100	1347	27
19,689	16,780	21,316	31,561	25,243	66%	1130	1407	27
19,734	18,607	20,396	30,744	77,345	26%	1237	1413	30
20,334	18,704	21,575	32,337	91,172	55%	1102	1287	26
21,018	17,305	22,894	30,867	33,786	58%	24	29	27
21,153	21,110	21,181	26,609	20,296	89%	1080	1373	26

* (for sorting by test scores)

AFFORDABLE ELITE COLLEGES

RANK	NAME	OVERALL SCORE	STUDENT LOAN DEFAULT RATE	GRADUATION RATE	GRADUATION RATE PERFORMANCE	STUDENTS RECEIVING PELL GRANTS
185.	Elon University (NC)	6	1%	82%	-3%	10%
186.	Carnegie Mellon University (PA)	6	1%	87%	-4%	14%
187.	Saint Louis University–Main (MO)	6	3%	71%	6%	14%
188.	Rensselaer Polytechnic Institute (NY)	6	2%	83%	-1%	17%
189.	Worcester Polytechnic Institute (MA)	6	2%	80%	5%	16%
190.	Wake Forest University (NC)	6	1%	88%	-3%	12%
191.	Denison University (OH)	6	1%	83%	-1%	16%
192.	NM Inst. of Mining and Tech (NM)*	5	5%	47%	-9%	26%
193.	University of South Florida–Main (FL)*	5	6%	53%	-8%	38%
194.	University of Tennessee (TN)*	5	5%	63%	-12%	28%
195.	Georgia College & State Univ. (GA)*	5	4%	57%	-15%	23%
196.	Millsaps College (MS)	5	5%	69%	-3%	22%
197.	Reed College (OR)	5	3%	78%	-6%	19%
198.	Southern Methodist University (TX)	5	4%	76%	-4%	17%
199.	St. John's College (NM)	5	2%	56%	-4%	32%
200.	Drake University (IA)	5	2%	76%	-1%	18%
201.	University of Pittsburgh–Pittsburgh (PA)*	5	3%	79%	-3%	18%
202.	Sarah Lawrence College (NY)	5	2%	74%	-1%	19%
203.	Rochester Institute of Technology (NY)	5	3%	63%	-5%	32%
204.	Loyola University–Chicago (IL)	5	4%	69%	-5%	31%
205.	Bard College (NY)	5	3%	78%	-1%	17%
206.	King College (TN)	4	6%	49%	-11%	36%
207.	Berry College (GA)	4	3%	60%	-13%	28%
208.	Colorado School of Mines (CO)*	4	2%	67%	-10%	19%
209.	Loyola University–New Orleans (LA)	4	3%	59%	-9%	28%
210.	Pacific Union College (CA)	4	6%	44%	-7%	40%
211.	Miami University–Oxford (OH)*	4	6%	80%	-0%	16%
212.	University of the Pacific (CA)	4	2%	60%	-9%	38%
213.	Bennington College (VT)	4	2%	64%	-7%	22%
214.	Butler University (IN)	4	1%	73%	-6%	17%
215.	Northeastern University (MA)	4	3%	78%	-6%	14%
216.	American University (DC)	4	2%	78%	-6%	14%
217.	Chapman University (CA)	4	3%	71%	-6%	21%
218.	Hendrix College (AR)	3	5%	68%	-10%	20%
219.	Milwaukee School of Engineering (WI)	3	3%	58%	-6%	28%
220.	University of Tulsa (OK)	3	5%	66%	-1%	17%
221.	University of San Diego (CA)	3	2%	75%	-5%	16%
222.	Texas Christian University (TX)	3	4%	74%	-6%	15%
223.	Baylor University (TX)	3	4%	73%	-7%	23%
224.	Shimer College (IL)	3	12%	34%	-11%	47%

NET PRICE annual family income $0–$75K	NET PRICE (annual family income, $0–$30K)	NET PRICE (annual family income, $30–75K)	NET PRICE (annual family income above $75k)	ENDOWMENT FUNDS PER FULL-TIME STUDENT	PERCENT OF APPLICANTS ADMITTED	ACT/SAT 25TH PERCENTILE SCORE	ACT/SAT 75TH PERCENTILE SCORE	MEDIAN ACT/SAT CONVERTED TO MEDIAN ACT*
21,974	19,012	23,265	32,481	20,098	53%	1123	1313	27
22,887	21,314	23,862	37,052	87,975	31%	1310	1453	32
24,913	23,952	25,389	32,885	60,751	66%	25	30	28
25,226	21,523	26,972	34,943	87,669	41%	1277	1407	31
25,739	21,651	27,809	35,751	96,666	56%			28
26,912	21,521	28,086	36,318	134,302	38%			31
33,547	32,822	36,495		281,084	49%	27	30	29
7,269	5,094	8,701	11,665	11,633	58%	23	29	26
8,842	6,580	10,693	16,062	8,700	42%	1053	1240	25
10,755	8,376	12,600	16,443	21,731	70%	24	29	27
10,920	8,882	12,019	14,661	4,310	72%	1053	1227	25
15,201	13,885	15,789	20,817	81,324	64%	23	29	26
15,638	11,871	18,339	37,079	290,887	39%	1303	1513	31
18,755	15,763	20,294	34,058	111,608	54%	1170	1353	28
20,137	17,461	22,301	35,092	0	85%			25
20,199	18,852	20,743	26,007	26,833	65%	24	29	27
20,872	17,626	22,112	26,822	81,773	58%	1167	1367	28
21,567	17,487	24,493	35,142	42,388	60%			26
21,952	20,051	23,167	29,648	44,308	59%	1100	1293	27
23,500	21,791	24,478	32,724	25,037	57%	25	29	27
23,687	19,500	26,979	37,463	42,416	35%			27
15,620	14,026	17,064	19,565	13,740	69%	19	25	22
16,381	15,160	17,208	22,026	385,265	64%	1053	1273	25
18,284	16,446	19,085	22,904	36,968	45%	27	31	29
19,053	17,534	20,227	24,186	55,454	62%	23	28	26
19,358	17,978	20,451	26,091	17,284	45%	873	1160	21
19,504	16,465	21,442	25,372	24,279	75%	24	29	27
20,146	17,700	21,946	34,314	27,924	37%	1053	1273	26
21,572	17,559	24,022	35,222	19,090	67%			25
22,582	22,347	22,718	28,538	32,751	67%	25	30	27
23,941	20,065	26,244	36,486	21,803	35%	1253	1400	30
25,259	23,377	26,183	36,601	37,130	43%	1167	1400	28
30,144	28,052	31,246	39,098	17,209	47%	1103	1293	27
16,164	14,649	17,050	23,377	106,837	83%	27	32	30
20,632	20,245	20,778	26,076	16,959	64%	24	29	27
20,677	18,469	22,114	26,386	192,756	40%	25	31	28
20,857	18,320	21,787	37,391	38,847	47%	1123	1293	27
22,201	19,818	23,590	33,153	127,669	44%	24	29	27
22,271	20,529	23,407	29,657	62,682	49%	24	29	27
26,304	24,983	27,361	27,834	6,206	50%			22

AFFORDABLE ELITE COLLEGES

* (for sorting by test scores)

BEST
COMMUNITY
COLLEGES

&

BEST-
BANG-FOR-
THE-BUCK
HBCUs

RANK	NAME	ACTIVE AND COLLABORATIVE LEATRNING	STUDENT EFFORT	ACADEMIC CHALLENGE
1.	Saint Paul College (MN)	80	71.3	61.5
2.	North Florida Community College (FL)	62.2	58.3	61.1
3.	North Dakota State College of Science (ND)	64.1	47	55.7
4.	Wisconsin Indianhead Technical College (WI)	62.5	54.3	58.8
5.	Lawson State Community College (AL)	65.8	59.4	59.3
6.	Missouri State University–West Plains (MO)	56.5	58.8	54
7.	Western Wyoming Community College (WY)	61.8	56.6	56.3
8.	Capital Area Technical College (LA)	63.5	55.7	51.9
9.	Snow College (UT)	65.2	50.8	52.4
10.	North Central Missouri College (MO)	57.1	59.2	53.2
11.	Linn State Technical College (MO)	58.8	47.6	46.7
12.	Halifax Community College (NC)	53.7	57.7	56.8
13.	Southeast Kentucky Community & Technical College (KY)	56.1	51.8	58.5
14.	Chipola College (FL)	52.9	55.2	53
15.	Grays Harbor College (WA)	57.5	55.8	60.3
16.	Kauai Community College (HI)	58	55.1	55.9
17.	Isothermal Community College (NC)	59.7	57.9	59.2
18.	Williston State College (ND)	56.6	49.6	50.1
19.	Williamsburg Technical College (SC)	62.5	55.7	54.7
20.	Mississippi Delta Community College (MS)	56.1	57.4	56.2
21.	Itasca Community College (MN)	59.9	52.7	51
22.	Cascadia Community College (WA)	67.3	53.5	56.2
23.	East Central Community College (MS)	54.4	53.9	53
24.	Washington County Community College (ME)	60.4	52.5	48.6
25.	College of Coastal Georgia (GA)	59.5	56.9	56.9
26.	Abraham Baldwin Agriculture College (GA)	56.3	53.6	54.3
27.	Dakota College at Bottineau (ND)	57.5	45.8	52.2
28.	Miami Dade College (FL)	55.8	55.7	54.7
29.	Cumberland County College (NJ)	53.7	52.5	55.1
30.	Bay de Noc Community College (MI)	55	55.4	52.9
31.	Hocking College (OH)	59.9	56.2	56.2
32.	Mayland Community College (NC)	51.5	53.6	51.3
33.	Umpqua Community College (OR)	61	58.5	62
34.	Itawamba Community College (MS)	50.5	50.3	50.7
35.	Bridgemont Community & Technical College (WV)	58.1	49.2	53.6
36.	Valencia College (FL)	52.6	54.2	53.7
37.	Southern Arkansas University Tech (AR)	52.4	55.1	48.1
38.	Vermilion Community College (MN)	54.9	51.6	52
39.	Robeson Community College (NC)	57.3	57.3	55.9
40.	Minnesota West–Granite Falls (MN)	54.5	48.1	47.9
41.	Ridgewater College (MN)	53.1	51.8	53.3
42.	Chippewa Valley Technical College (WI)	54.2	52.6	52.4
43.	Ashland Community & Technical College (KY)	53.9	53.2	51.7
44.	Green River Community College (WA)	58.8	55.7	54
45.	Texas State Technical College Marshall (TX)	56.6	48.9	48.8
46.	Tacoma Community College (WA)	56.6	53.3	56.6
47.	Highline Community College (WA)	55.1	57.1	53.4
48.	City Colleges of Chicago–Kennedy–King College (IL)	62.3	60	57.9
49.	Clinton Community College (NY)	51	55.3	56.8
50.	South Florida Community College (FL)	588	56.2	48.7

STUDENT-FACULTY INTERACTION	SUPPORT FOR LEARNERS	FIRST-YEAR RETENTION RATE	THREE-YEAR GRADUATION/TRANSFER RATE	CREDENTIALS AWARDED PER 100 FTE STUDENTS
71.7	66.2	52.6	47.0	24.9
65.1	67.4	56.9	56.0	40.7
60.1	52.4	71.4	46.9	60.2
59.1	51.7	65.4	50.8	44.4
59	57	58.9	49.3	18.2
59.2	57.9	59.2	49.8	40.5
58.7	53.4	49.7	76.6	31.1
57.2	64.5	55.7	45.8	28.3
53.7	55.2	54.6	74.3	43.8
53.7	53.8	60.1	58.2	41.6
57	50.3	76.0	59.3	63.6
60.6	60.2	60.6	42.8	20.2
57.6	58	54.3	42.5	43.8
53	56.5	65.9	57.9	44.1
55	55	60.8	37.3	31.1
54.5	59.5	54.3	37.1	40.8
58.1	63.6	54.7	12.1	20.1
61.5	56	52.5	35.2	64.5
61.7	63.9	39.8	33.6	23.9
55.6	59	56.7	29.6	32.7
52.2	54.4	55.6	61.9	47.1
50.8	51.6	56.8	53.1	29.6
53.5	55.8	67.7	50.1	34.9
55.4	45.6	53.3	56.6	67.9
57.8	54	55.0	30.6	28.0
59.4	56.5	53.7	43.9	32.2
55.2	58.8	49.5	66.7	48.7
56.5	54.9	61.6	35.7	32.8
55.8	56.4	63.6	39.1	37.3
56.2	51.8	55.4	44.0	48.6
57.7	56	48.2	31.0	32.8
58.4	61.3	65.2	48.4	20.8
54.1	49.4	46.5	33.4	29.7
59.1	60.1	64.0	40.7	37.9
63.8	53.3	43.9	39.5	46.1
51.1	52.3	66.0	52.5	40.2
53.5	58.9	59.9	48.2	43.5
54.2	55.9	49.0	65.2	42.5
56.3	57.1	56.0	25.1	24.6
57.7	53.3	64.9	61.1	42.9
53.1	52.2	58.7	59.2	44.3
52.6	51.3	57.7	59.9	46.4
61	55.5	58.9	31.9	33.7
53	49.8	55.8	54.0	32.2
56.5	59.3	57.7	49.3	38.9
55.4	52.4	54.0	47.4	30.3
54.2	52.9	56.6	47.6	30.5
58.8	53	39.0	38.5	13.0
55.5	51.1	51.7	43.9	40.6
54.1	54.6	54.1	57.6	56.6

RANK	NAME	OVERALL SCORE	STUDENT LOAN DEFAULT RATE	GRADUATION RATE	GRADUATION RATE PERFORMANCE
1.	Elizabeth City State University (NC)*	10	14.0	43.0	16.4
2.	Fayetteville State University (NC)*	10	11.6	32.0	5.2
3.	North Carolina Central Univ. (NC)*	10	12.0	39.7	6.3
4.	Tougaloo College (MS)	10	9.6	46.3	13.1
5.	Lane College (TN)	10	13.2	34.0	12.0
6.	Voorhees College (SC)	10	11.5	30.3	6.3
7.	Albany State University (GA)*	10	11.4	41.7	10.5
8.	Jackson State University (MS)*	10	11.7	41.7	10.3
9.	Claflin University (SC)	10	7.8	43.3	8.7
10.	Howard University (DC)	10	6.8	72.3	10.2
11.	North Carolina A&T State University (NC)*	9	11.4	40.7	4.7
12.	Winston-Salem State University (NC)*	9	10.0	39.0	2.9
13.	Tennessee State University (TN)*	9	9.3	35.0	0.4
14.	Rust College (MS)	9	19.2	30.3	5.0
15.	Savannah State University (GA)*	9	14.3	32.3	1.1
16.	Prairie View A&M University (TX)*	9	15.4	34.0	1.2
17.	Florida Memorial University (FL)	9	14.5	40.7	9.4
18.	Virginia State University (VA)*	9	12.4	40.3	6.5
19.	Wilberforce University (OH)	9	9.7	46.7	13.6
20.	Fisk University (TN)	9	11.9	52.7	10.0
21.	Spelman College (GA)	9	8.6	74.3	16.0
22.	Alabama A&M University (AL)*	8	9.9	32.3	-1.5
23.	FL Agricultural & Mechanical Univ. (FL)*	8	12.3	40.3	-1.1
24.	Southern Univ. and A&M College (LA)*	8	7.1	29.0	-1.0
25.	Norfolk State University (VA)*	8	13.4	34.0	0.6
26.	Alcorn State University (MS)*	8	11.2	34.3	1.5
27.	Lincoln Univ. of Pennsylvania (PA)*	8	16.6	38.0	3.9
28.	Fort Valley State University (GA)*	8	14.4	31.7	2.1
29.	Delaware State University (DE)*	8	8.6	35.7	-2.6
30.	Livingstone College (NC)	8	19.6	28.7	11.3
31.	South Carolina State University (SC)*	8	13.7	36.0	7.6
32.	Bethune-Cookman University (FL)	8	13.5	38.0	8.7
33.	Johnson C. Smith University (NC)	8	17.9	39.3	6.1
34.	Clark Atlanta University (GA)	8	8.4	41.0	5.1
35.	University of Arkansas–Pine Bluff (AR)*	7	21.4	25.0	-3.5
36.	Coppin State University (MD)*	7	14.1	16.0	-3.9
37.	Central State University (OH)*	7	20.2	23.3	-1.0
38.	Alabama State University (AL)*	7	13.1	25.3	-0.5
39.	Harris-Stowe State University (MO)*	7	18.8	9.7	-3.5
40.	Bowie State University (MD)*	7	8.2	37.7	-0.6
41.	Morris College (SC)	7	19.8	29.7	3.2
42.	Univ. of MD Eastern Shore (MD)*	7	14.2	31.7	-1.7
43.	Paine College (GA)	7	14.4	25.0	0.8
44.	Xavier University of Louisiana (LA)	7	8.0	48.3	-3.9
45.	Virginia Union University (VA)	7	15.9	30.3	3.9
46.	Bennett College for Women (NC)	7	10.2	41.0	1.4

HBCUS

BEST-BANG-FOR-THE-BUCK

STUDENTS RECEIVING PELL GRANTS	NET PRICE (all students)	NET PRICE (annual family income, $0–$30K)	NET PRICE (annual family income, $30–75K)	NET PRICE (annual family income above $75k)	PERCENT OF APPLICANTS ADMITTED	ACT/SAT 25TH PERCENTILE SCORE	ACT/SAT 75TH PERCENTILE SCORE
70.0	1,225	416	1,874	6,990	66.8	760	907
64.7	4,985	3,837	5,453	11,188	64.8	767	900
62.7	7,123	6,114	8,433	14,614	64.4	773	920
89.3	8,804	8,660	12,932	17,276	35.5	15	22
90.0	8,815	8,532	10,117		34.1	14	17
81.7	9,687	8,945	10,486	15,031	65.3		
76.7	9,715	9,381	11,141	13,901	41.8	793	927
74.7	9,783	11,402	13,589		36.4	17	20
77.7	11,682	12,905	12,489	12,306	36.1	778	987
43.0	19,125	17,628	22,922	24,249	54.1	940	1213
57.3	6,139	4,940	7,210	13,125	64.4	803	960
58.0	6,977	6,056	8,340	13,885	58.4	817	947
64.7	7,011	6,669	8,890	12,746	56.3		
84.7	7,897	7,849	8,738	12,175	37.4	15	19
74.0	8,504	7,930	9,770	13,056	79.5	800	940
65.7	8,996	11,073	12,571	14,015	40.1	757	907
83.3	11,522	14,921	15,170	15,750	54.9		
66.3	11,745	10,027	12,034	15,518	69.4	783	933
75.0	13,941	12,887	16,301	20,696	54.1		
56.3	19,161	18,961			56.5	17	23
47.7	27,871	25,570	29,736	33,516	38.1	945	1132
67.3	8,698	8,471	10,710	13,660	51.9	16	19
66.7	9,393	8,368	11,298	14,341	52.7	18	22
67.3	9,950	9,234	8,302	11,721	40.6	17	20
64.0	10,442	10,356	11,354	14,099	65.4	793	947
80.3	10,760	10,396	11,869	12,773	39.2	16	19
65.0	12,111	9,941			28.9	783	953
74.7	12,160	11,689	13,788	17,170	41.0	741	941
53.0	12,910	13,137	14,774	16,443	42.3	800	940
89.3	14,283	14,508	14,769	17,176	53.0	658	813
72.0	16,109	15,655		21,017	90.4	758	913
78.3	16,554	16,066	17,444	19,462	69.7	15	19
70.7	16,866	16,808	20,161	21,260	30.7	757	940
69.7	24,076	25,242	28,220	30,822	69.8	790	953
73.3	8,406	8,287	8,861	10,378	30.8	14	19
67.3	8,560	6,819	9,974	9,320	47.2	793	927
79.7	9,020	8,944	10,586	14,270	30.5	14	18
75.0	9,395	6,169	8,111	10,213	46.9	14	18
74.7	9,602	9,163	10,305	11,965	64.1		
47.3	11,468	9,134	13,885	17,872	49.9	813	967
89.3	11,788	11,545	13,158	16,546	44.3		
55.7	12,183	9,933	14,679	18,300	52.5	777	940
78.0	14,752	14,510	15,624	16,582	60.0	670	853
61.0	17,266	19,082	20,216	19,421	65.5	19	24
66.7	17,993	17,482	20,294	22,410	92.8	690	860
67.3	18,994	17,650	20,288	25,305	63.6		

RANK	NAME	OVERALL SCORE	STUDENT LOAN DEFAULT RATE	GRADUATION RATE	GRADUATION RATE PERFORMANCE
47.	Tuskegee University (AL)	7	8.7	45.0	4.6
48.	Morehouse College (GA)	7	19.9	55.7	7.6
49.	Lincoln University (MO)*	6	17.7	23.7	-6.1
50.	Kentucky State University (KY)*	6	16.0	20.0	-9.7
51.	Southern Univ. New Orleans (LA)*	6	11.4	17.0	-5.2
52.	Texas Southern University (TX)*	6	15.2	12.3	-9.9
53.	Langston University (OK)*	6	20.6	15.0	-7.9
54.	Mississippi Valley State Univ. (MS)*	6	10.6	24.3	-6.9
55.	Paul Quinn College (TX)	6	14.6	5.0	-21.7
56.	Wiley College (TX)	6	14.8	21.3	-4.6
57.	Grambling State University (LA)*	6	12.8	29.0	-3.8
58.	Bluefield State College (WV)*	6	16.0	27.0	-4.3
59.	Texas College (TX)	6	22.8	16.0	-3.7
60.	Cheyney University of PA (PA)*	6	17.4	23.7	-1.1
61.	Dillard University (LA)	6	7.0	27.7	-8.4
62.	Miles College (AL)	6	16.6	19.7	-2.9
63.	Jarvis Christian College (TX)	6	28.0	18.7	-4.7
64.	Edward Waters College (FL)	6	15.3	18.7	-3.4
65.	Saint Pauls College (VA)	6		16.3	0.3
66.	Shaw University (NC)	6	16.3	28.0	1.3
67.	Benedict College (SC)	6	21.5	27.3	1.3
68.	Stillman College (AL)	6	8.2	27.7	-1.2
69.	Hampton University (VA)	6	8.4	56.0	-2.5
70.	West Virginia State University (WV)*	5	9.8	25.7	-10.1
71.	Philander Smith College (AR)	5	12.5	26.0	-5.9
72.	Le Moyne-Owen College (TN)	5	14.6	13.3	-6.3
73.	Morgan State University (MD)*	5	14.7	29.7	-7.3
74.	Talladega College (AL)	5	22.2	21.3	-5.7
75.	Allen University (SC)	5	18.4	12.7	-9.0
76.	Univ. of the District of Columbia (DC)*	5	9.8	14.7	-4.1
77.	Huston-Tillotson University (TX)	5	20.5	23.0	-3.1
78.	Saint Augustines College (NC)	5	22.9	27.0	3.4
79.	Oakwood University (AL)	3	12.4	37.7	-7.2

STUDENTS RECEIVING PELL GRANTS	NET PRICE (all students)	NET PRICE (annual family income, $0–$30K)	NET PRICE (annual family income, $30–75K)	NET PRICE (annual family income above $75k)	PERCENT OF APPLICANTS ADMITTED	ACT/SAT 25TH PERCENTILE SCORE	ACT/SAT 75TH PERCENTILE SCORE
56.7	21,558	22,728	23,934		62.8	17	22
47.7	24,280	24,387	28,246	30298	64.2	923	1160
59.0	8,725	9,960	10,437	11647	78.9		
58.7	8,986	8,343	11,430	14634	33.5	15	19
75.7	9,057	7,212	8,270		28.8	16	19
72.0	9,211	13,397	18,395		42.8	727	900
71.7	9,474	9,281	10,913		59.3		
69.3	9,896	10,062			22.8	15	19
80.0	9,990	9,241			57.5	850	880
81.3	10,391	11,665	12,161	13927	45.1		
69.3	11,754	10,675	12,834	15405	42.8	15	20
69.3	11,912	10,960	11,186	11595	62.6	17	21
89.0	12,523	12,885	14,400	16619	48.4		
74.0	12,532	12,170	13,586	17868	58.2		
76.0	13,600	13,487	14,554	14875	41.6	16	20
82.7	13,687	13,326	14,550	17922	48.9		
83.0	13,688	15,202	14,485		48.0		
84.3	14,112	13,724	15,030	18563	24.7	14	18
80.7	15,628	14,672	17,075	17151	99.8	617	807
77.0	16,148	16,551	18,390	21907	46.6		
89.3	16,325	15,579	18,647		44.5		
81.0	17,424	17,070	19,910	21153	45.3	16	19
38.0	20,383	21,060	23,628		36.8	963	1097
43.7	7,951	6,918	9,221	9517	89.6	17	22
82.3	10,718	10,303	11,833	12350	69.0	16	20
76.3	11,267	11,369	11,663		33.9	14	17
64.7	12,203	10,873	14,450	17606	46.7	820	973
82.3	12,367	12,359	14,042		51.9		
90.3	12,561	12,959	14,001		54.1		
45.3	14,760	14,629	16,387		58.0		
68.0	16,147	16,466	17,008		80.1	703	900
71.7	23,165	22,997	23,645	26370	47.9	670	860
47.3	25,184	24,478	24,853	26828	42.1	17	22

5.

TROUBLED
WATERS

THE
COMMUNITY
COLLEGE
TRANSFER
SWAMP

To Transfer
Make a Plan

Find the pathways
and ask the right questions

What credits will transfer?

Does your university of choice have any "transfer pathways" in place?

How to balance work and school?

What's the value of getting an associate's degree?

How many students at the community colleges you're considering actually make the jump to a four-year college?

What are the requirements of the *DEPARTMENT* you want to study in?

Remedial classes? What?

Community colleges can propel you toward your career goal if you want a certificate or an associate's degree. And they are a much less expensive way to get these kinds of degrees than the vast majority of for-profit colleges. That's because the government subsidizes community colleges, and they're not expected to earn a profit, so the cost to you is relatively low. On the other end of the cost spectrum, for-profits, as the name implies, need to earn profits for their owners and make all their money from tuition, so the prices they charge to students are often three, five, or even ten times more than community colleges charge students.

Students also choose to go to a two-year college as a stepping-stonc to a four-year institution, and there are good reasons to do that. The first is access. If your grades weren't that great in high school, a community college might be your only option. That's okay. It can give you a chance to leave your spotty high school record behind you and work to be the best student you can. The other reason to consider community college as a first step to a bachelor's degree is cost. Plain and simple, it's apt to be less expensive. That's especially true if you know what you want to major in early on and take courses that are accepted for transfer.

At the same time, we dedicated a whole chapter to this issue (and called it "Troubled Waters"!) because if you intend to earn a four-year degree and you're starting at a two-year college, the truth is that you're in for a challenge. Three-fourths of students who start at a community college with the intention of earning a degree or transferring to a four-year institution end up doing *neither* after six years.[35] Even though 43 percent of the undergraduates in the United States are enrolled at a community college,[36] the process of transferring from a community college to a school where you can earn a bachelor's degree is often needlessly complicated and full of wrong advice and bridges to nowhere.[37]

But here's the good news: it's not impossible, so long as you have a strategy and pay attention to the rules. If you are able to transfer from a community college to a baccalaureate institution, then your odds of earning a bachelor's degree are every bit as good as those of students in the classroom with you at the university.

How to Make the Most of Your Transfer Process

Look at Transfer Pathways

Choose the university you want to transfer into, because then you can find out if there are articulation agreements or "transfer pathways" in place between a community college and the university. According to the American Association of Community Colleges, most if not all community colleges have articulation agreements with regional four-year colleges.[38] These agreements tell you which courses the four-year institutions will accept for credit.

A transfer pathway is like a road map between colleges, and it tells you all the requirements necessary to transfer. For some colleges in some states, it's clear and straightforward. Some universities even have *guaranteed admission* for transfer students who have completed pathways. Pathways are like contracts: they're not available at all colleges, nor in all programs, they're difficult to understand, and they are not always kept up to date. But if an agreement like this is available, it's a good deal and should be part of your strategy. Unfortunately, at many colleges, what you need to do to transfer is not clear and straightforward at all, which is why we think of this whole "transfer to a four-year college" thing as really murky and troubled waters . . . a swamp, and not a walk in the park.

Transfer Credits and Major Requirements

Know the *department* (not just the college) you want to transfer into at the four-year institution. We know you might change your mind, but here's why aiming for a specific program can be a worthwhile part of your strategy.

Credits that are *transferable* contribute to the sixty units you need to be accepted at most universities, but not all transferable credits count toward your major. *Applicable* credits are those that are transferable and also can be applied to meet a requirement in a university program. For example, you need to take a math course to be eligible to transfer, so you pick one from the dozens that are offered, making sure, of course, that it is transferable for credit. (Not all classes are transferable!) Later you find out that your friend, who's also transferring, took a different math class that was not only transferable but also applicable to his major. Both of you will be eligible to transfer, but he'll be further along the major road than you.

Transferable

Applicable

60 Credits

Community college classes might transfer to the university into one of two "buckets." Credits that can be applied to your major put you ahead of the game.

IS AN ASSOCIATE'S DEGREE THE FIRST STEP TO A BACHELOR'S?

Not necessarily. The courses you need to take to transfer may or may not be the same as those you need to earn an associate's degree. Coming from many community colleges, you can transfer to a four-year college without ever having earned an associate's degree. We know, that's confusing, so listen up. You do not need to complete an associate's degree to transfer to a university, but you do need to complete all the admission requirements of the four-year school you want to transfer into. These may or may not lead to an associate's degree.

Generally, community colleges offer a whole range of learning experiences designed for all kinds of people with different goals. There are classes for personal growth (weight training, photography), professional development (accounting principles, technical writing), and vocational training (geographic information systems, computer systems engineering). If your goal is to transfer to another college, you can't take just any classes. You have to take classes that the university you're transferring into recognizes for credit.

Partner with the Community College and Check out the Department

Alison Kadlec and Jyoti Gupta of *Public Agenda* write: "The best information about what will transfer is the department in the university to which you want to transfer. In many cases, even university advisors may not be well informed about what courses specific departments will accept."[39] So be persistent, ask questions, and go directly to the university department.

We're not just saying use the resources of the community college; we're saying make your community college your *partner*. We mean it. According to a research study by Public Agenda, finding accurate advice at the time you need it may be hard to come by, but students also report that there are many dedicated people in academic departments, counseling, career, and transfer centers who helped them every step of the way.[40] The trick is, you have to find them, and sometimes that's not as easy as it sounds. Some of our community college experts told us that advisors, though well-meaning, are often not well informed about the requirements for transfer. They also emphasized that the best place to get advice about the credits that count at the university is at the university department, not the general counseling offices.

Use the Available Resources

Don't be shy; you have a legitimate foot on both campuses because you're a current student at one and a prospective student at the other, and showing interest can increase your chances of being accepted. Make connecting—with university advisors, recruiters, counselors, and particularly personnel in the academic department to which you want to transfer—part of your strategy. Make time to do it, whether in person, by phone, by email, or by chat; however it works, build that bridge. In the end, you will have gained a degree as well as a whole lot of experience navigating bureaucracies that often have good people working in challenging conditions.

Prepare for the Math Assessment

If you did not pass Algebra 2 in high school, you have to do it in college, which is a pain. If it's not too late for you to meet that requirement before you graduate from high school, do it. If that's not in the cards, do not give up on yourself, please. It would be, as the old saying goes, like cutting off your nose to spite your face. Who would do that?

While you may be able to graduate from high school without passing Algebra 2 and with some pretty rough writing skills, a high school diploma doesn't make you college-ready.

Plan to Transfer in Two Years

We know most people don't do that for a whole lot of reasons. But full-time students have a much better chance of graduating than students who are part-time, so do what you can to go full-time. As

---

If My Goal Is a BA, Should I Get an AA, Just in Case?

It depends. On one hand, research by the Community College Research Center and Public Agenda suggests that it's a good idea because, statistically, with an AA or AS already under your belt, you're more likely to get a BA or BS.[41] This may be because you've proven to yourself (and everyone else) that you can achieve your goal step by step, so getting your BA or BS is one more step along a path you've already proven you can travel. Additional research suggests that the AA can give you a leg up in the job market until you get your BA.[42] If you want to earn a BA, our advice is to be as strategic as you can as you reach for that goal.

much as humanly possible, work less at a paying job and take a full load each semester. Here's one more tricky bit of math you should know about: Most colleges treat twelve credits as full-time, but this is not enough to graduate in four years because most degrees (and transfer requirements) are sixty credits. So if you want to earn sixty credits in four semesters, you need to take fifteen credits each term.

Lots of community college students work on top of going to school, so you won't feel alone on that score. Fifteen hours of work seems to be the magic number; too much more than that and you could be in danger of dropping out because the load is too great. Even if it means making some less-than-desirable sacrifices (a little more time living at home or skipping a few shopping trips), trust that it's worth it in the long run.

At the same time, we don't want to suggest that speed trumps learning. If fifteen credits are too many for you, maybe you can pick up six credits each summer. It's a bit of a balancing act, because statistically you're more likely to transfer if you stay on track. At the same time, the stronger your foundation, the more prepared you will be for your upper-division courses.

Map Your Path

Our experts suggest that you plan the courses you will take every semester until you transfer and take English and math in your first term even if they aren't your favorites. The truth is, they're a good

Frustrated? You're Not Alone

"A common source of frustration among students is the lack of coordination and communication among the various college offices that provide information and services. Combined with the out-of-date, unclear, or incorrect information often provided by these offices, this situation results in the waste of students' valuable time. Having to deal with the many offices responsible for different aspects of college operations and services is intimidating and confusing for most students."

SOURCE: PUBLIC AGENDA, "STUDENT VOICES ON THE HIGHER EDUCATION PATHWAY"

indicator of college success, and you need a strong foundation in both to graduate from college. Ask your partners at the community college counseling or transfer center for a "program map" to help you schedule your whole journey. This involves checking the requirements in the catalog, seeing what's available in the class schedule, and putting it all down semester by semester in your planner. Confirm your plan with the department advisors at your four-year college. The sample map on page 194 is similar to the tool used by Florida State University to help a business major map his path.[43]

An Academic Map for Transferring

This map is an example of a term-by-term course schedule for business majors, and though it's not specific to your community college, it gives you an idea of how to organize yourself each term. The sample schedule on the left serves as a general guideline to help students build a full schedule (fifteen credits) each term, and the milestones listed to the right are designed to keep them on course to graduate from a four-year college two years after they transfer. Several of our experts warned that keeping on course is up to you. As Dr. Lawrence Abele from Florida State University put it, "It is highly likely that the community college advisor will try to enroll the student in easier or fewer courses, but it will put the student behind or they end up having to take additional courses that they wouldn't have had to take if they met the milestones when they were scheduled. I find that

What Are Remedial, Developmental, and Accelerated Courses?

Remedial and developmental classes are classes that the college offers that are designed to get you ready for college-level work. They don't contribute to your degree or certificate, and that seems kind of weird, because after all, you'll be taking the class at the college, so you're probably thinking, It's a college class, right? Wrong. It's a class that teaches you stuff you need to know before you can succeed at college-level work.

Accelerated classes are those that combine remedial and college-level courses, and research suggests that you'll do a whole lot better in these courses than you would in the sequential remedial courses. If you can, get yourself in accelerated classes.[44]

Are You Making Milestones?

A Business Major's Sample Courses	Credit Hours	Area*
Term 1		
English Comp	3	B
Algebra	3	B
Microeconomics	3	M
Social Science	3	GE
Elective	3	GE
TOTAL HOURS	15	
Term 2		
English Lit	3	
Calculus	3	
Macroeconomics	3	
Elective	3	
Physical Science	3	
TOTAL HOURS	15	
Term 3		
Statistics	3	
Financial Accounting Principles I	3	
Microcomputer Applications	3	
Humanities course	3	
Elective	3	
TOTAL HOURS	15	
Term 4		
Managerial Accounting Principles II	3	
Business Elective	3	
History	3	
Foreign Language	3	
Marketing	3	
TOTAL HOURS	15	

*How do the credits count? Toward general education requirements (GE),
major requirements (M), or both (B)?*

Create a plan like this one, adapted to your major. Our experts strongly recommend that you have the departmental advisors at both the two-year and four-year schools sign off on your plan—and an actual signature would be best. This will allow you to be sure that you are meeting all the "area" requirements (different at each college) and taking the prerequisites necessary to get into upper level classes.

THE *OTHER* HELPFUL TOOL COLLEGE GUIDE

many advisors don't have high enough expectations, especially for students who want a four-year degree."

Danger Zones—and How to Navigate Them

1. At many community colleges, there are not enough classes to go around, and most colleges start registration months before classes start (especially for fall). Get advice about which classes to select early (as in very early—months before school starts), then get up at the crack of dawn and stand in line or go online when registration opens. We know that sounds crazy, but *do it*. The courses that everyone needs in order to transfer will fill up fast and leave the latecomers picking up doughnut crumbs along with the

What Is General Education (GE)?

General education is a pattern of courses that generally form the foundation of a four-year degree. These courses may be taken at either a two-year or four-year college. GE almost always includes English composition (aka English comp), social and behavioral science, and a humanities course, but there is no single common group of classes that make up GE, and many colleges have dozens of classes that may fulfill each requirement.

Don't plan your classes by scrolling through the college catalog to see what looks interesting. That would be like walking up to a gigantic buffet table when you're hungry. Without any guidance, you're likely to start with a chocolate éclair when what you really need is a taco with plenty of cheese.

Placement Tests

The test? What test? We know—you thought you dodged the test business by going the community college route. The thing is, because community colleges are largely open admission, students can have very different skill levels. You know that because you've been going to school for a lot of years already and you can see that not everyone learns at the same rate.

The placement test is designed to find out where you are in some basic skills, like reading, writing, math, and critical thinking. So take it seriously. We mean *really* seriously. Do not walk in tired or hungry or distracted. Ask if there are any test preparation materials you can review. (There almost always are—so be sure to ask. If they say there aren't any, ask why not.) Take the test when you're rested and as prepared as possible so that you do as well as you can. The better you do on that assessment, the fewer semesters you will have to spend meeting the remediation requirement. With the results in, register for the highest-level classes the school will allow you to enroll in (accelerated ones if possible). You want to do this for two reasons: studies show that people do better when they're challenged, and since remedial/developmental classes don't count toward your degree, you want to move through them as quickly as your skill level will allow. At the same time, don't pretend to know something you don't! Trust us, faking it (or worse, cheating) will come back to haunt you. It's much better to do what it takes to learn the material.

leftover classes. Registration woes are one reason most students don't succeed with their plan to transfer.

2. Developmental coursework is a challenge because it's frustrating to graduate from high school and be stuck in remedial college courses. That's why our experts strongly recommend that you try to get into *accelerated* courses, because they combine remedial and college-level work and you're much more likely to be successful in these more challenging courses.[45] Keep your eyes on the prize! These courses will improve your skills and make the rest of college easier.

3. Limited resources at the community college can knock you off track. While we suggested that you ask for help, we know that that might not be easy because of staffing challenges, particularly at peak registration periods. Persist. Plan in advance so that you're not going when the whole madding crowd is trying to get in to talk to someone. Go to those centers; make an appointment with advisors on both campuses. This is not bothering people; it's taking initiative and it's what successful people do.

4. Form a posse: motivate each other and study together. You know that 80 percent of your colleagues at the community college intend to transfer. You know most of them won't, so aim to be one of the ones who do and get together with a group of friends from your biology or economics class to study together. Persistence is the key; friends, study buddies, and fellow motivators help.

5. Connect with the university you'd like to transfer to, and make an appointment with the department you'd like to transfer to.

A Quick Checklist to Prepare for Community College

1. Check to see if your community college has a transfer agreement with the four-year college you want to go to. Ideally, the transfer agreement will include your intended major.

2. If there is a guaranteed transfer pathway, follow it. Confirm your courses with the department advisor at the four-year university.

3. Do not waste your time taking classes that neither transfer nor get you closer to an associate's degree.

4. You do not need an associate's degree to transfer to a university, but you do need to meet all transfer requirements, and an AA or AS may give you a boost.[46]

5. Try to take sixty units or credits in two years. Get in, get out, and stay the course all the way to your BA or BS.

6. Do not wait until you actually finish all of your coursework to apply to the baccalaureate university! Many university deadlines are in fall or early winter. Apply so that you can begin at your new school as soon as possible after completing all the coursework you need to transfer.

6.

THE
HERE
AND
NOW

//////////////////////////////////

TAKING STOCK
OF WHERE
YOU ARE

Your
Plan

Your
Resources

Go
Time

Your
Support

Your
Timeline

In this chapter, we want you just to think about why you're going to college. Think about your goals and what you like to do. Think about what you're doing now to get to where you want to be in the future. We know you've heard this before, but it's true, so it bears repeating: you're at a stage in your life where you're making decisions that will affect the rest of your life. If that seems intense, and even scary at times, it is. The most important concept to get your mind around is your purpose for going to college at all. Before you begin this chapter, answer the questions at the end of Chapter 2 (page 37) about why you're going to college. People who get through the bumpy bits and all the way to graduation have a purpose for being there. The first part of this chapter is about knowing what needs to be done; the second part has a couple of ideas that are motivating to students who are willing to work to achieve their goals.

THE KNOWLEDGE TO SUCCEED

Once you know why you're going to college, you need to do four things: (1) make a plan, (2) use all available resources, (3) get help, and (4) stick to a timeline.

Make a Plan (Ahem—a Really Precise, Realistic, Smart Plan)

Achieving a goal, *any* goal, requires a strategy. Athletes don't just get in shape; they develop specific objectives. They work out to develop certain abilities and sets of muscles, and then they measure the increase in their skills and strength daily, weekly, and monthly to achieve their fitness goals. They adjust their nutrition, they watch videos of themselves performing, they take time to recover from injuries. It's a whole regimen that hinges on what experts call "SMART" objectives: steps that are *specific, measurable, achievable, realistic,* and *timely.* The thing about SMART objectives is that they're not vague. An athlete doesn't say "I want to get in shape" and then leave it at that. An athlete works with her coach to outline a specific workout (four-minute wind sprints for forty-five minutes) that she'll do during a scheduled time (4:30 P.M. on Mondays, Wednesdays, and Fridays) to achieve a realistic goal (a five-minute mile by the track meet on August 1).

You need to do basically the same thing—only *mental*—to get ready for, get into, and get all the way through college. Using SMART goals can apply to all kinds of things, from completing the painstaking application process to filling out financial aid forms to making sure you're not just persisting in college but also making progress.

Remediation Is an Obstacle

You've taken college preparatory courses and your GPA is okay, but statistics suggest that six out of ten seniors will not be ready for college-level work in either English or math (or both).[47] That's crummy for a lot of reasons, and many of them aren't your fault. In fact, the problems may well have begun a long, long time ago when you couldn't understand what Mrs. Snarlypants was talking about and the whole situation made you decide that you were math-phobic or you couldn't learn to spell.

Nationwide, the biggest gatekeeper to college is Algebra 2. If you think this isn't fair, you have a lot of very well-educated researchers on your side who are thinking the same thing.[48] On the other hand, it's one of those obstacles that you have to deal with. Spend that energy! It will be well worth it, because if you can pass into college-level math *before* you go to college, you won't be wasting time or money taking classes in college that don't count toward your degree.

Same deal with English, though it's a little messier because many students also speak another language, which is an advantage in the long run. Read everything; write all the time. Ask for help. Grammar matters, spelling matters, and spell-check doesn't always know what you ~~mint to right~~ meant to write. No matter your major, communication skill is the multi-stranded thread that makes it possible for people far away from each other to share ideas and to work together in a global knowledge economy.

Wherever you are in your high school career, it's not too late or too early to plan. Every year take the most rigorous courses available. Seek academic help when you need it, because grades are one of the most important parts of your application. Get involved in ways that matter to you. And *take math every year*. No kidding. Taking it every year will significantly reduce the likelihood of getting to college without college-level math skills.

You see that there are quite a few tests listed here. The PSAT and PLAN are optional and cannot be used for your college record, but they're good practice, and the more you practice, the better you'll do. Nobody likes taking tests, and tests aren't, in fact, the best predictor of how you'll do in college, but let's be honest: standardized

College-going Activities to Plan

9th Grade Stay on the math track. Plan to complete Algebra 2 by 11th grade.

Get involved: volunteer, join groups, athletics, student government, or other activities.

Map the classes you expect to take before you graduate. Find out which AP or IB courses are taught at your school. Build a schedule that will include several of them.

10th Grade Take the PSAT or PLAN tests. They're optional and do not influence your college record, but they're good practice for the SAT and ACT tests you'll take next year. (Generally the PSAT score counts for the National Merit Scholarship competition only if you've taken the test your junior year.)

Are you taking or can you take AP classes? Talk to your teachers about taking the SAT subject tests. Practice tests are available from the College Board.

11th Grade Register with Collegeboard.com and SAT Question of the Day. Registering allows for electronic registration, and the SAT Question of the Day is good practice.

Take the PSAT in fall. By December the PSAT scores are in, and they are an excellent indicator of how you'll do on the SAT without additional study-ing. Also, the results show you what you did wrong, so you can review your errors and get help if you're making an error you don't understand. For the National Merit Scholarship competition, this is the year to take it.

Seriously look at the college landscape; start making your "big list" of colleges.

Take SAT subject tests in spring, if needed. The College Board has a sepa-rate book with a sample of each test, which you should take prior to taking the real subject test.

Prepare a résumé to help those writing your recommendations.

Attend college fairs.

Attend a financial aid workshop at the school or library.

Take the SAT or ACT in spring.

THE
OTHER
HELPFUL
TOOL
COLLEGE
GUIDE

Summer	Study for the SAT or ACT if you're planning to take it again in fall of senior year.
	Draft college essays.
	Visit possible college choices.
12th Grade	Narrow the big list down to four to ten colleges using the "four-way fit" and rankings worksheet.
	If you're thinking about early decision or early action, your timeline is short. (See Chapter 9.)
	Register for the Common Application if the colleges you're applying to use it.
	Put application deadlines on your calendar and submit applications on time!
	Follow both your high school's procedure and the colleges' requirements for sending recommendations and transcripts to colleges.
	Send your SAT or ACT scores through official channels with each application.
	Work on FAFSA 4caster (see Chapter 10) over winter break.
	Complete the FAFSA in January or as early as you can. Early birds have more options.
	CSS Financial Aid Profile is due in February—not all colleges require this, but if they do, they won't give you any funding unless it is filled out.
	Follow up with each college website to ensure your application materials have been received. Recommendations and transcripts go to the college directly from the recommender and your high school.
	March or April—If they haven't already, decisions will arrive; financial aid packages come, too.
	May 1—commit to a college.
	Take any required placement tests.
	Confirm with your high school that your final transcript goes to your college.
	Diligently read all communication from your college so you don't miss sign-ups for campus housing, orientation, registration, and other important notices.

THE
OTHER
HELPFUL
TOOL
COLLEGE
GUIDE

Are Standardized Tests Predictors of How You'll Do in College?

Nope. They aren't. Some colleges made the submission of standardized test scores optional for applicants and then they analyzed the results. "With almost 123,000 students at 33 widely differing institutions, the differences between submitters and non-submitters are five one-hundredths of a GPA point, and six-tenths of one percent in graduation rates. By any standard, these are trivial differences," conclude the study's authors. They go on to suggest that it's your high school grades that are the best predictors for your college success: "A clear message: hard work and good grades in high school matter, and they matter a lot."[49] If you want to find a bunch of colleges where test scores are optional, check out the website Fair Test, maintained by the National Center for Fair and Open Testing: www.fairtest.org/university/optional.

tests are part of the landscape right now, so take the test challenge like an athlete, and prepare. Build muscle and speed. Fine-tune your game. All that happens with practice, and it's our guess that 90 percent of the students reading this book will be able to pop their scores significantly by studying an hour a day during the summer or taking a free online course. Don't stop working out when the workout gets hard; that's when you're building your academic muscle.

Use All Available Resources

The most basic resource to which most people have regular access is the Internet. There's so much out there you can practically get seasick thinking about it. One resource that puts it all together is the College App Map.

After you've cruised the Web looking at college stuff, you might feel better, but you might feel worse because there's so much information out there you may feel like you're drowning. That's why you need to ask for help from someone who has been there. These resources are all over the place: your high school, your community, your family, your place of worship, the local public colleges. The thing is, they won't necessarily come to you, so take action and reach out.

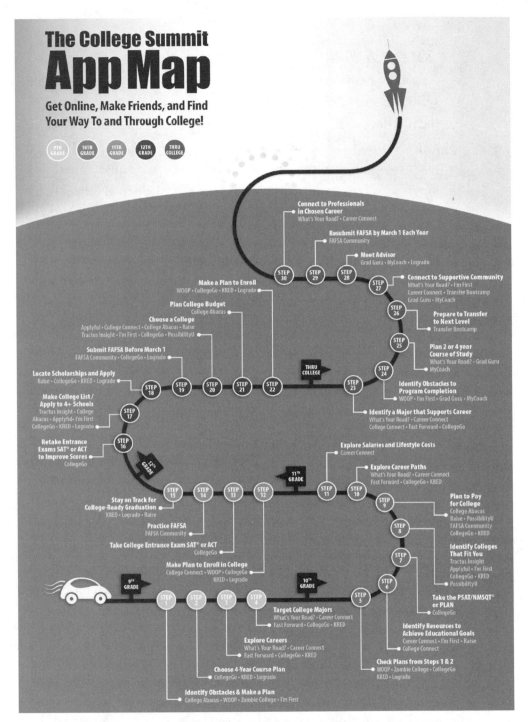

The College Summit
App Map

**Get Online, Make Friends, and Find
Your Way To and Through College!**

9TH GRADE · 10TH GRADE · 11TH GRADE · 12TH GRADE · THRU COLLEGE

Connect to Professionals in Chosen Career
What's Your Road? · Career Connect

Resubmit FAFSA by March 1 Each Year
FAFSA Community

Meet Advisor
Grad Guru · MyCoach · Logrado

Connect to Supportive Community
What's Your Road? · I'm First
Career Connect · Transfer Bootcamp
Grad Guru · MyCoach

Make a Plan to Enroll
WOOP · CollegeGo · KRED · Logrado

Plan College Budget
College Abacus

Prepare to Transfer to Next Level
Transfer Bootcamp

Choose a College
Applyful · College Connect · College Abacus · Raise
Tractus Insight · I'm First · CollegeGo · PossibilityU

Plan 2 or 4 year Course of Study
What's Your Road? · Grad Guru
MyCoach

Submit FAFSA Before March 1
FAFSA Community · CollegeGo · Logrado

Locate Scholarships and Apply
Raise · CollegeGo · KRED · Lograro

Identify Obstacles to Program Completion
WOOP · I'm First · Grad Guru · MyCoach

Make College List / Apply to 4+ Schools
Tractus Insight · College
Abacus · Applyful · I'm First
CollegeGo · KRED · Lograro

Identify a Major that Supports Career
What's Your Road? · Career Connect
College Connect · Fast Forward · CollegeGo

Retake Entrance Exams SAT or ACT to Improve Scores
CollegeGo

Explore Salaries and Lifestyle Costs
Career Connect

Explore Career Paths
What's Your Road? · Career Connect
Fast Forward · CollegeGo · KRED

Stay on Track for College-Ready Graduation
KRED · Lograro · Raise

Plan to Pay for College
College Abacus
Raise · PossibilityU
FAFSA Community
CollegeGo · KRED

Practice FAFSA
FAFSA Community

Take College Entrance Exam SAT or ACT
CollegeGo

Identify Colleges That Fit You
Tractus Insight
Applyful · I'm First
CollegeGo · KRED
PossibilityU

Make Plan to Enroll in College
College Connect · WOOP · CollegeGo
KRED · Lograro

Take the PSAT/NMSQT or PLAN
CollegeGo

Target College Majors
What's Your Road? · Career Connect
Fast Forward · CollegeGo · KRED

Identify Resources to Achieve Educational Goals
Career Connect · I'm First · Raise
College Connect

Explore Careers
What's Your Road? · Career Connect
Fast Forward · CollegeGo · KRED

Check Plans from Steps 1 & 2
WOOP · Zombie College · CollegeGo
KRED · Lograro

Choose 4-Year Course Plan
CollegeGo · KRED · Lograro

Identify Obstacles & Make a Plan
College Abacus · WOOP · Zombie College · I'm First

Steps 1–30 · 9TH GRADE · 10TH GRADE · 11TH GRADE · 12TH GRADE · THRU COLLEGE

The College App Map is connected to Facebook and provides a list of thirty
steps, or milestones you have to achieve each year in high school and college
to stay on the path to success. It also has a lot of links to award-winning apps
that'll help you keep track of your progress. Even if you don't want to download
all the free apps, it's a good overview of the steps you need to take to get all the
way through college. WWW.COLLEGEAPPMAP.ORG

Ask for Help

As you get more and more clued in to the college-going scene, it might seem like some kids started building their résumé s in preschool. By the time they're sixteen, they've been captain of a varsity team, served as president of four different clubs, performed at Carnegie Hall, and practically cured cancer. That's probably not you because, frankly, it's not most kids. But some students do have more help than others. They weren't born smarter, but they were born with connections, and that's not something they earned. They have parents who know the drill; they have counselors who know their name; someone in the family knows someone who knows someone who gets them the coveted summer internship. If that's not you, *you are not alone!*

Think about it: the kid who has it all has help. It's something scientists call social capital. Wealthy families have more than money: they have connections to summer jobs, the kids can afford to take unpaid internships, and they might have international experience because instead of working all summer they're traveling. Most of us don't have these kinds of opportunities or connections. Most of us have our families and our schools. We have our neighborhoods, churches, employers, and friends, all networks that are incredibly valuable to tap as you're preparing for college.

So that's where you start. If someone in your family went to college, get them on your team right away—ask if they are willing to answer questions you might have about applying and going to college. If you're the first in your family to go to college, you have to go a little further afield, but we're betting there are one or two people you've never thought to ask. On the College Board's website (bigfuture.collegeboard.org), click on "Get Started," then "Building a Support Network," then "The Scoop: What's a Mentor and How Do I Get One?" The site also hosts several videos to help you find people in your community to help you.

At your high school, even before you meet with your counselor, talk to your current teachers, the previous year's teachers, the librarian, and staff in the college and career centers if your school has them. Find

Choosing the Right College

Start with the exercises in Chapter 3 that guide you to the type of college that's right for you. Then use our rankings (Chapter 4) and the worksheets to pare down that confusing universe of all colleges to a manageable number that appear to be four-way fits for you. Getting down to the four to ten that you will actually apply to requires that you explore each college's website, but you can also get quick answers to a few of the questions you have from these sites.

> What race/ethnicity/age are the students? collegeresults.org (Ed Trust)

> What does the average student borrow? collegecost.ed.gov/scorecard (White House)

> What majors are available? nces.ed.gov/collegenavigator (National Center for Education Statistics)

> What about campus life? bigfuture.collegeboard.org (College Board)

out if there's a college-bound or community mentorship program that you could join. If you're in a community that has a National College Advising Corps, iMentor, or one of the many local or regional college access programs, you're in luck. Make the most of it.

Even if there isn't a formal program at your school, you can be proactive. When recruiters from public or not-for-profit colleges come to your school, make an effort to meet them because even though it sounds audacious, they're on your campus looking for students like you. Bring them a copy of your transcript and include your email address on it so they can get back to you. Recruiters love meeting students like you, so ask for their card and make them part of your team.

Prepare to see your counselor as if you're paying for the time she'll spend with you and you want to make the most of it. This is not as easy as it sounds. If you go to a big public high school, the average counselor is responsible for over 450 students, so he's likely to be overwhelmed and might not know who you are, let alone much about you.[50] In addition to there being few counselors for many students, counselors in public high schools only spend about 27 percent of their time on college conversations; at private high schools, it's twice that, with 54 percent of their time dedicated to college guidance. And many wealthy schools even have specific college counselors whose *only* job is to help students get into college. There's that social capital at work. To add to the challenge, Public Agenda has published a report on the state of advising in the United States, and overall it's pretty bad.[51] Sixty percent of young adults (ages twenty-two to thirty) rated their high school guidance counselors as fair or poor; in fact, high school counselors were seen as less helpful than teachers.

So there you have it: a pretty bleak picture. That's one of the reasons you will need support beyond the counseling office. When you show up with your questions ready to go, your counselor will know that you're a serious student with a no-nonsense goal, but even if she turns out to be a great resource for you, remember that ratio of one counselor to 450 students. Even a great counselor can't keep you on track on a day-to-day basis.

Finding help elsewhere is another task for your to-do list. We've put together a few questions at the end of this chapter to get you thinking about conversations you could have with people, but you should know in advance that not everyone will have the time, energy, or inclination to help you. Don't be dissuaded! You're on a mission here. It may be one of the most important conversations you have. There's a good chance that even if the person you ask can't help you, she might be able to give you a recommendation or two. Even by asking, you're growing your networking skills, which will help you become successful at every stage of your life.

Make a Timeline

A timeline is different from a plan, because a plan is what you'll do and a timeline tells you when you'll do it. The application deadline is a big one, but it's not the only deadline that matters, so you need to make sure you're aware of all of them—your admission and the money to pay for it is on the line. Really!

Here's the big picture: some colleges (not all) are getting hundreds or even thousands more applications—from *fully qualified* students—than they can accommodate. They don't need to keep the door open one minute longer than their website indicates because they have plenty of applicants to choose from.

But say you make the first deadline and then—hurray!—you get the happy email and you're in! It's not yet time to sit back on your laurels, because now there are the commitment deadlines. If you miss one of those, you could be counted out even though you were accepted.

This sounds like the stuff of nightmares, so let's think about it for a minute. Students can attend only one school, but they apply to several. College administrators know that not every student they admit will choose to attend their college, so they want a few assurances that you're as serious about considering them as they are about evaluating, admitting, and enrolling you.

This is why colleges require a few more steps to complete the enrollment process. Almost all colleges require that you commit by May 1, but in addition to meeting that deadline, some colleges require that you register for orientation or submit an enrollment deposit. All colleges will need your final transcript, which will be sent by the school over the summer and will show your successful graduation and your final GPA. Don't let that be a surprise to anyone. Unfortunately, we know that some students don't share everything with their parents. If you have failed a required class, for example, it's possible—even likely—that your admission will be rescinded. Your final semester grades should not include anything lower than a C, and only one or at most two of those. D's, F's, and for some schools even C-minuses risk the chance of the college rescinding your acceptance. After all, from their point of view, it looks like you ran out of steam. If a failing grade is explainable, don't wait for the college to contact you; let them know what happened.

The financial aid deadlines are also important to put on your timeline because the forms (which you'll read all about in Chapter 8) take planning to fill out, and some of the aid money that schools can give out is distributed on a first-come, first-served basis for qualified applicants.

This whole process sounds competitive, and it is. But when you think about it, it's also aiming to be fair, because every student has to meet every requirement by a specified deadline.

List Your Challenges

Feeling intimidated? Overwhelmed? When you think about college, does your brain flood with a million little things that all seem to be standing in your way? Don't panic. You're right on track. Lots of students feel that way, so researchers have developed a lot of techniques to help you deal with it.[52] One is called "mental contrasting," which is a way of thinking about a positive outcome while you're also thinking about knocking out the stuff that stands in your way. You're not just skipping merrily down the yellow brick road to an "everything is going to be fine in the end" dream—you're actually thinking about all the potholes you have to deal with on the way.

The idea is that thinking positively, smiling through adversity, and dreaming are great, but all that happy talk doesn't actually deal with the stark realities in front of you. With mental contrasting, you keep your eye on the goal but don't ignore the obstacles in your way. Your goal is college. Now we're asking you to list every last thing you can think of that is hard or challenging in your life and all the things you expect will be hard or challenging about getting to college and graduating. Your list will be different from ours, but here are a few ideas to get you started.

> **Family.** Families can be challenging in a whole lot of ways. Some parents aren't sure going to college is a good idea. Maybe they're afraid it'll cost too much. Or they're afraid you'll go too far away from home. Other parents are pretty sure college is a good idea, but don't know how to help you get there. Maybe they're harping on you constantly. Maybe they don't understand what's involved. Some teenagers feel overwhelmed with attention, and some feel like they didn't get enough. Either way, it's a challenge.

> **Money.** College is expensive. Often it's super-duper ridiculously absurdly expensive. In a lot of families, money is tight and parents can't contribute much to tuition. Maybe your family could use your salary if you just went to work full-time instead of going to college. Maybe

<continued>

you're afraid that if you go to college, your brother/sister/cousin won't be able to go. Maybe your family never talks about money, ever—it's like a big secret—but now you need all that secret info for the FAFSA.

> **Grades.** We know, the whole grade point average thing is stressful, but grades are important because they're an indicator of some combination of effort and ability. They also show a trend over time, and sometimes they show a pothole that is, in fact, explainable if you were going through a tough emotional or personal time.

> **Expectations.** Maybe someone in the neighborhood is wondering *What makes him think he's so special? Does he think he's better than everyone else?* Or maybe it's the opposite—maybe your family expects you practically to be the next president of the United States or their ticket to new riches. Managing other people's expectations can be tough.

> **Motivation.** You have stuff to do that you know you should be doing, but you'd rather be gaming. Or browsing. Or doing anything besides thinking about applying for college. Srsly.

> **Procrastination.** It's a habit. Habits can be broken. Break it. Today. Then it'll be easier to beat it tomorrow and the next day.

> **Tests.** Yuck. Nobody likes them. They're snapshots, not the whole picture.

> **AP classes.** Why? What's the point? Your friends have about half the homework you do.

> **Bad stuff.** It happens. Sometimes a lot.

> **Juggling act.** Too many obligations every day. School and work and family. Sometimes it's too much.

> **Technology.** You have a computer at home, but no printer, and anyway the computer is so old and slow it makes you crazy.

> **Friends.** You love them, but sometimes there's drama and everyone wants a little piece of your time and by the end of the day, there's nothing left.

> **Extracurricular.** You don't have any, and you know you're supposed to for scholarships and all that.

> **Work.** With all the hours you're working, there's not enough time to study. Or play sports. Or volunteer.

> **Volunteer.** The thing is, you would like to volunteer, but you just haven't. Or maybe the whole idea is a little frightening. Either way, you haven't done it.

Listing the obstacles in your way is a good exercise, because by getting them out of your head and onto a piece of paper, you can (1) ask for help and (2) strategize.

Sample Senior Timeline Table

College Name			
Take ACT or SAT			
Application deadlines			
ACT/SAT test scores sent to colleges			
Letters of recommendation deadline			
Follow-up with recommenders			
Letters of recommendation sent			
Counselor and school report deadline			
Follow up with counselor			
Program letters?			
Supplementary materials?			
Placement test?			
Interview?			
Financial Aid (FAFSA available)	*January 1*	*January 1*	*January 1*
Institutional Aid Form (CSS)?			
FAFSA due for financial aid			
Commitment deadlines	*May 1*	*May 1*	*May 1*

A GROWTH MIND-SET AND THE GRIT TO SUCCEED

You want to know what makes some people find success and achieve goals?

Effort. Trying harder. And in trying, they get smarter.

Maybe you don't believe that. Maybe you think that some people were just born smart and have an unfair advantage when it comes to mental muscles. Luckily for you, that is not entirely correct.

Carol Dweck, a psychology professor at Stanford University, has spent the last four decades doing research on how people learn.[53] She and the many researchers who work with her have found that people approach a challenge with one of two different mind-sets. Some people have "fixed mind-sets." They believe that qualities (like being smart) are carved in stone, which is to say you're born with the attributes you have and that's it—there's nothing you can do about it. Other people have "growth mind-sets." They believe that basic qualities, like being smart, "are things you can cultivate through your efforts." In other words, they believe that *trying* to get smart will actually make you smarter. As Dweck writes, "Even geniuses have to work hard to develop their abilities and make their contributions."[54]

During a presentation at Stanford's School of Education, Dweck put a slide up with one word on it: *YET!*[55] It's a word that, she said, you should use frequently, as in "I don't know YET!" or "I haven't mastered that skill YET!" According to Dweck, you can develop a growth mind-set by welcoming the struggle—and then persisting, puzzling, and fighting hard until you solve the problem at hand. When you encounter a question you can't answer or a problem that is difficult to solve, you might say to yourself: *I haven't built the brain muscle to answer that one . . . YET!* Which brings us to grit.

Getting from where you are to where you want to be takes effort. We're calling that "grit" because that's what researchers have been calling it. In 2013, Angela Duckworth, who is a psychologist and neuroscientist, won a MacArthur Foundation "genius" grant for "transforming our understanding of the roles that grit and self-control play in educational achievement." Check out her TED talk, or visit her website at the University of Pennsylvania, where you can take a test to see what your grit level is.[56]

Grit is perseverance. It's sticking to something through thick and thin. Even when it feels like everything is going horribly. Even when you feel like a huge failure. Even when you'd rather lie on the couch and watch reruns of pretty much anything instead of facing the real world. Getting up and fighting one more day? That's grit. The Duckworth Lab defines it as "the tendency to sustain interest in and effort toward very long-term goals."

When it comes to getting into college—and then making it through to graduation—you need a lion's share of grit, which, just like a growth mind-set, can be nurtured and encouraged. It doesn't necessarily get easier, but if you practice, you'll definitely get better at persevering. Now we've come full circle, back to the beginning: it might be true that you should "reach for the stars" and "believe in yourself" and all that jazz, but you should know right now that it's also going to take a whole lot of hard work. Sometimes it's going to be a slog. Sometimes you'll feel like crying. Sometimes you're going to feel like a failure. Trust us, *everyone* feels that way. But the ones who succeed keep fighting.

You Have to Fail to Succeed

Do not get mired in the idea that you will perish if you fail. You won't. Everyone who has ever done anything of value has failed at least once, and more often they've failed multiple times. In Silicon Valley, there's so much failure going on that the advice is to fail early, fail often, learn from your experience, and move on. The only thing you don't do is give up.[57] Before Thomas Edison figured out how to make an electric light go on and stay on, he developed 3,000 theories, and 2,998 of them didn't work. As Edison said, "Opportunity is missed by most people because it is dressed in overalls and looks like work."

Asking for Help

These questions are for brainstorming, not for asking all at once. Get your thoughts together first and do some research before you bring up a topic as a great unknown.

Parents

Talk about your goals for yourself. Ask what their goals are for you.

Talk about why college is the right choice for you.

Show them your purpose statement (Chapter 2).

Talk about your list of challenges. Are there any they can help you with? (see pages 213–16)

Ask what you can do to help them out.

Have a conversation about your timeline and deadlines.

Talk to them about the FAFSA (page 275).

Talk about affordability.

Teachers

Talk about your goals for yourself. Would they write a recommendation?

Do they have any career advice? Do they know someone you might be able to talk to in a career field that interests you?

Can they recommend someone to help you with the application process?

Would they be willing to proofread your essays?

Public Colleges

Attend a financial aid seminar. (Even if you don't plan to attend that college, go. You're welcome—public tax dollars are supporting this college.)

THE *OTHER* HELPFUL TOOL COLLEGE GUIDE

Asking for Help

Contact the admission or recruitment office. Ask any question you have.

Counselors/Advisors in Your High School

Share your college goals with them. Would they write a recommendation?

Look at your academic and extracurricular record together. Show them the SAT/ACT score range of the colleges you're thinking about. Ask for advice.

If any schools require interviews, ask if they can set up a mock interview for you to practice.

Friends

Ask friends to set up goals with you. Motivate each other.

Take the SAT or ACT together. Do the same with placement tests.

Go to the library and search for scholarships together.

Read each other's essays. Their win is your win.

Volunteer together.

Create study groups.

Share your calendars and keep each other on track.

A College Graduate

Ask what they wish they had known.

Did they face some of the same obstacles you are now facing?

Can they tutor you or help you find a tutor?

Would they read your essays? Would they write a recommendation?

Can they help keep you on track?

Do they have career advice?

What motivated them to stay on track?

7.

TASTING VICTORY

PREPARING TO SUCCEED

"Doing everything possible means being hard on yourself if you have to be."

Graduating from high school isn't the same as being ready for college.

Or, here's another way to think about it: if you're not prepared to take college-level courses the moment you step onto campus on your very first day of college, there's a good chance you won't graduate at all. *Ever*.

Harsh, right?

But it's true. Nearly 40 percent of students placed in remedial classes at a community college never even complete their remedial classes, much less earn a degree, according to a 2011 report by Complete College America.[58] Less than a quarter of community college students who begin their studies in remedial courses, and little more than a third of

four-year students who do the same, *ever actually walk across that graduation stage*. A lot of them get bumped out of the running before school even starts. (Every year, thousands of students who are accepted into college but placed into remedial classes simply never show up on the first day of school, according to the same report.)

So, basically, here's the reality: If you get to college and you're in remedial classes, don't panic. It means you're a survivor. You can beat the odds. Follow the advice in Chapter 6 to help you grow the mind-set and grit that will lead to success.

But if you're reading this and you're still in high school, listen up. You need to do *everything possible* to prepare yourself while you're still in high school—while the classes and resources you need are mostly free. That's particularly true in subjects like English and math.

If you know you're not great at algebra or you could use some extra help with that whole essay-writing thing, enroll in a summer course at the community college; sign up for free online resources; find someone to tutor you; advocate for yourself to get into the best possible classroom situation; ask your teacher, counselor, or principal for advice on where to look for help.

If getting yourself prepared means taking an extra class before or after school, do it. It's not going to be fun, but remember, *not* getting yourself college-ready before college only lowers your chances of graduation, and it also means that you'll have to take those same classes while you're *in* college. That'll be unpleasant, too, only in that case it's both unpleasant *and* expensive, since you'll be paying for every unit and the remedial courses won't even count toward your degree.

Preparing for college isn't just about the classes. If you're angling for a selective four-year college, you've got to do more than clear the bar for remedial classes.

So with that short pep talk, here's a list of what to do in high school so that you not only avoid skidding down that remedial slippery slope but actually climb up past where you need to be. (Why not graduate from high school more than college ready? Why not be ready for your *second* year in college?)

Like everything else in this book, none of these steps is easy, and all of them require *you* to be personally motivated. Get after it.

THIRTEEN THINGS YOU MUST DO IN HIGH SCHOOL TO BE READY FOR COLLEGE

Take Math Every Year

We said it before and we'll say it again: Take math every single year in high school, and at least (and definitely) take Geometry, Algebra 1, and Algebra 2. We know, you may not be *required* to take math your senior year, or if you're really a whiz, you may have finished your school's graduation requirements sooner than that, but take a math class every year anyway. Why? Because if you have to take a math placement test before college, you're much more likely to do well if you haven't let your math skills languish for a year. And even if you don't have to take a placement test, most colleges require you to pass math classes in college, and again, those are going to be way easier to pass if you haven't been busy forgetting what the hell a quadratic equation is for a year or two.

Get Yourself a Tutor

You may have noticed that there's been a bit of a boom in the tutoring business, with dozens of tutor-matching services on the Web. It's like online dating—you pop in your zip code and you get a list of tutors. They're even on Craigslist, so shop around. (Remember to be safe! Meet strangers in public places like the library or coffee shop, or bring a friend along the first time you meet someone you found online.) There's no sense in paying for a tutor whose teaching style doesn't match your learning style. You can also tap into an electronic tutor on an as-needed basis 24/7, for which you essentially pay by the minute. It can be pretty affordable, because instead of spending an hour, you only pay for the five minutes of help you need.

If you can't afford to pay a tutor, pick up the phone and call the local colleges, public and private. Sometimes students work as tu-

MYTH BUSTERS FROM THE COLLEGE BOARD

Myth: I can't take AP because the courses I need are not offered at my high school.

Reality: There may be opportunities to take AP courses outside of your high school. Talk to your counselor about taking a course elsewhere or online through an approved provider.

Myth: I can't take AP because no one has recommended me.

Reality: If you think you're ready to take an AP course, then you're ready to advocate for yourself—just talk to a teacher or counselor. And don't back down, even if you encounter some resistance.

Myth: I can't afford to take an AP exam.

Reality: The College Board, which runs the AP system, aims to make exams affordable for everyone. Fee reductions for students with financial need, as well as state and federal subsidies, are available.

SOURCE: COLLEGE BOARD

tors for hire, and sometimes tutoring is part of a volunteer project, so they're actually actively looking for people like you. Help them find you! Connecting with a college student gives you an extra bennie—you can learn the subject and also ask your tutor all kinds of questions about college that he or she probably already knows the answers to. Don't be afraid to get creative if cost remains an issue; the barter economy is alive and well. Think about what skills you could trade for someone's time and help. Do you know a foreign language? How to sew? How to fix cars or bikes? Walk a dog?

Finally, for the courses you're struggling in, there are probably students who understand the material better than you. Ask your teacher to recommend someone in class to help you. Meet them during lunch or after school; most students are delighted to help others.

Sign Up for Outside Classes

It's possible to get a jump on earning a bachelor's degree—and get the whole degree done in less than four years—if you take some classes at your local community college while you're still in high school. Work with your counselor and college advisors to make sure the courses you select are transferable. If you're a diligent student, you could earn a degree in three years!

You also might want to strengthen your academic credentials by taking some free classes through Khan Academy, a nonprofit educational website (www.khanacademy.org). There are thousands of classes offered, from organic chemistry to art history. The short videos are like sitting next to the smartest kid in the class who's showing you her work. Pause. Scroll back. Ask a question. It's like doing a few mental push-ups . . . relaxing in a weird kind of way.

Get Your AP On

If your high school offers Advanced Placement courses, take them. They fulfill a high school requirement, and if you get a certain score on the end-of-the-year subject test, then you might earn college credit at the same time. Some students who take lots of AP classes actually start their first year in college as a sophomore, which should make your eyes light up with dollar bills. (Whether or not an AP translates to college credit depends on the college, so look it up!) Even if you don't get college credit, AP courses are a good way to stretch academically, and admission counselors love to see AP classes on your transcript. It's evidence of being a serious student—just what they want!

A lot of kids tell themselves they're not smart enough for those classes, but if you're motivated, we repeat: do it. Ask your counselor if you can register for an AP class. If the answer is no, ask why. It could be a space issue, or it could be that you didn't clear an invisible bar and you need to know what that bar is so you can prepare to jump it. If you're up for a challenge, don't wait to get invited and don't let the cost of the tests stop you (there are ways to get those tests paid for). See the "Myth Buster" box, and if you've got it, go for it.

Are You Fluent?

Students who are native speakers of Spanish, French, Chinese, Japanese, or German can take the AP test in that language without taking a class at all. If you're fluent and you can read and write in one of these languages, you should easily earn a 4 or 5. If you make arrangements in advance, schools can order the test to be administered along with the other AP tests on the schedule.

Challenge Yourself

Same deal as the AP. Don't wait to be invited into honors or International Baccalaureate (IB) classes. If you think you can hack it, review your preparation for these courses, march into your counselor's office, and ask if you can sign up. Maybe you're a candidate; maybe you'll have to wait till next year. Honors programs sometimes allow students in at the end of the semester or at the beginning of the year. If you're not quite making the cut, let your teachers know you'd like to be ready to move to honors classes as soon as you can, and ask them to help you get there.

Be a Hoarder

But not with clothes and shoes and old newspapers. Hoard badges, certificates, and licenses instead. Check out Open Badges (open-badges.org), where you can collect badges for being a "Code Whisperer," an "Editor," a "Div Master," or a "Super Styler," depending on your ability to demonstrate your coding skills and build your own Web projects.[59] You like medicine? Get certified in CPR or first aid. You get the idea; you're building your résumé while you do what you like to do anyway.

Be a Test Master

If you had never seen a bicycle and you got on one for the first time and tried to ride up a hill, you probably couldn't do it. If you turned the bike around and coasted downhill, you might be able to go a ways, but you'd probably look pretty funny with your feet out trying to balance. Taking the SAT or ACT is kind of like riding a bike: the more you practice, the easier it gets. So good advice is just to take practice tests several times, say six. By the seventh go at it, you'll be coasting downhill with alacrity and you'll know just how to use your gears to pump uphill.

On the other hand, when you're getting on a bike for the first time, it helps to have someone give you a little guidance, and that's where the test prep classes come in. There are dozens of them: group classes, one-on-one tutoring, live online, on-site, streaming video, combinations of video and one-on-one. Do your homework before you spend a few hundred dollars. You need to know if full-length practice tests are available (how many?) and what kind of feedback you'll get (and how frequently?). How will you communicate with instructors: Email? Live chat? Some companies offer money-back guarantees if a student doesn't get a higher score, so they're pretty confident they can teach you something that will help you. What you may learn is not so much content as test-taking tips.

For more test-prep fun, download the SAT and ACT Question of the Day apps. Well, okay, maybe not *fun* exactly, but it's kinda fun— especially when you get to stump your family and friends. Check your school's career center or library, where there are often resources and staff who know the drills that have helped others before you. In the end, all this practice will make you a whole lot less wobbly on test day.

Don't Be a Couch Potato

There's no one-size-fits-all answer to the question of how many extracurricular activities you should engage in. Some students (and their parents) get so tied up in how something will look on a résumé or a college application that they forget whether or not it's even a worthwhile thing to do, or if you're learning anything at all. The fact is that participating in sports, clubs, and the arts are all great ways to spend time and sure beat watching reality TV on your couch. And if you choose a sport, a club, and a random pastime—maybe volunteering with old folks, hiking, stamp collecting, or painting murals—that you actually *like* doing, chances are you'll get pretty good at all of them. You may even be rewarded for your efforts with recognition, varsity letters, or invitations to play music, produce a video, or speak to organizations. So basically, our advice here is don't sit around. Do something with your life that you actually like doing. If that's playing the piano, working for the school newspaper, and gardening at the local community garden patch, do it. Is it making pottery and fostering homeless dogs? Do that instead. There's no "right thing" to do, and it's going to look way, way better on your application to be a leader or a recognized specialist in one or two things than to have dabbled in everything while not really getting good at anything at all. In other words, if you're choosing between joining one or two organizations that you really enjoy and where your presence matters or joining five or six that you really don't care about and where no one would miss you if you didn't show up, choose the first option.

Get Out into the World

Internships prepare you for careers by giving you work experience in a field of your choosing. Volunteer work allows you to participate in a project designed to help others. They're different, but they're similar in that both expose you to the world of work, provide insight into what might become career options, and generally don't pay (or don't pay very well). Hospitals, libraries, schools, and parks typically need volunteers and, particularly if you're interested in those fields, you can gain valuable insider experience through interning or volunteering. If you're thinking of teaching, there are lots of places where you'd be needed badly. Becoming a teacher's assistant, tutor, or advisor could give you insights on how to manage a classroom or develop a dynamite lesson plan.

Have Not-So-Lazy Summers

We know that it might sound good to spend the summer loafing around with your pals like you used to. But sorry. That ship has sailed. If you want to get into college—and be college-ready once you get there—you've got to make goals for your summer, both physical and mental. Write a blog, take an art class, make a video, read everything you can find, learn harmonica, train for a marathon, make a map of the bike routes around your town, do an internship, read *War and Peace*, or make it your job to know what's going on in the world.

One way to think about your summer is to ask yourself this question: would *you* recommend you? You should expect a lot from yourself, so spend a little time thinking about the letter of recommendation you would like someone to write about you. Then set about living up to your own expectations and use your summer to help you become that person. At the end of each summer, update your résumé. Don't overdo it, and be truthful. But the exercise of having what you've done written down will produce something helpful to give the teachers you eventually ask to write recommendations for you.

Build That Bridge

Some colleges invite some of their admitted freshmen to what's known as a summer bridge program. These programs vary in length, content, and quality, but they're all designed to provide a little extra help to admitted students before they arrive in the fall. If you're first in your family to go to college, or if your high school doesn't send a whole lot of students to four-year colleges, or if you were admitted but just barely made the cut, a lot of colleges will reach out to you and ask if you want to come to their summer bridge program. Should you go?

The short answer is yes. Especially if it's mandatory. A few schools that make their bridge programs mandatory even offer a small stipend to students to compensate for loss of summer employment. (Check the fine print!) And the longer answer is yesssssss. (We kid, we joke. Ha. But really.) We don't know what the program at your college is, but if you were invited, or you think it might be fun, or you're even a little bit nervous about that first week of school, just go. What's to lose?

Here's what to expect. Summer bridge programs can be as short as one week or as long as six weeks. Some involve staying on campus and some don't. The itineraries at different programs vary a lot. Most introduce new students to mentors, tutors, other students, staff, faculty, and administrators. Some also give you the quick-and-dirty on where the important buildings are, info on what will be expected of you in the lab or in class, and some advice on study skills and time management. At the very least, they're a good way to meet other students who will be in your class, scout the campus, find out where to find the best burgers, sniff out the best hikes, or track down the cafés with the best live music.

Don't Slack Off

Having prattled on about tutors and extracurriculars and preparing for tests and all that, we feel obliged to add what you already know: your GPA is still the single most important piece of information about you in your college application. So don't undermine your academic preparation by spending too many hours doing anything else—even if it's totally worthwhile, like volunteering or playing an instrument or training for a marathon. Of course, if you can do all those things, too, then go for it, but it's a balance that you're going to strike on your own. And remember that if the scale is tipping—"I can *either* participate in an event *or* get an A in Algebra 2"—choose your grades first. Colleges look most favorably on students who have already demonstrated that they can effectively juggle academic achievement and a life beyond the library, but the truth is, if you don't have the grades, if you're not prepared, if you're not totally, completely college ready, then ignore most of the advice in this chapter and *hit the books*.

8

FAMILIES ARE COMPLICATED

THE TRICKY BUSINESS OF TRANSITIONS

Whose Future is it Anyway?

For many people, "parents" might not mean your Mom and Dad, or even any mom or dad. Maybe you have guardians, grandparents, aunts, uncles, or older siblings whom in some ways you consider your parents. Whether they're biological, adopted, or part of an extended family, if they went to college, they might have some idea about what you're going through. But for lots of parents—even the ones who went to college—the application and financial aid processes are totally intimidating and a maze of decisions they might not feel ready to help you make. Which colleges should you apply to? How do you know if they're the right colleges for you? How are you going to pay for it? What if you're not accepted? Are you prepared? Will it be worth it?

How much debt will you have when you graduate? Can you afford it? Lots of questions that can turn into *lots of stress* in a hot second.

If your parents have always been there for you—picking you up when you fell down, packing your lunches for twelve years, helping you with your high school homework, calling teachers when you failed a test—your road ahead could be bumpy because you and your parents will have to get used to lots of changes. If your parents expect a lot from you but weren't really the type to be involved, you're actually in luck this time. You've had to learn a thing or two about independence already, and if you've internalized some high expectations yourself, that will help you through the challenges ahead. And if you've got parents who don't expect much and aren't very involved, here's your chance to really take control of shaping the future you want for yourself.

Then there's your parents' level of education, which is a big deal because it has to do with whether or not they have the knowledge and confidence to help with college decisions. If they went to college, they may have it all mapped out for you, including the degree they've decided you'd like best. They may have chosen *the* school for you. If they haven't been to college themselves or are relatively new to the United States, they might see that it's important for your future and they may want to be totally supportive, but they might not be able to help you much.

Some parents will be downright hostile to the whole idea because, after all, you could go to work right now and start bringing money in for the family. William G. Tierney, co-director of the Pullias Center for Higher Education at the University of Southern California, has mentored local students for many years. He recalled "one young man who was accepted into some really good colleges and his father, who worked at the 98-cent store, got really angry. Why did he do that? He could get him a job right now at the 98-cent store!" Dr. Tierney talked to the young man's father to help him understand why college would be a much better option for his son.

Not everyone has an advocate, so you may be the one who has to help your parents think differently. It can be hard, particularly because your parents are facing the daily demands of supporting you and others, and they're feeling the pinch. A dollar earned today looks a whole lot better than a maybe-dollar in the future. They may be reading news stories about well-educated baristas who are feeling as if their degree wasn't worth it.

One way to answer that question is to show them unemployment statistics, which are in the news a lot. Even during the height of the recent recession (2009–10), research showed that a "bachelor's degree is one of the best weapons a job seeker can wield in the fight for employment and earnings . . . unemployment for students with new bachelor's degrees is an unacceptable 8.9 percent, but it's a catastrophic 22.9 percent for job seekers with [only] a recent high school diploma—and an almost unthinkable 31.5 percent for recent high school dropouts."[60]

So when your parents ask if it's worth it, the honest answer is a resounding yes. We asked Sandy Baum, one of the authors of College Board's 2013 report "Education Pays," that question. You can show your parents all the research behind her answers, but here's the cheat sheet: A college degree is absolutely worth it economically. College graduates have better jobs, are employed more, make more money, and are more satisfied with the work they do. But they're not just sitting around watching their income grow. They're more involved with their families and their communities. College graduates are just plain healthier . . . and more satisfied with life. All this might convince them, but really, we think what they really want to know is why *you* want to go to college. Why is it worth it for you?

So as you plan, talk to them about how you see your future, because no matter where your parents fit on the sliding scale of involvement with your life, you going to college is not happening in a

Kaitlyn's Parents

Emotionally there? Yes. Practically there? No!

"My parents didn't go to college, and even though they wanted me to go, they didn't know what to do. We had no idea that there was a 'college bound' process. My parents, who had always known everything and had always been there for me, suddenly knew nothing. It was scary for them, and I was really lost."[61]

vacuum. It's a transition for the whole family, and it's important to be aware of that.

TRANSITIONS

Going from high school to college is tricky business. Your parents might be freaking out because you're more self-sufficient or independent than you were just a few months ago and they wish you were still a kid. Or it might be the opposite—now that you're almost a legal adult, maybe your parents are starting to put all kinds of pressures and responsibilities on you. Your ideal career might not match what your parents have in mind, or maybe they're worried that if you go away, you will grow apart.[62]

The truth is, this whole process is just plain complicated, and we can't promise to help you navigate all of it. All we can say is that you're in good company. While your experience is unique to you, some themes are pretty common. So much so that college programs are built on the idea that all "traditional age" college students (ages seventeen to twenty-one) are changing both who they are and what they want at a rapid pace. Here are few things that might be going down in your kitchen these days.

You and Your Parents Disagree on What Kind of College You Should Attend

This happens a lot because lots of parents have in mind the kind of college they want their kid to go to. Often it's because of a certain academic program, or because it's centered on a certain faith, or because it's nearby. You should probably consider those schools because chances are your parents want what's best for you, but you should also think about what school *you* want to go to.

Your parents are right when they say that college is about going to class, learning, and setting yourself up for a career and a successful life in the "adult" world. But it's *also* about the reasons in the "Considerator" list (page 10). It's about nurturing deep friendships, meeting people who are different from you, and opening up to being part of something bigger than you. It may sound cheesy, but that's all part of developing your identity as an adult. Finding a college that will give you the experiences you need to grow is an important conversation.

Your Parents Worry That College Is Just About Beer, Drugs, and Hooking Up

You can't pretend that the social scene doesn't exist. And it's true that some students on some campuses *do* waste their college years. But that doesn't have to be you; in fact, promise yourself that it won't be. Consider a story that Dr. Tierney told us about a young man who spent four years at college, graduated, and then came back "with his tail between his legs."[63] Why was he ashamed? Not because he didn't get his degree—he did. But because "he drank his way through college. He didn't have a résumé. He didn't have anything to show for it. After four years of college, he didn't know a single person he could ask for a letter of recommendation." This young man had passed his classes, but after it was all over, he knew he hadn't taken advantage of the opportunities there for him, so he went back to his mentor, asking for help. That was a good move on his part—and now this particular young man is back on track. Let your parents know that you're aware of the dangers and that this will not be your experience.

Your Parents Are Intimidated and Find the Whole Process Stressful

This reaction is understandable, but assure them that you've got this. Share with them the planning process we mapped out in Chapters 6 and 7. Show them your plan, your calendar, and your timeline, and ask for their help. If they've been to college themselves, chances are they've forgotten a lot of the details about the admission process, and in any event things have changed and gotten more complicated since they went through it. If they have never been to college, you can help them understand what you're up to. If they are able and want to help you, they will be delighted that you're taking the initiative.

Digging in and taking responsibility for the application process has two beneficial effects for you, too: it prepares you to succeed at college, where you have to go through a whole lot of similar processes (registering, following through with financial aid, etc.), and it demonstrates for your parents that you have the will, ability, and persistence to take on responsibilities, so they'll trust you more.

Your Parents Are All Up in Your Grill

You'd be surprised by how common this is. Admission personnel tell us that it's not unusual for parents to call their office pretending to be you. Or worse. If your mom or dad is proofreading your essays, that's great. If they're writing those essays or if they're calling the colleges on your behalf, it's time to take a few deep breaths and have a talk. Make it clear that you want their help; they can be the most valuable members of your team. But let them know that this has to be *your* journey, driven by *your* decisions, and that, while you very much appreciate their support, you're (about to be) an adult now. (See the sidebar "Legally Adult.")

When You Say "College," the Tears Start Flowing

Lots of moms and dads have a very hard time coming to terms with the fact that you'll be leaving home. We talked to one young woman whose mother let her go more than six hundred miles away to college on one condition: that they talk on the phone every day, and they did. This is not, however, necessarily optimal, either for your parents or for you. As researchers Karen Levin Coburn and Madge Lawrence Treeger write in *Letting Go: A Parents' Guide to Understanding the College Years,* "It is so easy for parents to succumb to the temptation to micromanage—to check up on a son or daughter's daily activities and emotional state. In doing so, of course, they deprive their children of the most long-lasting knowledge they can gain: the knowledge of how to live independently, form their own points, make their own decisions and mistakes, and ultimately make their own commitments to personal and political values, a vocation, [or] another human being."[64]

Legally Adult

One of the conversations you need to have with your parents is about the Family Education Rights to Privacy (FERPA) Act. According to FERPA, once you turn eighteen or attend a post-secondary institution, you become responsible for your own records. This means that while you will know how you're doing in your college classes, professors cannot tell your parents, the registrar's office will not release your academic record, and the dean's office will not share behavioral records with them unless you have authorized it.

For some parents, particularly those who have been on the homework hotline every night, this is a choke point, but it's the law. It's not time to panic, it's time for you to guide them to understand what the law permits and what it doesn't. The U.S. Department of Education explains, "FERPA is a Federal law that protects the privacy of student education records. . . . [It] gives parents certain rights with respect to their children's education records. These rights transfer to the student when he or she reaches the age of 18 or attends a school beyond the high school level."[65]

Though your parents might not be thrilled to know that the federal government does not allow them to see your transcript without your permission, it's important for you to have a conversation so that they understand that FERPA is not designed to keep them in the dark; it's designed to protect your privacy. No one can get access to your student records without your knowledge and clear consent: not prospective employers, not fake prospective employers, not the media, not a blogger, not nosy Aunt Flo from Tuscaloosa. Your parents should be reassured because even though the school can't release the information, you have access to your records 24/7 and you can authorize the release of information directly to them. In fact, an important part of FERPA is that it gives you the right to review your own records.

For a sample FERPA third-party release, see page 246.

When You Say "College," All Your Parents Hear Is "Money Money Money"

College is expensive. It's often really, really expensive, and it's a huge financial burden for most families. We get it. Chapter 10 goes in-depth into the process of paying for college, but in order for you to find a "financial fit," as we outlined in Chapter 3, you need to have a conversation about affordability with your folks. This is hard. We talked to over a hundred students, and by far the most difficult conversation they had to have with their parents was the one about money. Parents were reluctant to share and students were reluctant to ask, but you have to have these conversations. On the practical side, you need family income information for the Free Application for Federal Student Aid (FAFSA), but on an interpersonal level, you need to understand how your college experience impacts the whole family.

Start the conversation with our rankings. Your parents can see that the price of college varies—and it varies considerably depending on which income bracket your family falls into. Just flipping through the rankings pages will help the conversation, which may go from "Yikes! We could never afford that!" to "Wow, what a deal!"

After you have a general idea of college costs and maybe some idea of the family budget, play around with the interactive calculator from the federal student aid website (studentaid.ed.gov).[66] To figure out what dollar figure you should drop into each category, go to a prospective college's financial aid website and check out their cost of attendance, using the cost (not the sticker price!) that is average for your income bracket.

One part of the financial calculation that you should talk to your parents about is how long it will take you to earn your degree. Though graduation rates are calculated based on six years, it's possible to earn a bachelor's degree in *four* years if you earn fifteen credits each semester or take summer classes.[67] Many students take fewer credits so they will have more time to devote to difficult classes, because they couldn't enroll in the classes they wanted, or because they only wanted to go to classes Tuesdays and Thursdays after ten. Others are taking fewer credits because they're working. That brings us to the question of whether it's wise to work while you're in college. For financial reasons, you may have no choice. There are pros and cons, so it's something you should discuss. For some research on the subject, take a look at the sidebar "To Work or Not to Work" in Chapter 11, page 308.

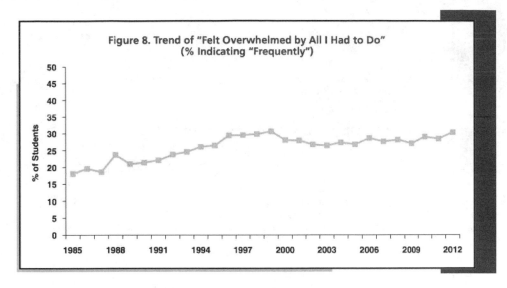

Figure 8. Trend of "Felt Overwhelmed by All I Had to Do"
(% Indicating "Frequently")

According to a 2012 survey conducted by UCLA researchers, "Many academic habits tied to success in college are on the rise, but more students (30 percent) were frequently overwhelmed by all they had to do as high school seniors; especially women (40 percent); 18 percent of men reported entering college feeling overwhelmed."

SOURCE: CIRP FRESHMAN SURVEY—HIGHER ED RESEARCH INSTITUTE

A LAST NOTE

There are lots of reasons parents fret and those worries will be different depending on your family's financial situation, cultural background, and educational experience, as well as a whole lot of personal reasons. You are embarking on an adventure, and no matter what happens, you'll grow. Your parents will grow, too, and on occasion, you may both feel a little overwhelmed. According to a national study conducted by UCLA, 30 percent of freshmen do. You may be in that 30 percent, so if you're feeling like it's hard, you're not alone.[68]

Nobody can know what the future holds, but to the best of your abilities, you can prepare for it. Talk about what you're worried about, and work with your parents to make a plan that supports your goals and helps keep everyone on the same page.

SACRAMENTO STATE

California State University, Sacramento
Office of the University Registrar
6000 J Street • Lassen Hall 2000 • Sacramento, CA 95819-6056
T (916) 278-8088 • F (916) 278-6453 • www.csus.edu/registrar

STUDENT CONSENT FOR RELEASE OF INFORMATION

_____   _____
Student Name (Last, First, MI)   Student Identification Number

The _Family Educational Rights and Privacy Act_ (FERPA) of 1974, as amended, seeks to guarantee both a student's right of access to education records, financial aid records, and financial records, and the confidentiality of student information. Institutions may not disclose information contained in education records without the student's written consent except under certain conditions. A student's record may be released to parents, guardians or other third parties by providing a written authorization or consent.

STUDENT CONSENT FOR RELEASE OF INFORMATION

I hereby **give my consent** for my parent, guardian or other third party, as named below, to have access to my education, financial aid and financial records. This consent will remain in effect until rescinded.

_____   _____
Student's Signature   Date

PARENT/GUARDIAN/THIRD PARTY:_____
                                                                    Please Print

STREET ADDRESS:_____

CITY _____ State _____ Zip _____

STOP! Withdrawal of Consent Only

STUDENT WITHDRAWAL OF CONSENT FOR RELEASE OF INFORMATION

STUDENT WITHDRAWAL OF CONSENT FOR RELEASE OF INFORMATION

I hereby **withdraw my consent** for my parent, guardian or other third party as named above, to have access to my education records, effective immediately.

_____   _____
Student's Signature   Date

07/13 Registrar

The Federal Education Rights and Privacy Act is designed to protect confidentiality. If you're eighteen, and you would like your parent, guardian, or any other third party to have access to your records, you need to allow it.

*Release forms will vary from campus to campus.

THE OTHER HELPFUL TOOL COLLEGE GUIDE

9.

GETTING IN

DEMYSTIFYING
COLLEGE
ADMISSION

THE COLLEGE

ADMIT ONE

OF YOUR CHOICE

The YouCanDoThis Ticket Company

Think of the admission process like a video game. You've got to get by the checkpoints, collect the badges and weapons, move to the next level, battle an array of zombies and armed thugs, and save planet Earth, all in the right order. If your attention lapses or you make too many wrong moves, you get knocked out (though in video games, unlike college admissions, you don't actually lose anything if you do). Once you know the rules and the obstacles that can get you off track, you can win this thing, but it takes focus, effort, and time.

The admission process is a game where organization and strategy matter, and no matter how quickly you work, it's going to take a year. A full year. It'll begin when you're a junior

9th Grade

Start academic and financial planning

10th Grade

Research: know the expectations

11th Grade

✦ Visit colleges
✦ PSAT/SAT/ACT

Summer

✦ Work, write essays
✦ Explore careers

12th Grade

✦ Apply!
✦ Commit!

and you start researching colleges, planning a financial strategy, and figuring out your goals. The applications become available in fall of your senior year and by early winter, all your applications will be in. Between fall and spring of senior year, you'll fill out and submit all financial aid paperwork, follow up with recommendation letters, continue your usual extracurricular, work, and volunteer activities, and you'll do all of this without losing your mind while maintaining your GPA. If something has to go, don't let it be your mind. Lose the extracurricular stuff. Then comes spring.

This chapter begins with a glossary, then takes the application apart so that you know what you need to do. We include a glimpse of what happens behind closed doors in the admission office, because knowing what they're looking at can help you stay on track, avoid danger zones, and get admitted to colleges that fit you academically, financially, socially, and physically.

Admission Glossary

Application Deadlines

These are set by each college so there is no single date you can put on the calendar. Generally, the last day to apply is in late fall or early winter of your senior year. To make matters slightly more complicated, a whole raft of "supplemental materials," like your school report (sent by the counselor) and letters of recommendation (sent by the recommenders), need to be submitted separately. The deadlines for that stuff may be different from the application deadline, but getting all those different pieces in on time is your responsibility and no one else's. Colleges use customer relationship management (CRM) tools, so that they can manage multiple communications with their prospective students, and some colleges have ways that you can check the progress of your

Beware the Plague of Senioritis

Lots of students start to run out of steam in their senior year. They take fewer classes, or fewer hard classes. They start to play hooky in the afternoon and let their grades drop. But listen up: that can't happen to you. While it may seem like no big deal—by then you will already have submitted your applications, right?—keeping your GPA up (or raising it) will actually give you *more* options in the spring of your senior year, when the acceptance letters start rolling in. Remember that your admission to the college was conditional on you meeting certain requirements, and failing to meet those requirements could mean your acceptance is rescinded. They can un-accept you if you get a D! If you end up on a waitlist, those spring grades really matter. So buckle down. Keep focused, and enroll in challenging courses rather than easy electives. Our experts suggest that it's better academic preparation to take an advanced math class than almost anything else, regardless of your interests or intended major. It's a long, hard road, but don't give up when you're almost to the finish line.

application online. Is it complete? Are they missing a transcript or a letter of recommendation? Some of the messages they send will require a response from you, so even though email is an old technology, check it. Frequently.

Common Application

The Common Application is a single application template that over five hundred colleges use, and it allows you to provide standard information and answer questions that are asked by all member colleges. Most of the colleges using the Common App also require college-specific information, which is unique to the college. For each application, there is a fee unless you request and qualify to have your application fee waived.

Comprehensive Review (aka Holistic Review)

Your application to schools that use a comprehensive or holistic review will include more opportunities for you to let them know who you are and what you can bring to the school. Sometimes schools

Who Should Write Letters of Recommendation?

Colleges are academic institutions, so ask teachers who know you as a student recently—junior year or first semester senior year are best. You don't really want to go back to freshman year unless you have an ongoing project or something that demonstrates your extraordinary academic prowess. Advisors you've worked with in clubs and organizations who know your academic work as well as your extracurricular, organizational, and visionary capacity are also good. If you have a hole in your academic record, like a particularly bad semester, and a counselor knows the backstory, you might want to ask her.

Respect the teacher's time. A well-written letter of recommendation is like writing an essay. Give your teachers time to do it well, and also give them the option of saying no to you. There can be all kinds of reasons a teacher can't write a letter for you, but trust us: you don't want someone writing your recommendation who doesn't *want* to write it. You'll come off sounding less awesome than you are. If possible, ask to see the letter. As one of our experts said, "Too often, believe it or not, counselors write form letters and fill in a student's name. Often enough they mess that or the university name up."

After you've asked, follow up with each recommender a week or two before the deadline, and then a couple of days before the deadline, to make sure the letters actually have been sent. Remember that your teachers and coaches and counselors are busy people. If they forget to send in your letter of recommendation, that may be their fault, but it's *your* application. Use your timeline and planner to stay on top of it.

offer interviews for prospective students. These are often with alums who live near you or recruiters who travel. If they offer you an interview, go for it. It's a great opportunity. Read everything you can about the college before you go. Practice answering the question "Why are you interested in *our* college?" And dress nicely, like you're going for a job interview.

The National Association for College Admission Counseling has analyzed what goes into a college's holistic decision process, and grades in college prep courses top the list as the most important element of every application. It's not just the grade they're reviewing, it's also the rigor of the courses you've chosen to take. How you respond to essay or short-answer questions also matters. As one of our experts told us, "More and more institutions ask short-answer questions, which are read by trained staff to determine the applicant's 'grit' or ability to persist in the face of adversity. These reviews may determine admission as well as aid packages and, at some institutions, the availability of support services. It is important to answer the questions directly and honestly; don't try to provide the answer you think the reviewer is expecting."[69]

Decision Plans

Some colleges have their own standard, while others allow you to choose from three kinds of decision plans: regular, early action, or early decision.

> **Regular.** The vast majority of students apply using the regular decision plan, which gives time to compare financial packages before committing to one college. Regular decision deadlines are generally in fall or early winter, with most between December 1 and February 1, and decisions arrive in late March or April. This gives the college a chance to see your first-semester senior grades. While not all colleges that process "regular" admission look at first-semester senior grades, all colleges confirm your admissibility with your final transcript that includes both semesters of your senior year.

> **Rolling admission.** If the college has a rolling admission policy, the dates may be less strict and notices are sent out as applications are read.

> **Early action (EA).** You apply early and get your decision early (usually in December), but you don't have to commit until May 1. This sounds like a great deal—who wouldn't want to know early? If your junior year record is excellent, your application is in tippity-top, A-plus shape,

and you know this school meets your four-way fit requirements, go for it. If you're not sure about the college, or if your application will be stronger with your senior grades, you should probably wait.

> **Early decision (ED).** This one is binding, meaning a commitment is made the moment you submit your application. You can only apply ED to one college, because if you're accepted, you're committed to enrolling. Many colleges don't offer ED because students don't have a chance to compare financial packages. Once you're accepted ED, you must withdraw all other applications.

The Decision

As we mentioned, in most cases colleges will notify you of their decision on your application sometime in March or April of your senior year. The exceptions are, as outlined above, if you apply EA or ED to a school, or to a school with a rolling admission policy.

> **Admitted.** You're in, but don't celebrate too early! Every admission letter is *conditional*: you're admitted only if you follow through on your classes (either at high school or at your other college if you are transferring), pass everything you said you were taking, and didn't lie on your application. If your schedule changes and you've had to drop a class that you had intended to take, contact the colleges and explain why. A personal reason? A scheduling conflict? Either way, contact them and explain why you're not following through with something you had planned. They will find out anyway when your final transcript doesn't match what the midyear report said you were doing, and it's much, much better to make sure your application honestly reflects you. If a college decides to rescind its acceptance after May 1, you could be left with few options.

> **Deferred.** If you decide to apply EA or ED, you could be deferred, which means that the college will look at your application again during the regular cycle. At this point, there's nothing more to do, because in general the application is considered complete once it is submitted and there is no opportunity to provide supplemental information. They have what you sent and it's in their court.

> **Waitlisted.** If you are waitlisted, you're not in, but you're not out, either. If you really want to attend the school, contact them, express your interest, and, if they allow it, provide additional information that will strengthen your application. For example, let them know if you have earned any awards or recognition, or if you've been promoted or given a raise because of your contributions to your workplace. If a portfolio was part of your application and you know it's stronger now, ask if they would consider reviewing it. Don't bombard them! Don't ask anyone to step in and fight for you, but if you're very interested and you have something more to tell them, let them know. If space becomes available, the college reviews waitlisted candidates to see which ones will be pushed over the edge into the admit group.

> **Admitted for spring term.** Some schools, particularly state colleges, will admit you for the spring term. This can be a good deal for you if it's absolutely the school you want to attend. If you're interested, ask at the four-year college if there are any courses you can take at your community college that will meet lower-division requirements.

> **Denied.** Receiving a denial is hard even if you half expected it because it was a reach and you knew it. Give yourself a day to mope, but then get back to the big picture.

Think about your other options, other schools that might actually be a better fit, because most students with a plan *do* make it into the college that is best for them.

Rejection

It's safe to say that rejection is not something people line up to experience for the fun of it. When it happens you have to figure out ways not to feel crummy, and to do that you have to hog-tie the "I'm a failure" monkey clinging to your back and unleash the one that says, "I can learn something from this."

There are a lot of researchers working in this area, and one is Martin Seligman, who was the president of the American Psychological Association and has been dubbed the "father of positive psychology." Seligman says that all humans talk to themselves to explain life events, and one of the themes he writes about in his research (and talked about in a TED talk) is that when either positive or negative events happen, optimists and pessimists use two sides of the same gauge, which Seligman dubs the "Three P's."[70]

"Pessimists," Seligman wrote, "tend to react to negative events by explaining them as *permanent, personal, and pervasive.* Failed a test? It's not because you didn't prepare well; it's because you're stupid. If you get turned down for a date, there's no point in asking someone else; you're simply unlovable. Optimists, by contrast, look for specific, limited, short-term explanations for bad events, and as a result, in the face of a setback, they're more likely to pick themselves up and try again."[71]

Guess what? When something good happens, the pessimists and optimists reverse the gauge. Optimists see it through the lens of the Three P's, and pessimists figure it's a fluke! You get the picture. It's not about changing the denial; it's about changing your reaction.

Appeal

If you think you were denied because there was an error, or if there are extenuating circumstances that you would like to explain, you may wish to appeal the college's decision. Every campus will have an official appeals process, so do your research before you pick up the phone.

Enrollment Deposits

After you have made your choice, some colleges require that you submit a non-refundable deposit, which is generally an advance on your first semester's tuition. If you qualify for an application fee waiver and the timing of the deposit is a financial hardship, work with the school to waive or defer your deposit.

> ### If I Am Applying Regular Decision, Is It Better to Apply Early?
>
> It's best to apply when your application is complete and as good as it can get. That means it's been written, rewritten, polished, and proofread. Don't rush to be first if taking more time on your essay or personal statement will make it better. Quality beats quick every time. For colleges that do rolling admissions, the earlier you apply, the earlier you hear.

Fee Waivers

If you qualify, you can be excused from paying for applications and tests through fee waivers. (For details on whether you qualify, see the box "Do Not Let Application Fees Stop You!" on page 49, and sample fee waiver request, page 50.)

Orientation

Most colleges offer orientations in the summer before you enroll, and it's a great way to confirm the "fit." Make every effort to attend; after all, you're making a big commitment, and at orientation you will meet other students, faculty, and staff, get to know the campus, and find out a little about the campus culture. Some schools require an enrollment deposit, but you are not locked into attending a college simply because you attended orientation.

School Report

Not every high school offers the same classes, clubs, and Advanced Placement opportunities. The school report (submitted by a school official, often your counselor) is designed to show college admission officials your achievements within the context of your school. Have you stretched yourself to take the most challenging classes available? What's the counselor/student ratio? What percentage of graduating seniors go to a four-year college? Knowing this allows the admission office to see how you have made the most of whatever school environment you're in.

Student's Demonstrated Interest

This is sometimes used by colleges as a measure of how serious you are about them. You've visited and interacted with their website; you've taken a tour of campus; you've followed up with an admission counselor. Some colleges track all of this information and use what they perceive to be your interest as part of what goes into evaluating your application for admission. On the other hand, many colleges don't track it at all; the best advice on this is don't sweat it. If you're interested in a college, visit it, ask questions, ask for a tour—do everything you would do because you're genuinely interested in the college. Maybe they're tracking your interest level; maybe they're not. To have parents calling multiple times says a lot about parental involvement, but it says nothing whatsoever about *your* interest.

Should I Send My Test Scores Early?

Advice from the College Board: If you know which schools you'd like to send your scores to and are comfortable sending your scores in the spring of your junior year, go ahead and do it. Several of our experts suggested that you send scores in your junior year to as many potential schools as you can afford. Sending the scores does not obligate you to apply or attend, and some colleges see this as a sign of interest. They may also use scores to qualify you for special campus visit programs, information sessions in your hometown, or scholarships.[72]

The Application Process

In Chapter 3, we encouraged you to look at the whole group of colleges out there through the lens of your goals. First semester of your senior year, it's time to get down to business.

How Many Colleges Should You Apply To?

Some students arrive at their first semester of senior year with a pretty long list; others have a tidy, short list with just one or two colleges. Whatever the length, every school on your list should meet your four-way fit criteria: each college is appropriately academically challenging, socially comfortable, and the right distance from home in a location and with a climate you can handle. In short, you can see yourself on any of these campuses. On the critical measure of financial fit, you need to make an educated calculation based on that college's net price calculator. An easy way to do this is through the College Abacus website (www.collegeabacus.org). Remember, the cost will not be the sticker price, so don't rule out a college without checking out the cost *to you*.[73]

If your list is on the short side, we'd like to encourage you to explore a little more and stretch your list to *at least* four schools, which is the number of colleges SAT and ACT allow you to send your scores to for no additional charge. If your list is long, don't worry about cutting it down yet, but do sort it into reach, match, and safety categories. The College Board recommends that you apply to at least one safety, a couple of matches, and a reach.[74] (See pages 54–5.)

Review the priorities in your four-way fit worksheet (pages 65–66). What happens if you decide that you can go a little farther afield? What happens when you find out that an academic reach might be a financial fit after all? You get the idea: while you want to narrow your list, you don't want to narrow it so much that you won't have options.

What's Included in a College Application?

They're all different. While we mentioned that more than five hundred schools use what's known as the Common Application, a lot of those schools also require extra material that's unique to just them. Just like any application, a college application asks a lot of personal questions, like where you were born; your race, religion, and ethnicity are optional. The colleges need to know where you are and how to get in touch with you, of course. They also ask questions about your family and your educational history and whether you speak any other language. Academic information includes your GPA, class rank, current courses, honors and awards you've received, and ACT or SAT testing results.

Is It Better to Get an Easy A or Risk Getting a B in a More Challenging Course?

The advice is to take the most rigorous schedule you can and take responsibility to learn the material—not just to pass the test, but to learn it in a way that would enable you to teach it to someone else. If you learn to understand, your foundation for college will be much stronger. Bottom line? Challenge, but don't overwhelm yourself. Athletes who don't push themselves when they train will get injured when they compete, and scholars need to do the same.

The SAT and ACT

Which test you choose to take may depend on what's offered in your area, or a teacher or counselor who knows you well may recommend one or the other.[75] Some students take both. While deciding which one to take is up to you, don't put it off, and don't let the cost be a deterrent since fee waivers are available. Get the waiver from your high school, because the school counselor is the person who verifies that you qualify. Taking the tests spring term of your junior year is recommended, because if you're happy with the results, you're done, and if you're not, you have first semester senior year to have another go at it.

After you take the test, you should be aware that you may receive mailings from several colleges. These schools have purchased the names of students who fit certain criteria they desire. You should consider those schools—they think you're a good candidate for admission. At the same time, their solicitation is not a guarantee

Fee Waivers

✦ SAT and ACT will allow you to send four scores at no charge; additional scores cost $11.25 per college.

✦ Some state schools allow you to apply to multiple campuses using a fee waiver.

✦ Fee waivers are available for qualified students completing the Common Application and those completing the separate applications required by some colleges.

To qualify, you (or your family) must meet one of the requirements (see box "Do Not Let Application Fees Stop You!" in Chapter 3, page 49, and sample fee waiver request, page 50)

that you'll be admitted. They've seen one piece of what you bring to the table, but they don't have the whole picture yet. And don't be pressured. Recruiters who pressure you have their own agenda.

Personal Statements, Short-Answer Questions, and the Essay

All the parts of your application should work together. After all, the professionals who are reading it will read the whole thing, and you can correctly assume that they're intelligent and want to get to know you a little through what you write. So here's some advice about how to make each section of your application add to the overall picture.

> Choose an essay topic that allows you to use your own voice to show something about you that you would like the reader to know. Don't use the essay to rehash information provided elsewhere on the application.

> The personal statement is not just about experiences but also about how those shape you and what you have become and will do because of them. Be prepared to explain that clearly.

> More and more institutions ask short-answer questions to provide readers with a more complete picture of the student's circumstances, challenges, and ability to persist in the face of adversity.

Give yourself the summer to think through what you would like an admission committee to know about you, and write some drafts. The Common Application, which releases its essay questions on August 1, caps the word count at 650. The prompts for the 2014–15 cycle are listed below.

> Some students have a background or story that is so central to their identity that they believe their application would be incomplete without it. If this sounds like you, then please share your story.

> Recount an incident or time when you experienced failure. How did it affect you, and what lessons did you learn?

> Reflect on a time when you challenged a belief or idea. What prompted you to act? Would you make the same decision again?

> Describe a place or environment where you are perfectly content. What do you do or experience there, and why is it meaningful to you?

> Discuss an accomplishment or event, formal or informal, that marked your transition from childhood to adulthood within your culture, community, or family.

A first draft of any essay is almost always pretty rough, and as Mark Twain noted, writing short is a whole lot more difficult than rambling on. Plan to rewrite even your short answers several times, and be sure someone else has proofed your work.

The College Admission Essay: Writing for Real

Dr. Mary Adler, Professor of English, California State University, Channel Islands

THE FIRST THING you should know about writing a college admission essay is that you are writing to real people who are going to make decisions that matter. If you treat it like a typical high school essay, even one dutifully written for a good grade, you'll miss the boat. For this essay to succeed, you have to locate your passions, to figure out what makes your story unique, one that only *you* can tell: It's the personal in *personal* statement. The stakes are high, because the essay is the one application piece that represents you as a human being, capable of curiosity, compassion, and change. As the admission staff at Princeton put it, your essay is where you convey "what you care about, what commitments you have made and what you've done to act on those commitments."[76]

Good writers often start out with writer's block because they lack a sense of audience. We've told you that these essays matter, that they can give you an edge, but who reads them? Typically your application is read by a professional admission counselor, and a few schools have a committee structure. It may surprise you to know that the way to impress a reader is *not* by looking up multisyllabic words in a thesaurus and *not* by quoting impressive phrases from writers like William Shakespeare. Nope. Your audience is rooting for *you*, not the thesaurus or Shakespeare. They want to get to know *you*, to hear *your* personality come to life through *your* voice, to experience *your* story of growth and reflection. The staff at Wellesley College suggests, "Your goal should be to make members of the Board of Admission feel as though we're sitting down at the table together to discuss your interests and aspirations. We're keen to know your story."[77]

(continued)

The College Admission Essay (continued)

To tell your story well, start early. Extra time will allow you to think more in the beginning and to edit more at the end. Start by *talking it out*. Find someone who will listen—a friend, relative, co-worker, teacher—and talk over a range of ideas that fit the prompt on the application. Take notes as you talk, since great ideas have a habit of disappearing in an hour or two. As you think about turning points, realize that even a small event can become a vehicle for change.

Next, you'll need to find a way to help your reader experience both past events *and* how those events have shaped your values, commitment, and decisions today. Try free-writing about both. Start by jotting down memories of those events, capturing specific details such as dialogue, colors, and sensations. Then write your reflections on those events, according to the prompt. Spend more time on the second part than the first.

This fast writing, where you don't pause to edit, is where *your* voice will come out, where you'll find the specificity, rhythm, and personality to reach your audience. It's more work, because you'll still need to go back over your notes, highlight which sections to use, and decide on an order. But this essay is worth the work.

There's no advantage to getting all the way to the maximum word count; a tightly written, clear answer is infinitely better than a rambling series of sentences. Abbreviations are fine, but this isn't a tweet.

In the short-answer section, make every answer *add* to your application; don't just repeat what you've said before. You would be surprised by the number of students who waste an answer by just saying again and again what they wrote in an essay or on their list of extracurricular activities.

Websites for More Information on the Personal Statement

www.cws.illinois.edu/workshop/writers/tips/personalstatement/#questions
The Writing Center at the University of Illinois at Urbana-Champaign provides, among other resources, a list of personal inventory questions that will guide you in generating information prior to writing.

https://owl.english.purdue.edu/owl/resource/642/01
The Writing Lab at Purdue University provides comprehensive advice for getting started. Later, you can go back to OWL and use it for grammatical and style help when editing and proofreading your statement.

www.cmu.edu/hpp/apply-to-schools/personal-statements/tips.html
Carnegie Mellon University's Health Professions Program has terrific guidance on how to choose a focus for your personal statement and how to frame that focus.

http://students.berkeley.edu/APA/PERSONALSTATEMENT/blunders.html
This UC Berkeley site includes a helpful list of things to *avoid* doing in your personal statement.

What About Extracurricular Activities?

You're not in school 24/7, so how do you spend your time? Sports? Music? Clubs? Volunteering? Work? Family responsibilities? Extracurricular accomplishments show a college something about who you are outside of the classroom. They strengthen college and scholarship applications because they allow you to emerge as an individual who cares about something beyond yourself. Unfortunately, some students try to look like they're superhuman and fall into the exaggeration trap. Don't go there because, well, it's a lie, and besides, the quality of your engagement trumps quantity. Being a member of a dozen clubs doesn't mean as much as being actively engaged in a few that you really care about. A question to ask yourself about your involvement is this: would they miss you if you didn't show up?

Other students have major family and work obligations that limit the time they can spend in after-school activities, and colleges understand that. If your extracurricular activity is taking care of younger siblings or working at night, write about that. But don't shortchange yourself on the school front, either; there are plenty of ways to become a valuable member of your school community during school hours.

After the Fat Envelope Arrives

For some students, going from admitted to committed is a short step. Others have options that need more analysis. By April of your senior year, you'll have all your choices in front of you along with the financial aid offers, that final piece of the puzzle. Take a look at how the colleges stack up against one another. You should have all the information for the four-way fit worksheet (page 65); some of your colleges may be out of the running because their aid package was almost all loans. Another college may gain in rank because they have awarded you a handsome scholarship. Revisit all the important reasons you have for choosing a college—and don't slip into thinking that you have to go where your cousin went or your friends are going.

Your Decision

This is all logical and there may be a clear winner, but there's another part of the decision that sometimes doesn't fit so neatly into boxes. It's the emotional tug, and you need to talk about those feelings alongside looking at the facts. Let your parents know why, for you, the social fit means going a little farther away, or why the academic fit is better at a particular school. The best advice is to make a decision with the long term in mind.

How's the Fit?

SCHOOLS >>>	1.	2.	3.	4.
ACADEMICS				
FINANCIAL				
SOCIAL				
PHYSICAL				
TOTAL:				

THE *OTHER* HELPFUL TOOL COLLEGE GUIDE

May 1: National Decision Day

May 1 is the day that you need to commit to a college and it's standard across the country, so don't miss it. While some colleges may accept a few stragglers, many don't because they have admitted more than they can accommodate. Even state schools are under no obligation to admit you if you fail to meet their deadlines. Some commitments include enrollment deposits, which are deducted from your first semester's tuition. Because all colleges share the May 1 commitment date, colleges that don't hear from you will assume that you're going elsewhere and your space will become available to someone on the wait list.

Final Senior Transcript and School Report

Before you leave your high school, make sure that your counseling office knows the college you've committed to so that the final school report goes to the right college. On the college side, admission professionals will verify that you did what you said you were going to do and that you didn't do something you shouldn't have done. If you failed a required course or had behavioral issues, or if your official transcript doesn't match your self-reported data, your admission could be rescinded. This is unfortunate all around, but it does happen. If you have a serious and compelling reason that explains why you failed or dropped a required course, let the college administrators know. Sometimes circumstances beyond your control are explainable.

Remember, You're Not Done Yet!

After May 1, your college will begin sending you information about possible placement tests, orientation, and other welcome-to-the-college events. At some colleges, all incoming freshman students are assigned to read the same book during the summer. A lot of the stuff the college sends you will require your attendance or attention—these are administrative hurdles and you have to clear them. At the very least, make sure the college can get in touch with you (not your parents) and that communications are not getting caught in a spam filter or piling up unnoticed. You've gotten this close; how terrible would it be to mess up now?

Orientation is an opportunity to get familiar with the campus culture and meet some future classmates. Some orientations include class registration, and some may be described as required or mandatory. The National Association of Student Financial Aid Administrators (NASFAA) advises us that if orientation occurs before the start of the academic year, it cannot be covered with financial aid.[78] If attending orientation would be impossible for you without financial help, check with your financial aid office to see if institutional aid might be available to cover the cost of attending.

Placement Tests: A Definite Danger Zone

After you're admitted, but before you're allowed to enroll, you might have to take placement tests. This will depend on the college, but the fact is more than half of the students who graduate from high school have not met the requirements for college-level math and/or English. As a result, many colleges require that students take a placement test before they enroll in classes. *If you are required to take a placement test and you don't, it's possible that you may not be able to enroll in classes even if you have been admitted!*

Yikes! How can they do that? Remember, all admission letters are conditional, because students are admitted *before* they graduate from high school. Graduation is a condition, and in some cases so are placement tests. If you don't meet the conditions that were explicated in your letter of acceptance, the college may not allow you to enroll. If they didn't tell you exactly what the conditions of your admission were in your admission letter, you can argue with them, but try not to go there. Ask as many questions as you need to up front to avoid unpleasant surprises.

Read everything, respond quickly, and never forget to thank the people who help you—both those at your high school and the new staff whom you may not have met in person yet. Now you're on your way to college, ready to be part of the village helping other kids who will follow your lead.

10.

IT'S ALL ABOUT THE BENJAMINS

HOW TO PAY FOR COLLEGE

$$$

KEEP
CALM
AND
THINK
ABOUT
MONEY

The best time to deal with the money issue is *before* you apply, because even though it's your education, the financial picture is bigger than you. It includes the whole family, and it's complicated. Dr. Sandy Baum, a researcher at George Washington University and the Urban Institute and co-author of the College Board's report "Education Pays," says, "You have to think of college as an investment in yourself. For the typical student, the investment pays off very well over a lifetime, not just financially, but also with a more fulfilling life."[79]

The financial aid process is complicated, award letters are difficult to compare, and there's a whole vocabulary attached, which is why we've included a separate financial glossary here as well. In this chapter we take apart the whole system, beginning with the first document you have to submit, the Free Application for Federal Student Aid (FAFSA): what it is, why you need it, and why you need to get it to the colleges as soon as you can complete it accurately (the earlier the better). Next, we'll show you how financial aid packages can be very different from one college to the next. Then we'll get into the sticky issue of college debt: how much is too much? We'll explain the growing availability of income-based loan repayment plans that guarantee your college loans will not bankrupt you even if you choose a career that doesn't pay a lot. We'll give you some advice on budgeting and how to take advantage of the available tax write-offs, so by the end of the chapter you will have a pretty good idea of whether or not a college should make your financial fit list. Some will, and some won't. Our advice is that if you reach academically and stick within your affordability range, you'll have a win-win situation.

WHAT IS FINANCIAL AID AND HOW DO YOU GET IT?

Financial aid is money you can use to go to college, and everyone can get some—even people who think they can't. It comes in two basic types.

GRANTS & SCHOLARSHIPS

LOANS

So that's it: two piles of money you don't have to pay back—grants and scholarships—and one pile of money you do have to pay back—loans. (Federal Work-Study doesn't really fit in either stack, see page 283.) We'll get into the details of these stacks of money later in the chapter, but of course you want the free money—everybody does. That's why you have to fill out this annoying form called the FAFSA. Some grants are awarded based on need: that is, how much you and your family earned. Others are awarded based on merit: that is, high GPA, playing concert-quality clarinet, etc. Scholarships are also "free" money, and may be awarded for all kinds of different reasons, but let's not get ahead of ourselves. Most people could use a little financial help, and whether you're going for grants or some scholarships, the first step is often the FAFSA.

FAFSA

We said that filling out the FAFSA (www.fafsa.gov) is annoying, because you have to collect a lot of tax documents and you have to talk to your parents about money—and that's always a pain. But filling out the FAFSA isn't rocket science; it just takes time. Some students don't take the time to fill it out, but that's one of those short-term moves that make no sense in the long run, because you can't get grants without it or federal student loans without it. Even families that won't get any grant aid should fill out the FAFSA because federal loans have more flexible repayment plans. You'll need parental help to fill it out, but the hassle is worth it.

Six Tips from Dr. Baum

1. Think of college as an investment in yourself.

2. Borrow only what you can afford.

3. Assume that tuition will go up—say 5 percent per year—and work that into your affordability calculation. (It may not, but if you plan, you're covered.)

4. Beware of bait-and-switch, which is when the financial aid package is a lot more generous your first year than in subsequent years. (Ask if your scholarships are likely to be renewed.)

5. Tuition and fees are fixed prices, but you have choices in how you budget your room and board and other living costs.

6. Most students should avoid private loans, which have variable rates.

The Federal Student Aid website (http://studentaid.ed.gov/fafsa/ filling-out#get-help) does a very good job of walking you through the process. Remember that the first *F* in FAFSA stands for "free," so don't pay anybody to do this for you. If your parents need the form in Spanish, that's also available on the www.fafsa.gov site. If you need help, use the free tools on the site, which include help and hints on every page. And if you click the "Help" icon with the big question mark, you can have a live chat in English or Spanish.

Part of the challenge here is that as a dependent student, you will need to get a whole bunch of financial details from your parents. Even if your parents aren't helping you pay for college, you are still considered a dependent student for financial aid purposes until you're twenty-four unless you're in foster care, are under guardianship, or have dependents of your own.

Below is the list of documents that you will need to fill out the FAFSA. You will not send these documents, but you should keep them in a file, readily available, in case your submission is selected for verification. Being selected for verification is one way that the government audits the process and it's nothing to worry about, but if you're selected, get your documents to the financial aid office so that they can release your money to you. If you're eligible to receive a Pell Grant, you're more likely to be selected for verification, so stay organized.

It probably doesn't need to be said, because you are well aware of how interconnected the world is, but cheating on the FAFSA (by either lowering your family's stated income or increasing dependents) is unwise, since your FAFSA application is linked to your family's IRS filing. Also, some colleges routinely verify all financial aid requests.

Gathering the Documents and Information Needed to Apply for Financial Aid

You will need to collect the following:

◆ Your Social Security number. (It's important that you enter it correctly!)

- Your parents' Social Security numbers if you are a dependent student. The FAFSA does *not* ask (or care) about parents' citizenship status, but if your parents don't have a Social Security number and the system doesn't allow you to proceed by putting zeros in the appropriate box, you may have to file a paper application, which will delay the process.

- Your driver's license number if you have one.

- Your Alien Registration Number if you are not a U.S. citizen.

- Federal tax information or tax returns, including IRS W-2 information for you (and your spouse, if you are married), and for your parents if you are a dependent student:
  - IRS 1040, 1040A, or 1040EZ
  - Foreign tax return if applicable
  - Tax return for Puerto Rico, Guam, American Samoa, the U.S. Virgin Islands, the Marshall Islands, the Federal States of Micronesia, or Palau, if applicable

- Records of your untaxed income, such as child support received, interest income, and veterans' non-education-related benefits for you, and for your parents if you are a dependent student.

- Information on cash; savings and checking account balances; investments, including stocks and bonds and real estate but not including the home in which you live; and business and farm assets for you, and for your parents if you are a dependent student.

The FAFSA4caster

We recommend that before you talk to your parents, you play around with the FAFSA4caster, http://studentaid.ed.gov/fafsa/estimate. You can use it just like a calculator—change the input and you'll change

The CSS Profile

You will need the information on the FAFSA (and a little more) if you're applying to colleges that also use the CSS/Financial Aid Profile. The CSS Profile is in addition to, not instead of the FAFSA, and it's designed to help the colleges give away their institutional funding according to the college's guidelines. There's a tutorial available on the College Board website that will guide you through the process, and as with the FAFSA, there are help buttons on every page (http://student.collegeboard.org/css-financial-aid-profile). Filling out this form is about as fun as clipping a Gila monster's toenails, but you gotta do it if you want a chance to get any scholarships directly from the college. There's a cost involved for each profile: $25 for the first college and $16 for each additional college, but if you qualify for a fee waiver you can fill it out once and send your profile to eight colleges for free.

the output. It doesn't save any information, so you can try it out with as many variables as you want. The 4caster asks some questions about your family and your family income, and if you don't know that yet, just put in some numbers so when you're with your parents you can show them how it works. When it gets to the calculation page, three boxes will be blank: state grants, college grants, and scholarships. You won't know the whole scholarship picture until spring of your senior year, but after you finish working through this chapter, you should have a good idea if you qualify for state grants. So pop some numbers in there and you'll see how they impact the bottom line. (You should also start scoping out scholarships junior year, and it's never too early to know what's available.)

After your FAFSA has been processed, you'll get your Student Aid Report (SAR) and you can check to be sure it's correct. If it's not, follow the procedures to correct or submit additional information. Once it's correct, the SAR shows your expected family contribution (EFC), which is the most important number the FAFSA will give you.

EXPECTED FAMILY CONTRIBUTION (EFC)

The EFC is how much the federal government (and the schools) believe your family can contribute to your education. (Though many researchers view the EFC as more of a way to ration scarce aid dollars than to accurately measure need.) As a general rule, the higher the family income and the more assets a family owns, the higher the EFC. This seems logical, except that the EFC often seems to be much more than a family can actually *afford* to pay without going into too much debt or without putting too much stress on the family members left at home. In most cases, a school will not give you need-based aid to cover the EFC. If, for example, the EFC states that your parents can afford to pay $10,000 a year, in all likelihood your parents will have to come up with that amount.

When you find the gap, that's when hard decisions have to be made. Parents can borrow additional money (see the sidebar "Parent PLUS? Or Parental Problem?" on page 288), but is it worth it?

The other number that will influence how much aid you get is how much your school costs; this is called the cost of attendance.

COST OF ATTENDANCE (COA)

For all colleges, the cost of attendance includes the same elements: tuition and fees; housing and meals; and allowances for books, supplies, transportation, loan fees, and dependent care. Because all colleges use the same definition, you can compare COAs between colleges for the average student. (Remember in Chapter 4 where we were comparing schools by net price? Net price is simply the COA minus grants and scholarships.) The COA includes some costs that will be pretty much the same for everyone (tuition and fees), but other costs are different for each student. Transportation, for example, can be next to nothing if you live on campus; on the other hand, it could be a lot if you commute, or if your college is far from home and you plan to fly back for holidays and breaks. Where you choose to live can make a big difference—on campus or off; with family or in a shared house or apartment. These are all part of an estimated COA, but they are also discretionary choices that bring your costs up or down.

COA is a key factor in determining how much of some forms of financial aid you receive. (Pell Grants, which we'll discuss shortly, are not affected by COA.) The higher the COA, the more aid you need, because the simplest way to think about the aid you get is:

COA – EFC = Need

Take the cost of attendance (COA) and subtract your expected family contribution (EFC) and what you get is how much more money you need. The college's financial aid award will cover some portion of this need, but take a close look at what they're offering, because some colleges may offer you lots of grants and scholarships (great!), and some will offer you nothing but loans.

Need – Financial Aid Award = Unmet Need

After you subtract your financial aid award from your need, what you have is called "unmet need." Sometimes there's a small gap. . . and sometimes there's a gap so big that you can't afford to consider

College Abacus shows how Akeelah's family income reduced the price of a couple of colleges.

Laurence Fishburne Angela Bassett Keke Palmer

AKEELAH
and
the
BEE

Akeelah's college search

Akeelah and the Bee *(2006) follows a young girl from South Los Angeles in her quest to win the Scripps National Spelling Bee.*

At **College Abacus**, we were curious to explore what an extraordinary student like Akeelah might expect in financial aid when applying to college. As a first-generation minority applicant from a low-income background, financial aid is likely to provide key support for Akeelah's matriculation, persistence and completeion at a four-year college.

that college. Don't stop at the sticker price, but do compare aid packages! To see how an estimated financial aid package will influence your actual cost, check out the College Abacus website.

For the presentation, the fictional family's financial data was put in the College Abacus tool, then three Los Angeles area colleges were selected—a community college (LA Mission), a public university (University of California, Los Angeles) and a private college (Pomona). This is what came up:

You can see that while Pomona's sticker price was $62,230, the estimated net price for Akeelah was $4,400.

UNPACKING THE FINANCIAL AID OFFER

Akeelah still has to take a look at what's in the financial aid packages at each college, because "free" money (grants and scholarships) is of course preferable over a whole bunch of loans that will take years to repay. With less debt, she has a significantly greater chance of graduating in four years if she chooses one of the four-year options. Grants are gifts, and it's money you don't want to leave on the table, so let's take a look at the different grants that are out there.

Pell Grants

The federal Pell Grant program is for students with financial need. The maximum Pell grant award varies year to year. For the 2014–15 school year, it was $5,730 annually. How much you actually get depends on two factors: your need (based on the information you provided in the FAFSA) and how many credits you're taking. If you're taking at least twelve semester credits (or the equivalent at your school) during the term, you're considered full-time; six credits makes you half time. If you're not considered full-time, your Pell award is adjusted to reflect some fraction of the full-time status.

But watch out! Remember that while earning twelve credits per semester is considered full-time for financial aid purposes, if you only take twelve credits each term, it will take you five years to graduate, since the average bachelor's degree requires a total of 120 units. If you're trying to stay within a tight budget, you should calculate what an extra year of tuition, room, board, and all the rest will cost you. At the same time, if you're working and going to school, fifteen credits might be too many. It's a balancing act, but one that has a financial component you can calculate.

Another thing to look out for is that you cannot receive more than one Pell Grant each semester, even if you're attending two colleges simultaneously. So if you thought it was a good idea to get a few courses out of the way at the community college while you're enrolled at the university, use your Pell Grant where you're enrolled full-time. If you're enrolled part-time at both schools, use it where the COA is higher.

Federal Supplementary Educational Opportunity (FSEOG) Grants

Students who are Pell-eligible and have the most financial need could receive from $100 to $4,000 in Federal Supplemental Equal Opportunity Grant (FSEOG) funds, which are federal funds administered by the campus. If FSEOG funds are available, they are limited, and it's likely that the college will run out of FSEOG funds before it runs out of students who qualify. To give yourself the best chance at these funds, submit your FAFSA in January, and make sure that the institutional code is listed for each school that you want to receive the information. In most cases, the early birds get the FSEOG.

Federal Work-Study

Federal Work-Study (FWS) is not a grant and it's not a loan, but it is a program that helps students offset the cost of their education by working, either for the college on campus or for a nonprofit off-campus. If you qualify for FWS, you can earn some tax-free dollars, and that could make your college experience more affordable, so definitely check it out. Be aware, however, that there are two big flaws in the program that might limit your ability to benefit from it.

First, for political reasons, work-study dollars tend not to flow to the campuses and students that need them most. Florida State University, for instance, receives less than one-fifth as much work-study money as Columbia University, even though Florida State is five times bigger and has a much higher proportion of low-income students, according to researchers at the Community College Research Center.

Second, while a certain percentage of work-study jobs are supposed to be community service-oriented—allowing you, for instance, to earn money tutoring or mentoring poor kids at a nonprofit— in practice, colleges tend to hoard work-study money for cheap on-campus labor. So if you're lucky enough to get a work-study job, it'll probably be answering phones in the bursar's office or handing out towels at the school gym. Not that there's anything wrong with those jobs. It's good honest work and there's often enough downtime so that you can get some studying done. But if you want a work-study job that actually involves community service, you'll probably need to ask for it, and one might or might not be available.

Merit Aid

Merit aid is one of the biggest chunks of money colleges offer students and the percentage of students getting it is on the rise. Merit aid goes to all kinds of students for all kinds of reasons. Some financially needy students receive it because they have talents and accomplishments schools are looking for—high GPAs and test scores, astounding musical or athletic ability, or a history of leadership. But students from middle class and affluent families can qualify for merit grants, too. In fact, it's the financial aid such families are most likely to get. Frankly, it's a little bit of a racket since schools often use merit aid to lure students from wealthy families who have enough money to pay full near-tuition. But regardless of your family background, you should do what you can to maximize the amount of merit aid you're offered. That means, first and foremost, keeping your GPA up. It also means building your other skills and talents, and making sure you highlight them in your application.

Danger Zone: Scholarship Scams

If you've "won" a scholarship but they ask you for money, it's a scam. Sometimes they'll call what you need to send them a "disbursement fee" or "redemption fee" because, they say, they need to pay the taxes on your prize. It's all baloney.

Or it's a "scholarship for profit" racket—you send just $5 and about ten thousand other people send $5, and then they give away $1,000. If you feel like wasting $5, give your uncle $5 and ask him to buy a lottery ticket for you. Alternatively, if the money is eating a hole in your pocket, give that $5 away.

Life has no guarantees, and neither do scholarships. If someone "guarantees" you money if you just pay them a little something up front, run—don't walk—the other way. This could also be true of some "free" scholarship or financial aid seminars. We went to one and nobody asked up front for money, but it was pretty clever how they made it seem like they could help you get more federal money if they helped you with the FAFSA . . . for a small fee, of course. Remember, the first *F* in FAFSA stands for "free."

State Grants

State grants may be need-based, merit-based, or a combination of both and the early bird really does get the worm. Some states have deadlines in February or March; others are first-come, first-served. Just like the federal grants, they don't have to be repaid. But some may have certain restrictions. State grants, for example, may require that the student use the funds in her state of residence. Some state grants are tiered, giving more funding for higher GPAs. Check your state's website; they're all listed on the U.S. Department of Education website (www.ed.gov).

Service Grants

There's money available to offset tuition or forgive loans for those who complete a term of national service or who sign up for Reserve Officer Training Corps (ROTC) or the military. Two years in AmeriCorps, for example, could yield a benefit worth more than $10,000 in student loan relief or college tuition, and over 120 universities match these funds. ROTC could earn you up to a full four-year scholarship, and the G.I. Bill provides up to $35,000 (tax free) for servicemembers that can be used for educational expenses. For details on how serving others can benefit your financial situation, check out Chapter 13.

Scholarships

Scholarships do not have to be repaid, there are lots of them, and diligent students with outstanding GPAs really do get checks in the mail from corporations, communities, individuals, foundations, clubs, and churches. Don't ignore them, especially the ones that might have a smaller pool of applicants—a parent's workplace, your place of worship, community-based foundations. But you shouldn't focus on scholarship applications at the expense of studying for the SAT or maintaining your GPA, because it's your academic record

that will qualify you for merit aid grants, which are like scholarships in that they don't have to be repaid. Many colleges award them as part of a financial aid package for students with a strong academic record.

If an application is required for a scholarship, the big winners don't just throw their name in the ring with a generic essay that sounds like a recycled English assignment or a cut-and-paste from a previous effort. And statistically you won't get much if you simply register for the no-essay-required scholarships. But if you approach the scholarship search as if it's a job and custom-fit each application, it could yield some rewards. It's also a crapshoot: you might get nothing, but for sure you'll get nothing if you don't put yourself out there. Some students who really go for it end up with a whole lot of money that they would not have had if they hadn't been willing to put in some effort. Scholarships are also a great networking opportunity, because organizations like to know the students they're funding. Consider your pre-college scholarship search the first step toward building a standout résumé for your post-college employment search. Scholarships you get will not only make you look impressive on paper for years to come but also can open doors and expand your network of people to tap for internships, jobs, and advice.

Loans

Loans might appear in your financial aid package as just one more line that reduces the unmet need. But don't be fooled. Loans are not like grants or scholarships. They have to be repaid. On the other hand, you also have to realize that taking on *a reasonable* amount of debt is fine, and even a good thing. A few loans might give you an opportunity that you never would have had if you hadn't been willing to invest in your future.

The Institute for College Access and Success (TICAS) advises that if you decide to, or feel like you have to, go the loan route, use all the *federal* loans available before going to a private loan from a commercial bank. Interest rates may vary, but federal loans have more flexible repayment plans, and that's often critical. The best kind of loan to get if you qualify is a subsidized federal loan—the government pays interest on the loan while you're in school, and you don't have to begin repaying the loan until six months after you've graduated. Most loans are unsubsidized, which means that you have to start paying the interest as soon as the loan is disbursed. Federal (not private) loans can also be repaid as a percentage of your future income, which is hugely important. You have to make the arrangements, but it means that if by choice or bad luck you don't make a large income as an adult you won't go bankrupt paying off your student loans.

Lots of students invest in their future by borrowing, but the National Association for College Admission Counseling recommends that you be *very* careful if you're considering borrowing a

Parent PLUS? Or Parental Problem?

Rachel Fishman, Policy Analyst,
Education Policy Program, New America Foundation

Even with all the financial aid you can get from grants and student loans, there's often a gap between what you're getting and what a high-cost institution will cost you. Some students ask their parents to help by taking on a Parent PLUS loan, but before you do that, there are a few things you should know.

Parent PLUS loans often come with much worse terms than student loans. They have higher interest rates and aren't eligible for flexible income-based re-payment plans. Also, PLUS loans are basically impossible to get rid of. Even if your parents file for bankruptcy, they'll still have to pay off these loans.

On your part, you need to make sure that you have applied for and received all of the grant aid to which you're entitled. Work diligently and strategically on scholarship applications, and appeal to the financial aid office on the chance that additional funds might be made available to you. If you've done all of this and a gap still remains, you may have to make the difficult decision to attend a more affordable college.

lot of money to go to a private for-profit college. Their studies show that on average, bachelor's degree programs at for-profit colleges cost 20 percent more than similar programs at flagship public universities, associate's degree programs at for-profit institutions average four times the cost of the program at a community college, and students at for-profit colleges end up with significantly more debt than students at nonprofit institutions.[80] According to TICAS, "National data show that the vast majority of graduates from for-profit four-year colleges (88%) took out student loans, and they borrowed an average of $39,950—43 percent more than graduates from other types of four-year colleges."[81] Given this, it probably won't surprise you that, with few exceptions, most for-profit colleges don't do very well on our Best-Bang-for-the-Buck rankings.

The U.S. Department of Education has two public federal student loan programs: Direct Loans and Perkins Loans.

Direct Loans

For all Direct Loans, the U.S. Department of Education is the lender.

Direct Subsidized Loans are loans made to eligible undergraduate students who demonstrate financial need. The loans are intended to help cover the costs of higher education at a college or career school.

Direct Unsubsidized Loans are loans made to eligible undergraduate, graduate, and professional students, but in this case, the student does not have to demonstrate financial need to be eligible for the loan.

Direct PLUS Loans are loans made to graduate or professional students and to parents of dependent undergraduate students to help pay for education expenses not covered by other financial aid.

Perkins Loan

The Federal Perkins Loan Program is a school-based loan program for students with exceptional financial need. For Perkins Loans, your college is the lender, but it hasn't gotten new money in years and may be eliminated.[82]

How Much Debt Is Too Much?

Student loan debt is climbing, and it's a concern all around. The Project on Student Debt reports that "seven in *10* college seniors who graduated in 2013 had student loan debt, with an average of $29,400 per borrower."[83] The College Board suggests that as a rule of thumb, your parents shouldn't take on *total* debt exceeding 37 percent of their income, and that your monthly loan repayments should not add up to more than 10

Beware the Private Loan Trap

The Institute for College Access and Success advises, "Private student loans are one of the riskiest ways to pay for college. They have much more in common with credit cards than they do with federal student loans. Private loans typically have variable interest rates that are higher for those who can least afford them and they lack the important consumer protections and repayment options of federal loans."[84]

to 15 percent of your starting monthly income after you graduate. Chapter 11 is all about employment after college, and different occupations command different earnings, of course. One way to get a general estimate of what your salary after graduation might be is to go to the National Association of Colleges and Employers (NACE) website, which provides a free Job Seekers Salary Calculator. Pick a profession, select a region, and project that you have a BA. To estimate your monthly loan payments and evaluate repayment plan options, visit studentaid.gov/repayment-estimator.

Repayment Plans

If you are taking out loans, it's very important to keep in mind from the start what your (or your parents') obligations will be when you graduate and it comes time to pay back the loans. Here are the available options based on your specific circumstances (e.g., income, employment status, whether you are in graduate school, etc.).

Deferment. Postpones repayment of the principal balance for up to three years for people facing unemployment.

Forbearance. Allows you to postpone or reduce your monthly amount for a limited time, up to five years.

Extended repayment. Available to students whose outstanding principal and interest exceeds $30,000.

Public service loan forgiveness. Borrowers employed in public service jobs (government, public safety, law enforcement, public health, public education) are eligible for loan forgiveness after making 120 on-time monthly payments.

Income-based Loan Repayment

Here's something most adults, even many college admissions experts, don't know because back in the day it wasn't available—but it's hugely important for you. If you take out federal student loans to finance your college education, you will have the option of paying back those loans as an affordable percentage of your future income.

Here's why that's important: with the "income-based repayment" option, your college loans won't be a crushing financial burden to you, regardless of how much you borrowed for college or how much you earn afterward.

Here's how income-based repayment works. The more you make, the higher the percentage you pay, though you'll never pay more than ten percent of your income. The lower your income, the lower the percentage you pay. If you earn, say, $50,000 a year, you'll devote 6.5 percent, or $271 a month, to paying off your loans. If you earn $30,000, you'll only pay 4 percent, or $104 a month, though it'll take you more years to pay the loan off. If you earn only a poverty-level income, around $18,000, you'll pay nothing, though interest on your unpaid portion might still accrue. (To see what your payments will be at different income levels, check out the Department of Education's Repayment Estimator: studentloans.gov/myDirectLoan/mobile/repay ment/repaymentEstimator.action#view-repayment-plans). And if, after twenty years, you've still not earned enough to pay back your loans (that's probably not going to happen, but it could), then the remaining balance of your loan is forgiven.

Now, that doesn't mean you should borrow more than you need— that's always a bad idea. But here's what it does mean, according to college finance policy expert Alexander Holt of the New America Foundation.[85] First, don't be afraid to finance your college education with federal loans. It's a good investment and under income-based repayment you'll be able to afford it. Second, make sure you max out on your federal loans first before turning to private loans, because the income-based repayment option only applies to the former, not the latter (in fact, there's almost no good reason to finance an under-graduate degree with private loans).

Income-based repayment is not something you have to think about or do anything about now. You apply for it only when the time comes for you to start paying back your loans. But when that time does come, you have to be proactive. You may have to ask your loan servicer to give you the forms (they have a habit of not telling you). And you need to reapply every year, otherwise you'll have to pay the standard, non-income-based amount, which could be higher.

APPEAL PROCESS

When you compare your financial aid awards, you will see that the different colleges have packaged your financial aid in different ways. You can compare these side by side on the Financial Aid U Cost Comparison Worksheet (page 295).[86]

If you think a college has made an error, check with that college's financial aid office. If your circumstances have changed, let them know. If going to the university depends on the aid package and your package is not enough, you can file what's called an appeal. There will be procedures for doing this, and the college is under no obligation to match the package another college might have offered you. But if you do want the college to reconsider its offer, use their appeal process. Appeals can be effective, though you will need to provide documentation if you're appealing based on changed circumstances. Ron Lieber wrote about the "appeal season" for the *New York Times* (April 5, 2014), and the bottom line is that colleges do listen, though perhaps selectively. It's really impossible to calculate your odds, but Lieber's reporting suggests that you should give it the good old college try. Particularly "if similar schools offer radically different amounts, it's worth finding out if there was an error."[87] You have nothing to lose by asking and everything to gain by putting together documents that support your appeal.

THE OTHER COLLEGE GUIDE

TAX BENEFITS FOR EDUCATION

Tax relief for families paying tuition, fees, and some course-related expenses is available through both credits and deductions. One tax expert told us that in his experience, families aren't using this as much as they could. You could get up to $2,500 back easy as pie, so it's worth your effort. Here's a snapshot.

Credits. If you're enrolled at least half-time and you're pursuing a degree or credential, your parents will be eligible for the $2,500 American Opportunity Credit (AOC) to help defray the cost of your college expenses. Eligible expenses include tuition and fees, books, supplies, and equipment. Up to 40 percent ($1,000) of that credit is refundable, so if you don't have a tax liability, you can get as much as $1,000 back just for filing! The other $1,500 of the AOC reduces your taxes. A second type of credit available, called the Lifetime Learning Credit, is $2,000, and it's good for students who are only taking one course, or not pursuing a degree.

Deductions. Congress has discretion over whether tax deductions are extended from year to year. In the past, deductions have been available for tuition and fees and they also may be available on qualified student loans.

You don't have to remember all of this at once—it's a lot of information! The important thing to keep in mind is that when tax season rolls around in the spring, you (and your parents, if they are contributing to your education costs) should revisit your eligibility for credits and deductions as you prepare to file your taxes. Doing so will most likely bring you valuable savings.

SATISFACTORY ACADEMIC PROGRESS

Colleges must enforce strict guidelines because they are distributing federal dollars, and taxpayers want to see that it's going to good use—they don't want to pay students to play Frisbee or hang out in the dorms and forget about going to class. That's why there's a guideline called "satisfactory academic progress" (SAP). It essentially means that you have to be making adequate progress toward your degree. The institutions have some flexibility on how they define SAP, but in general, students cannot exceed strict time limits, they must pass a significant number of classes, and they must abide by limits on taking courses as credit/no credit (or pass/no pass) rather than for an actual grade. If you're planning to stop for some period of time, make it easy on yourself by filing all the official paperwork with both the records and the financial aid offices so that it doesn't appear as though you're not making SAP.

THE BOTTOM LINE

Finances are just one piece of the college fit puzzle, but for most families, they're a big and important piece. They're also usually a scary piece, but the more you stay informed, the more you'll notice the fear turning into power to make some major life decisions. Community college may be the least expensive way to go, but it could also be an expensive detour if you don't get out of it what you want. An expensive college may seem like a dream come true, but if the financial aid package doesn't fit your budget and going there would leave you climbing a mountain of debt, it may not be worth it, either. In spring of your senior year, when all the financial aid packages are unwrapped, with the guidance and resources we've recommended here you and your parents will have a pretty good idea of the college that makes the most sense for all of you in the short term and over the long haul.

Cost Comparison Worksheet

Use this worksheet to compare the financial aid award letters you received from different schools. The worksheet will help you compare financial aid packages side-by-side to determine the cost to you and what out-of-pocket expenses you may have to pay.

	1.	2.	3.
NAME OF COLLEGE:			

COST OF ATTENDANCE	1.	2.	3.
Tuition & Fees	+	+	+
Room & Board	+	+	+
Books & Supplies	+	+	+
Personal Expenses	+	+	+
Transportation Expense	+	+	+
TOTAL COST OF ATTENDANCE	=	=	=

FINANCIAL AID SOURCES: GRANTS/SCHOLARSHIPS		1.	2.	3.
Federal Grants	Federal Pell Grant	+	+	+
	Federal Supplemental Educational Opportunity Grant (FSEOG)	+	+	+
	TEACH Grant	+	+	+
State Grants & Scholarships		+	+	+
Institution Grants & Scholarships		+	+	+
Outside Grants & Scholarships		+	+	+
TOTAL GRANTS/ SCHOLARSHIPS		=	=	=

NET PRICE OF ATTENDANCE	1.	2.	3.
Total Cost of Attendance			
Total Grants/Scholarships	−	−	−
NET PRICE OF ATTENDANCE	=	=	=

OTHER FINANCIAL AID RESOURCES		1.	2.	3.
Federal Work Study		+	+	+
Student loans	Federal Direct Subsidized Loan	+	+	+
	Federal Direct Unsubsidized Loan	+	+	+
	Federal Perkins Loan	+	+	+
TOTAL OTHER FINANCIAL AID RESOURCES		=	=	=

REMAINING COST OF ATTENDANCE	1.	2.	3.
Net Price of Attendance			
TOTAL Other Financial Aid Sources	−	−	−
REMAINING AID TO BE PAID	=	=	=

THE OTHER HELPFUL TOOL

COLLEGE GUIDE

Glossary of Financial Aid Terms

Accreditation: required for institutions to be able to give federal financial aid.

CSS Profile: a financial aid profile by the College Board that is used by students to apply for non-federal financial aid from some colleges and scholarship programs.

Cost of attendance (COA): includes tuition and fees; room and board; and allowances for books, supplies, transportation, loan fees, and dependent care. Cost of attendance minus grants and scholarships equals net price.

Dependent student: for financial aid purposes, a dependent student is considered part of a parent's household.

Direct loan: loans offered by the U.S. Department of Education. They may be subsidized or unsubsidized.

Disbursement: payment of federal aid funds to the student by the school.

Enrollment status: percentage of full-time that you're in school. Financial aid award is adjusted based on this status. Generally "full-time" is twelve units per semester, but you need to complete fifteen units per semester to graduate in four years.

Expected family contribution (EFC): a number used by a school to calculate how much financial aid you are eligible to receive, if any. It's based on the information you provided in the FAFSA. It is not the amount of money your family will have to pay for college, nor is it the amount of federal student aid you will receive. The EFC is reported to you on your Student Aid Report and is used by colleges to award aid.

FAFSA (Free Application for Federal Student Aid): form used by the U.S. Department of Education for all students seeking financial aid.

FAFSA4caster: provides an early estimate of your student aid eligibility.

Federal methodology: the formula used to calculate the EFC for students; the higher your income + assets, the bigger your EFC.

THE
OTHER
HELPFUL
TOOL
COLLEGE
GUIDE

Glossary of Financial Aid Terms

Fees: college costs that are in addition to tuition (e.g., student health fee).

Financial aid package: a combination of loans, grants, and scholarships that schools offer to students. Some students' aid package may include work-study.

Grant: funding that does not have to be repaid if the student completes the courses for which the grant money was awarded:

> *Federal Supplementary Educational Opportunity Grants (FSEOG)* are need-based and disbursed as part of campus-based aid and not all schools participate.

> *Pell Grants* are available from the federal government to students who meet guidelines for financial need.

> *State grants* vary and are need-based, merit-based, or both. Some state grants can only be used at the state colleges and universities.

> *Teacher Education Assistance for College and Higher Education (TEACH) Grant:* can help students pay for college if they plan to become a teacher in a high-need field in a low-income area.

Independent student: for financial aid purposes, a student who is considered separate from any parent.

Loan: funding that is available and must be repaid over time with interest:

> federal student loans come from the federal government.

> private student loans are nonfederal loans, made by a lender such as a bank, credit union, state agency, or school.

Loan forgiveness programs: government programs that erase outstanding debt in return for a student's work in certain fields.

Merit aid: discounts that a college awards to an admitted student. Awards are based on achievement or talent, not financial need.

Need: the difference between COA and EFC. (See also Unmet Need.)

Net price: an estimate of the actual costs that you will need to pay during the school year to cover education expenses at a particular school. Net

THE *OTHER* HELPFUL TOOL COLLEGE GUIDE

(Continued)

Glossary of Financial Aid Terms

price is determined by taking the institution's cost of attendance and subtracting your grants and scholarships.

Pell Grant: a financial aid award made by the federal government to students who meet guidelines for financial need.

Scholarship: a gift of money that does not have to be repaid:

> merit-based: awarded based on academic achievement or a combination of academics and a special talent.

> need-based: awarded based on students' and families' financial need; normally determined by submitting the FAFSA.

> career-based: awarded to students interested in pursuing a specific career.

> college-based: offered by a specific college or university, usually as a result of academic or personal achievements. Can be partial or full.

Stafford Loan: federal government loan for students who have financial need. They are part of the Federal Family Education Loan Program (FFELP) and may be subsidized or unsubsidized.

Student Aid Report (SAR): a summary of the information you submitted on your FAFSA. You will have a chance to correct it, and once it's correct, it will contain your EFC, the number that's used to determine your eligibility for federal student aid.

Subsidized loan: a type of Stafford Loan on which all the interest is paid by the government until the student graduates.

Unmet need: the difference between cost of attendance and what a student can afford to pay, including all grants and scholarships.

Unsubsidized loan: the borrower pays the interest, which begins to accrue from the date of disbursement.

Work-study: a type of financial aid usually available on a limited basis, which allows students to pay some of their expenses by working on or off campus.

11.

CARPE DIEM

MAKING THE MOST OF YOUR FIRST YEAR

FUN
CREATING
YOUR FUTURE   WORK
FREEDOM   RESPONSIBILITY   STRUCTURE

a little thing called balance

TIME

Get ready. Your first year of college, no matter where you go, will probably be unlike anything you've ever experienced, and lots of students are really thrown by the changes.

When they get there, some students have the OMG moment: suddenly finding themselves out of their comfort zone, homesick, facing academic challenges, trapped in a small room with a weird roommate or cruising endlessly for a parking place, and on a campus where everyone seems to be going somewhere with intent and you're not even sure where the bathroom is. Not everyone will make it through their first college year. That's understandable, because not everyone has thought about what going to college really means. Though there's a wide range of retention rates at different institutions:[88] on average about 65 percent of the freshmen at public institutions and 67 percent of the freshmen who start at private institutions will return for a second year.

It's crummy to think that over 30 percent of your classmates will not make it past their freshman year, but the other side of that statistic is that *most kids do make it* and you can be one of those. The ones who make it have a plan. They strategize—they graduate with a good GPA, manageable debt, and a network of friends and professionals who will be lifelong connections to a fulfilling social and professional life. None of this happens by accident. Successful students learn how to manage their time; they know the college rules and use them to select courses that lead to a degree; they figure out how much they can work without blowing the academic scene; they have a healthy social life; and they move into their second year with friends who share their interests and a mentor who can guide them. You can do all of this.[89]

WHAT TO DO WHEN YOU MISS HOME

Not everyone is a residential student, but if you do go away from home, you might feel a little homesick. According to a UCLA study, 66 percent of first-year students feel "lonely or homesick," so you have to think of homesickness as an allergy that lurks in residence halls and you have to prepare to combat it.[90] Here's the antidote: don't go home. You're in the process of making your college home, and you need to give yourself time to take root. Sometimes what's happening at home makes it harder, like the family pet dies. This is a terrible thing to think about, but sometimes it happens because you got Snickerdoodles when you were in kindergarten and now she's ninety-one in dog years. Your parents and grandparents and friends may send out a little SOS that they miss you and your laundry, but trust us: it's better if you don't give in. Get to know some commuter students who live in the area and let them show you around. Or go downstairs, put the coins

Six Tips for First-Year Success

1. When the homesickness bug bites, do your laundry.

2. Write your purpose for being in college on the mirror and look at it every day.

3. Think of time like money, spend it wisely, and account for it.

4. Strategize your way through any remediation required of you. You *can* do it.

5. Work fifteen hours (or less) a week.

6. Stick to your plan to earn your bachelor's degree.

in the machine, do your own laundry, and spend Friday night hanging around. Chances are pretty good that you're not the only one who's missing family and friends. Chances are equally good that as you give yourself time, you will grow roots and friendships—with kids who live in the area, and possibly even others who live in or are from other countries—and it won't be long before your college will feel like home and you'll miss it when you leave.

MANAGING YOUR FREEDOM

It's likely that during your first college year, you're going to struggle with managing your time. After all, it's not like high school, where you have to show up in the morning and dutifully go to six classes in a row before being released for the day. And it's not like working full-time, where you have to show up in the morning and put in your eight or nine hours of work before clocking out. Most college students have a much looser schedule. Some have only two or three hours of classes on any given day, and many have one day a week when they don't have any classes at all. Many of you also will have responsibilities that mean you're rushing from class to work to helping out at home, and for you the whole idea of "free time" is totally ridiculous.

If you are a full-time student (according to the National Center for Education Statistics, 77 percent of students at four-year institutions are full-time), you may have some free time and you'll need to manage it—and not get sucked into wasting many an afternoon on Angry Birds, sports, or just hanging out in the residence halls.[91] If that sounds like you, you're in good company. According to Postsecondary Education Opportunity's analysis of the American Time Use Survey, about 48 percent of students struggle with managing their time. On average, most students study for just 3.3 hours a day, which includes "1.7 hours taking classes and 1.5 hours doing research or homework outside of class."[92] Compare that with the 4.3 hours per day that students are spending on sports and leisure activities, and, well—*yikes.*

What this data snapshot should tell you is this: you've got to go into college with your eyes wide open. Being a full-time college student will give you an enormous amount of freedom, but it also means an enormous amount of responsibility. You'll be managing more time than you ever had before, but that's okay—in fact, it's great, it's liberating!—so long as you think of college as a full-time learning experience. Just because you're not required to show up and *be* some-

Time Use of Full-Time College Students on Weekdays Ages 18 to 24 Years 2003–2012

"[I]t is with much puzzlement and a great deal of concern that we learn that full time college students spend an average of 3.3 hours per weekday on educational activities. These activities include 1.7 hours per day taking classes, and 1.5 hours per day on research and homework. This pattern has held year-after-year for the last eight years in data conducted by the Census Bureau and sponsored by the Bureau of Labor Statistics."

POSTSECONDARY EDUCATION OPPORTUNITY

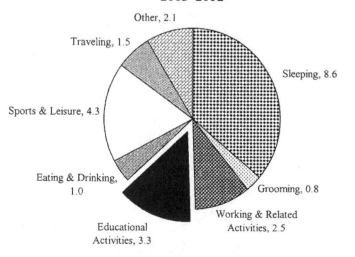

where—in class, at work, at the library—doesn't mean you don't need to be spending that time *studying* and *working*. In fact, being a full-time student should be a solid forty-plus hours a week going to class, hitting the books, reading, researching, writing papers, and otherwise studying. That's eight hours a day. Count 'em—*eight*.

If you do that, if you clock in your study time Monday through Friday, chances are, you'll probably do well in your classes. And the good news is, you'll *still* have time for *sixteen* more hours of working out, hanging out, sleeping, eating, chillin', or participating in whatever campus activities you'd like. However you divide up your day, just make sure you don't shortchange the studying part. If you've made it to college, then you're *paying* for your education in time and money. (Even if you're not the one paying, *somebody* is.) Your job for the next four years is to get an education that will set you up for success.

TIME MANAGEMENT, ROLES, AND GOALS

This time management business is worth getting good at because being at college is like being self-employed, and how much you earn in the long run has a lot to do with the choices you're making every day. Here are two questions that good managers ask themselves:

1. How am I spending my time now? Some first-year programs start students out by asking them to track what they do for a week: every day, every hour, every minute. It can get kind of obsessive, like those step-tracking devices, but it's an illuminating experience. How much time do you really spend gaming? Exercising? Studying? Sleeping? Reading? Socializing? Eating? Walking from A to B? (Is that why you're late to class?) Locating your car keys, house keys, or cell phone? (Is there a solution to that?) You get the idea—

before you start managing how you *should* use your time, figure out how you *are* using it.

2. What are my goals? Are you striving for a specific GPA? Do you have any physical fitness goals? Would you like to really master a technical skill? Get better at writing? Excel in your math class? Keep in touch with Grandma? Find friends? Improve a talent? Read 100 percent of your class assignments? Join a study group? Start an Ultimate Frisbee team? You'll probably gain steam as you make you make your list—don't stop! Write down everything you *think* you want to do.

Now take that unwieldy list and chop it up. First, sort it into goals for each of your various roles. Your goals as a student? An athlete? A son or daughter? A friend? An employee? An artist? Divide the page so you can see how your roles influence your goals.

Next you need to prioritize. This is the hard part. What's most important? There's no single answer to that question. Sleep is important, but so are studying, socializing, and being a good son/daughter/friend/colleague.

Each goal includes tasks related to it. Those tasks are what you put in your planner.

THE TWO BOOKS (OR WEBSITES) OF RULES

You will have a lot of freedom at college, but you would be wrong to assume that it's anarchy on campus. In fact, colleges are very rule-bound places, and all the rules about academics and behavior are published in either the **college catalog** or the **student handbook**. These were once printed tomes, and many still are, but they're also online, so your chances of pulling the ignorance card are eliminated. The catalog itself is more than a book—it's the college's contract with you *as long as you remain continuously enrolled at the institution.* If you stop out for a while? New catalog year, new contract, possibly additional requirements. Make a note of your catalog year, because the requirements you must meet to remain in good standing and earn your degree are all delineated in that catalog.

CLASSES AND CREDITS

The class schedule is published before the start of each term and is usually a searchable database where the classes are all listed with the days, times, credit hours, and instructors. Many of the professors will be listed on ratemyprofessors.com, so you can check out some students' opinions, which are just that: opinions, submitted anonymously. Some classes will list the instructor as to be announced (TBA), and you have to roll with that: could be great, could be a challenge.

Most colleges number courses to indicate level, with the 100-level classes indicating they're for first-year students. Sometimes AP scores earned in high school will allow you to go directly to a higher-level course. If you can do that, congratulations—you're saving time and money!—but be aware that the instructor will assume that you, and everyone else, has covered material taught in the prerequisite and may move at a fairly rapid pace.

Crossing the Remediation Bridge

Many colleges require that most (or even all) students take a placement test to see where you are in math or English, and you need to take the tests seriously. Use the Khan Academy's free online resources (www.khan academy.org) to review before the test, or to supplement a course you're required to take after the results are in. Check to see if you have options: Can you take the class at the community college? Does your college offer a summer program? Strategize so that you will have crossed that bridge by the end of your first year.

To Work or Not to Work, That Is the Question

Dr. Sandy Baum, who has written extensively on college finances, suggests that you could be better off financially over the long haul if you limit work so that you can graduate in four years.[93] This calculation is necessarily individual, but according to a report by Public Agenda, "more than half of those who left higher ed before completing a degree or certificate say that the 'need to work and make money' while attending classes is the major reason they left." The report goes on to say, "The problem often begins in the first year. Of those who fail to graduate, more than 6 in 10 report that the statement 'I had to work as well, and it was too stressful trying to do both' described their first year of school; more than a third say it describes their first year a lot.'"[94]

On the other side of the issue, internships and career-related experiences can set you up for future employment, so spending some time working (especially paid internships) may, paradoxically, contribute to a good outcome. Baum's colleague and University of Pennsylvania professor Laura W. Perna writes, "Quantitative studies consistently show that retention rates are higher for students who work a modest number of hours per week (ten to fifteen) than they are for students who do not work at all or those who work more than fifteen hours per week. Research also shows increased academic success for students working on rather than off campus."[95]

Developmental courses may be numbered 0–99 (or not numbered at all) and are part of what Complete College America calls the "bridge to nowhere": remediation.[96] Nationwide, 20 percent of freshmen who go directly to four-year colleges need remediation, and if you're at an open-access or less selective school, the percentage may be much higher. The thing to know right from the get-go is that remedial classes are not college-level coursework, so they won't count toward your degree. Check with your financial aid office about how remedial units count toward your eligibility status for financial aid. According to the National Association of Student Financial Aid Administrators, "Sometimes remedial coursework is baked into a program of study. If it is, financial aid can count toward those courses. If it is not, students are not eligible for aid for those courses."[97] As we said before: Don't give up on yourself. You can do this.

As a rule of thumb, a credit hour measures the amount of time you spend in class. If you're taking fifteen credit hours per term, you're in class or lab for fifteen hours a week, but every class will have work that needs to be done outside of class. Many of your instructors will tell you how much time they expect you to be spending on their class alone, but as you just read, the American Time Use Survey seems to suggest that a lot of students are either geniuses or slackers, so take that time element with . . . well, a bag of pretzels. How much time you actually need to get the most out of a class will depend on the rigor of the course, the instructor, your preparation and learning style, and *your own commitment to your education*. We put that in italics so you would trip on the whole idea that a lot of this is riding on you. However long it takes you, making the most of your first year means coming to class prepared and giving yourself time to research, write, and understand and do that again and again.

So that you set yourself up to graduate in four years, the experts we spoke to recommend taking fifteen credits each semester, though this advice will vary if you're at a campus that uses a quarter or trimester system or your major requires more than 120

Office Hours

Every professor, administrator, and campus professional we talked to said that you should go to the instructor's office hours at least once during the first term. Ask for clarification on a point made in class. Review a recent assignment or ask how you might improve. Asking for help is not a sign of weakness. On the contrary, it's evidence that you are in college for the right reasons. Chances are the prof will be glad to see you and may even become one of your mentors along the way.

credits. That being said, your advisor, who knows both your college and your academic record, may suggest that you take fewer classes while you acclimate to college life and build a solid GPA for yourself. For financial aid purposes, you're considered full-time if you take just twelve units a semester.

Figuring out how to balance your course load with your life obligations has to do with the academic credit count, but it also has to do with the types of classes you're taking and the expectations of each instructor. This is where the **syllabus** comes in. A syllabus is a course outline and should describe what students are supposed to be learning in the class and how that learning will be measured (essays, tests, lab results, performance, portfolio . . .). A syllabus also indicates how assignments are weighted for grading purposes. Is the final exam worth 50 percent of your grade, or maybe 100 percent? Do you have a choice of taking a test or doing a term paper?

Don't just float by this information; think about it. What will you be reading? How many essays will be assigned? Is there a midterm? Is there an in-class final? A take-home final? When you're planning your schedule, look at the requirements for *all* your classes. Do you really want to be taking five finals, each worth 100 percent of your grade, at the end of the term?

The syllabus is not quite the contract that the catalog is because dates and assignments can change, but it should give you a pretty good idea of what you can expect from the course and what the instructor expects from you.

The last tool that you need to be aware of is the **academic calendar,** because one day can make a huge difference. Here's the summary: Colleges allow students to add and drop classes at the beginning of the term, but there comes a day (noted in the academic calendar) when you're on the official roster, which is recorded in the registrar's office. If you just walk away from a class—even if you tell the instructor—and haven't filed the official campus paperwork or completed any required online forms or other procedures, you may find that you earned an F on your official record because you remained officially registered in that class. If too many weeks have passed, dropping a class may be prohibited, or you may be allowed to "withdraw," which will result in a W on your permanent record. All of these rules will be clearly stated in the catalog, so read it! Remember, that's your contract, and ignorance is not a defense.

A final note on dropping classes: while you may be able to drop classes without impact on your academic record, you need to be aware of your credit count for financial aid. If you've accepted aid as a full-time student and you drop below twelve credits, you need to contact your financial aid office because you will have to repay the difference between full- and part-time status.

SCHEDULING YOUR CLASSES

Advisors tell us that when you schedule your first-term classes, you should meet a requirement, explore what might become your major, and choose a class you find interesting. Beyond that, we suggest that you challenge yourself without setting yourself up for months of crazy stress. That means skipping the easy A for the class that promises to teach you how to be more analytical or communicate more thoughtfully. Laszlo Bock, Google's hiring guru, said that once you're at college, "make sure that you're getting out of it not only a broadening of your knowledge but skills that will be valued in today's workplace. Your college degree is not a proxy anymore for having the skills or traits to do any job."[98] If you begin doing that in your early college years, you will set yourself up for a successful career in college and beyond.

If there is a first-year seminar, you may want to consider signing up for it. These classes are often an opportunity to deepen your understanding of your purpose and motivations, while learning how to learn. Not all first-year seminars will be stellar, but when they are, they're definitely worthwhile. According to the Association of American Colleges and Universities, the "highest-quality first-year experiences place a strong emphasis on critical inquiry, frequent writing, information literacy, collaborative learning, and other skills that develop intellectual and practical competencies."[99] If your seminar has these traits, it's categorized as a "high-impact practice," and it could set you up for learning for the rest of your life.

CLASSES THAT ENGAGE STUDENTS: HIGH-IMPACT PRACTICES

You won't find any class labeled "high-impact practice" (HIP), but administrators know what they are, and we thought you should, too. HIP is academic jargon for practices that help students learn, make the most of their experience, and keep them motivated and on track to graduate. Some HIPs (like service learning) may be a part of a formal class; others (like internships) are graded and part of your academic curriculum, but they occur in a work environment. Still others, like the first-year experience, are a HIP by themselves. We've listed five HIPs along with their definitions below; these classes might be available to first-year students on your campus.

First-year seminars and first-year experiences are always small, so you really get to know the faculty and the students in your group. A really good first-year seminar will get you thinking, writing, and researching. You'll work collaboratively as a team, so you'll gain that skill as well. Some first-year seminars focus on a cutting-edge topic or a faculty member's own research.

Learning communities encourage you to think across courses and challenge you with "big questions" that go well beyond the classroom. You will take two or more linked courses as a group and work closely with one another and with your professors. Many communities explore a common topic or readings, and some deliberately link liberal arts and professional courses, while others feature service learning.

Writing-intensive courses emphasize writing at all levels of instruction and across the curriculum, including final-year projects. You'll be encouraged to produce and revise various forms of writing for different audiences in different disciplines.

Collaborative assignments and projects combine two key goals: learning to work and solve problems in the company of others, and sharpening your own understanding by listening seriously to the insights of others, especially those with different backgrounds and life experiences. Approaches can include study groups within a course, team-based assignments and writing, and cooperative projects and research.

Service learning and community-based learning offer field-based "experiential learning" with community partners. Often it is a required part of the course. The idea is to give you direct experience with issues you are studying and with ongoing efforts to analyze and solve problems in the community. A key element in these programs is the opportunity you will have to both apply what you are learning in real-world settings and reflect in a classroom setting on your experiences. These programs model the idea that giving something back to the community is an important college outcome, and that working with community partners is good preparation for citizenship, work, and life.

BEYOND THE ACADEMICS

You're going to college for the academics, but a whole lot of learning goes on outside those classroom walls. Making the most of your first year means engaging in opportunities to lead and collaborate. If you're having any trouble connecting with people, finding help, or locating the right opportunity, find the Office of Student Affairs. One VP of student affairs defined her team's role as "helping you graduate." Student affairs professionals know what's going on, and they can help you find whatever it is you're seeking.

HEALTH AND WELLNESS

When you're not feeling well, life falls apart in so many ways. It's easy to say take care of yourself, be safe, drink plenty of water, and

First Lady Michelle Obama on the Power of Education

First Lady Michelle Obama spoke at Bell Multicultural High School in Washington, D.C., November 12, 2013. Here is an excerpt from her remarks.

ONE OF THE MOST IMPORTANT THINGS you all must understand about yourselves is that those [difficult life] experiences are not weaknesses. They're not something to be ashamed of. Experiences like those can make you stronger and more determined. They can teach you all kinds of skills that you could never learn in a classroom—the skills that will lead you to success anywhere in life. But first, you've got to apply those skills toward getting an education.

So what does that mean? That means, first and foremost, believing in yourselves no matter what obstacles you face. It means going to class every single day—that's what I did—not just showing up, but actually paying attention, taking some notes, asking questions.

It means doing your homework every single night—I did—studying hard for every test, even if it's not your favorite subject. It means reaching out to your teachers and counselors and coaches and asking for help whenever you need it. And when you stumble and fall—and I guarantee you, you will, because we all do—it means picking yourself up and trying again and again and again.

All of that is on you. You've got to own that part of it. You've got to step up as individuals. Because here's the key: if you step up, if you choose to own your future and commit to your education, and if you anything stand in your way until you complete it, then you will not only lead our country to that North Star goal, but you will lead yourselves to whatever future you dream of.

eat your vegetables. You know the drill. The truth is, college is a really healthy time of your life, but stuff happens, and the American College Health Association tracks it by surveying college students.[100] Of the 130,000 participants, 91 percent said that their health is good, very good, or excellent. There are a few complaints—allergies (19 percent), back pain (12 percent), sinus infections (15.6 percent)—but for the most part college students are good to go. Several factors can really impact academics, with the biggies being anxiety (19.7 percent) and stress (28.5 percent), which, when you think about it, is a totally appropriate response to the level of change you're going through.

The survey shows that finances are a stressor, too (7.3 percent), but not as much as the Internet and computer games, which affect academic performance 11.7 percent of the time. Work, at 14.7 percent, is a little more stressful than relationships, which come in at 9.7 percent. Concern for friends or family has a 10.4 percent effect. Sleep difficulties (19.4 percent) are worth noting because organisms that don't have adequate rest don't deal with stress very well. It's called sleep deprivation, and for the health of your mind, body, and spirit, try to avoid torturing yourself.

ACTUAL VERSUS PERCEIVED: WHAT'S REAL AND WHAT'S NOT

Another piece of the American College Health Association survey shows that what students are really doing is very different from what other students *think* they're doing. This is good for you to know, because if someone suggests that *everyone* is drinking, smoking, and getting high, you'll know that it's simply not true. Then, like a genuine over-the-top card-carrying nerd, you can cite some statistics. It's interesting, for example, that 58 percent of males never used marijuana, but only 10 percent of students thought that was the case. Students think everyone is drinking a lot more than they are, too, since 93.5 percent perceive recent drinking, but only 64.8 percent actually did drink in the last thirty days.

You'll probably have a lot of people talking to you about the dangers of alcohol, and the part about being underage is real; it's the law, and in some schools it's really, really, absolutely enforced, no kidding, as in zero tolerance. Remember the catalog? Read the part about drugs and alcohol before you do something regrettable. Unfortunately, about 35 percent of the survey participants did something they regretted while under the influence—males and females in about equal numbers. They did other dangerous things, too, like had unprotected sex (22.7 percent) or physically injured themselves (15.7 percent). And lots of people drank so much they forgot altogether what they did (31.9 percent). That's a tough look in the mirror the morning after.

A RECAP

Despite, or perhaps because of, all the time students have available in college, nearly half of all first-year students struggle with effective time management and a third have a hard time developing effective study skills.[101] For too many students this adds up to too much, and they leave before their sophomore year begins.

On the other hand, most students not only survive, they thrive. They don't ignore all the obstacles and pitfalls on the road, but they don't lose sight of their goal, either. How can you make the most of your first year? Connect with at least one mentor; build relationships with students who share your goals; and, like Michelle Obama said, step up, choose your own future, and commit to your education.

12.

KEEP UP THE GOOD WORK

EMPLOYMENT AFTER COLLEGE

What does success look like to you?

Your degree will get you a better-paying, more satisfying job than you would be able to land without that sheepskin, but the diploma is only the final chapter of a much bigger story of your college years. What did you learn? What skills did you develop? Who are your lifelong friends, and which faculty know you by name well enough to write a letter of recommendation? Career counselors often ask students to engage in the imagination exercise we began the book with—where do you see yourself in five, ten, or fifteen years, and what do you need to do to get there? So even before you start lining yourself up for employment, consider what success looks like to you.

Defining success is tricky because there are some external markers, for sure, but there are also indicators that aren't so clear. People whom others consider to be successful often have a lot of stuff to show for it, but "success" defined as fame or fortune may not be synonymous with leading a fulfilling or happy life; if it were, all those celebrity rehab centers would go out of business. Measuring your success against societal norms is a bit of a trap, and it's one that Americans fall for a lot, as Barry Schwartz writes in his excellent book, *The Paradox of Choice*.

At the same time, you need to make a living—so you have to think about money. Career counselors will often ask whether you would rather have more money or more free time. Would you rather be working where you can make the most money, or would you rather be working where you can be close to family? Would you rather be working in an office in a collaborative team, or would you rather have the opportunity to travel? Using your college years to line yourself up for future employment and the kind of life you want after college is a many-stranded, multiyear project. One good place to begin is connecting with people you admire.

The How-to Guide to Networking

Let's be honest. There's no right way to network. There's no secret handshake. You have to start with the people you know—your teachers, parents, your friends' parents, your boss, your boss's boss, your boss's friend on Facebook—and simply expand from there. If you have a goal (like going to graduate or professional school, working in the White House, or becoming a chef), then share it with people. Ask everyone for advice. Ask if there is anyone *they* think you should talk to, then go share your goal with that person, too. You get the idea.

If you get discouraged, just remember that Bill Gates didn't build Microsoft himself. He started it with the kid who was his backyard

buddy when they were growing up. Barack Obama didn't get to the White House by himself. He used every inch of his network and then he leveraged the power of social media. There are countless others of a less famous variety who have done the same in order to leverage their smarts and skills into a successful project, job, or life. That's what networking is. And building a network is part of what college is all about.

Does Your Major Lead to a Career?

Choosing a major is a big deal because it's a stepping-stone, and it's silly to think they all lead to the same place. Obviously they don't.

What Does Success Look Like to You?

1. Jot down a few people you consider to be successful. (You can know them personally, or not.)

2. Write a few words about why you consider them to be successful.

3. Do you admire them? Why or why not?

4. Do you think there's a difference between "successful" and "happy"?

5. Do you think you might have different goals for personal success and professional success?

Thank heavens—petroleum engineers are not whom you go to see performing at Carnegie Hall.

You'll often hear people talk about following your passion, which is totally fine even though it may be completely irrational. Passion means "a strong and barely controllable emotion or an intense desire or enthusiasm for something." Even though it's not grounded in reality, passion really does drive people to succeed, and nobody's suggesting that you settle for a major because it's lucrative and not what you love to do. But we are suggesting that you look very realistically at how you defined success in the exercise above and think seriously about whether or not following that passion is likely to get you there.

If you're passionate about playing football, for example, that's terrific, because you know how to be a team player and you're probably in great shape. Deciding that you're aiming to be a pro football player *for a living* could be problematic because statistically, your chances of going from high school star to the NCAA to the NFL are .09 percent. Ouch. We just threw a wet blanket on some of the 310,000 high school seniors nationwide who play football.[102]

The point is, it is totally copacetic—even healthy—to have a passion that is not necessarily your lifeline. Many successful people have a range of interests and even passions, and though some become hobbies that produce supplemental income, it's also possible to think strategically about how to leverage your passion to support your career. Athletes, for example, often make great managers, excellent sports journalists, creative videographers, and fabulous coaches because they understand the game and they know what it takes to be a team. Artists make extraordinary teachers, writers, Web designers, and game developers because they understand what motivates, excites, and enraptures people.

So do you need to abandon your passion in favor of a career? One graduate we spoke to leveraged her passion for dance into a lifelong career in physical therapy. Choosing a major solely because it has good employment prospects is not likely to result in a fulfilling life. On the other hand, the stakes are real: you need a job after you graduate so it's best to gather as much information as you can before you commit yourself to a course of study that won't get you where you want to go. The bottom line is that your major needs to sustain your interest like a hobby, and it needs to be a foundation for your success—however you define it.

Beyond Mastering Your Major

College is the time in your life to explore all sorts of interests. Take electives that are not part of your major but may be complementary. Or expand your horizons by taking classes about a subject you know nothing about, taught by faculty who are known to change students' worldviews. Check into the opportunities available to study abroad for a semester, an experience that can stretch your network around the world. Depending on the program, tuition is often paid by your college, so your financial aid may not be affected, and travel scholarships are sometimes available.

You might also consider signing up for a domestic exchange program at another U.S. campus. Some state schools with multiple campuses have short-term intrasystem transfers available. Getting out of your comfort zone can lead to both personal and professional growth, because these experiences require initiative, nurture a spirit of adventure, and foster flexibility—attributes that are desirable in friends as well as professional colleagues.

It's What You Know and What You Can Do

Whatever your major, when you're looking for a job, it's helpful to know what employers think. According to a Gallup-Lumina study, "Eighty-four percent of business leaders say that the amount of knowledge a candidate has is very important in hiring decisions . . . and only nine percent of business leaders say where the candidate received their degree is very important in hiring decisions."[103] Brandon Busteed, who leads the development of Gallup's education work for employers, noted that "it's not about where you go to college, it's about *what you know*. It's about *how you do* college."[104] The National Association of Colleges and Employers (NACE) polls employers annually to determine the kinds of skills they want their new hires to have: the ability to work in teams, make decisions, solve problems, plan, organize, prioritize, and verbally communicate top their lists annually. Other sought-after skills include research, analysis, technical, writing, and selling skills.[105]

As you make your way through college, see how you're doing on developing some of these skills. If you have them, how would you demonstrate that you have them? What skills (different from these) will be necessary in your field? How can you showcase them?

The "How" of Finding a Job

Career Center

The journey begins, not surprisingly, at your school's career center, which you should visit during the first weeks of your freshman year.

Not the second semester of your senior year, when you begin to see that the educational pipeline you've been moving through ends at a cliff. Avoid the cliff by talking to the professional staff or using the college-to-career guides available at the career center. Over time, you'll use this center to broaden your network, meet alumni, go for internships, hone your résumé—and learn to fly. All the time students make the mistake of not (or barely) utilizing campus career resources. Don't let that be your story.

On your first visit, here's the question to ask: "What kinds of jobs does this major lead to?" They'll know the answer to that question, and they also can give you access to one more piece of the puzzle: alumni in your intended major. They usually can do this because most campuses have an internal network, alumni network, or LinkedIn Alumni network that you can log into from your student portal.

Even before you have totally decided on a major or a career, log into the alumni network and search by career or occupation and see who's out there. If you have a question, reach out to alumni who are doing the kind of work you may want to do one day. This is a good way to grow your professional network at the same time as you get advice from recent (and long-ago!) graduates. On the alumni side, participation is voluntary, so don't think of yourself as being pushy; the purpose of networks is to connect people through time and space, and many alums would welcome the opportunity to give someone the help they wish they'd had.

Informational Interviews

The career center also can help set you up with informational interviews. These are not job interviews; they are conversations designed to help you get guidance from people working in fields you aspire to be in. They're learning opportunities, so don't worry about needing to know everything before your conversation; at the same time, the more preparation you put into it, the better your outcome will be. A great place to start these is with graduates of your own institution who are in careers you would like to pursue.

Internships

Internships are another good way to get an insider's view, but you should know there's some controversy surrounding them because many, particularly in the nonprofit sector, are unpaid. This is one of those realities that aren't altogether fair, because who can afford to work without getting paid? The Department of Labor issued guidelines in 2010, but according to a 2014 investigation by ProPublica, those guidelines aren't really being enforced.[106] Some companies get around the no-pay rule with a semantic shift by calling unpaid workers "volunteers" instead of interns.

There's another side to this story, too. Lots of students have broken into fields because of the experience and connections they made through unpaid internships. At the time the guidelines were issued, thirteen college presidents—including New York University president John Sexton and University of California president Mark Yudof—wrote to Labor Secretary Hilda Solis to ask that the agency reconsider its plans to step up enforcement. "The Department's enforcement actions and public statements could significantly erode employers' willingness to provide valuable and sought-after opportunities for American college students," the administrators wrote. "While we share your concerns about the potential for exploitation, our institutions take great pains to ensure students are placed in secure and productive environments that further their education. We constantly monitor and reassess placements based on student feedback."[107]

According to NACE's *2014 Internship and Co-op Survey*, "nearly 97 percent of employers plan to hire interns and/or co-ops during 2014."[108] If you do choose to take an internship—whether paid or unpaid—make the most of the opportunity. You'd be surprised how many students don't know the basics, so here's a cheat sheet.

1. Dress appropriately. (If you're not sure what the dress code is, ask.)

2. Act like the employee you want to become one day.

3. Always be on time.

4. Be observant. Pitch in where you can.

5. Ask your supervisor how you can be most helpful, especially when there doesn't seem like anything needs doing immediately. (Do they have a long-term project you could help with?)

6. Work your internship like it's a job, and work it so that everyone will miss you when you leave.

7. Keep in touch after you go. If a job comes up, you want to make it easy for them to find you! Plus, when you need letters of recommendation, your former boss is a great person to ask.

What Kinds of Jobs Are Out There and Where Can You Find Them?

According to a study by the Georgetown University Center on Education and the Workforce, "Between 80 and 90 percent of job openings for college-educated workers are now posted online. For college graduates, online job advertisements are a viable tool for connecting real people with real jobs in real time."[109] Not surprisingly, the most in demand career clusters are managerial/professional office, and Science, Technology, Engineering, and Math (STEM). Together these two clusters represent over 60 percent of the jobs for college-educated workers. College-educated workers with expertise in software development and information technology are in the highest demand in the online college-educated labor market.

Knowing the types of jobs available and the skills employers want nationwide is a good place to start, but you need to dig deeper into the picture to see what's available where you want to live, then pace yourself. Give yourself time to explore various career options while you're in college and don't forget to enjoy yourself. One of the key secrets of a successful college experience is this: Some of the things you do will contribute to you being a good candidate to be hired for

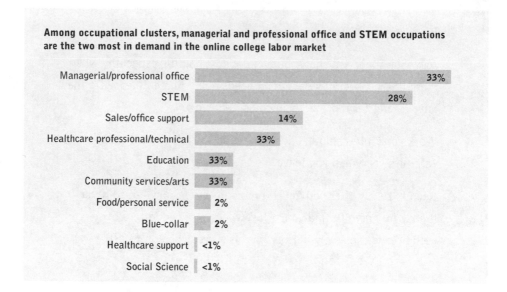

Among occupational clusters, managerial and professional office and STEM occupations are the two most in demand in the online college labor market

Occupation	Percentage
Managerial/professional office	33%
STEM	28%
Sales/office support	14%
Healthcare professional/technical	33%
Education	33%
Community services/arts	33%
Food/personal service	2%
Blue-collar	2%
Healthcare support	<1%
Social Science	<1%

The Online College Labor Market, shows that one out of three jobs posted online for college graduates are "managerial or professional," and several majors feed this pipeline. Jobs open specifically in STEM occupations come in close behind with 28 percent of the postings. Due to rounding, the percentages sum to more than 100 percent.

GEORGETOWN UNIVERSITY CENTER ON EDUCATION AND THE WORKFORCE, ONLINE COLLEGE LABOR MARKET:WHERE THE JOBS ARE, 2014

a job. And some of what you do during your college years will help you do a better job once you're employed.

Participate in crew, soccer, or any other sport. Being a member of the team is not necessarily a résumé builder for a software firm. On the other hand, that experience taught you how to train, how to make tough decisions, how to work collaboratively, and sometimes how to let others take the glory. These skills may not be the ones that get you in the door, but they're worth working on because they'll make you a better person—at work, in your home, and in your community.

Take a Futurist's View

Change is inevitable. Some of our routine daily tasks, like driving our own cars, may seem quaint in a few years, and we're sure you can think of several habits your parents have (like a newspaper de-

Software developers (applications) are the most in demand; there were 125,000 online job ads for software developers in the second quarter of 2013.

Occupation	Number of online job ads
Software developers, applications	125,000
IT professional, NEC*	76,000
Sales representatives, wholesale and manufacturing	63,000
Registered nurses	50,000
Accountants/auditors	49,000
Computer systems analysts	48,000
Medical and health services managers	47,000
Managers, NEC*	47,000
Sales managers	38,000
Financial managers	37,000

You can also look at the market based on numbers of jobs. Not surprisingly, the tech world is the top of this list, but there's also demand in the health and financial sectors.

GEORGETOWN UNIVERSITY CENTER ON EDUCATION AND THE WORKFORCE, ONLINE COLLEGE LABOR MARKET:WHERE THE JOBS ARE, 2014

livered to your door) that you won't share when you live, as you will, in your "smart" home. It's also true that behind each of these innovations, there are thousands of college graduates who are making it happen.

As the world changes, it's likely that you will make several career moves in your life. According to the Bureau of Labor Statistics, young adults born in the early 1980s held an average of 6.2 jobs from ages eighteen to twenty-six, and for you it may be more. The jobs may be vertical promotions, building on one another, or they may be moves from one career path to another; either way, lifelong learners who can work collaboratively, think critically, and communicate effectively will be in demand.

Setting yourself up for future employment is about doing what you can do to build your résumé, but it's also about knowing what's out there. When the competition is tough, the applicant who knows the most about what's needed in the position will have the advantage. Research is critical, and it can't be random—each résumé you submit and every conversation you have in an interview setting has

Be Careful What You Post

In this socially connected world, sometimes what matters is not who you really are, but who you appear to be. Social media has made everything about everyone so visible and so public that it's not surprising to hear that coaches and employers use it to find out a little bit more about potential recruits or hires. It's up to you to know what's out there about you and to manage what you can. What photos of you landed on Facebook? Would you mind if your future boss saw you dressed like that? (Or with *that* in your hand?)

On the flip side, social media can be a powerful tool for getting a job. Learn to use it well and you have all the advantages that a well-run campaign has. Do you appear professional? Would the boss be proud to add someone like you to her team? The way to set yourself up for employment in the future is to cultivate your talent and to learn all you can about the world, about the industry you hope to break into, and about people—from all walks of life, from all kinds of backgrounds, from where you've been and where you hope to go.

to communicate your interest in the job for which you're applying. A stock cover letter isn't going to get you an interview, but a well-crafted letter that connects *your* specific experience to *their* job just might get you over the transom.

So imagine you're about to graduate, you're applying for a dream job, and you know that you are not the only person seeking this position. In fact, you have it on good authority that there are about seven hundred applications from college graduates in the queue. What's on your résumé that makes it stand out? What letters of recommendation do you have? Who could say something about your work ethic? Who in your network is the right reference for this job? Does someone in your network work there? How does your résumé demonstrate your skill set? What does your cover letter say about your fit for *this specific* job?

That's it. That's how you line yourself up for future employment: become the person you would hire.

13.

DO UNTO OTHERS

//

NONPROFIT AND PUBLIC SECTOR CAREERS

to be of service

Perhaps you're the kind of person who has a spark of idealism in them, who wants to devote a year or two (or maybe even your whole career) to serving others. If so, you're not alone: the National Conference on Citizenship reported that young people today are the most service-oriented of any generation, with a 43 percent volunteer service rate compared to a 35 percent rate among baby boomers.[110]

Maybe you'd like to work for, say, a nonprofit that weatherizes homes for the poor. Or in a government agency that keeps our air and water clean. Or maybe you want to join the military, helping to protect the country against the threat of terrorism. Or, likely, you have no idea yet. Indeed, figuring out how to sift through the myriad options available can be a daunting task. Not to mention the common perception that such do-good pursuits require a good deal of personal sacrifice. And, sometimes they do! But in this chapter we're going to show you how serving others—be it your community, your country, or the world—can also be a service to yourself.

We are going to be exploring three "buckets" of service. First we'll look at *national and community service* opportunities, which encompass programs like AmeriCorps and the Peace Corps. Next we'll look at *military service*, specifically through the Reserve Officer Training Corps (ROTC) program. And lastly we'll explore *public service*, which include internships, fellowships, and jobs within the federal government.

We'll tell you not only how to get involved but also what tangible economic benefits come from participating in these experiences. We're talking about money to pay some (and maybe even all) of your college tuition bill, preferential hiring perks, opportunities for free travel around the world, and more. Consider this your selfish guide to selfless service.

NATIONAL COMMUNITY SERVICE

Yonah Lieberman, a twenty-two-year-old graduate of the University of Michigan, grew up with a passion for social justice. The state-mandated community service requirements he had in high school helped him to develop an interest in service, and when he got to college, he really had the opportunity to discover what social change meant to him. Yonah decided to apply to AmeriCorps after he graduated, and he was placed in New York City, working as an advocate for low-income tenants across the five boroughs. "I'm really happy," says Yonah. "It can be challenging, but it's amazing to see the impact we can have after just one year. It's really helped me figure out what I want to do."[111]

Laura Cowie, a twenty-three-year-old AmeriCorps volunteer, graduated from the University of Maine at Farmington and decided to devote a year to service. She's spent the past year working as a volunteer and mentor with ninth graders in an underprivileged Miami high school. She began the year as a classroom tutor and finished her service as a co-teacher. Laura says the best part of her year was getting to be part of her students' lives, which consequently changed hers. "Doing a year of service really changed my plans," said Laura. "Before I never considered working for nonprofits as a career, and now I am pretty committed to doing it."[112]

The primary way to get involved in national service is to join AmeriCorps, the federal program that annually places eighty thousand individuals in service roles throughout the country, doing valuable work while earning a paycheck and other benefits, including tuition grants. You can get involved right after high school, beginning at age seventeen. Many students take a gap year between high school and college to participate in an AmeriCorps service program.

The program lasts for ten months to one year, though you sometimes have the option of extending your service for additional years if you're interested. There are hundreds of programs in the AmeriCorps network; some are national programs, like AmeriCorps NCCC, which trains and sends teams of young people to respond to natural disasters. Others are set up as partnerships with nonprofit groups—AmeriCorps members might work for, say, City Year, tutoring and mentoring students in low-income schools, or for Big Brothers/Big Sisters, mentoring at-risk youth. Many are state based.

For a good overview of how AmeriCorps works and its various related programs and opportunities, spend some time on its website, www.nationalservice.gov/programs/americorps. For AmeriCorps-related service opportunities in your state, visit your state service commission's website, too. A list can be found here: www.nationalservice.gov/about/contact-us/state-service-commissions. The site www.americorpsalums.org has lots of good information, too. And for a lengthy and detailed list of AmeriCorps-related programs that includes the specific benefits each provides, go here: www.sa.sc.edu/communityservice/longterm/.

The Benefits

AmeriCorps is not volunteer work, but a real job with real benefits, including a living allowance based on the poverty-level income for a single individual in the area where you're stationed. For Laura living in Miami, making a few lifestyle changes, such as riding her bicycle, walking, and taking the bus, made living on her stipend quite comfortable. In some big cities, however, you'll potentially need to supplement the monthly stipend with some additional cash.

AmeriCorps also includes a grab bag of other benefits, including a chance to travel and see a different part of the country (some programs will even cover up to $1,000 in relocation expenses). Many also provide subsidies for child care if you need that, as well as health and dental coverage. In addition, you have the opportunity to get on-the-job training in skills ranging from carpentry to CPR, database management, fund-raising, and team leadership. Networking is another benefit that pays for years as you build relationships with volunteers, co-workers, nonprofit leaders, and alumni. "Everyone I've been working with has been really excited to help me figure out my next move," said Yonah. "I've been getting a lot of help from my network."

Successful participation in AmeriCorps allows you to receive an end-of-service benefit in the form of the Segal AmeriCorps Education Award, which can be used to repay a qualified student loan or to pay the current cost of attending a qualified institution of higher education. The Segal AmeriCorps Education Awards are equivalent to the maximum value of the Pell Grant for the award year in which the term of national service is approved. For the 2014 fiscal year that value was $5,730. What's more, AmeriCorps participants currently may earn up to the value of *two* full-time education awards and have seven years from the date they earn it to use them. So two years of national service can earn you more than $10,000 in student loan relief or additional higher ed tuition. (If you do not want the Education Award, you have the option of receiving their $1,200 end-of-service cash stipend.)

More than 120 universities also provide scholarships to national service alumni or matching tuition funding to the AmeriCorps scholarship. Other colleges waive application fees, and some even reserve a few spots and provide a full scholarship to AmeriCorps alumni. A comprehensive list of schools that match scholarship funding for AmeriCorps alums can be found at the Corporation for National and Community Service (CNCS) website, http://1.usa.gov /1igHR8Y. Many schools will give additional scholarships throughout your education for service and leadership. So if you start with service, keep it up—it can really pay off.

A recent survey by AmeriCorps Alums (the national network that connects the nearly one million alumni of all AmeriCorps programs) found that AmeriCorps positively influenced most alums' professional trajectories. AmeriCorps alumni overwhelmingly say that AmeriCorps significantly shaped who they are today. Nearly all alums (88 percent) believe their AmeriCorps service was among the most significant professional experiences of their life, including nearly half of alums age thirty-six or older who strongly agree with this statement. Upon graduating from AmeriCorps, alumni believe they gained valuable workplace skills (64 percent strongly agree), and they want a career that impacts the world around them (72 percent strongly agree).[113]

Like everything else these days, acceptance into national service programs is competitive. In 2011, there were 582,000 applications

Which Loans Qualify for Relief?

Qualifying student loans under the Segal AmeriCorps Education Award include Stafford Loans, Perkins Loan, William D. Ford Direct Loans, Federal Consolidated Loans, Supplemental Loans for Students, Primary Care Loans, Nursing Student Loans, Health Education Assistance Loans, and loans from state agencies, or state institutions of higher education. A school is qualified to accept the award if it is a Title IV institution. (This includes most colleges, universities, and graduate schools.)

for 82,000 AmeriCorps positions. Only one in four applicants is accepted into City Year. But don't be discouraged—there are many opportunities, and likely there's a good fit for you, especially if you're interested in an adventure. Programs in smaller cities and towns tend to be less competitive, and some positions do go unfilled. There are definitely opportunities out there!

Another national service program to consider is the Peace Corps, which was established by President John F. Kennedy in 1961 with the goal of encouraging mutual understanding between Americans and people of other nations and cultures. Unlike AmeriCorps, you generally need to have a four-year college degree to participate. If you join the Peace Corps, you could be sent to one of over seventy countries for twenty-four months to do all sorts of volunteer work with foreign governments, schools, nonprofits, NGOs and more. (Note: You don't necessarily get to choose your region or country, although your preferences are taken into consideration).[114]

Being a Peace Corps volunteer comes with all sorts of practical benefits and though your college graduation is a long way off, you might want to look into them. There is no fee to participate, and it gives you the opportunity to travel to and from your country of service completely on the government's dime. You also receive a monthly living and housing allowance, full medical and dental coverage, paid leave for family emergencies, and forty-eight paid vacation days. There are also unique benefits toward graduate study you can take advantage of if you become a Peace Corps volunteer.

In the job market, Peace Corps and AmeriCorps VISTA alumni (though not other AmeriCorps alumni) are entitled to certain preferential hiring privileges: for one year after your service ends you can receive non-competitive eligibility when applying for federal jobs. This means that if you meet the minimum qualifications for a position, then you do not need to go through all the hoops of the normal competitive hiring process.[115]

Ironically, those who give a year of service or more may be less burdened by educational debt than those who took a more traditional path from high school to college to full-time employment. Not only that, but your service may help get you into competitive colleges or graduate schools because you've demonstrated you're committed, and when faced with adversity, you persevere. While some programs do not allow you to have a job outside of service, most do—which might mean you can save additional funds for books, fees, and tuition before you start college or grad school.

MILITARY SERVICE

Alyson Ochs graduated from Indiana University–Purdue University's ROTC program in 2011 and in 2014 was stationed in Afghanistan as an ER nurse in a forward surgical team. She describes the experience as one of the greatest in her life—an honor that has allowed her to meet lifelong friends and has provided her with invaluable career skills. The U.S. Army paid for Alyson's full nursing school tuition, and she plans to go back to medical school later to become an ER doctor, again with the military's financial help. If not for the army, Alyson says, she "would have a very difficult time affording medical school."

For Alyson, the on-the-ground job experience she is able to get through her military service is invaluable. "I literally worked well beyond any civilian nurses with some of the best surgeons in the country, working on soldiers and those in need." Alyson's team, consisted of twenty people, treats injured U.S. and NATO troops as well as Afghan soldiers, police, and civilians, performing life- or limb-saving surgeries.

If you're qualified and eligible, joining the military can open a lot of doors for your entire life. Today, 2.5 million individuals serve in the U.S. military, with 1.4 million on active duty in the four armed forces and 1.1 million in the reserves.

It can be very difficult to join the military. Today's military (both active and reserve) make up less than 1 percent of the U.S. population. About 75 percent of Americans between the ages of eighteen and twenty-five are ineligible because of physical fitness, educa-

Army	Navy	Marine Corps	Air Force
Large-scale and long-term ground operations	Naval security, transport, and force projection	Rapid naval deployment and ground operations	Air and space operations

The branches of military service.

tional, medical, or criminal reasons, or because of drug or alcohol abuse. While not everyone will necessarily serve in combat, the military recruits new members under the assumption that they're recruiting for a general-purpose job, so the fitness requirements apply to the entire armed forces.

That being said, for those interested in or already heading to college, joining the military can go a long way to help you pay for that. Military officers, who account for about 15 percent of the armed forces, almost always hold undergraduate degrees, and some hold master's and doctoral degrees. All officers are educated in ROTC programs or service academies like the Naval Academy and West Point.[116]

Unlike the Peace Corps and AmeriCorps, if you have certain skills that the military particularly wants, they may offer you more financial incentives. The bottom line, though, is that for those with plans to continue education beyond high school, serving in the military means you can access a substantial pool of money to pay for college and graduate school and to repay your student loans.[117] For a detailed list of some of the educational benefits you can get by participating in military service, check out this webpage: www.military.com/join-armed-forces/military-vs-civilian-benefits-college.html.

While it's a good idea to click through the various service websites, it's strongly recommended that you meet in person with a military recruiter before you apply. You can begin this process in high school by finding a recruiter through the JROTC, which is a high school leadership program run through the Army. When you get to college, many universities have programs and actual offices that host ROTC programs; you can simply call the university and ask, approach a recruiter, or ask someone to reach out for you. Once you're in college you can decide to join ROTC up until the start of your junior year—generally you need to have two years remaining in school, although there are some exceptions. (If you decide after you graduate from college that you want to become an officer, there are some compressed training programs you can participate in, but at a certain point the military might not want you because of age considerations.)

Other benefits of being a scholarship cadet include a shorter service obligation (just three years of active duty, as opposed to four years for scholarship winners) and eligibility for post-9/11 GI benefits (scholarship winners don't become eligible for GI benefits unless they stay past their service obligation). Alternatively, both scholarship and non-scholarship cadets can choose to serve in the National Guard or Army Reserve. Being in the reserves is only a part-time commitment, so it can be done in conjunction with grad school or many full-time jobs.[118]

Henry Chen, who recently finished the ROTC program at Johns Hopkins, chose to serve in the Maryland National Guard concurrent with his graduate school studies. "Through ROTC I was able to graduate college free of student debt, which enabled me to pursue an M.A. degree rather than being forced to find a full-time job immediately after graduation," he says. While he acknowledges that ROTC was a major time commitment in college, Henry credits it immensely for teaching him efficient time management skills.

After you complete your military service, there are some major advantages for veterans when it comes to securing competitive federal employment. Veterans' preference gives qualifying veterans a legal hiring preference in federal appointments over other applicants. Moreover, there is no limit on how many times you can apply and

ROTC Terms of Service

In some branches of the service, such as the U.S. Army, you can try out ROTC for up to two years without any commitment on either end. Committing is called "contracting." Non-contracted cadets are full participants in their battalions and get academic credit but must either contract or leave ROTC by the beginning of junior year. The earliest chance to contract is the summer before your freshman year. A contracted cadet may or may not have a scholarship. Scholarship cadets get a full-tuition scholarship from the time of contracting until graduation. (If you contract in the second semester of your freshman year, you can get five semesters of tuition scholarship, not six.) Non-scholarship cadets don't have free tuition but still have a job waiting for them at graduation.

claim an entitlement to veterans' preference.[119] And for some jobs, being a military veteran gives you an incredibly advantageous credential and network, especially if you want to work in the national security field. "You may come out of a very elite university, but you might have no ramp into the State Department leadership or the Pentagon policy office or the [Capitol] Hill staff," said Phil Carter, a senior fellow at the Center for a New American Security and an Iraq War veteran. "The military offers you that." Henry Chen adds that ROTC "definitely helps to convey a sense of responsibility and maturity" which is attractive to potential employers. And ROTC offers many internship opportunities. Henry was placed as an intern in the Defense Intelligence Agency the summer after his junior year, and several of his friends have had the opportunity to travel to countries like China, Thailand, and Slovakia on cultural deployments with the Army while in college.

PUBLIC SERVICE

When you think "federal government," you probably think Washington, D.C., and that would not be wrong. But what you might not be aware of is that 85 percent of federal government jobs are outside of the Washington, D.C. area; fifty thousand federal government employees even work abroad, distributed among more than 140 foreign countries.[120] And work is available for almost every interest and skill, whether that's physics, art, or event planning.

The great thing is, you don't have to wait until you graduate from college before trying your hand at—and gaining the benefits of—a public service career. In 2010, President Obama issued an executive order creating the Pathways Programs, an initiative that provides students in high school, college, graduate programs, and other qualifying educational institutions with paid opportunities to work in federal agencies. The programs were created in order to better attract talented and diverse students and recent graduates into government work, and to create ways that make it easier to transition them into long-term employment later on.[121]

Juny Canenguez, a recent graduate of George Mason University, has spent the past two years working as a Pathways intern at the U.S. Department of State. Now that she's out of college, she's in the process of being converted into a formal employee with the federal government, thanks to her time as an intern. "It was amazing," said Juny. "I'm now being recruited to the civil service, and my long-term plan will be to join the Foreign Service," which will allow her to be posted as a diplomat oversees. Juny says that one of the highlights of her internship experience was getting to regularly meet other civil servants and Foreign Service officers, hear about their experience, and get their advice.[122]

Channing Martin, a former Pathways Program intern in the U.S. Office of Personnel Management (OPM) was hired immediately after her internship ended into a permanent, full-time position at OPM; she now works as a program and management analyst with OPM's Student Programs.[123] "As a high schooler I was always really interested in diversity and inclusion issues, and when I realized this intern program existed," says Channing, "I was really attracted to that." Channing spent her yearlong internship on a rotation between different departments, having the chance to get her feet wet in a broad range of governmental tasks and responsibilities. She got to experiment with things ranging from understanding the role of performance management to supporting efforts to expand equal pay and learning how to write requirements for database systems. Channing did all this while balancing her time as a full-time student; she spent her second year in Carnegie Mellon's public policy graduate school living in D.C., interning during the day and taking classes by night.

"Interning for the federal government allows you to check out exactly what kind of work they do and decide if it resonates with you," said Tim McManus, vice president of the Partnership for Public Service. "If you go and do an internship at the EPA or the Department of Energy, you'll be exposed to not just the mission but the way the agency works. Is the culture one that is good for you? Is it fast-paced? Is it too slow? You have the ability to see for yourself."[124]

While there are also unpaid internship and volunteer opportunities to work in the federal government, and your state and local governments may offer some paid and unpaid jobs, too, the Pathways

Which Federal Agency Should I Apply to for Paid Internships and Jobs?

There are hundreds of federal agencies. Some you've surely heard of, like the State Department; others, like the Federal Mediation and Conciliation Service, you probably haven't. Almost all of them do important work. But frankly, some of them are better run than others. What you want to do is limit your search to the ones likely to give you the best experience.

If you want some help understanding the various agencies you should visit the Partnership for Public Service's site www.bestplacestowork.org. This website compiles information based on a survey of 376,000 civil servants who were asked questions such as whether their agencies had high or low morale, enough resources to do their jobs, satisfactory work-life balance, and more. You can also go through the site and see how different agencies, from large ones to small ones, compared with one another. In addition, you can read reviews from federal employees about what they think of their jobs and work environments and find links to each agency's website that will give you information on the kind of work it does specifically.

Program offers unique benefits to individuals who are considering going into public service that cannot be found anywhere else. Unlike these other options, a successful completion of a Pathways Program allows you to receive what is known as "noncompetitive eligibility" when applying for federal jobs. This means that Pathways participants are eligible to have their internships converted to a permanent position without having to apply through USAJOBS. This is a big advantage in the job market. Typically when you apply for a federal job through the normal hiring process, you are competing with *thousands* of other applicants. So the preferential hiring benefit you can receive through the paid Pathways Programs is incredibly valuable. It's competitive to get in, but worth it.

To apply to a Pathways Program position, first you should create an account on USAJOBS.gov, which is the official federal jobs search engine. Thousands of government job announcements are posted on this site, including a description of duties, minimum qualifications, benefits, and application instructions. (There are about thirty thousand vacant positions on USAJOBS.gov on any given day.) Just type "Pathways," "recent graduate," or "internship" into the keyword search on USAJOBS.gov or visit an individual agency's website to begin applying. You also can search on USAJOBS.gov by geographical region and preferred work schedule. (Some federal jobs offer alternative work schedules like telecommuting.) The USAJOBS Pathways website is www.usajobs.gov/StudentsAndGrads. From there, click either "Find Internships" or "Find Recent Graduate Jobs." Also, try using the résumé builder tool on the website, which will give you tips to help ensure that your job application is as successful as it can be. In addition, you should check out the Partnership for Public Service's one-stop-shop site for information on federal internships and jobs.

Other major benefits that come from working for the federal government include opportunities to pay off your student loans on top of your normal salary. There are two main ways to do this: the Federal Student Loan Repayment Program and the Public Service Loan Forgiveness Program. Through the former, participating agencies may pay you up to $10,000 a year—for a maximum of $60,000—toward the payment of your student loans. In return, you need to work at that agency for a minimum of three years.[125] (Your participation in the Pathways Programs can count as one of those three years.) Then, through the Public Service Loan Forgiveness Program, if you work in a public service job for at least ten years (which can include federal, state, or local government jobs, a 501(c)(3) nonprofit organization, a public child or family service agency, or even a private organization that provides public service such as public interest law services or public health), the government will forgive the remaining balance of your loans![126]

"I think the beauty of the government is that any type of person, anyone that is interested in *anything* can work here," said Channing.

CONCLUSION

The skills and training you can get from participating in military service, national service or public service can take you almost anywhere you want to go in life, even if you ultimately choose a for-profit career. Mrim Boutla, co-founder of More than Money Careers, works to show students and college career centers how financial and social impact concerns can be combined for millennial employment opportunities. She sees that too many individuals are operating under the outdated assumption that mission-driven work cannot be applied all over the job market throughout your life. According to Boutla, many hiring personnel like to see prior commitments to service—this type of demonstrated dedication conveys a lot to an employer about what kind of person and worker you are.[127] Additionally, companies are increasingly looking for employees with experience working in adverse conditions and with diverse groups. Many companies—including Comcast, Deloitte, and others—actively recruit AmeriCorps alums just for this reason.

So should you consider service? That's a question only you can answer. Review your goal statement. Think about your purpose.

Mission-driven opportunities are not for everyone. There could be financial, educational, and professional benefits in it for you, but if you're in it only for you, you probably won't make the cut.

To many, making a life is more than making a living, and you may want to explore that concept. If you're thinking about taking a gap year between high school and college, research your opportunities thoroughly—you can start with the two dozen opportunities we've listed here, talk with your counselor, and visit the college and career center. Some volunteer programs are designed for students during winter or spring breaks; others might take a whole summer.

The experience itself can be personally transformative and expose you to opportunities that those taking more traditional paths never see. The decision is yours to make for all the right reasons.

50 SCHOOLS YOU SHOULD KNOW ABOUT

MIDWEST

#2 College of the Ozarks

At College of the Ozarks, a four-year private liberal arts school of about 1,357 undergraduates, Christ is at the center of academic and social life. Chapel is part of the curriculum at C of O, and services are held every Sunday at 11:00 a.m. The school offers forty-two majors and ten pre-professional programs. The leading majors are business, education, nursing, and agriculture. The 15:1 student-to-faculty ratio allows professors and advisors to form meaningful connections with students, who cite these relationships as one of the most positive features of C of O.

Here's the thing about College of the Ozarks: it's free. But here's the thing about life: nothing's free. The cost of tuition is taken care of by grant money and work education. Students are assigned campus jobs that are frequently tailored to their majors—from milking cows (the milk will eventually be made into ice cream) to communications roles in the admission office. Agriculture majors often work at the C of O hog or beet farm, both of which supply fresh food for the dining hall and a local farmers' market. Every semester students are asked to put in one full forty-hour workweek to help further develop a solid work ethic. Ninety percent of students come in demonstrating financial need, and for many, C of O offers their one chance to graduate with a debt-free degree.

The Ozarks are a beautiful, lush stretch of Missouri with plenty of bodies of water to help students stay cool in the humid Missouri heat. C of O is in rural Point Lookout and overlooks Lake Taneycomo. It's a quick ten-minute drive from Branson, which offers family fun, touristy amenities, and great jobs for students.

Spiritual and patriotic growth saturates most corners of life here. The school has a zero-tolerance rule for tobacco, alcohol, or drug use (on and off campus), a dress code, and a 1:00 a.m. curfew. The Keeter Center on campus provides patriotic education including a program in which veterans share with students their personal experiences in service. Many students travel to nearby Springfield, Missouri, to find some off-campus fun.

#5 Illinois State University

Illinois State University is a public university in the twin-city community of Bloomington-Normal, Illinois (sometimes dubbed BloNo), with 17,749 undergraduates. Among the most popular majors at ISU are elementary education and special education. In fact, one out of every eight teachers in Illinois has a degree from ISU, which has an education research lab school that offers future teachers hands-on experience working in elementary and high schools. Other popular majors include business administration, psychology, accounting, criminal justice, finance, and nursing. The College of Business is in *BusinessWeek*'s top one hundred, and business majors report a superior experience due to small classes and direct collaboration with professors. Increasingly the school is focused on study abroad and has expanded the scholarship money available for the same. ISU has support services for first-generation and low-income students that keep students chugging along toward a degree. Ninety-four percent of students who utilize these services return to BloNo for their sophomore year of college.

About 81 percent of students receive some sort of financial assistance— the school doles out about $30 million in institutional grants and scholarships. The school finances about $19 million in jobs, allowing about six thousand students to earn wages on campus. Only 2.8 percent of Redbirds default on their student loans.

Together, Bloomington and Normal have 167,699 residents. Situated in the corn-soaked heartland of the United States, the twin communities take pride in their midwestern hospitality and values. The Bloomington train station offers Amtrak trains to locations all over Illinois and Missouri. Chicago, St. Louis, and Indianapolis are no further than a three-hour drive.

Diversity at ISU is on the rise, up by 13 percent from 2012 to 2013, though 80 percent of the student body remains white. Redbirds are known for being very serious . . . about their bar scene. ISU has been ranked as the third-best party school by Princeton Review, and the students themselves rank the nightlife as the best feature on College Prowler. Athletics aren't really a huge deal at ISU, but they have about 388 student organizations, from Redbird Bodybuilding to Nerf Club.

#7 University of Michigan–Dearborn

More than fifty years ago, when the Motor City was spinning at full horsepower, the University of Michigan–Dearborn was founded as an upper division of accountancy and engineering for Ford Motor Company. Today, the University of Michigan–Dearborn still has connections with Ford but now offers over a hundred undergraduate degrees. UM-Dearborn offers the "ultimate scholarship" in the form of more than seven hundred co-ops—paid internships that also count for academic credit. Students are able to gain real experience at Ford Motor, Ernst & Young, DTE Energy, and Apple. Sixty percent of the students who participate in the co-op programs receive a permanent job by graduation. Back on campus you'll find student-to-teacher ratios of 15:1 and classes with an average of twenty-four students.

Numbers are on your side, because the majority of all UM-Dearborn students receive some form of financial aid, and for every tuition hike, UM-Dearborn makes a point of increasing access to scholarships and grants. One such scholarship, the Opportunity Scholarship, ranges from $2,000 to a full ride and is given to students from school districts where over 70 percent of students qualify for free or reduced-price lunches. In June the school holds transition workshops to ease the jitters common among incoming freshmen and to give future students a more thorough understanding of their financial aid options.

UMD is just fifteen minutes from downtown Detroit, a favorite destination for recreation and nightlife. Public transit stops right at UMD, and campus shuttles can drop you around campus, though most students prefer to drive because the shuttles are infamously tardy. Although UMD is largely a commuter campus, brand-new private apartment-style housing now sits between campus and the nearby mall.

On-campus service engagement is unusually high at Dearborn. Students can volunteer their time at the on-campus food shelter or on any of six alternative spring break trips. Strolling through campus, it's common to see students offering a friendly smile or hello. The campus is fairly diverse, with a strong Arab American presence. The school preaches inclusion, not diversity. The vice chancellor noted that in forty-five years in higher education, he has never seen such fluidity between races and groups.

#8 Wayne State College

Wayne State College started in 1891 as a tiny teachers college in a Wayne, Nebraska, storefront and has grown into a liberal arts college with 3,500 students majoring in some ninety programs. Still, the college remains an education powerhouse, pumping out about one in ten Nebraska teachers. With an education program in the top thirty in the nation, WSC has its teaching majors substitute in actual classrooms before they even begin student teaching. A small setting allows for an 18:1 student-to-teacher ratio, and class sizes average twenty-one students. Wayne offers a mentoring, advising, and tutoring program (through TRIO) for first-generation and low-income students, who are more than 60 percent of all students. These programs help create plans for academic success and make positive connections on campus that help steer students around the red Solo cups, financial struggles, and other common distractions.

WSC is all about serving up a private school education with a public school price tag. It offers the most affordable tuition in the region, and it doesn't believe in jacking up tuition costs every year. In addition, the school gets tremendous support from the state, so 85 percent of students are awarded some sort of financial aid. WSC is part of the Midwest Student Exchange Program, which means if you are not from the great state of Nebraska but hail from elsewhere in the Plains, you may be able to enroll at a reduced price.

Wayne is a friendly town of about 5,500 residents who wholly embrace the WSC Wildcats. The campus is wedged between Norfolk and Sioux City, both about forty-five miles away. In July, Wayne catches chicken fever. Don't worry, the Chicken Days aren't dangerous—that is, unless you consider eating contests, cluck-offs, and joining in the world's largest chicken dance to be dangerous.

Wayne State College is the cultural hub of the area. The Student Activities Board throws over four hundred events a year, including casino nights and shows by comedians and hypnotists. WSC also hosts WillyCon, the biggest sci-fi convention in the area. Local bars offer student discounts, and Wildcat Wheels, a free taxi service for students, will cart you home after a long night. Overall, students find WSC a comfortable place to spend these precious years.

#11 Michigan State University

Michigan State University, a public institution educating 38,000 students, is the third-best university at "turning brilliant ideas into marketable gold mines," according to an independent study by the Product Development & Management Association. MSU's Institute for Entrepreneurship provides capital to launch student businesses, and the school has a whopping 275 study-abroad programs to choose from, including ones in Antarctica and Cuba. MSU is recognized as a top research facility, and the U.S. Department of Energy chose it to design and establish a $720 million facility that will advance understanding of rare nuclear isotopes and the evolution of the cosmos. So whether you are an aspiring despotic dictator or just super-interested in the cosmos, MSU could be the school for you.

MSU understands that a Pell Grant won't cover all your costs. The Spartan Advantage Program supplements Pell Grants and covers excess costs related to tuition, books, and room and board. And there's more. MSU's Child Care Grant helps cover the high cost of keeping your rugrats safe and happy while you obtain a degree, and the Detroit Compact Scholarship, which covers the full cost of tuition and fees, supports students who have their sights set on college from their first year of high school.

MSU's campus is beautiful, especially in the fall, when the trees lining the Red Cedar River change from Spartan green to varied shades of yellow and orange. East Lansing, with almost fifty thousand residents, is full of small-town charm. While local buses are not always timely, they provide affordable transit during the frigid winter months. There are also Greyhound and Amtrak stations within walking distance from campus. All in all, you can't go wrong with a city that invented chocolate cheese.

Sports are a big deal at the Big Ten. On game day, school spirit is palpable and East Lansing is covered in a sea of green and white. Besides having the buffest mascot in the biz and being well versed in the art of tailgating, over half the student body is involved in service learning. And when you consider the university's several sustainability awards, MSU is crawling with friendly do-gooders.

#21 Indiana University–Bloomington

Indiana University is a large public university in Bloomington, Indiana (or B-town, as many Hoosiers call it). If you are part of the almost 50 percent of college students who enter school undecided, IU has something that may suit you: the Individualized Major Program, wherein students create their own major by choosing courses like they're ordering at Chipotle—except there's less guacamole involved and definitely less stress. Want to earn credits before the academic year even starts? IU's Intensive Freshman Seminar will give you a jump on meeting friends and getting acquainted with the responsibilities of college life. At most institutions graduate students monopolize coveted research positions, but at IU interested first-years can get their hands on serious equipment and spend six to eight hours a week in a research lab. There's even the STARS program that allows undergrads to get a faculty science mentor.

Tuition at IU is a flat fee of about $10,000, so you can take anywhere from twelve to seventeen credit hours for the same price. The school boasts a high graduation rate, and through the GradPact program the school will foot the bill for any additional tuition costs if the class offerings make it impossible to graduate in four years. Recognizing how confusing and deceptive financial aid letters can be, IU's go so far as to detail how much a borrower's monthly payment would be after graduation. The school offers a personal finance course that walks students through topics like insurance, investing, and home ownership. About 68 percent of students receive some form of financial aid, and for Pell Grant recipients, IU offers the Pell Promise award, which takes care of any tuition or fees not covered by their Pell Grant.

Bloomington is a cool, artsy town of about seventy thousand people tucked into southern Indiana's green flowing hills. *Travel+Leisure* says IU is one of the most beautiful college campuses, with its charming red-brick paths, carved limestone structures, and picturesque clock tower. Typical of the Midwest, the weather is relatively unpredictable and extreme within defined seasons.

Hoosiers care about their athletics. So much so, in fact, that IU passed a student athlete Bill of Rights to protect their education. The men's basketball team has racked up five NCAA championships and although game tickets are expensive, lots of students suck it up to support their team. The largest collegiate bike race in the United States, the Little 500, inspired the 1979 movie *Breaking Away*, a movie that depicts what 1970s B-town was all about. Although IU's student body is largely white, it does include students from all fifty states and 130 countries, and valued cultural resources—the Asian Culture Center, the Latino Cultural Center, the Neal-Marshall Black Culture Center, the Leo R. Dowling International Center, and the GLBT Student Support Services office—are available.

#22 University of Wisconsin–Eau Claire

University of Wisconsin–Eau Claire is a midsize public university (about 10,300 undergraduates) that emphasizes the importance of hands-on, real-life experience. Blugolds are required to complete thirty hours of service learning in their four years, a policy that gives students a taste of the wider world. The Center of Excellence for Faculty and Undergraduate Student Research Collaboration gives undergrads the chance to work on projects that most students don't experience unless they go to grad school.

UW–Eau Claire grads have an extremely low loan default rate—about 2.4 percent—possibly the result of the one-on-one attention from financial aid officers. The school encourages budget appeals if students' circumstances change unexpectedly, and financial aid experts have the opportunity to explain the weight of loans so students don't wind up blindly checking a box to receive thousands in loans without professional guidance. The university gets how crushing debt can be, especially for middle- and low-income families. When tuition increased recently, students whose estimated family contribution was less than $7,000 received a grant to offset the price hike. The school has $8 million in funding to pay students to work on campus in jobs often treated as learning experiences.

Eau Claire is where you want to be on a warm summer day. The campus is a fast twenty-minute drive from friends at UW-Stout and an hour and a half away from the Twin Cities. The bus system is easy and convenient, but students recommend having a car to venture off campus.

There are always people hiking the Chippewa River trail, floating down the river, or frolicking at Mt. Simon Park. When the sun goes down, students hit nearby Water Street for late-night fun. The Blugolds have the largest Division III marching band in the nation, and the school's well-traveled choir has given UWEC the rep of being "Wisconsin's Singing University." Intramural sports are also quite popular. UWEC works to make the campus a welcoming place for everyone, with LGBTQ resource centers, diversity mentors, and targeted scholarships.

#28 University of Northern Iowa

The University of Northern Iowa is a midsize public school of about 10,380 undergraduates. UNI's accounting program, whose students earn higher-than-average pass rates on the professional exam, is a popular choice. The College of Education is also a draw, complete with courses of study to become everybody's favorite PE teacher or a no-baloney fitness trainer. UNI hosts the state's only program in gerontology (the study of aging), and other popular majors include criminology, interactive digital studies, political science, and communication disorders. UNI's John Pappajohn Entrepreneurial Center gives students the funding and support they need to get their dream ventures off the ground; it has contributed to the creation of over 50 student businesses.

While all three of Iowa's public universities recently implemented a tuition freeze, UNI offers the most affordable tuition, fees, and room and board. Student loan indebtedness has decreased by about 10 percent in the last three years, contrary to the 6 percent yearly increase in loan debt nationwide reported by The Institute for College Access and Success. Taking into account several variables affecting graduation (including income level, loans, and average ACT/SAT scores), the graduation rate is 5 percent higher than expected.

Cedar Falls is an affordable town (average rent is $759 per month) of 39,260 people. It has the convenience of a big city and the allure of a small town. Panther country (UNI) is two hours from Des Moines and three hours from Minneapolis. Waterloo Regional Airport is only about ten minutes from campus. Walking around campus is a breeze, but to get around town most students drive. The blustery Iowa winter can be brutal, but the beautiful campus and friendly atmosphere keep the student body planted winter after winter.

The school is 87 percent white and 57 percent women, with five hundred international students, mostly from Saudi Arabia and China. Greek life isn't a huge deal here, though it's available. Men's football brings fans to the UNI Dome—and to the parking lot to tailgate. In a beloved UNI tradition, "campaniling," students rendezvous in the shadow of the bell tower to share a kiss. Legend has it that a brick falls off the tower for each student who doesn't swap spit under the campanile by the time they graduate. And there's a lot more going on besides kissing. Panthers know how to get down: they started a dance phenomenon called "the Interlude" that even Michelle Obama found infectious.

#44 University of Wisconsin–Madison

The University of Wisconsin–Madison has one of the best reputations of any flagship university in the Midwest. Their brand holds prestige all across the globe—Jiao Tong University in Shanghai, China, named it in the top twenty schools worldwide. The university is well connected and offers job fairs where students can get face time with Fortune 500 companies. The most popular majors are biology, economics, political science and government, psychology, speech communication, and rhetoric, and the Center for

Measuring University Performance ranks UW-Madison among America's best public research universities. Over 80 percent of Badgers receive their diplomas in six years or less. For a jump start on preparing for college and a taste of college life, first-generation students or those from low-income families can participate in the College Access Program during their sophomore and junior years in high school. Madison also has several organizations that support those same students on campus through advising, mentoring, and tutoring.

UW-Madison has a midrange price tag compared to other Big Ten schools (University of Nebraska is the least expensive and Pennsylvania State University carries the highest sticker price). The bulk of financial aid at UW-Madison comes from loans. While graduates accrue an average $26,625 of debt, only about 1.1 percent of those students default on their student loans. In the 2012–13 school year, 61 percent of students received a scholarship of some sort.

Madison, Wisconsin, one of the greenest cities in the United States, is the quintessential college town. If you opt for the type of wheels that come with a bell and a helmet, you're in luck: Madison was voted one of the most bike-friendly cities in America. The campus is about an hour and a half from Milwaukee and less than three hours from Chicago. But in this town, you'll have pretty much everything you need.

With five lakes, 260 parks, and 150 miles of hiking, biking, and running trails, Badgers are never bored. Whether your speed is beer pong at the Kollege Klub, shopping at the Dane County Farmers Market, or exploring Museum Mile, there's plenty to keep you busy. Public service is preached all over campus, and UW-Madison is the top producer of Peace Corps participants among large universities. Famous for being LGBTQ friendly, the campus has a center that hosts events and supports the community. Game day is everyone's favorite day. The campus becomes awash in cardinal red for hockey and football alike. And don't worry if you don't know how to Bucky (Madison's contribution to the "Dougie" dance phenomenon), because someone will teach you.

#25 University of Illinois at Springfield

University of Illinois at Springfield, the smallest campus in the U of I system, features much smaller class sizes than you're likely to find at Champaign-Urbana or Chicago. In fact, most classes have less than twenty students, so one-on-one attention is easy to come by. UIS curricula center on an active learning approach, so lessons are more hands-on, with less of the professor-lecturing-student dynamic. The top majors are business, computer science, psychology, biology, accountancy, and criminal justice. Engaged citizenship is part of UIS's core, and students are required to participate in service learning, a study-abroad program, or an internship. Springfield, the state capital, is a prime location for students interested in politics and public service. UIS has been facilitating internships with the state legislature and other local NGOs for forty years. UIS has the lowest tuition among schools in the U of I system. Over 69 percent of students receive aid through scholarships, grants, loans, or student employment.

Springfield has a population of about 116,250 people and has a small-town feel with lots of historical museums, including the Abraham Lincoln Presidential Museum. There aren't a lot of recreational activities until you're of age to hit up Springfield's nightlife. Springfield is relatively safe and the campus crime rate is low. Reasonably priced buses take students around town, but many recommend bringing a car.

UIS is young, established in 1969. The school is constantly developing its sense of community and identity, so students have the opportunity to be part of shaping traditions that will live on for generations to come. Greek life just came on the scene in 2013, and there are four organizations and counting. UIS gets diversity bragging rights: about 50 percent of each incoming class identifies as being from an underrepresented group. Students can opt to live in unique living-learning communities that support their UIS experience, including one geared toward first-generation students that supplies peer advising and tutoring.

NORTHEAST

#1 Baruch College–CUNY

Baruch is a public college in New York City with more than fourteen thousand students. Princeton Review ranks Baruch in the top twenty-five for entrepreneurship, and the School of Business, the largest business school in the United States, is highly respected. The School of Arts and Sciences has a culture all its own, encompassing forty areas of study from journalism and mathematics to political science and performing arts. In the city that never sleeps, students have access to world-class writers and performers who offer master classes, lectures, readings, workshops, and concert series right on campus. The integration of notable professionals is happening all over campus: a former New York City comptroller recently joined the faculty in Baruch's School of Public Affairs.

Baruch is one of the fifty most affordable schools with the best return, according to Affordable Schools, and the Education Trust ranked Baruch College in the top five for affordability, accessibility, and graduation rates. By today's standards, its tuition costs are bordering dirt cheap, at just over $6,000 for the year. New York state's Tuition Assistance Program (TAP) awards 96 percent of its state-grant aid to students with high financial need. These students are eligible for $5,000 toward tuition. And City University of New York's (CUNY) Search for Education Elevation Knowledge (SEEK) program, an effort that has helped make Baruch one of the most diverse schools in the entire nation, supports students from low-income backgrounds who would not be ordinarily admitted into the college. Baruch College is twenty-first on President Obama's scorecard for top colleges when it comes to value and affordability.

Baruch is in Manhattan, so the city is the campus. Central Park might serve as Baruchians' version of a quad, and Broadway theaters are only a ten-minute subway ride from campus. Most students commute to campus on public transportation—it's a five-minute walk from the number six train subway station on 23rd Street.

Baruch is shaking it up on the demographic front. Uniquely, white students are a minority at this school, with 35 percent of students identifying as Asian, 13 percent as Hispanic, and 10 percent as black. Even though most of the entertainment comes from the lively surroundings, the school recently took over the East 25th Street block to create a plaza for Baruch students; it now hosts an annual Spring Fling. There's no massive student center offering a hangout hub. Instead Baruch students are likely to congregate at nearby Fitzgerald's Pub.

#7 New Jersey City University

New Jersey City University, with 6,400 students, is a public university about four miles from the Statue of Liberty. It's good to be an aspiring registered nurse at NJCU: they have an accelerated one-year program for those who graduated with a different degree and want to trade it in for scrubs and a stethoscope. Nursing majors have access to resources at the newly renovated science building, a $34 million endeavor that includes new lab science and media arts technology. The university is an approved center of play therapy, a burgeoning area of child psychology. Under a new commitment to break down the barriers for underrepresented student groups to study abroad, the school is working toward equal opportunity for all students to populate their Instagram feeds with tapas and the leaning Tower of Pisa. Popular majors include accounting, business administration, corrections and criminal justice, psychology, and a range of nursing studies: registered nursing, nursing administration, nursing research, and clinical nursing.

Some students at NJCU feel that financial aid at NJCU is a bit of a headache. However, the net price is reasonable and the school offers a few unbelievable scholarships for the state's overachievers. The School of Business, for example, offers a full ride, a laptop, and funding for two study-abroad experiences to all students who are accepted into its honors finance program, and nurses-to-be are offered $10,000 scholarships for the aforementioned accelerated program. All in all, about 85 percent of full-time undergraduates are offered some combo of scholarships, grants, and loans.

Jersey City is a bustling city just beyond the skyscrapers of Manhattan. The main attractions are cultural, with many live performances to choose from and lots of history to explore. From Ellis Island and Lincoln Park to trendy farmers markets filled with fresh produce, exotic meats, and artisan baked goods, there's plenty to occupy your time. Transportation abounds—hopefully you won't mind the never-ending commuter traffic and loud honking. The local bus system has a stop right in front of campus, and there's a light rail stop five minutes away.

The university has a variety of club athletics, including softball, golf, bowling, volleyball, and the recently added women's tennis team. Students can be found dipping at salsa club, sonkaling at the taekwondo club, or participating in any number of activities led by more than twenty campus organizations. Greek life is not raging at NJCU, but there are nine active organizations on campus. Whether you're looking for other Christians, Muslims, Caribbeans, Haitian students, black students, or gay students, you're likely to find a club for you at NJCU.

#11 Penn State Wilkes-Barre

Penn State Wilkes-Barre was originally founded to educate engineers who would improve safety measures for the local mining industry. Today, the school offers bachelor's degrees in six programs: administration of justice, business, electrical engineering technology, English, surveying engineering, and information sciences and technology. The school has a tight-knit community of six hundred undergraduates that affords students an intimate learning environment while offering access to (the first two years of) the main campus's 160 degree programs and all of its study-abroad programs. Average class size at Wilkes-Barre is about eighteen students.

The small student body allows for individual advice and attention based on each student's specific financial situation. One in eight freshmen receives an academic scholarship. The seven hundred scholarships at Penn State Wilkes-Barre range from a couple hundred bucks to $4,000. Upon applying to Wilkes-Barre, all students are automatically considered for a host of scholarships.

Wilkes-Barre is a fairly industrial city, with the campus tucked safely away out in the country. If you find that Wilkes-Barre is not your scene, it's not too hard to transfer to any of Penn State's twenty-three other campuses.

Penn State Wilkes-Barre is primarily a commuter campus. Men dominate the school, with women making up just 24 percent of the student body. The school's orgs include an outdoor recreation club, ROTC, a student alumni association, business club, campus activity board, student newspaper, engineering club, and fitness club.

#13 Ramapo College of New Jersey

Ramapo College is a midsize public university near New Jersey's Ramapo Mountains. The school is often mistaken for a private school because of its intimate network of students and interdisciplinary structure. Ramapo has been recognized as a military-friendly school, as it works well with veterans to sort out things like transfer credit, financial benefits, and other situations specific to their circumstances. Students interested in saving the planet can gain hands-on experience at the Ramapo College Sustainable Education Center. The center focuses on solar and wind energy, recycling and composting, and ecological agriculture. Nursing majors at Ramapo train in the Valley Hospital, recognized as a center of excellence in nursing.

Two-thirds of Ramapo's students receive some form of financial aid. Students from low-income backgrounds may qualify for Pell Grants, and New Jersey residents may qualify for Tuition Aid Grants of up to about $7,000. First-year students involved in the Educational Opportunity Fund program (for low-income and/or high-performing community college students) can send their tuition bill back to Ramapo after federal grants and scholarships have been applied, and the school will pick up what remains.

Ramapo College of New Jersey sits on the border of New York and New Jersey. You can get the best of both worlds on a campus in a rural enclave that's also only an hour from New York City. The school has shuttles to the city, local shopping centers, and a train station. In the winter, getting around campus can be difficult due to icy hills and mountainous terrain.

Many students at Ramapo pack up on the weekends and head for some home cooking and more comfortable beds. Tuesdays and Thursdays are the nights to get social at Pub 17. Even though Greek housing is off campus, going Greek at Ramapo continues to be a popular choice, with twenty-five organizations to choose from. Ramapo has more than a hundred student clubs, ranging from Ramapo Pride to the less traditional Ramapo College Beekeeping Club. Journalism students and all those who like to hear themselves talk can join Ramapo's radio station, WRPR-FM, or Ramapo College Television and Video. Ramapo's music programs include five different choirs that travel all over, from the Philippines to the Czech Republic.

#14 University of Maine at Farmington

University of Maine at Farmington is a small public liberal arts and teachers college in central Maine. With just two thousand students, the college's student-to-faculty ratio is 14:1. In contrast to many undergrad programs, all classes are taught by actual professors, not graduate assistants. UMF began as a teaching school 150 years ago, and education is still one of the most popular majors here; students can choose to focus on early childhood, elementary, school health, secondary, or special education. UMF has a strong liberal arts core and prides itself on the collective creativity of its students, who have opportunities to display their work at the UMF Art Gallery and the Emery Community Arts Center. It's not uncommon to find guerrilla art exhibits strung throughout the campus.

Ninety percent of all full-time students at UMF receive financial aid. The average aid package is just over $12,000, and Maine has a deal with the rest of New England and Canada to give students in the region a tuition break of $4,900. The school offers over a hundred scholarships, and Maine's Native American population can go to UMF free of charge. UMF's extensive network of student employment programs creates jobs for more than half of all students.

On the foothills of the mountains just off the Appalachian Trail, students ski, swim, hike, and climb their way through what Farmington has to offer. In an already safe town, UMF takes care to provide extra dorm security and escort services for students. UMF offers shuttle services from campus to coach bus lines that run throughout Maine and to Logan Airport in Boston. There are also shuttles to the local Walmart and supermarket.

UMF is a true blend of artsy and outdoorsy. Local poets, artists, musicians, actors, and filmmakers are the lifeblood of a thriving art scene in Farmington. Students can get their creative juices flowing with dozens of artistic groups on campus, from Film Club to the Writers Guild. It's not just artists who fall in love with Farmington. *Fly Rod & Reel* rated UMF as one of the top ten universities in America for fishing. And not to worry—UMF also has all the typical religious, political, and student clubs, while downtown Farmington has everything you need, from funky retail shops to a late-night Taco Bell.

#15 University of Vermont

The University of Vermont is one of the oldest universities in the Northeast and educates just under ten thousand students. UVM prides itself on being a public Ivy, with over 70 percent of the student body coming from the top 25 percent of their high schools. The university has several well-regarded, innovative programs linked to both land and water. The Rubenstein Ecosystem Science Laboratory on the banks of Lake Champlain serves as a teaching and research facility. The school has been recognized for its groundbreaking research on whales and their place in marine ecosystems, and it owns four farms where agriculture majors learn the business of farming in an actual dairy cooperative. UVM's extremely active career services center provides advisors who emphasize the importance of service learning, and it has a website and database devoted to placing students in internships. With resources typically found at major large universities, UVM still maintains an average class size of twenty-four and a 15:1 student-to-faculty ratio.

Less than 2 percent of Catamounts default on their student loans. Maybe it's because they are raking in the dough not long after college. The average mid-career grad is earning over $80,000, and the *Wall Street Journal* noted that students with a UVM degree have a high chance of gaining entry to top medical and business schools like Harvard, Yale, and University of

Pennsylvania. Nearly all freshmen receive some sort of financial aid, which usually averages around $20,000.

Burlington, home to the band Phish and to Ben & Jerry's ice cream, has about forty thousand residents. The town is fairly progressive and quite passionate about great food and the great outdoors. The *New York Times* and the *Huffington Post* have named Burlington as a top city for outdoor activities, and *Travel I Leisure* ranked Burlington as the number one college town in the entire nation.

Students at UVM are engaged and committed to making their community healthier, more sustainable, and, yeah, a bit more hip. UVM students make full use of Lake Champlain and the surrounding mountain ranges for recreation. Skis, snowshoes, canoes, and camping equipment are available for rent right on campus. The school offers a mind-blowing fifty-four sports, including crew, sailing, and quidditch. AERO, one of 170 clubs, is an alternative energy racing club that engineers a fully electric racecar every two years. Local values are absorbed by the campus: selling bottled water has been banned and 12 percent of all campus food is locally sourced, fair trade, or has a low environmental impact.

#17 Holy Family University

Holy Family University is a small private liberal arts university in Philadelphia committed to teaching students responsibility toward "God, society and self." Holy Family emphasizes open-mindedness with an eye toward students thriving in multicultural settings. With just over two thousand students and a student-to-faculty ratio of 12:1, plenty of personal attention is available. Most students are headed toward the health professions, education, or business. For those wanting to jump into the workforce as quickly as possible, Holy Family has accelerated programs for bachelor's degrees in business administration, nursing, and criminal justice. Students in the communications program have access to a TV/radio broadcasting studio outfitted with manual and robotic HD video cameras, a digital video editing room, and a Mac lab. Co-op and internship programs have enabled students to work with the Philadelphia Flyers, NBC, and the *Bucks County Courier Times*. An impressive 87 percent of students who participate in HFU's co-op program receive a job in their field right out of college.

The vast majority of full-time undergraduates receive some kind of need-based financial aid. The average scholarship or grant award to students is almost $14,000, and grads are getting jobs at a 10 percent higher rate than the rest of the nation. Scholarships are a mix of merit- and need-based, and two grant programs are available for students from low-income backgrounds. The amounts vary but go up to $36,780 for high-need students.

Holy Family is located in a more subdued and suburban part of Philadelphia and has three campuses throughout the area with shuttle service between the locations. There are bus stops right outside of campus and a train station down the street to serve the large commuter population at Holy Family. Students report feeling safe on campus, and campus security patrols the area regularly.

HFU offers a friendly, warm atmosphere with an environment geared toward growing personally, academically, and spiritually. Females outnumber males by a factor of more than three. About 44 percent of the school population identifies as an ethnic minority. The school has choir, dance, drama, theater, a student newspaper, and sports. The Tigers battle in the NCAA's Division II.

#28 University at Buffalo–SUNY

SUNY Buffalo is one of only two State University of New York campuses in a major city (the other is the University of Albany). The student body is made up of nearly ten thousand undergrads, and with an average class size of twelve to fifteen students, you can get a personalized education from one of their 160 programs in a stimulating urban context. One of many experiential training programs, a notable feature of the school, is based at Campus House: a social club for faculty and a training program for hospitality majors where students learn key aspects of hospitality management. You'll find the state's largest social work program here, and education is also a favorite program of study. Future teachers can work at the Center for Excellence in Urban and Rural Education exploring improvement initiatives in underserved areas, and trendsetters in the Fashion and Textile Technology Program spend three years on campus and one year studying their specialty at the Fashion Institute of Technology in New York City. The school has multiple resources on campus to help students market themselves in the workforce. Across fields alumni seem to fare pretty well when it comes to employment. Recent years have seen mechanical engineering grads hit a remarkable 100 percent job placement rate.

More than half of students at Buffalo qualify for Pell Grants, and nearly three-fourths of students receive some sort of financial aid. The school has two merit scholarships and twenty-one departmental scholarships. The Buffalo born-and-raised may qualify for the Say Yes to Education Scholarship, which covers the remaining tuition bill for Buffalo public school alums from low-income backgrounds after federal aid is applied.

The school is located about twenty minutes from Buffalo Niagara Airport. Students say the area is very safe, but it is still a big city after all. Staying alert and the buddy system are never bad ideas. Buffalo is one of the biggest cities in New York, and so the setting is probably better suited to those who'll embrace the grit of a major city over students seeking endless green pastures.

SUNY Buffalo's active campus life has forty clubs, despite generally being a commuter school. Greek life is visible and diverse, with lots of students choosing to rush one of the twenty organizations that are responsible for a healthy portion of the campus nightlife. The surrounding area is not lacking in clubs, bars, boutiques, and restaurants. The museum district of Buffalo is just across the street, and the Buffalo Zoo is a mere a four minutes away by car.

#35 Towson University

Towson University is a large public university twenty minutes outside of Baltimore, Maryland. As a leader in cyber operations, it has been deemed a center for excellence by the National Security Agency, a distinction afforded only thirteen other institutions. Cyber Ops majors often have first pick at highly sought-after NSA internships, and the school's proximity to the nation's capital gives students the opportunity to intern at some of the most prestigious political, civic, and business establishments in the country. Prior students have interned with the White House, Johns Hopkins Hospital, the National Institutes of Health, MTV, the *Today Show*, and the Baltimore Orioles. Students have access to cutting-edge technology, including 3-D printers for rapid manufacturing, prototype assembly, or creative design. The UTeach program links students with expert faculty mentors and varied avenues to discover exactly where their passions and talents lie. To better accommodate commuters, expanded course offerings at the northeastern Maryland campus are in the works. An award-winning advising program begins from the moment students step foot on campus via the First Year Experience, which includes a course requiring periodic meet-ups with specially trained advisors.

While institutional grants award low-income students with up to $9,000, these grants are highly selective, so students are more likely to receive aid from the many departmental scholarships. Check out the TUTORS work-study program for supplemental funds; it pays well above the Maryland minimum wage for tutoring elementary kids in Baltimore City. To ensure that students understand the weighty responsibility of accepting loans, the financial aid office provides mandatory entrance counseling. Combined with chances to discuss repayment options on the way out, it's evident that loan literacy is highly valued at Towson.

USA Today ranks Baltimore as one of the best cities for college students based on diversity, degree attainment, arts and leisure, cost of living, and professional opportunity. While not known for its sterling safety record, Towson makes sure that entering Fort Knox is easier than entering any one of its dorms uninvited.

Towson has two hundred clubs, many with dedicated coaches and advisors. The dance team has consistently won national championships since 1999, and the school runs its own version of *The Apprentice*: The Associate (hopefully with better hairdos). Teams work on complex company cases with the likes of Bank of America, McCormick, Target, and Sherwin-Williams. With an NCAA Division I sports scene, there's lots of fun to be had rallying around the Towson Tigers. Football and lacrosse games are frequent favorites.

#41 Bloomsburg University of Pennsylvania

Bloomsburg University of Pennsylvania is a medium-size public university in rural Pennsylvania. While the school has over fifty majors, business is a particular strength here, and students going that route have access to the Ziegler Institute for Professional Development, a career center where students can seek advice and avail themselves of resources like résumé workshops. In 2011, Bloomsburg University built the Benner-Hudock Center for Financial Analysis, where students learn business data literacy through technology (e.g., virtual investing programs and stock analytics programs). Second-year students have the opportunity to participate in Sophomore Experiential Learning, which enables students to job-shadow for twenty to forty hours in work environments such as Comcast's corporate headquarters.

To subsidize the already below-average cost of tuition, BU offers $2 million in scholarships. Those who are pretty sure they want to spend the next decade in army green can apply for the Army ROTC Scholarship, which pays tuition, fees, and a monthly stipend in exchange for a combined eight years in active duty and the reserve. SOLVE, the work-study placement office, helps students keep tuition costs in a manageable place by hooking students up with on-campus work-study gigs. It also connects them to paid opportunities at nonprofits and businesses off campus, ranging from the United Way to film studios.

Altogether, the rural Pennsylvania atmosphere is quaint and beautiful, though some say the students and the local residents don't always see eye to eye. There is reliable shuttle service from the campus to key locations in town. Bring your rain boots, because when it rains in Bloomsburg it pours, apparently for days.

Bloomsburg has a friendly small-town feel. Lots of schools throw that phrase around to make their backdrops sound charming, but BU's the real deal. It's a great fit for students who love their provincial roots but want the resources of a larger university. Although 81 percent of the campus is white, and the university had a notable bout with racial intolerance in the early 1990s, the school now has an equity task force to help ensure that all students feel safe and welcome and are treated equally and respectfully. There are nearly a dozen organizations devoted to the education and inclusion of underrepresented groups, including the Black Cultural Society, the LGBTQA Commission, a Spanish club, and a gospel choir, to name a few. BU has twenty-nine Greek organizations and 250 student clubs and organizations, including NCAA intercollegiate sports teams and community government.

#1 Berea College

Berea College, located in Berea, Kentucky, is profoundly unique. Founded by abolitionists in 1855 and known to be the first interracial and coed school in the South, it has consistently prided itself on an adherence to Christian values and being open and accepting to all people. Practicing what they preach might just be an understatement: all admitted students receive full four-year tuition scholarships, and service learning is a must, made possible through various course offerings that count toward Berea's "active learning experience" requirement. The most popular of Berea's more than thirty majors reflect the diversity of experiences and interests on campus: industrial production technology, psychology, and studio and fine arts are favorites. Designing your own major is an option, as is completing an engineering dual degree program with either Washington University in St. Louis or the University of Kentucky. Just over sixteen hundred students means the student-to-faculty ratio is quite small, 11:1. All in all, Berea does a fantastic job of meeting the needs common to many of its students. The overall graduation rate is strong, and—given that so many students are the first in their families to attend college and have often faced major social and economic challenges—the actual graduation rate is 25 percent higher than the expected one.

A large endowment and small student population are what enable Berea College to make such a remarkable commitment to its financially under-privileged community, though students also receive money from outside sources to meet economic needs beyond their tuition costs. The vast major-ity of incoming freshmen (99 percent) qualify for Pell Grants. In return for the generous financial assistance the school provides, all students have to work ten to fifteen hours per week at an on-campus job all four years. The school also funds up to 75 percent of study-abroad costs for those who take advantage of the program.

Berea, Kentucky, is a small town in the truest sense, with a population of 13,561. Known for its art festivals, this tight-knit Appalachian community has a distinct cultural identity that's almost bucolic. Eighty-eight percent of students live on campus, so everyone becomes quite familiar with each other. For students in search of a community-oriented college that feels connected both internally and to the outside world, Berea may be a good choice. True to its inclusive form, Berea offers a sustainable living area, the Ecovillage, which provides family housing for students and even has a child care center.

Although Berea works hard to accommodate students from all backgrounds, its racial and ethnic diversity is about average. Even still, *Black Enterprise* magazine ranked Berea as one of the best colleges in the nation for African American students, and its gender diversity is balanced too—females account for 57 percent of students. Fifty-three percent of students come from outside of Kentucky. There are some athletic teams, but sports are not particularly popular. Students admit that Berea doesn't quite offer a typical college social life, yet they find plenty of ways to keep busy through several dozen clubs—finding Appalachian cultural crafts or a personal training meet-up are equally probable on Berea's campus.

#2 Texas A&M University–College Station

With one of the largest undergraduate populations in the country, Texas A&M in College Station, Texas, ranks second in the South on our "Best Bang for the Buck" list primarily because of its exceptionally high graduation rates and affordable cost to students. Its enormous size provides students with endless academic opportunities. It boasts over 120 majors for students to choose from and has been specially recognized for its engineering and business programs. A *New York Times* survey reveals that Texas A&M graduates are some of the most sought after by business leaders worldwide, and the *Wall Street Journal* found that Texas A&M ranks second in the nation for having the most-sought-after graduates in the government and nonprofit sectors as well. An 80 percent graduation rate and a retention rate of 92 percent reveal that Texas A&M students truly value being "Aggies," as they're known. Part of this triumph can be attributed to the Academic Success Center, which helps students plan coursework and learn strategies and offers financial advice and other support. Texas A&M was originally a military institution and is consistently ranked as one of the most military-friendly colleges; the student body has a large number of veterans.

Beyond networking, loyal Aggie alumni provide funds that have built an exceptional endowment for the school. Tuition for in-state students is low (not so much for out-of-staters), and approximately 71 percent of students receive financial aid. Texas A&M gives out some of the largest National Merit Scholarships in the country and therefore draws many of these scholars. It also has a Regents' Scholars Program, which is a need-based program for two thousand first-generation college students. These students have an amazing 90 percent retention rate. Fourteen thousand students have part-time on-campus jobs.

College Station is, well . . . a college town: a 100,000-person city dominated by Texas A&M students and often referred to as "Aggieland." The region, much like the student body, is largely conservative and Christian. *Kiplinger* ranks College Station as the third-best midsize U.S. city with regard to housing costs, access to schools, and access to health care. *Forbes* also ranks it nationally as the sixth-best midsize city for business and careers. The campus is residential, with most students living on campus or nearby.

So just how large is Texas A&M? There are currently 44,072 undergrads who are involved in over eight hundred student groups—plenty of room to find your niche. While the school is composed of primarily white, conservative, Christian students from Texas, the university works to welcome students from all walks of life through diversity seminars and a Difficult Dialogues Program. There are some fifty student groups dedicated to various aspects of African American and Latino student life, along with other identity-related offerings. Texas A&M's culture is in large part defined by the highly anticipated football games, for which there is no shortage of related traditions. For example, before the first big home game there's the "First Yell," which features events, an entertainer, and a midnight yell practice. Good times.

#6 The University of Texas at El Paso

The University of Texas at El Paso is a large public Hispanic-serving institution situated in the very western tip of Texas. The National Science Foundation named UTEP one of six minority institutions in the country that merit the title "Model Institution for Excellence," numerous groups and magazines have claimed that UTEP-educated engineers (most of whom are Hispanic) are extremely well qualified, and the Carnegie Corporation gave UTEP one of its eleven Teachers for a New Era research grants. UTEP offers seventy-one bachelor's degrees within fifty-seven majors. Among the most popular programs are business management and marketing, education (particularly multilingual education), health professions (particularly nursing), engineering, and biology. UTEP also has exceptional theater arts programs. Many students avail themselves of undergraduate research jobs to help finance their education. Ninety percent of the school's law school prep students get into law school, and UTEP sends more Mexican American graduates to medical school than almost any other institution.

The average net price at the University of Texas at El Paso is $3,258 (96 percent of students are in-state). Fifty-nine percent of UTEP students receive Pell Grants (which also contributes to the low net price). One-third of students come from families who have a yearly income of $20,000 or less, and 78 percent receive some kind of financial aid. While the loan default rate is high, 71 percent of aid comes from grants and scholarships. In-state students whose families earn under $30,000 can likely take advantage of the UTEP Promise, which can pay full tuition and fees for those who qualify, and there are a fair number of academic scholarships as well.

El Paso, Texas, is at the very western tip of Texas, right at the border of Texas, Mexico, and New Mexico. A large city with 672,538 citizens, it has a small-town feel, and natural beauty is easy to find, with the Franklin

Mountains and their state park just outside the city for those who love out-door activities (and don't mind the sometimes scorching heat). The desert climate makes for clear skies and beautiful sunsets, and unlike many south-ern cities, there is a blend of cultures—Native American, Hispanic, and Old West among them. The campus is built into a hillside overlooking the Rio Grande, allowing students to see just over the river into Mexico. Many students live off campus since there is a lot to do in the city, though the large number of school events do provide that campus community vibe.

Because it was originally a school of mining and metallurgy, students are known as the UTEP Miners. The university has just over 23,000 students, 96 percent of whom are from Texas; a great many (55 percent) are first-gen-eration college students, and almost four-fifths are Hispanic. Campus life is lively, and basketball and football are hugely popular. Fun fact: UTEP was the first school in the South to racially integrate its intercollegiate sports teams. In 1966, the men's basketball team won the NCAA national cham-pionship, and their story is documented in the film *Glory Road*. Football fans enjoy Minerpalooza, a huge annual festival surrounding the start of the football season. UTEP seems to have it all, from dinner theater shows like *Footloose* to community service to Greek life (present but less so than at many southern schools).

#11 Lane College

Lane College in Jackson, Tennessee, is a historically black college. A small private Christian liberal arts college open to people of all backgrounds, Lane mostly educates African American students. Although its graduation rate isn't high, costs aren't either, making it an affordable option. Lane College offers just fifteen majors, so students should do their research to make sure that at least one of these majors is a good fit for them. However, there may be a little extra time to decide which path to take because the school's general requirement courses sometimes take students a year or two to complete. Business administration and management, biology, and crim-inal justice are popular majors, and Lane also offers students unique op-portunities to study homeland security, law enforcement, and firefighting. Originally founded to educate freed slaves, Lane College continues its tra-dition of bettering the individual and society through spiritual and ethical learning. It's important to note that while freshman retention and gradua-tion rates are quite low, when the challenges many students face are taken into account Lane College's actual graduation rate is 12 percent higher than expected. The student-to-faculty ratio is 17:1, and many students offer glowing reports of how caring the faculty are and how eager they are to help students improve.

Lane is committed to educating students from financially underpriv-ileged circumstances—nearly every student is from a low-income family. Ninety-eight percent of students receive financial aid, 90 percent receive

Pell Grants, though only 14 percent receive scholarships. All in all, the net price comes in at $8,815. Ninety-one percent of incoming freshmen take out loans, and the default rate on loans overall is rather high. Off-campus jobs are the best way to supplement funds, since there are no on-campus jobs available to students.

Jackson is a small city of about 67,000 residents in western Tennessee between Nashville and Memphis. Like the school, the city is a religious one, with over two hundred churches of various denominations. The music history of the city is rich and is commemorated annually with the Shannon Street MusicFest. It's an affordable city, so while 61 percent of Lane students live on campus, those who choose not to will find very reasonably priced housing off campus. Some students have complained that both Jackson and Lane College have high crime rates, leaving students feeling unsafe. There are police officers regularly stationed around campus for added safety.

Nearly all of the fifteen hundred students at Lane are African American, though the student body is a diverse one in terms of geographic origin, sexual orientation, and religious denomination. Men and women are equally represented, and 34 percent of students are from outside of Tennessee. Many students say the social and night life is decent, particularly because of the location in Jackson. Greek life is a small scene at Lane, and while their Division II athletics are not wildly popular, the basketball team typically draws fans. Lane has rules some students find too strict—a curfew (11:00 p.m. during the week, 1:00 a.m. on weekends), a no-tolerance policy for alcohol and drugs on campus, no visitors (either from other dorms or from outside of the school), and students must attend Wednesday chapel ten times per semester. Still, several students feel the rules are meant to protect them and are in line with a Christian education. Despite the regulations, there are still outlets for fun. And as students point out, studying takes up much of their time anyway!

#12 Jackson State University

Jackson State University is a well-regarded historically black public research university located in Jackson, Mississippi. Jackson State has five undergraduate colleges hosting thirty-seven different majors, and as of 2014 it will be the only school in Mississippi with an undergraduate program in biomedical engineering. With a number of opportunities for research, it is one of only two HBCUs recognized by the Carnegie Classification of Institutions of Higher Education for their high research activity. Although the graduation rate (41.7 percent) is below the national average, it's high on our list in part because the undergraduate studies program is doing a lot to get all of its students into caps and gowns, with a range of supportive programs that advise, tutor, and mentor students. The First-Year Experience is aimed at freshman retention, the W.E.B. Du Bois Honors Program offers first- and second-year students more challenging classes to choose from, and a summer bridge program provides new students the chance to get ahead by earning six to nine credits in science technology, engineering, or math.

The net price of the institution is lower than most at $9,783, making it an appealing option for financially strapped students and families. About 74.7 percent of students receive Pell Grants, and 38 percent get institutional grants. Some combo of grants and loans is generally what makes up the packages of the 94 percent of students who receive some form of financial aid; however, merit- and need-based scholarships are available via the Thurgood Marshall College Fund, which awards money to students at its forty-seven member schools. About a quarter of Jackson State's incoming students end up taking out loans, and their default rate is higher than at most schools. Work-study jobs are available to help out with college costs and could be a good way to borrow a little less.

Jackson, Mississippi, is a midsized city, with about 175,000 people. The state's capital, it is a business, historical, and cultural center, and *Forbes* ranked it the third "Best Bang for Your Buck" city among large U.S. metropolitan areas. Students report that the city doesn't offer them much in the way of activities but that they find people there very friendly and encouraging of Jackson State students. Only 31 percent of students live on campus, while others choose to find a place to live in the city's low-cost housing.

Ninety-two percent of Jackson State's 6,675 students are African American, female students are slightly more prevalent at 62 percent, and 35 percent of students hail from outside of Mississippi. Students get extremely geared up for their Jackson Tigers Division I sports teams, particularly the football team. Greek life is present but doesn't dominate social life. Tech-savvy students might be interested to know that Jackson State has been recognized as a technologically advanced university and has the only Apple-authorized campus store in Mississippi. Jackson isn't exactly a party school, but a fair amount of nightlife on campus makes it pretty easy to have a good time on the weekends.

#14 Oklahoma State University

Oklahoma State University, home of the Cowboys, is located in Stillwater, Oklahoma, and is full of wildly spirited students. OSU's low tuition (particularly for in-state students) and its above-expected graduation rate make it an enticing choice. Well known for its business and marketing, agriculture, and engineering programs, OSU also has unique and excellent programs in architecture and in hotel and restaurant administration. Design firms in the South ranked OSU in the top ten for its School of Architecture, while the *Journal of Hospitality and Research* ranked OSU's School of Hotel and Restaurant Administration eighth in the world. Its environmental science program is also one of the best offered in the country, and students seeking research opportunities will likely be impressed by the Henry Bellmon Office of Scholar Development and Undergraduate Research, which offers scholarships, guidance, and freshman-year research opportunities; it even helps students compete for major national and international awards. OSU's graduation rate is slightly above the national average, and it maintains above-average graduation rates for Hispanic, African American, and Asian American students. Notably, it leads the nation in bachelor's degrees earned by Native Americans.

In-state tuition is only $7,650, while out-of-state tuition remains significantly higher, $18,860. OSU does a good job overall of meeting students' financial needs. Seventy-eight percent of students were given some form of financial aid, and of that aid 28 percent is state grants, 30 percent is federal grants, and 42 percent is scholarships. Homegrown students are provided with numerous state-based support options, including Oklahoma's Promise, a program that can cover full tuition for select students who apply in eighth, ninth, or tenth grade. OSU sweetens the deal with the Cowboy Covenant, an additional $1,000 renewable cash scholarship available to Oklahoma Promise students. For out-of-state students, OSU has the Nonresident Achievement Scholarship, which is based on ACT/SAT score and GPA.

Forty-seven thousand residents form the tight-knit community of Stillwater, which might be best described as having a small-town feel and lots of small-town charm. People are open and generous, ready to say hi to anyone passing by on the sidewalk. *CNN Money* ranked Stillwater as one of the top places to live in 2010 in the United States. Eskimo Joe's is a popular haunt that was voted the third-best college sports bar in the country by *Sports Illustrated* and best post-game college hangout by *Sporting News*. While newcomers or outsiders may be inclined to call it a podunk town, Stillwater defenders highlight that the famous country-western singer Garth Brooks (an OSU alumnus) got his start playing at the Tumbleweed music venue there. It's a small town with a lot to offer.

Like many southern state schools, OSU is a large, football-loving campus. The strong Christian and conservative community is full of students who are passionate and prideful about their university. Football games draw massive crowds of loyal fans, decked out in orange to rally and support. OSU is also known for its wrestling team, which has won more championships in any single sport than any other university (thirty-four NCAA championships, to be exact). There's also a rodeo team, which competes in the National Intercollegiate Rodeo Association. The school is definitely a diverse place, though most of OSU's twenty thousand students are white (72 percent white, 6 percent Native American, 5 percent African American, 5 percent Hispanic, 2 percent Asian American). Ranked the fourteenth-most-religious university in the United States by the Princeton Review, OSU doesn't have any actual formal religious affiliation. Greek life is a major part of the social scene, and many students acknowledge a divide between Greek and non-Greek students on campus. Fun fact: OSU is home to the largest student union in the world—a portion of which is associated with the School of Hotel and Restaurant Administration.

#23 Texas State–San Marcos

Texas State–San Marcos, located in southern Texas, has a very low net price, making it affordable to almost all students, but particularly those in-state. The School of Criminal Justice, the School of Journalism and Mass Communication, and the McCoy Business College offer well-regarded programs at a school that has seventy-three majors within twenty-seven distinct fields of study. Some of the most popular majors include business/marketing, the social sciences, visual and performing arts, communications/journalism, and parks and recreation. Forensic anthropology and geography are also unique programs that catch the attention of many students. The graduation rate remains about average at this 35,000-student campus. Texas State is also military friendly, educating a fair number of veterans as well as students in Air Force and Army ROTC programs. The study needs of such a large student body are accommodated well by a seven-story campus library.

While Texas State offers an array of grants, scholarships, work-study opportunities, and loans, perhaps its most unique financial opportunity is the Bobcat Promise: free tuition and fees to incoming in-state freshman whose gross family income is $35,000 or less. Fifty-seven percent of students receive some kind of financial assistance, and Texas State meets about 76 percent of its students' financial need. Even without much financial aid, students are likely to find costs at Texas State much more manageable than at many other schools: in-state tuition is $7,732 and out-of-state tuition is $16,888.

The city of San Marcos, with a population of about fifty thousand, is a quickly growing midsize city with a somewhat suburban feel. San Marcos is home to the largest outlet mall in Texas, offering a destination to students in need of a break from campus. San Marcos is only thirty miles from Austin and forty-nine miles from San Antonio—students can access the best of both cities (buses run between San Marcos and Austin) while enjoying the less bustling environment in San Marcos. Like the campus itself, much of San Marcos has natural parks and recreational areas.

Social life at Texas–San Marcos is marked by its diversity. Forty-two percent of students are students of color, nearly 30 percent of whom are Hispanic/Latino. Less diverse are the geographic origins of students—over 90 percent of Bobcats are from Texas. A lure for many who know they'll need an outdoor break from the books, the San Marcos River runs through the campus and adjoining Sewell Park. Students engage in all kinds of water activities such as tubing, kayaking, and boating, and those who don't love the water have a great time hanging out in the park, playing outdoor sports, sunbathing, and picnicking. Greek life is not much of a presence at Texas State, but football is extremely popular and tailgating at the games is a regular activity in the fall. Students also have ways to engage beyond the confines of campus during the Bobcat Build, a large annual community service project.

#26 Tennessee Technological University

Tennessee Technological University (aka Tennessee Tech or TTU) is a medium-size public university in Cookeville, Tennessee. Primarily known for its engineering and technology programs—mechanical engineering and computer science, to name just two—it offers many academic programs, ranging from nursing and exercise science to fine arts programs working with fibers, glass, metal, and wood. A new, unique major at TTU, World Cultures and Business, combines humanities, international finance, and economics, and has been recognized by the American Association of State Colleges and Universities. Agricultural majors at TTU can get hands-on experience at the Tech Farm. Undergraduate research programs on campus expose students to state-of-the-art facilities and innovative faculty focusing on economic development, energy systems, natural resources, health care, and STEM disciplines. Each of the six undergrad colleges has its own success center where students can seek academic advising.

With relatively low tuition, an above-average graduation rate, and a below-average loan default rate, Tennessee Tech provides students with a solid, affordable education. The net price at Tennessee Tech is about $11,369, which is relatively low and partially the result of a large number of in-state students. Approximately two-thirds of TTU students receive financial aid. Of those who do, their packages are 64 percent grants and scholarships and 36 percent loans. Just over a third of students receive Pell Grants. TTU also provides scholarships based on high school academic performance; a few, including the Soaring Eagle Scholarship, are meant for out-of-state students. *U.S. News and World Report* ranked TTU students as having the least amount of debt of all southern schools.

Cookeville is a small town of about 25,000 that sits eighty miles east of Nashville. It has both rural and urban areas, and while students bemoan that the town doesn't offer much of a nightlife, lovers of the outdoors are never at a loss. Cookeville is surrounded by three lakes, and there are gorgeous mountains, state parks, and rivers nearby. If that doesn't tickle your fancy, Nashville is less than two hours away.

Many students find that TTU is the perfect size. With about ten thousand undergraduates, there is always someone new to meet, yet familiar faces can be found all around. TTU is composed of mostly white students (83 percent) and students who are from Tennessee (88 percent). The gender balance leans toward males, who make up about 56 percent of the student population. Sports on campus are moderately popular. Fans come out to most games (especially football), and there's an annual tradition called the Blizzard before their big rival basketball game, where students throw "Tech Squares" (toilet paper) into the air all at once. But there isn't overwhelming widespread support, despite what the mascot's name, Awesome, might lead most to believe. Greek life is definitely present and defines certain circles, but it's not a major fixture of the social life. Students say there's no wild nightlife, but fun is always possible, like hanging out at a popular off-campus destination, Rodeo Bob's, which has a country feel and caters to its college student customers.

#13 Alice Lloyd College

Towns like Pippa Passes, which shares its name with a Victorian verse, are surely few and far between. Formerly Caney Creek, the small settlement was rechristened by Alice Spencer Geddes Lloyd, a lifelong social reformer who arrived in Appalachia with the hope of providing opportunities for people throughout the region. Her mission, to foster the success of "mountain people," continues to define her namesake, Alice Lloyd College. ALC emphasizes leadership education and community involvement, a sensible and crucial philosophy given the economic stagnation across central Appalachia. Students enrolled in the most popular major, education, may also choose to enroll in the Teacher Education Program, which culminates in the creation of a professional portfolio and Teaching Performance Assessment. ALC is part of a statewide effort to improve business conditions in its poverty-stricken region. A formal Leadership Education Program requires professional dress every Tuesday, and accounting and business majors are encouraged to connect with the Appalachian Entrepreneurial Development Program. There are also dual-degree options in the nursing, pre-dental, and pre-veterinary tracks. Impressively, 96 percent of ALC graduates are either employed or enrolled in another degree program, and 83 percent eventually find employment somewhere in the region. Think about that alongside the fact that 60–70 percent of students in each freshman class are the first in their families to attend college.

Tuition at ALC is guaranteed for any qualified student from one of the 108 counties of central Appalachia. This scholarship, in tandem with federal and state aid, covers the cost of tuition for most students, and explains why so many ALC graduates are relatively debt-free. While room, board, books, and food still cost upward of $3,700 per semester, minority students from the region can qualify for grants that will cover some of this additional cost. For other students with additional need, a long list of endowed scholarships is available; it is important to keep in mind that several of these consider the status of "professed Christian" to be just as important as GPA. Students are also required to work a minimum of ten hours per week while enrolled. The most unique facet of ALC's aid policy is its support of post-graduate education. The Caney Scholars Program incentivizes exceptional undergraduates to stay in the region by providing financial support to those who pursue full-time post-graduate studies in Kentucky. Selected students can even live free of charge in University of Kentucky housing! ALC is truly an appetizing choice for prospective students seeking to remain and make change in their home region.

Pippa Passes is located in remote and rural eastern Kentucky. Mountains surround the campus, a potential haven for those who love the outdoors. One overlook adjacent to the college, called High Rocks, is a frequent field trip for the college's hiking club.

ALC's identity is strongly rooted in its Christian-based morals and ethics. Dormitories are strictly segregated by sex, and a curfew (midnight on weekdays, 2:00 a.m. on weekends) is enforced. Those looking to go out for some fun or a scene will face difficulties, since the nearest action is in Pikeville, over an hour away by car. ALC's culture more or less invites a lack of diversity, and since its policies are designed to attract regional applicants, it follows that enrolled students come overwhelmingly from white, rural, and Christian households. Most extracurricular activities either are service-oriented or pay homage to Appalachian culture or the Christian faith. The Voices of Appalachia Choir, touting a repertoire of traditional gospel and bluegrass pieces, tours in the spring and frequently performs at school events. Several groups cater to students interested in worship and missionary work. Few alternatives exist for students less inclined toward faith-based pastimes. There is, however, an active arts community, with many students involved in theater, photography, and creative writing. The nearby towns of Hindman and Whitesburg are home to centers that support local artists and artisans. The college also operates an FCC-licensed radio station that broadcasts on campus and in nearby towns.

SOUTHEAST

#1 East Carolina University

East Carolina University (ECU) is a large public university located in Greenville, North Carolina. ECU comes in first in the Southeast rankings because of its good graduation rates and solid academic performance—all at a low net price to students. ECU boasts the largest nursing program in North Carolina, and many students come to ECU to study health sciences. ECU was originally founded as a teacher training school in 1907. Sure, academics here are challenging. But fear not—ECU has free private tutoring services. The tutoring center is equipped to support students in all disciplines, though it's especially popular for students feeling challenged by hard sciences, computer science, and math. ECU also makes regular use of Starfish, a software program through which faculty can talk to students informally online to keep the lines of communication open.

ECU is part of the University of North Carolina system, which means lots of benefits for in-state students. A whopping 82 percent of the ECU undergraduate student body is from North Carolina. Like many other state schools, the cost for out-of-state students is not as low. While ECU doesn't offer specific first-generation scholarships, it is the single largest participant in the UNC grant program, which allows the university to enroll a higher proportion of people in financial need. Also, ECU makes concerted efforts to financially educate its students to help them develop a pragmatic attitude toward money. For example, freshmen are encouraged to take a one-credit college success class that teaches students debt management and fiscal responsibility. Hence it's not so surprising that there's a low student loan default rate among graduates.

The main campus of ECU is located in the heart of Greenville, North Carolina. Town-gown relations are fantastic—purple and gold, the university's colors, can be found throughout the city. The university also provides for buses and shuttles that take students across campus and town free of charge. When these shuttles aren't running, ECU offers individually scheduled Safe Rides for students to get from A to B without worry. Never getting too cold or too hot, Greenville enjoys mild weather all year round, though the city tends to be humid and it rains a lot. (Nothing is perfect, right?)

Students love ECU because of the atmosphere both on and off campus. Although there are 27,000 students, the relatively small campus of 530 acres fosters a community environment in which students can bond and thrive. Athletics at ECU are very popular, and football games are the best places to find good team spirit—upward of fifty thousand people come from all over to watch ECU play.

#2 North Carolina State University at Raleigh

The North Carolina State University at Raleigh (NC State) is a large public university, particularly notable for its high retention and graduation rates, prestigious academic programs, and post-graduation job opportunities—all at a low net price. NC State is strongest in the STEM disciplines, as well as architecture, design, and business management. The university encourages its students to participate in (paid!) internship or co-op programs before graduation, and their engineering college is where some of the best opportunities on campus are found. NC State is one of the three schools that make up Research Triangle Park in North Carolina, an area that's become quite attractive to high-tech companies and entrepreneurs with its multiple research facilities and institutions. The potential direct pipeline to great job opportunities is a major selling point for NC State.

NC State offers an extremely low net cost for a flagship research institution. According to Vice Provost Louis Hunt, NC State is able to give its students bang for the buck by strategically prioritizing their funds toward what most enhances student success—classrooms, labs, and excellent faculty. In terms of aid packages, apart from federal financial aid and aid offered by the state of North Carolina, NC State offers the Pack Promise program. It guarantees that low-income students will receive financial aid packages consisting entirely of scholarships and grants, and it includes support like the Goodnight Scholarship for middle-income students. Access to their great scholarships is competitive, so be sure to impress by filing your forms early and correctly.

The university is located right by downtown Raleigh, a city consistently ranked as one of the top places for young professionals. It's safe to say students won't run out of activities, whether on or off campus. NC State's very own Wolfprowl bus service takes students to and from downtown Raleigh on weekends for free. Students should be careful and smart when walking around at night, even though emergency security services all around campus provide additional safety. The hot, humid summers and cold, occasionally snowy winters bring pleasantly mild springs and falls in between.

NC State's campus spans a massive 2,110 acres. Students at NC State seem to be pretty happy—the freshman retention rate is 92 percent. While the majority of students are white, the university does sponsor many cultural student organizations where students can find their niches and bond over shared cultures and experiences. The university also provides academic and social support services for low-income and first-generation students. There's additional tutorial support, mentoring, coaching, and financial literacy workshops. Students come together by cheering on the Wolfpack at sporting events—football and basketball (both Division I) are particularly popular, and school spirit is never lacking.

#3 University of Georgia

The University of Georgia (UGA) is a public flagship university located in Athens, Georgia, and is well respected for its high-caliber academics and research facilities. You might say UGA is a powerhouse on the academic front—it's produced twenty-three Rhodes Scholars since 2012, and five Marshall Scholars in the past decade. With seventeen undergraduate colleges housing 170 majors for students to choose from, exploring your interests is certainly possible here. The strongest majors range from biological sciences, landscape architecture, and business to fine arts, performing arts, and journalism (UGA's Grady College of Journalism is home of the Peabody Awards). Student reviewers on one site, College Prowler, overwhelmingly agreed they were generally impressed by the high caliber of UGA professors. Upon arrival, first-year students are placed in small seminar groups (about fifteen students) with faculty members who have designed courses to engage students, smooth their transition from high school to college, and establish relationships with faculty and fellow students. The topics are not what you might expect, with seminars on Moneyball, Internet memes, and even the zombie plague (a public health course, of course!).

UGA proudly boasts a good number of students on financial aid. In particular, it receives many high-achieving students from Georgia who are recipients of the HOPE and Zell Miller scholarships, which help keep the brightest from Georgia in Georgia. Of the 2012–13 freshman class, 85 percent of the students hailed from Georgia, and a full 99 percent of those Georgians were HOPE and Zell Miller recipients. UGA has also teamed up with Coca-Cola to offer a scholarship specifically for first-generation students.

Athens is also consistently rated as one of the best college towns in America. On UGA's large, historic campus, you'll find architecture in the Federal, Classical, and antebellum styles. There's a sense that everything and everyone in town revolves around the school. UGA's Sanford Stadium and Stegeman Coliseum, home to its football and basketball teams, respectively, were used in the 1996 Summer Olympics.

Above all, UGA students like to have fun. The Georgia Bulldogs football team, basketball, and gymnastics team are particularly popular, and students take their collegiate sports very seriously. The university has been working to make the student body reflect the world a bit more, but as of now the school is largely white. Still, for students from underrepresented backgrounds there is mentoring support, along with workshops on study skills and time management, and the Freshman College Experience summer bridge program features an introductory course that fulfills core curriculum requirements while also allowing students to familiarize themselves with the collegiate experience. With over five hundred student organizations, students have several ways to shape their campus lives. Students looking for a unique experience can apply to live in the Franklin Residential College, a community based on the Oxford and Cambridge model, in which students live and learn together.

#4 University of Florida

The University of Florida (UF) is a large state school in Gainesville, Florida, with great academics, lots of school spirit, and a vibrant on-campus social life. UF is a rather prestigious public university: in 2001 the educational consulting center Howard Greene & Associates assessed UF as providing an education comparable to that of Ivy League colleges. With numerous research opportunities, UF is far above the bar in geography, environmental studies, engineering, and science. It also offers the first entrepreneurially centered living-and-learning academic community in the United States. The business school is touted as one of the best and a particularly good choice for accounting majors, with a high pass rate (76.8 percent) and average score (79.9) on the CPA exam.

UF makes certain its doors are open to students needing financial aid. The university offers a range of grants and scholarships, particularly to Florida residents, with some available for out-of-staters. The Florida Opportunities Scholarship (FOS) program is available for three hundred in-state first-generation college students and pays any tuition, fees, and board costs remaining after awards such as the Pell Grant and the Florida Bright Futures Scholarship. FOS students benefit from peer mentoring, financial education, career and life coaching, and faculty who provide academic tracking and coaching throughout the year to help students avoid falling through the cracks. Fun fact: UF's ROTC program, founded in 1905, is one of the oldest in the nation.

With over nine hundred buildings sitting on two thousand acres, this school is *big*. But don't worry about getting around! Nine bus routes of the Gainesville Regional Transit System serve the campus, and anyone with a university-issued ID doesn't have to pay a penny to use them. A corner of campus is listed as a historic district in the National Register of Historic Places, and the many other beautiful, historic buildings make UF a pleasurable place to pass four years—even in the hot, humid, and sometimes rainy weather.

UF was the #6 party school in the 2014 Princeton Review, and the social scene is undeniably one of many reasons its students love their school. Its 96 percent freshman retention rate is among the highest in the country, and UF isn't lacking when it comes to ethnic and cultural diversity on campus. The student body is just under 60 percent white (still a majority), with sizable populations of Hispanic, African American, and Asian students. The school is building up its support for first-generation and racial and ethnic minority students by providing transition programs for new freshmen, peer mentoring projects between prospective and current students, and increased financial assistance. Gators are extremely proud of their school, particularly in the realm of sports—it's the only school in the country to finish among the nation's top ten in each of the last twenty-eight national all-sports standings.

#9 Appalachian State University

Appalachian State University is a large public university located in the rural college town of Boone, North Carolina. It gets a major thumbs-up for its welcoming campus atmosphere and good support of students in need of financial support. It was originally founded as a single-purpose teacher training college, and education training remains a popular major among students today. Appalachian makes good use of its history and surrounding environment to enhance its academics. The university's Department of Sustainable Development is also the oldest in the country. Upon arrival, first-year students are enrolled in small seminar classes to help equip them with the creative and critical thinking necessary for university-level classes.

Appalachian also offers the Learning Assistance Program, which provides individual and small-group academic services to students with varying needs, from first-generation students and athletes to students with language challenges or disabilities.

Appalachian awards a number of need-based and college scholarships to incoming students. The ACCESS program, for students whose family's income is below the current poverty line, covers the difference between grants such as Pell and state grants and the cost of tuition and board. More than just money, it also provides individually tailored support programs for every student: special orientation groups, transition classes, advisors, and mentors. Since its inception, these programs have been very successful. In the 2013–14 academic year, almost half of ACCESS scholars made the dean's or chancellor's list. Appalachian also visits North Carolina high schools to assist young people in the college application process and is part of a collaborative effort to make college visits possible for low-income and first-generation students.

Appalachian has a physically large campus that encompasses thirteen hundred acres in rural Boone, a college town with a population of thirteen thousand; Appalachian itself enrolls around fifteen thousand undergraduates. The campus has a dynamic vibe for living and learning and is surrounded by beautiful rivers and mountains that make it a dream for hikers and nature lovers. Appalcart, a free bus system, gives students access to a number of bus routes on and off campus. The beautiful springs, summers, and falls are balanced out by long, cold winters—snowfall in Boone averages three feet every year.

Even after digging out from under mounds of snow, Appalachian students seem to like it here and stay pretty focused. The freshman retention rate is 87.6 percent, and according to NC Appalachian Collaborative for Higher Education director Jennifer Wilson-Kearse, 84 percent of students who went on a college tour at Appalachian ended up enrolling there. There isn't much racial diversity on campus, though according to one current student, the student body and faculty alike welcome students from all walks of life with open arms and are generally very liberal-minded. School spirit is the name of the game, and the Kidd Brewer Stadium (nicknamed "the Rock") is constantly flooded with both students and out-of-towners whenever there's a football game.

#10 University of North Carolina at Charlotte

UNC Charlotte is a public research university and is the largest institute of higher education in North Carolina. Its seven colleges, including an honors college, offer a total of over 170 undergraduate programs. UNC Charlotte makes sure to track students in academic need so they can help keep them in school before things go terribly awry and it's too late. The Students Obtaining Success (SOS) program reaches out to students on academic probation and provides free peer mentoring tailored to the specific needs of individual students.

In-state students are entitled to a vast amount of federal aid disbursed through the state, which has enabled UNC Charlotte to become one of the best values in the region. UNC Charlotte also offers a number of merit, athletic, departmental, and outside scholarships, and its BEST (Building Educational Strengths and Talents) program provides first-generation and other select students with academic advising and tutoring, leadership development, and career services. The highly competitive Levine Scholarship provides room and board to fifteen high-achieving students all the way through—that's right, the full four years.

Charlotte is the largest city in North Carolina, and the UNC campus occupies a nice-size chunk—one thousand acres. The city has many restaurants and activities students can choose from, and as a result, the campus's vibe is more urban than collegiate. Still, UNC Charlotte's campus remains rather self-contained: there are no major roads running through campus, and there are several man-made lakes throughout the heavily wooded landscape. The weather is mild, although this area is no stranger to rainfall.

UNC Charlotte's campus, while not very ethnically diverse (about 78 percent white), maintains a large number of groups, academic clubs, and organizations, including multicultural and Greek ones, that bring students together. The sports facilities are excellent, and the university's Division I sports teams—specifically the men's basketball team—is always flooded with fans at every game.

#13 University of Virginia–Main Campus

The University of Virginia (UVA) is a large public university located in Charlottesville, Virginia, that enjoys a reputation as prestigious as any Ivy League school's. UVA offers broad and high-caliber offerings that easily rival those of private universities, but they come at the price of a public university. How's this for catering to a wide range of interests: the most popular majors are the social sciences and business management (UVA has the fourth-highest pass rate in CPA exams across all programs of all sizes in the country); the school is part of a coalition dedicated to increasing the number of minority students graduating with STEM degrees (the Virginia–North Carolina Alliance); and UVA's student body produced the highest number of Peace Corps volunteers among medium-size universities.

UVA meets the full financial need of both in-state and out-of-state students, according to university spokesperson McGregor McCance. With a need-blind admission policy—meaning that a student's ability to pay is not even considered until *after* an admission offer is extended—each applicant's achievement and potential reign supreme. UVA goes the extra mile to support low-income, first-generation, and underrepresented students. UVA grads, through the Virginia College Advising Corps (part of the National

College Advising Corps), head to high schools throughout Virginia to assist students with their college and financial aid applications, scholarship searches, and the transition to college.

UVA is located in a suburban college town, about a ten-minute drive from downtown Charlottesville, where residents and students alike shop, dine, and enjoy concerts, among other leisure activities. In Charlottesville you'll experience all four seasons, so be prepared to layer up or scale back depending on the time of year.

The freshman retention rate at UVA is 97.5 percent, well above average, suggesting that student satisfaction runs pretty high. Despite UVA's reputation for catering to students from elite white backgrounds with insular circles on campus—which isn't entirely false—the school offers many on-campus resources and events that support a variety of students and interests, such as Fall Fling, a largely African American student event, and Fall Blast, which draws a big Hispanic crowd. There are over a hundred on-campus organizations that cater to different social and cultural groups, in addition to first-year transition programs and faculty and peer mentor programs—both of which can prove invaluable for first-generation students. Most who begin UVA end up finishing, and notably it has the highest African American graduation rate in the country for a public university. Fun fact: UVA's teams are called the Cavaliers, but the unofficial mascot is the Wahoo, a fish that is believed to be able to drink twice its body weight!

#14 James Madison University

James Madison University (JMU) is a large public university in Harrisonburg, Virginia, known for its rigorous academics and research facilities. Undergrads at JMU have full access to faculty and research facilities, allowing them to explore and engage their interests on a deeper level than is typically possible. JMU's strongest programs include educational training (it was originally founded as a women's teachers college), business management, engineering, and the STEM disciplines. JMU operates with an eye toward how students will fare after graduation. The Student Success Programs help students of varying majors find internship and career opportunities, and their brand-new Success Center houses writing and communications centers, tutoring areas, and health care and counseling centers; it even has space for peer assistance study sessions, whereby strong students tutor others in the same major who are having some trouble.

JMU is most affordable if Virginia is your home state. The financial aid program at JMU is not as extensive as at many of the colleges we've highlighted. Their first-generation scholarship is currently offered to just thirty students, and its Centennial Scholars Program to endow low-income students funds about 180 students per year across all undergraduate and graduate classes. They do, however, have in place good systems and programs to keep anyone getting aid knowledgeable and up to date on their obligations.

Students can monitor their student loan database to track their financial progress, and JMU's Financial Education Committee educates students on managing their finances through popular classes and social media outreach. The upshot? Relatively low loan default rates might mean these efforts are worthwhile.

JMU has a large campus with well over a hundred buildings on its 721 acres. In the Shenandoah Valley you'll find no shortage of nature. Newman Lake and the Edith J. Carrier Arboretum, an urban botanic preserve, are both located right on JMU's campus. For anyone with an adventurous spirit and an itch to get off campus, Harrisonburg public transport takes students around campus and around the city.

Students tend to do quite well during their years at JMU because of a nurturing environment conducive to both academic and social growth. Thanks to its continuous efforts to expand and diversify, JMU has more than doubled its student body, faculty, and staff in the last decade. According to student reviewers, the student body is "ambitious but not obsessed"—performance is important, but so are other aspects of campus life and community involvement. And if you can't find what you're looking for, JMU is the type of place that encourages students to develop new organizations and create their own initiatives to further enrich the school experience for everyone.

#16 University of Mary Washington

The University of Mary Washington is a small, public liberal arts and sciences university that prides itself on a nontraditional learning environment and a serious focus on service. A major benefit of going to Mary Washington is that with a student-to-faculty ratio of 14:1, students have more opportunities to work closely with faculty members and build meaningful relationships. Professors are constantly encouraged to work with students in innovative ways, and according to provost Jim Levin, lecturing is more the exception than the rule. Close faculty guidance is complemented by strong advising support, and we don't mean your average help-you-pick-classes automaton. From day one, designated success coordinators get to know your interests and strengths to help you through college and into the real world on the other side. Popular majors include history, American studies, political science, and international affairs—not surprising, given its location in the heart of Fredericksburg, Virginia, less than an hour and a half from Washington, D.C. Mary Washington is one of the few universities in the United States that offer an undergraduate program in historic preservation—most programs are graduate level—and Fredericksburg offers ample opportunities for fieldwork. The school is also pushing boundaries with regard to integrating new technology in a number of ways from the way that subject knowledge is actually shared to cutting-edge personalized training programs for students to sharpen their own tech skills for the future.

While Mary Washington has fewer financial aid programs for students than do large public universities, there are other forms of support for students from economically disadvantaged backgrounds, both before and after college. The Student Transition Program operates a six-week summer program in which students can take college-level classes (for credit!) to help them get up to speed about expectations during the first year. After freshman year, STP remains an ongoing resource for students through counseling and programming.

The campus's Jeffersonian architecture showcases its deep historical roots. For instance, Brompton, now the home of the university's president, was a field hospital during the 1862 Battle of Fredericksburg. While Fredericksburg itself may be quiet, D.C. is just an hour and a half away by car. Unfortunately, student reviewers report the free campus buses are not particularly reliable, so make friends who have cars. The weather is typical for the region—a nice sampling of all four seasons.

#17 Elizabeth City State University

Elizabeth City State University (ECSU) is a small public HBCU located in Elizabeth City, North Carolina. We here at the *Washington Monthly* are big fans of this college—we've included ECSU in our Best Bang for the Buck college rankings for the past two consecutive years. ECSU offers thirty-six baccalaureate degrees spread across its four schools. While its graduation rate remains a relatively low 43 percent, it exceeds the expected graduation rate by a whopping 16.4 percent when you crunch the data to account for the challenges students face. The freshman retention rate nears an impressive 79 percent, in large part because ECSU offers a variety of academic initiatives to train, retain, and graduate students who come to college with low academic standing. Students in the MERIT Program come to college with GPAs lower than 2.0 and are strategically partnered with faculty and staff who help them persist in a college environment both academically and socially. MODEL Scholars also come to college with GPAs lower than the state requirement and are enrolled in summer programs designed to smooth their transition from high school to college. ECSU is devoted to cultivating in students the academically focused attitude that's crucial to success.

ECSU is part of both the University of North Carolina system and the Thurgood Marshall College Fund, both of which provide funding that shaves down the costs for students. ECSU has an exceptionally low net price of $1,225. In the 2012–13 academic year, 97 percent of students were receiving some sort of financial aid, and 84 percent of all undergrads were receiving grants or scholarships.

Along with its small student body, ECSU also has a small campus of about two hundred acres. Its rural setting in northeast North Carolina is near the Virginia state line and coincides with a catchment area that represents the poorest counties in the state.

Between 2009 and 2010, ECSU's enrollment increased almost threefold, from 1,358 to 3,118 students—a far cry from its original size in 1891 when it began as a training school for twenty-three African American teachers and had just two faculty members and a $1,900 budget! The majority of the student body remains African American, although the school is becoming increasingly diverse along racial and religious lines. Most students are from North Carolina, with a small percentage from elsewhere (generally Virginia and Washington, D.C.).

#20 Georgia Institute of Technology–Main Campus

The Georgia Institute of Technology (GA Tech) is an elite public university located in Atlanta, one of the South's major urban centers. It offers a huge return on investment: you can earn a prestigious degree and have a great shot at a well-paid job right out of school, all at a low net price. Academics at Georgia Tech are no walk in the park, but students believe it's worth the struggle—evidenced by the 94.8 percent retention rate. A remarkable 58 percent of the student body majors in engineering at Georgia Tech. Georgia Tech has teamed up with HBCUs, Spellman and Morehouse among them, to create a pipeline for dual degree opportunities. About 60 percent of Georgia Tech students study abroad each year, and the school has far-reaching international connections in its own right, with satellite campuses in France, Ireland, China, and Singapore. Students are encouraged—not required—to take part in a three-year co-op program that involves paid internships for one semester during each year.

The prestige of a Georgia Tech degree does not carry an eye-popping price tag. The state of Georgia offers the HOPE and Zell Miller scholarships to all Georgia residents with a minimum GPA of 3.0 and 3.7, respectively. The G. Wayne Clough Georgia Tech Promise Program covers the full cost of attendance for families earning less than $33,300 a year. Georgia Tech also spends a good portion of its endowment in (we think) the best way possible—to defray costs for those with financial need. A big chunk goes to the President's Scholarship Program, which in addition to a scholarship (for in-state and out-of-state students) has lots of perks: trips, mentoring, faculty and alumni networking events, specialized courses. The catch? It goes to the top 2 percent of high school students, and you've got to apply early action in October to be considered. Want to study abroad but worry about the cost? Assistance for your overseas adventures comes with the aid offer, and Georgia Tech will even credit you if the tuition ends up being cheaper . . . so it's actually possible to go abroad for a semester *and* save money at the same time!

A medium-size campus of four hundred acres located in midtown Atlanta, Georgia Tech's dynamic location has an urban vibe and offers students abundant ways to fill their free time. It's really the best of both worlds once you step onto campus—lots of greenery and mostly low-rise buildings provide a contrast to and respite from the city. Atlanta weather is known to fluctuate wildly throughout all four seasons, which doesn't quite fit the Sunbelt stereotype.

Students at Georgia Tech are career-driven, but more supportive of each other than competitive. High graduation rates and low default rates among loan borrowers signal that students are doing rather well during and after college. While it can feel like the student body lacks diversity in some regards, the energy and atmosphere seem open to all walks of life, which is encouraging since the school is trying to ramp up its gender and racial diversity. For those new to the college world, there are first-year transition seminar courses; a campus organization, First Gen, that has regular events and fund-raisers; and the Team Coach program, which provides peer mentoring and academic support throughout freshman year. The Division I sports are a major draw, but lest you forget the real heart of the school, every year several students vie for the InVenture Prize, a competition to develop and showcase inventions for a cash prize of $20,000 and a free patent filing.

WEST

#1 University of Washington–Seattle

The University of Washington–Seattle (UW Seattle) campus is a large, highly reputable public university in downtown Seattle, Washington. Established in 1861, UW Seattle is one of the oldest public universities on the West Coast. Particularly strong in the sciences (ahem, all you pre-med and science lab types), UW Seattle is considered a public Ivy and has since 1974 been the largest recipient of federal R&D funding among public universities and second among all public and private universities. (In 2013, this amounted to over $1 billion!) The college has sixteen different schools and offers eighteen hundred undergraduate courses each quarter. Students who want academic help can visit CLUE, the university's free, late-night peer tutoring center. The Student Support office also has an extra Instructional Center Program that offers group and one-on-one tutoring, particularly in traditionally difficult subjects like the STEM disciplines and writing, and provides post-graduate advising as well.

UW Seattle is generous with its financial aid across its campuses, thanks to the high number of institutional and state grants available. About one-third of undergraduates are low-income or first-generation students. The Husky Promise, which supports almost ten thousand students on all the UW campuses, provides Washington residents from low- to middle-income households with institutional grants and scholarships that help cover tuition and board costs that federal and state grants can't. Once at UW Seattle, students can also apply for other scholarships, and the Student Support and financial aid teams set aside an emergency fund should students need it at any point. Student Support also provides one-on-one holistic academic and social advising to ease the transition to college and connect students directly to opportunities like study abroad, specialized majors, jobs, and internships.

UW Seattle's campus was ranked by *Slate* and *Travel+Leisure* as one of the most beautiful college campuses in the United States. Its location in downtown Seattle makes it easy for students to pursue a range of interests on and off campus. Seattle is a popular tourist destination and is especially well known for its vibrant music scene and great coffee (and hip coffee shops).

Even though Seattle catches a lot of flak for being gray and rainy, students at UW Seattle seem happy there. It boasts retention and graduation rates of 93 percent and 80.3 percent, respectively, and the university makes sure students from all ethnic and socioeconomic groups are proportionately represented at the school. Educational workshops and celebratory cultural festivals are quite common, and UW Seattle's outreach and recruitment team carries this cultural enrichment beyond campus, collaborating with many high schools and middle schools to expose students to the diverse campus culture. Greek life and Division I athletics are popular on campus, but neither are a must for a healthy and active social life.

#2 Brigham Young University–Idaho

Brigham Young University–Idaho is a private, religiously affiliated university in Rexburg, Idaho. BYU-Idaho is known for its unique Three Track System, which divides the academic year into three 14-week semesters. Each track consists of two consecutive semesters, and students can enroll in classes over the fall/winter, winter/spring, or spring/fall semesters. When students aren't in school, the university helps them find internship programs. BYU-Idaho is noted to be one of the top internship providers in the country, with its strong internship search database and specialized faculty coordinators who facilitate students' individual internship searches.

The Three Track System allows for a more efficient use of resources and enables the school to sustain a low net price for its students. What's more, BYU-Idaho is hardly stingy with its financial aid resources, thanks to the generosity of its donors. Specific colleges and departments also offer their own academic and merit-based scholarships, which they are happy to award to deserving students. As long as all the necessary paperwork is filled out, it should be smooth sailing if you qualify.

With over fifteen thousand undergraduates enrolled in any given semester, BYU-Idaho is the largest private university in the State of Idaho, and the campus itself spans over two hundred acres with over forty buildings. Rexburg has been ranked one of the safest cities in the country, so if BYU is for you, tell your parents they can chill out and stop worrying. Winter sports are particularly popular, and students frequent the nearby Grand Targhee and Kelly Canyon ski resorts for quick getaways.

BYU-Idaho is owned and operated by the Church of Jesus Christ of Latter-Day Saints and strongly emphasizes individual and spiritual growth. Students are required to follow a strict honor code and to behave in line with LDS teachings. Ninety-nine percent of students belong to the LDS Church, and the majority are white. A significant portion of students take hiatuses from school to serve as missionaries, and the university holds weekly devotional services to enhance student participation in the religious community. Although BYU-Idaho no longer takes part in intercollegiate sports, there are organized intramural sports that foster student interaction and provide some recreational relief.

#3 University of California–Irvine

The University of California–Irvine is a large public university located in Irvine, California. It is a prestigious university and has an admit rate of 45.6 percent, which is low relative to other state universities. UC Irvine is a member of the Association of American Universities and is considered a public Ivy. UC Irvine offers eighty-seven different undergraduate programs in twelve schools, and its most popular majors are in the biological sciences. UC Irvine graduates have gone on to win three Nobel Prizes in chemistry and one in physics. The university also encourages its students to extend their learning beyond the campus gates, as it has strong semester and summer internship and study-abroad programs around the United States and the world.

As part of the University of California system, in-state students can benefit from federal, state, and UC-wide grants and scholarships as well as low tuition costs. The UC Blue and Gold Opportunity Plan provides full tuition and student services fees for California residents whose families earn less than $80,000 a year, and should students need more funding they can apply for it. The new Middle Class Scholarship Program applies to students whose families earn less than $150,000 and helps to cover up to 40 percent of UC Irvine's fees. According to student reviewers, financial aid is easy to attain and officers at UC Irvine are helpful. In fall 2013, 58 percent of enrolled students were first-generation college students, which is a good indicator of UC Irvine's financial benefits.

Irvine is an affluent suburb in Orange County, California. This is not your typical college town, but it's a safe place to live and it's near Newport and Laguna Beaches, so break out the swimsuits! There is not a lot of public transportation available, so be sure to bring a car, save up for one, or make friends who have them.

UC Irvine's freshman retention rate is an impressive 93 percent, which is a strong indicator that students are quite content here. The Student Support Services offer summer bridge programs for incoming freshmen, provide one-on-one advising and coaching services for students (particularly first-generation or low-income students) to further ensure academic and social success, and host regular roundtable discussions for first-generation and low-income students to meet fellow students and to address any questions that they may have. The student body is diverse, with the majority being Asian American, followed by white and Hispanic students.

#4 University of California–Davis

The University of California–Davis is a large, prestigious public teaching and research university. UC Davis is also considered a public Ivy by many, and as a result is becoming increasingly selective. It boasts ninety-nine undergraduate majors, divided into the Colleges of Agricultural and Environmental Sciences, Biological Sciences, Engineering, and Letters and Science. It is strong in research, boasting a faculty with members of the National Academy of Sciences, American Academy of Arts and Sciences, American Law Institute, Institute of Medicine, and the National Academy of Engineering. Its Department of Viticulture and Enology, which studies the science of grape growing and winemaking, has made significant contributions to the world-famous California winemaking industry.

All students can apply for federal grants, and in-state students in particular can apply for generous state and UC grants and scholarships as well. The Blue and Gold Opportunity Plan and Middle Class Scholarship Program, available to all students in the UC system, offer aid to students from families earning less than $80,000 and $150,000 a year, respectively. The Aggie Grant Plan, unique to UC Davis, is created for students whose families earn between $80,000 and $120,000 a year, and will cover at least 25 percent of their system-wide tuition and fees with gift aid.

With just over 7,300 acres, UC Davis's campus is the largest within the UC system. It contains a number of buildings specially designed for specific disciplines (such as the Equestrian Center and Animal Sciences Building) and also has an arboretum, art statues, and a popular performing arts center. It enrolls a total of just over 34,000 students, including post-graduates, which makes it the campus with the third-largest enrollment in the UC system. The city of Davis itself is largely influenced by the university, with a ratio of students to long-term residents of 1:4. It's a very politically liberal place, generally speaking, and a bicycle-friendly city—an affordable option for college students. For those who don't like bikes, though, UC Davis has its own bus services, Unitrans, operated and managed entirely by students! Unitrans runs double-decker buses (like those formerly in London) and offers free transportation around the city.

UC Davis has an ethnically diverse campus, with Asian American and white students accounting for the largest percentage of the student body. Although the freshman retention rate is an impressive 92 percent, the graduation rates for Hispanic and black students are markedly lower than those of their peers—something to bear in mind. There are over five hundred student organizations, and the Associated Students of UC Davis, the university's undergraduate student government, is one of the most generously funded student governments in the country. It has its own executive, legislative, and judicial branches—a big plus for all of you future politicians and lawyers. KDVS, the school's student-run radio station, is quite popular. In the past it has aired historic interviews with Angela Davis and then-governor Ronald Reagan.

#13 University of Washington–Bothell

UW Bothell is a branch campus of the University of Washington, the public state university system. The school prides itself on operating like a private liberal arts college at a public school price. Classes are small, and the administration and faculty are dedicated to each student's success in all areas, from academia to hands-on community- or research-based learning to career searches. For first-year students, the university offers the Discovery Core, a three-quarter-long seminar in which students are introduced to the university's resources and expectations, create their first portfolios, and establish relationships with faculty. UW Bothell's largest programs are in interdisciplinary studies and the STEM disciplines. Its Student Success Center offers advice on career and internship searches, community-based learning, study abroad, merit scholarships, and help on writing and quantitative learning—all for free. UW Bothell historically accepts many transfer students, most of them from surrounding community colleges; they expected nine hundred incoming transfers in fall 2014 alone.

Like UW Seattle, UW Bothell offers the Husky Promise program, which provides Washington residents from low- or middle-income households with institutional grants and scholarships that help cover tuition and board money where federal and state grants can't. In the 2013–14 academic year, 46 percent of the student body were first-generation college students. UW Bothell also admits students who would not normally meet UW admission standards but who have potential, and requires them to enroll in an academic transition program to familiarize themselves with university resources and academic expectations, as well as to engage in mentorship programs and peer study sessions. The university's advising team requires students to establish individual relationships with Student Success advocates who mentor and promote students throughout their college careers, and this has proven particularly useful for first-generation students whose families may not be familiar with the ins and outs of college.

UW Bothell shares its suburban campus with Cascadia Community College in the small city of Bothell, which has just over 33,000 residents. Bothell's unemployment rate is very low, and the city is home to many high-tech companies with whom the university partners to enhance student success both in college and after graduation. It's surrounded by many natural getaway spots and is only about twenty miles away from the city of Seattle, a popular destination for students in search of entertainment or a quick getaway.

With just over four thousand undergraduates, UW Bothell's student body is the largest of all the University of Washington system branch campuses. It has a diverse campus, with white and Asian students in the majority. The university's Diversity Outreach and Recruitment Team organizes cultural events and empowerment workshops and invites motivational speakers to campus to further break down barriers. Most important, students love UW Bothell because they are surrounded by like-minded students in an environment where they can get involved and see the changes they want on campus.

#24 Arizona State University

Arizona State University is a large public university in Phoenix, Arizona. Originally founded as a teachers college, ASU now has a number of nationally acclaimed programs: its engineering programs are among the strongest in the country, and business, education, public affairs, and art and design are also well regarded. The campus has strong research facilities, especially those focused on entrepreneurship and start-ups, space exploration, and biology. Larger classes are par for the course here, given the massive student body. The university recently launched a widely touted first-year success coaching program, in which incoming students form relationships with coaches who provide advice and guidance to the university's resources, such as tutoring, supplemental instruction, and career services.

ASU is generous when it comes to financial aid, particularly for in-state students. Apart from federal and state grants, students can also be considered for institutional scholarships—all they need to do is fill out the form, and the financial aid office will sort out the rest. In particular, the Obama Scholars Program is offered to students who meet the Pell eligibility threshold, and promises to cover the cost of tuition and fees, housing, meal plans, and books for up to four years, provided that recipients maintain satisfactory academic progress. The College Attainment Grant Program covers tuition and fees for entering freshmen from Arizona high schools. About 10 percent of the fall 2014 freshman class will be eligible for these types of financial aid scholarships. While in college, ASU students can also become eligible for many merit scholarships or other renewable funds.

ASU is the largest public university in the United States by enrollment, with several buildings spread across downtown Phoenix. Many of its buildings feature a modern urban design, and some are fused with commercial and retail offices. The campus is big on practicing sustainability, and many students travel on and off campus via bikes and light rail. Phoenix has a subtropical desert climate, with very hot summers and warm winters—the city is nicknamed "Valley of the Sun" for a reason!

With a huge student body that's incredibly ethnically diverse, ASU takes great care to offer an environment that brings students together. Their impressive freshman retention rate of 80 percent is in part supported by faculty who aim to integrate the experiences of students, tying academic learning to residential living as well as campus organizations so that students can interact with related people and ideas in and outside the classroom for a more encompassing education. The university has over eleven hundred clubs and organizations; Changemaker Central, an organization for entrepreneurs and innovators, is particularly popular across all of ASU's campuses. The ASU Sun Devils also compete in Division I athletics and enjoy lots of fans around campus.

#26 University of Utah

The University of Utah is a large public university in Salt Lake City, with serious funds for R&D. Known as "the U," it offers seventeen specialized programs, nearly a hundred departments, and over thirty interdisciplinary programs in which students can find their niche. Its architecture and medical schools are also the only accredited programs in Utah in their respective fields. Something else grab your fancy? Students can also create their individualized major under the Bachelor of University Studies program. Its class sizes are small, with an average student-to-faculty ratio of 13:1. VP of academic affairs Martha Bradley also attributes much of students' academic success to the U's unique first-year learning communities. These communities offer two-semester-long learning environments in which at most thirty students work on critical learning skills, familiarize themselves with the university's resources, and access tutors and mentors. Some programs span multiple years, and students can even shadow professionals and research with faculty. Although this is an optional program, almost three out of four students take part, and the university is constantly striving to refine the program. The U also has student success advocates and tutoring programs that can help any student who may need help in his or her academic path.

The U offers a generous amount of merit, diversity, and need-based scholarships to both in- and out-of-state students. The Larry H. and Gail Miller Scholarship offers a full ride (including tuition, books, housing, and even study abroad) to traditionally underrepresented or first-generation students. The Presidential, Honors Entrance, and Eccles Scholarships also offer near-full ride scholarships to students in need. The best thing about The U's financial aid program, though? It's easy to navigate. Simply complete the FAFSA and UFORM (the university's own financial aid form) and you can become eligible for an array of scholarships, determined by the financial aid office. The U also offers numerous scholarships to encourage student retention and graduation once students are in college. The university offers scholars to all students in learning communities as incentives to stay in school and graduate in a timely manner.

The U's campus takes up a mere fifteen hundred acres, tiny in proportion to the large student body. A large proportion of students live off campus from as early as freshman year, but the university is currently building more and more freshman dorms to foster community spirit. It is located in a metropolitan area, and there are a number of campus shuttles that can transport students around and off campus for free. The U is big on sustainability: the university makes sure to use green power in its energy consumption, and its Bicycle Master Plan has launched a number of policies and programs promoting bicycle ridership among its students. There are a bunch of things to do around Salt Lake City as well: the zoo, amusement park, golf course, and ski resorts are just a drive away.

Although the U has a student body of almost 25,000 undergraduates, the university fosters student community through academic opportunities and interest groups. The freshman retention rate is an impressive 87.5 percent. Learning communities play a large part, and according to Bradley, the likelihood that LEAP and Diversity Scholars Programs students will continue in college is around 6 to 10 percentage points higher than other mainstream students. The University of Utah "Utes" compete in Division I football, and students love showing their school spirit at football games. There is a fierce Utah-BYU rivalry, and the annual Utah-BYU football game is often referred to as the "Holy War" by sports commentators. The U also has an active student association that organizes festivals and dances to bring students to campus. The majority of its student body are white, with Asian and Hispanic students in the minority and a very small percentage of black students. Although the U is not a religious university, there are many LDS Church members at the university.

#29 Evergreem State College

Evergreen State College is a small, public liberal arts college in Olympia, Washington, famous for its nontraditional, holistic classroom experiences. The majority of its entering class at any given time is transfer students (55 percent) rather than first-year students (45 percent), many coming from community colleges throughout Washington. Evergreen is well known for its experimental teaching techniques, which allow students to grow and find themselves as individuals. It operates on a quarter system, and each quarter students enroll in one sixteen-credit multidisciplinary program instead of separate classes. The programs have a central theme, and students learn about related subjects. Evergreen's strongest fields of study are environmental studies, sciences, and public policy. There are typically twenty-five students per program, with two or three instructors. Students at Evergreen find they are able to gain a deep understanding about particular subjects that interest them. There are no grades or GPAs. Rather, professors issue narrative evaluations, eliminating grades as a source of competition and encouraging students to work collaboratively. If you, like most new students, come from a traditional high school, fear not! Evergreen has a robust orientation program to ease newbies into their approach to learning. Also unique is Evergreen's Academic Statement, which is the only academic requirement for graduation. Upon entry students write a short essay explaining what they want to gain from college, which is then revised every year. Prior to graduation, students submit a short goal statement that appears on their final transcript, giving students a hand in how they are presented on paper to graduate schools and prospective employers.

Evergreen's interdisciplinary approach to various topics and small class sizes provide students with an education similar to that in private colleges, but at a much lower sticker price. About half of Evergreen's student body comes from low-income households, and about 30 percent are first-generation students. Evergreen has dozens of scholarships and tuition awards, many of which specifically support low-income and first-generation college students. The college also provides a number of additional scholarships to students already at Evergreen, with at least sophomore standing, who may be at risk of dropping out due to financial problems.

Evergreen's small student body, just over four thousand students, occupies a comparably small space of a thousand acres. The campus is located in the city of Olympia, Washington, where it rains frequently. The city has a vivacious local community, with plenty of trails and parks for those interested in nature. Evergreen's own campus also contains a large tract of undeveloped land along the Puget Sound waterfront, providing a good natural laboratory for students doing scientific research. Olympia is also just a day trip away from popular cities like Seattle and Portland.

The majority (three-quarters) of students at Evergreen are from the state of Washington. Students from community colleges can transfer credits to Evergreen without losing time toward graduation. The campus is located near a military base, and there is also a growing population of veterans here. While most students are white, there's still lots of diversity, with people from all walks of life and different socioeconomic backgrounds. Notably, 20 percent of its student identify as LGBTQ. Evergreen hosts lots of educational workshops and celebratory events for mingling and to raise awareness of a range of issues and topics. The administration hosts many academic and social advising programs that support a smoother transition for underrepresented students into university life. Fun fact: many Evergreen alums are widely known and highly respected creatives, including *The Simpsons* creator Matt Groening, *Hey Arnold!* creator and *Rugrats* writer Michael Bartlett, and musician Macklemore, to name a few.

#30 Western Washington University

Western Washington University is a large state university in Bellingham, Washington. First established as a teachers school for women in 1886, Western now offers seven academic colleges for undergraduates, focusing on business and economics, fine and performing arts, humanities and social sciences, sciences and technology, environment, education, and interdisciplinary studies. Notable academic programs include its environmental studies and interdisciplinary studies colleges, fine and performing arts, and the sciences (engineering and marine biology in particular). The Huxley College of the Environment was the first college dedicated to environmental science and policy in the nation, and many of its students go on to graduate school after leaving Western. The Fairhaven College of Interdisciplinary Studies offers an alternative, holistic academic program in which students enroll in interdisciplinary programs revolving around one central theme rather than separate classes, and instead of grades instructors give narrative evaluations of the students. Western's engineering program offers its nationally recognized vehicle design class, and the university runs its own marine biology center on the Pacific Ocean. Western has a traditionally good relationship with employers: many outside employers have asked Western to create more interdisciplinary programs that allow students to transfer skills into the workforce. Western also collaborates with faculty members to keep track of the academic progress of all students, ensuring that the student can get help—financial, academic, or social—at any stage of his or her college career. Should a student want to pursue a major not offered at Western, the university can advise on other good colleges to which students can later transfer.

Despite lower state education funding and higher national tuition costs, Western's cost of enrollment has, thankfully, been flat for the past ten years. Western is also a participant in Washington State's large need-grant program. Prior to admission, the university awards many need-based, achievement-based, and diversity scholarships to high school students from both Washington and other states, such as the President's Scholarship and Computer Science and Math Scholarship for Women. After admission, individual departments also award grants and scholarships upon application.

Western has a modest campus of 215 acres, which allows the large student body to interact frequently. The campus has many state-of-the-art facilities, such as an arboretum (which it shares with the city of Bellingham), performing arts center, electronic music studio, and air pollution lab, among many others. It also has a prized collection of outdoor and indoor public art sculptures, funded by both public and private donors. Bellingham itself is a large city with a damp and temperate climate. For all you explorers, Bellingham is also in close proximity to both outdoor areas such as the San Juan Islands and large cities such as Seattle and Vancouver, British Columbia.

With a student body of fourteen thousand and over 230 student organizations, Western students will have no trouble finding things to do on campus. They can also start their own group if they can't find one that suits their particular interest: Western's student-run, dedicated student affairs organization, the Associated Students of Western Washington University, provides funding, space, and services to many student groups. Because Western enrolls many historically underrepresented students, such as first-generation students, veterans, adults, and students with disabilities, the Office of Student Outreach provides an advising program that pairs students with their individual advisors and can receive extra counseling opportunities if need be. Many of Western's alumni have gone on to the creative industry.

#35 University of Hawaii at Hilo (UH Hilo)

UH Hilo, one of the ten branch universities of the University of Hawaii system, is a small public university in Hilo, Hawaii County. Making the most of the wealth of nearby natural resources, the school is strong in the sciences, particularly marine biology and geology, and students often use their surroundings as a "living laboratory." Hilo's College of Pharmacy is the only Accreditation Council for Pharmacy Education (ACPE)–approved school in the state of Hawaii and the Pacific islands. UH Hilo makes concerted efforts to educate global citizens, and it is a partner of the Semester at Sea program, in which students spend four months taking classes on board, docking at several ports to take part in excursions or service learning projects. Classes (on land) at UH Hilo are small, with an average student-to-faculty ratio of 15:1, giving students a chance to form close relationships with faculty and with each other.

UH Hilo places extra emphasis on providing financial aid to in-state students during the admissions process, but once admitted, the university offers good support to out-of-staters in need. Hawaiians can apply for the Hawaii B Plus Program, the Hawaii Student Incentive Grant, and UH Hilo Opportunity Grants, for which approximately five to six hundred students in the university are currently eligible; there are also on-campus job opportunities and guidance about finding them.

Overlooking Hilo Bay, on top of the Mauna Loa and Mauna Kea volcanoes, UH Hilo occupies a large campus (755 acres) relative to its small student body of less than four thousand. It has a very low crime rate. Hilo itself is the largest settlement on the island of Hawaii, and while it is sometimes called a city, it is not an officially incorporated city and has no municipal government. The climate is generally hot, humid, and rainy.

UH Hilo's location at the crossroads between North America and Asia has allowed the university to develop a diverse environment: the student body consists of local Hawaiians, U.S. continentals, and international students from over forty countries. That being said, the student body is primarily white, Asian, and Pacific Islander, with black and Hispanic students a minority. While campus is quiet, the administration has deliberately beefed up orientation and social programs for first- and second-year students to offer more opportunities to socialize. The relationship with the local community in Hilo is also good: blurred lines between campus and the community make for a healthy blended environment in which students can develop their interests. The local art scene in Hilo is particularly lively and appealing to students.

ACKNOWLEDGMENTS

Thanks to so many of my colleagues who I have had the pleasure to work with as an educator, a counselor, and a dean. My most heartfelt thanks goes first to my daughter, colleague, and editor, Haley Sweetland Edwards, whose editing and encouragement kept me on track; and to my co-author and editor, Paul Glastris, without whose energy, vision, and guidance this book would not have come into being.

Thanks to countless students who have taught me so much about what it means to have a dream and go for it. A special thanks to the seniors at Oxnard and Camarillo High Schools, who shared with me their worries, concerns, questions, and hopes as they navigated their next steps. I hope this book—and the people you'll find to help you—will guide you through the many choices you're facing. Sincere thanks to the National Resource Center for the First-Year Experience and Students in Transition and the many presenters at the "First Year Experience" conference who are seeking, finding, and implementing strategies to support students. I owe a huge debt of gratitude to my colleagues and friends at California State University Channel Islands. Collaborating with you to build a university where thousands of students are finding a pathway to their dreams has been a privilege.

Finally, thanks to the scores of experts, colleagues, and friends whose research, work, and wisdom informed and inspired me: Lawrence G. Abele, Leah Alarcon, Anthony Lising Antonio, Kathy Asher, Lauren Asher, Betsy Barefoot, Sandy Baum, Kathy Beckham, Gary Berg, Michael Berman, Sandy Bieler-Rao, James Blackburn, Bob Bontrager, Kevin Buddhu, Anthony Carnevale, Amanda Carpenter, Zoe Corwin, Joe Cuseo, Nick Edwards, Marie Francois,

ACKNOWLEDGMENTS

John N. Gardner, Dennis Geyer, Nancy Grant, David Hawkins, Don Hossler, Nicole Hurd, Davis Jenkins, Kristen Jennings, Jennifer Keup, Michelle LaFrance, Jim Maraviglia, Donna Maygren, Jan Minimum, Tom Mortenson, Ken O'Donnell, Damien Pena, Ginger Reyes Reilly, Richard Rush, Wm. Greg Sawyer, Luke Schultheis, Robert Shireman, Allison Stark, Charles Spence, William G. Tierney, Kaia Tollefson, Vashti Torres, Kristan Venegas, Barbara Wagner. Thank you to each of you for your time, insights, and encouragement.

—*Jane Sweetland*

Though I share a byline, the truth is that my wonderful co-author Jane Sweetland researched and wrote the vast bulk of this book based on an outline I sketched out with then–*Washington Monthly* editor Haley Sweetland Edwards, who, in an inspired flash of nepotism, suggested her mother. As a former teacher, counselor, and university dean who wrote her doctoral dissertation on student motivation, Jane had an almost spookily perfect résumé for the assignment, and the knowledge she gained from her years of direct experience with students and their challenges suffuses every page. This book was made possible by a generous grant from the Kresge Foundation and by the enthusiasm and deep knowledge of its managing director for education programs William F. L. Moses. Bill said early on that we would be in great hands if we could get The New Press to publish it and he was right: thank you Marc Favreau and Tara Grove.

The Other *College Guide* is in many ways a "news-you-can-use" version of the more policy-oriented College Guide and Rankings that the *Washington Monthly* magazine has been publishing annually since 2005 (and which my friend Steve Waldman told me years ago we ought to turn into a book). So I owe a debt of thanks to the editors, writers, and staff of the *Washington Monthly*, past and present, whose labors have built the franchise. They are too numerous to mention individually but I would be remiss if I didn't single out Kevin Carey, guest editor of that issue for many years now; Robert Kelchen, data manager for both the magazine and book versions; Jamie Merisotis and Kevin Corcoran of the Lumina Foundation, who have generously supported the magazine's higher education coverage and become members of the *Monthly* family; and *Washington Monthly* publisher Diane Straus Tucker and senior editor Phillip Longman.

Interns play a huge role at the *Washington Monthly* and contributed mightily to this book. Rachel Cohen reported and wrote chapter 13 ("Do Unto Others"). Piper Janoe, Alaina A. Lancaster, and Alexandra Ma wrote the profiles of individual colleges, with an assist from Amanda Hobson. Summer Jiang fact-checked the entire book.

I'm grateful to Mary Bruce of AmeriCorps Alums and Tess Mason-Elder of Civic Enterprises for providing vital research for chapter 13; to Michael Dannenberg and Mary Nguyen Barry of Education Trust for help with chapter 4; and to my *patriote* Elias Vlanton for shrewd advice along the way.

—*Paul Glastris*

NOTES

1. CHOOSING TO GO

1. Kristan Venegas, phone interview, March 4, 2014. Dr. Venegas is an associate professor of clinical education and research at the Center for Higher Education Policy Analysis at Rossier School, University of Southern California. Her research focuses on college access and financial aid for low-income students of color.

2. Robert Shireman, "A College Considerator: Factors to Weigh in Contemplating College Affordability," California Competes, April 2014, http://californiacompetes.org/wp-content/uploads/2014/04/A-College-Considerator.pdf. In a conversation with the author on February 25, 2014, Shireman said, "Is it a good idea to show a potential college student that her poor showing in high school is an indicator that she will struggle in college, too? We do worry about discouraging people with data that may or may not apply to them. On the other hand, it does not seem appropriate to keep the data from them if it can inform their decisions."

2. MOVING UP IN THE WORLD

3. Sandy Baum, Jennifer Ma, and Kathleen Payea, "Education Pays 2013: The Benefits of Higher Education for Individuals and Society," College Board, 2013, https://trends.collegeboard.org/sites/default/files/education-pays-2013- full-report.pdf.

4. Anthony P. Carnevale, Stephen J. Rose, and Ban Cheah, "The College Payoff: Education, Occupations, Lifetime Earnings," Georgetown University Center for Economics and the Workforce, Washington, DC, August 5, 2011, http://cew.georgetown.edu/collegepayoff. The press release about the study says, "According to the study, individuals with a bachelor's degree now make 84 percent more over a lifetime than those who have just a high school diploma, up from 75 percent in 1999. Today, bachelor's degree holders can expect median lifetime earnings approaching $2.3 million. By comparison, workers with just a high school diploma average roughly $1.3 million, which translates into a little more than $15 per hour." "New Study Finds That Earning Power Is Increasingly Tied to Education," press release, Georgetown University Center on Education and the Workforce, August 5, 2011, https://georgetown.app.box.com/s/q61zgkvohht6ehtk2psh.

5. Since 1983, ACT has collected a comprehensive database of first- to second-year retention rates and persistence to degree rates. These rates provide national benchmarks for institution type and level of selectivity. Data are compiled by ACT from the ACT Institutional Data Questionnaire, an annual survey of information collected from two-year and four-year postsecondary institutions. http://www.act.org/research/policymakers/pdf/retain_2012.pdf.

6. Some points are from the White House Initiative on Educational Excellence for Hispanics, "Graduate! A Financial Aid Guide to Success," May 2014, http://www.ed.gov/edblogs/hispanic-initiative/graduate-financial-aid-guide-to-success.

7. Steve Piscitelli, "More than Academic Skills to Succeed in College," presentation at the First-Year Experience Conference, San Diego, California, February 15–18, 2014. Steve Piscitelli explains hitting the reset button: www.stevepiscitelli.com/htrb-hit-the-reset-button.

8. "O*Net Online," U.S. Department of Labor, www.onetonline.org.

9. "Career Clusters Internet Survey," National Association of State Directors of Career Technical Education Consortium, http://www.careertech.org/career-clusters/ccresources/interest-survey.html.

10. Anthony P. Carnevale and Ban Cheah, "Hard Times: College Majors, Unemployment, and Earnings," Georgetown Center on Education and the Workforce, May 2013, https://georgetown.app.box.com/s/9t0p5tm0qhejyy8t8hub.

11. Anthony Lising Antonio's research addresses many of the issues currently facing American higher education, including a better understanding of how students and families gather and digest information about college admissions and college going to make crucial college choice decisions. The author interviewed him on February 24, 2014, at Stanford University.

12. "Fast Facts" from the National Center for Education Statistics, U.S. Department of Education, http://nces.ed.gov/fastfacts/display.asp?id=84. The total number of degree-granting institutions in 2010–11 was 4,599, with 2,870 four-year colleges and 1,729 two-year ones. The College Board's 2014 handbook lists 3,979 colleges, universities, and technical schools. "To be included, an institution must be accredited by a national or regional accrediting association recognized by the U.S. Department of Education and offer some undergraduate degree programs—at least an associate degree."

13. Harold T. Shapiro, *A Larger Sense of Purpose: Higher Education and Society* (Princeton, NJ: Princeton University Press, 2005), 74.

14. Information about state regional college tuition discounts is available from the National Association of Student Financial Aid Administrators (NASFAA), http://www.nasfaa.org/students/State___Regional_College_Tuition_Discounts.aspx.

15. National Association for College Admission Counseling, "The Low-Down on For-Profit Colleges," http://www.nacacnet.org/issues-action/LegislativeNews/Pages/For-Profit-Colleges.aspx. "For-profit colleges are run by companies that operate under the demands of investors and stockholders. These institutions are privately run and exist, at least in part, to earn money for their owners. Nevertheless, for-profit colleges can receive up to 90 percent of their revenue from federal student aid."

16. National Student Clearinghouse online data and communication with Afet Dundar, PhD., Associate Director, February 11, 2014.

17. Christopher M. Mullin, "Why Access Matters: The Community College Student Body," Policy Brief 2012-01PBL, American Association of Community Colleges, Washington, DC, www.aacc.nche.edu/Publications/Briefs/Pages/pb02062012.aspx. "Community colleges are open access and do not, with the rare exception, build a student body. As this brief points out, the open door philosophy not only benefits students attending community colleges, but also benefits other sectors of higher education."

18. Anne Kim, "A Matter of Degrees: In the Future World of 'Credentialing,' Do You Still Need College?," *Washington Monthly*, September/October 2013.

19. Elias Vlanton is a veteran teacher at Bladensburg High School in Maryland and was awarded an honorary doctorate of letters from Saint Mary's College of Maryland for successfully assisting low-income students with attending college. Email, July 17, 2014.

20. Federal Trade Commission, "Choosing a Vocational School," August 2012, www.consumer.ftc.gov/articles/0241-choosing-vocational-school.

21. This chapter focuses on choosing a four-year college because most people who choose community colleges select one in their area. On the role that community colleges play in providing access to higher education, see Mullin, "Why Access Matters."

22. Conversation with Anthony Lising Antonio, February 24, 2014. Antonio's research also investigates the impact that increasing racial and cultural diversity is having on higher education.

23. James L. Marviglia, associate vice provost for marketing and enrollment development, Cal Poly San Luis Obispo, interviews April 2, and May 9, 2014.

24. Phone interview with David Hawkins, director of public policy and research, NACAC, March 5, 2014. See also "NACAC Applauds Sen. Harkin's Findings on For-Profit Colleges' Wasteful Abuses," NACAC press release, July 31, 2012, www.nacacnet.org/media-center/PressRoom/2012-Press-Releases/Pages/NACAC-Applauds-Sen.-Harkin%E2%80%99s-Findings-on-For-profit-Colleges%E2%80%99-Wasteful-Abuses.aspx.

25. Gallup and the Lumina Foundation, "What America Needs to Know About Higher Education Redesign: The 2013 Lumina Study," February 25, 2014, 18, www.gallup.com/strategicconsulting/167552/america-needs-know-higher-education-redesign.aspx.

26. Sandy Baum, interview, January 31, 2014, Washington, DC.

4. THE *OTHER* COLLEGE RANKINGS

27. Pew Research, "The Rising Cost of Not Going to College,' February 11, 2014, www.pewso cialtrends.org/2014/02/11/the-rising-cost-of-not-going-to-college.

28. David Leonhardt, "Is College Worth It? Clearly, New Data Say," *The Upshot* blog, *New York Times*, May 27, 2014, www.nytimes.com/2014/05/27/upshot/is-college-worth-it-clearly-new-data-say.html.

29. Pew Research, "The Rising Cost of Not Going to College"; Sandy Baum, Jennifer Ma, and Kathleen Payea, "Education Pays 2013: The Benefits of Higher Education for Individuals and Society," College Board, 2013, https://trends.collegeboard.org/sites/default/files/edu-cation-pays-2013-full-report.pdf.

30. David Leonhardt, "Even for Cashiers, College Pays Off," *New York Times,* June 25, 2011.

31. Leonhardt, "Is College Worth It?"

32. To establish the set of colleges including in the rankings, we started with the 1,727 colleges listed in the U.S. Department of Education's Integrated Post-secondary Education Data System as having a Carnegie basic classification of research, master's, baccalaureate, and baccalaureate/associate's colleges and are not exclusively graduate schools. We then excluded 134 colleges that reported that at least half of the undergraduate degrees awarded were not baccalaureate degrees, and eleven colleges with fewer than a hundred undergraduate students. We excluded the five military academies because of their unique missions. Finally, we excluded colleges that had not reported any of the three main measures used (percentage receiving Pell Grants, graduation rate, net price) in the past three years.

33. Hispanic-serving institution (HSI) is a formal designation that applies to 370 accredited non-profit two- and four-year colleges nationwide. While other minority-serving institutions (i.e., HBCUs and tribal colleges and universities) were founded for the purpose of educating their target populations, HSIs earn their designation based on enrollment demographics alone, according to the College Board Advocacy and Policy Center.

34. "About Historically Black Colleges and Universities," Thurgood Marshall Fund, 2012, www .thurgoodmarshallfund.net/about-tmcf/about-hbcus.

5. TROUBLED WATERS

35. Community College Research Center, Teacher's College, Columbia University, "Community College FAQs." The FAQ "What percentage of community college students obtain a bachelor's degree" says this: "According to a recent study by the National Student Clearinghouse, 15 percent of students who started at two-year institutions in 2006 completed a degree at a four-year institution within six years." The figure that 81 percent of students who enter higher ed through community colleges intend to earn a bachelor's degree comes from L. Horn and P. Skomjsvold, "Web Tables: Community College Student Outcomes: 1994–2009," NCES Publication 2012-253, November 2011, National Center for Education Statistics, U.S. Department of Education, Washington, DC.

36. "Trends in College Spending 1999–2009," Delta Project, www.deltacostproject.org/sites/default/files/products/Trends2011_Final_090711.pdf.

37. "Student Voices on the Higher Education Pathway," Public Agenda, www.publicagenda .org/files/student_voices.pdf. For more on the transfer process, see Stephen J. Handel and Ronald A. Williams, "The Promise of the Transfer Pathway: Opportunity and Challenge for Community College Students Seeking the Baccalaureate Degree," College Board Advocacy and Policy Center, October 2012.

38. Davis Jenkins leads the Community College Research Center's involvement in Completion by Design, which is working with colleges in four states to increase college completion. Conversation with author, March 24, 2014.

39. Alison Kadlec and Jyoti Gupta, "Indiana Regional Transfer Study: The Student Experience of Transfer Pathways Between Ivy Tech Community College and Indiana University," Public Agenda, April 2014.

40. "Student Voices on the Higher Education Pathway."

41. Peter M. Costa and Elizabeth Kopko, "Should Community College Students Earn an Associate Degree Before Transferring to a Four-Year Institution?," Working Paper No. 70, April 2014, Community College Research Center, Teachers College, Columbia University.

"Nationally, nearly two thirds of community college students who transfer to four-year colleges do so without first earning an associate degree. And while over 80 percent of all entering community colleges indicate that they intend to earn a bachelor's degree, only 15 percent end up doing so within six years."

42. Clive Belfield's research demonstrates that having an AA or an AS will give you a boost in the labor market and will be something to fall back on if you don't earn a bachelor's degree, or until you do. Clive Belfield, "The Economic Benefits of Attaining an Associate Degree Before Transfer: Evidence from North Carolina," Working Paper No. 62, July 2013, Community College Research Center, Teachers College, Columbia University.

43. Lawrence G. Abele, provost emeritus and director, Institute for Academic Leadership, Florida State University, prepared the sample map to help you think through how the courses you're taking now prepare you to complete all the requirements for your degree or for transfer. Dr. Abele emphasized the need to have your personal plan reviewed by departmental advisors at both the two- and four-year institutions.

44. Many students never cross to the finish line because they can't get past the remedial gatekeepers at the starting gate. See "Report on Remediation: Higher Education's Bridge to Nowhere," Complete College America, April 2012, www.completecollege.org/docs/CCA-Remediation-final.pdf.

45. In a sample of over 150,000 students in community colleges in the Completion by Design initiative, 13 percent of college-ready students earn a bachelor's degree in five years; this figure is 2.5 percent for students who are referred to developmental education. Sung-Woo Cho, Community College Research Center research associate, personal communication, 2012.

46. Belfield, "The Economic Benefits of Attaining an Associate Degree Before Transfer."

6. THE HERE AND NOW

47. "Beyond the Rhetoric: Improving College Readiness Through Coherent State Policy," HigherEd.org, 2010, www.highereducation.org/reports/college_readiness/gap.shtml.

48. Anthony P. Carnevale, Georgetown University Center on Education and the Workforce, conversation with author, Washington, DC, January 31, 2014.

49. William C. Hiss and Valerie W. Franks, "Optional Standardized Testing Policies in American College and University Admissions," February 5, 2014, www.nacacnet.org/research/research-data/nacac-research/Documents/DefiningPromise.pdf.

50. Statistics are from American School Counselor Association, "2007 to 2008 Student to School Counselor Ratios." "Although professional groups such as the American School Counselor Association say that a student-counselor ratio of 250 to 1 is optimal, this is far from the typical state of affairs in most public schools. In California, the ratio is closer to 1,000 students for every counselor available. In Arizona, Minnesota, Utah and the District of Columbia, the ratio is typically more than 700 to 1. Nationwide, the average is 460 to 1." "Can I Get a Little Advice Here? How an Overstretched High School Guidance System is Undermining Students' College Aspirations," Public Agenda, 2011, 3, www.publicagenda.org/pages/can-i-get-a-little-advice-here.

51. "Can I Get a Little Advice Here?"

52. Paul Tough, How Children Succeed (New York: Houghton Mifflin, 2012). "The intervention, which goes by the rather clunky name of Mental Contrasting with Implementation Intentions, or MCII, was developed by NYU psychologist Gabriele Oettingen and her colleagues. . . . It means concentrating on the obstacles in the way. Doing both at the same time, Duckworth and Oettingen wrote in a recent paper, "creates a strong association between future and reality that signals the need to overcome the obstacles in order to attain the desired future . . . the next step is creating a series of implementation intentions" (92–93).

53. Carol S. Dweck, Mindset: The New Psychology of Success: How We Can Learn to Fulfill Our Potential (New York: Ballantine, 2008).

54. Carol S. Dweck, "Even Geniuses Work Hard," Educational Leadership 68, no. 1 (September 2010): 16–20, www.ascd.org/publications/educational-leadership/sept10/vol68/num01/Even-Geniuses-Work-Hard.aspx.

55. Carol Dweck, "Mindsets: Increasing Educational Equity and Opportunity," presentation at the Brown Bag Lecture Series, Stanford Center for Opportunity Policy in Education, Palo Alto, CA, February 24, 2014.

56. "TED Talk—Angela Lee Duckworth," www.pbs.org/wnet/ted-talks-education/speaker/dr-angela-lee-duckworth; The Duckworth Lab, University of Pennsylvania, https://sites.sas.upenn.edu/duckworth/pages/research.
57. Steven Blank, *The Startup Owner's Manual* (Pescadero, CA: K&S, 2012), 25. "Failure will happen. It is a normal part of the startup process."

7. TASTING VICTORY

58. "Report on Remediation: Higher Education's Bridge to Nowhere," Complete College America, April 2012, www.completecollege.org/docs/CCA-Remediation-final.pdf. "Nearly 4 in 10 remedial students in community colleges never complete their remedial courses. Research shows that students who skip their remedial assignments do just as well in gateway courses as those who took remediation first."
59. Anne Kim, "A Matter of Degrees," *Washington Monthly,* September–October 2013, 46–49.

8. FAMILIES ARE COMPLICATED

60. Anthony P. Carnevale, Ban Cheah, and Jeff Strohl, "Hard Times: College Majors, Unemployment and Earnings: Not All College Degrees Are Created Equal," Georgetown University Center on Education and the Workforce, January 4, 2012, http://cew.georgetown.edu/unemployment.
61. Kaitlyn Cotton graduated in 2013 with a degree in psychology and business administration. She has since accepted full-time employment. Phone conversation with author, March 7, 2014. "As a freshman, I hardly went to class first semester. I partied all the time. At the end of my first semester I was on academic probation with a 1.3 average and my mother said she wouldn't be paying any more because I was just wasting my time and her money. I had to figure it out. I had to have a reason to be in school. That's when a friend and I volunteered at AmeriCorps. I credit all my success and everything I've done to that experience of getting out and finding that I was needed. My grades shot up because I had a reason to be there, but there was a balance, too. I was working thirty hours a week with a federal work-study job on campus and another job outside and I was taking 15 units. I had to get really strategic."
62. Barbara K. Hofer and Abigail Sullivan Moore, *The iConnected Parent: Staying Close to Your Kids in College (and Beyond) While Letting Them Grow Up* (New York: Simon & Schuster, 2010).
63. William G. Tierney, co-director, Pullias Center for Higher Education, conversation with author, February 19, 2014.
64. Karen Levin Coburn and Madge Lawrence Treeger, *Letting Go: A Parents' Guide to Understanding the College Years* (New York: Harper, 2009).
65. Family Educational Rights and Privacy Act (FERPA), U.S. Department of Education, www.ed.gov/policy/gen/guid/fpco/ferpa.
66. If you click on the "Budget" link on the federal student financial aid website (http://studentaid.ed.gov) you will find several links to resources that will help you anticipate costs and balance your budget.
67. Six-year graduation rates are consistent with financial aid regulations, which allow students to receive federal funding for their degree to a maximum of 150 percent of the time it should take to earn it. In addition, most majors require 120 semester credits; however, a student is considered full-time if he takes just 12 credits each semester. This makes it possible to be a full-time student for four years without completing a degree.
68. This infographic is from the Cooperative Institutional Research Program's Freshman Survey 2012 report by John H. Pryor, Kevin Eagan, Laura Palucki Blake, Sylvia Hurtado, Jennifer Berdan, Matthew H. Case. CIRP is part of the Higher Education Research Institute at the University of California Los Angeles.

9. GETTING IN

69. Luke D. Schultheis, vice provost for strategic enrollment management, Virginia Commonwealth University, email, July 21, 2014.

70. Martin Seligman's TED talk, "The New Era of Positive Psychology," was filmed in February 2004, www.ted.com/talks/martin_seligman_on_the_state_of_psychology.

71. Paul Tough, *How Children Succeed: Grit, Curiosity, and the Hidden Power of Character* (New York: Houghton Mifflin, 2012), is an inspiring read, showing the intersection of research and practice.

72. "Score Reporting and Score Choice," College Board, http://sat.collegeboard.org/register/sat-score-choice.

73. Colleges award financial aid in spring after students have been admitted, but you can get a pretty good idea if the college is likely to be within reach for your family by checking our Best Bang for the Buck rankings. Use College Abacus or the college's net price calculator to get an estimate that takes into account your specific financial situation.

74. "Access to Opportunity," College Board, http://professionals.collegeboard.com/guidance/access-to-opportunity. The decision is a big one and some students want to keep all options open for as long as possible. In the end, while you might have a top choice, you should know that you are a fit and can get a good education at every one of your choices.

75. According to the ACT website, "The ACT is an achievement test, measuring what a student has learned in school. The SAT is more of an aptitude test, testing reasoning and verbal abilities" (http://www.actstudent.org/testprep). However, the SAT is currently being revised and a new SAT is scheduled to launch in 2016.

76. Trustees of Princeton University, "Admission Requirements," 2014, www.princeton.edu/admission/applyingforadmission/requirements.

77. Trustees of Wellesley College, "Application Essay," www.wellesley.edu/admission/apply/essay.

78. NASFAA spokesperson telephone conversation with author, April 21, 2014.

10. IT'S ALL ABOUT THE BENJAMINS

79. Interview with Sandy Baum, January 31, 2014, Washington, DC. Baum has written and spoken extensively on issues relating to college access, college pricing, student aid policy, student debt, affordability, and other aspects of higher education finance.

80. National Association for College Admission Counseling, "For-Profit Colleges: What to Know Before You Enroll: A Guide for Students," www.nacacnet.org/issues-action/LegislativeNews/Documents/For-Profit%20Student%20Brochure.pdf.

81. State-by-state and college-level data can be found in the Institute for College Access and Success, "Student Debt and the Class of 2012." Calculations are by the Project on Student Debt on data from U.S. Department of Education, National Postsecondary Student Aid Study, 2011–12, http://projectonstudentdebt.org/state_by_state-data.php. "From 2008 to 2012, debt at graduations (federal and private loans combined) increased an average of six percent each year."

82. Federal Student Aid is an office of the U.S. Department of Education and offers a website loaded with links that can help you understand different types of financial aid. See http://studentaid.ed.gov/types/loans.

83. Institute for College Access and Success.

84. Lauren Asher, president, Institute for College Access and Success, conversation with author, February 26, 2014.

85. Interview with Alexander Holt, New America Foundation.

86. The National Community Tax Coalition (NCTC) is the nation's largest, most comprehensive membership organization for community-based organizations offering free tax and financial services to low-income working families. Financial Aid U (FAU) is one of its national college access programs, supported by the Citi Foundation, to reach low-to-moderate-income students and their families by providing financial awareness around postsecondary education. The program goals of FAU are to help students: understand that college can be affordable via federal and state financial aid, enhance the awareness of the public of the barriers faced by low-to-moderate-income students who desire to go to college, and develop recommendations to simplify the FAFSA as well as align the FAFSA and tax preparation process. As of 2014, it has assisted over 8,000 students and their families with applying for financial aid and provided access to over $71 million in federal and state aid to support their college educations.

87. Ron Lieber, "Appealing to a College for More Financial Aid," *New York Times*, April 4, 2014.

88. ACT, "National Collegiate Retention and Persistence to Degree Rates," 2012, http://www.act.org/research/policymakers/pdf/retain_2012.pdf. "These rates provide national benchmarks for institution type and level of selectivity . . . [though] selectivity ranges may vary from one institution to another."

89. Much of this chapter was informed by presenters at the First Year Experience Conference, February 15–18, 2014, San Diego. The annual conference provides a forum for higher education professionals as they work to support student learning, development, and success in their first college year.

90. "The First Year Is a Big Deal," infographic from 2011 CIRP Freshman Survey and 2012 Your First College Year Survey, www.heri.ucla.edu/infographics/2012-YFCY-Infographic.pdf.

91. National Center for Education Statistics, *Digest of Education Statistics,* Table 303.70: "Total Undergraduate Fall Enrollment in Degree-Granting Postsecondary Institutions, by Attendance Status, Sex of Student, and Control and Level of Institution: Selected Years, 1970 Through 2012," http://nces.ed.gov/programs/digest/d13/tables/dt13_303.70.asp.

92. Postsecondary Education Opportunity, January 2014, http://www.postsecondary.org/last12/243_912pg1_16.pdf. The data for this PEO study was collected from the American Time Use Survey from 2003 to 2012.

93. Conversation with Sandy Baum, Washington, DC, January 31. 2014.

94. Public Agenda, "With Their Whole Lives Ahead of Them: Myths and Realities About Why So Many Students Fail to Finish College," www.publicagenda.org/files/theirwholelivesaheadofthem.pdf. "The number one reason students give for leaving school is the fact that they had to work and go to school at the same time and, despite their best efforts, the stress of trying to do both eventually took its toll. More than half of those who left higher ed before completing a degree or a certificate say that the 'need to work and make money' while attending classes is the major reason they left."

95. Laura W. Perna, "Understanding the Working College Student," American Association of University Professors, July–August 2010, www.aaup.org/article/understanding-working-college-student#.U2VXPF6SSxo.

96. "Report on Remediation: Higher Education's Bridge to Nowhere," Complete College America, April 2012, www.completecollege.org/docs/CCA-Remediation-final.pdf.

97. Conversation with NASFAA spokesperson and personal correspondence, April 23, 2014.

98. Thomas L. Friedman, "How to Get a Job at Google: Part 2," *New York Times*, April 19, 2014.

99. George D. Kuh, *High-Impact Educational Practices: What They Are, Who Has Access to Them, and Why They Matter* (Washington, DC: AAC&U, 2008). An excerpt is at http://accreditation.ncsu.edu/sites/accreditation.ncsu.edu/files/Kuh_HighImpactActivities.pdf.

100. American College Health Association–National College Health Assessment II is a national research survey organized by the American College Health Association. Results can be reviewed online. www.acha-ncha.org/docs/ACHA-NCHA-II_ReferenceGroup_ExecutiveSummary_Spring2013.pdf.

101. "The First Year is a Big Deal" infographic from 2011 CIRP Freshman Survey and 2012 Your First College Year Survey, www.heri.ucla.edu/infographics/2012-YFCY-Infographic.pdf.

12. KEEP UP THE GOOD WORK

102. National Collegiate Athletic Association, "Probability of Competing Beyond High School," September 2013, http://www.ncaa.org/about/resources/research/probability-competing -beyond-high-school.

Probability Of Competing Beyond High School

Student Athletes	Men's Basketball	Women's Basketball	Football	Baseball	Men's Ice Hockey	Men's Soccer
High School Student Athletes	538,676	433,120	1,086,627	474,791	35,198	410,982
High School Senior Student Athletes	153,907	123,749	310,465	135,655	10,057	117,423
NCAA Student Athletes	17,984	16,186	70,147	32,450	3,964	23,365
NCAA Freshman Roster Positions	5,138	4,625	20,042	9,271	1,133	6,676
NCAA Senior Student Athletes	3,996	3,597	15,588	7,211	881	5,192
NCAA Student Athletes Drafted	46	32	254	678	7	101
Percent High School to NCAA	3.3%	3.7%	6.5%	6.8%	11.3%	5.7%
Percent NCAA to Professional	1.2%	0.9%	1.6%	9.4%	0.8%	1.9%
Percent High School to Professional	0.03%	0.03%	0.08%	0.50%	0.07%	0.09%

These percentages are based on estimated data and should be considered approximations of the actual percentages.

103. Gallup and the Lumina Foundation, "What America Needs to Know About Higher Education Redesign," February 25, 2014, www.luminafoundation.org/newsroom/news_ releases/2014-02-25.html#sthash.iEqvRXoe.DdHmCKrO.dpuf.

104. Ibid.

105. "The Job Outlook for the College Class of 2014," National Association of Colleges and Employers, (NACE) Bethlehem, PA.. For more detail about this survey and its findings, go to to the NACE website (www.naceweb.org) and click on press releases.

106. Kara Brandeisky and Jeremy B. Merrill, "How the Labor Department Has Let Companies Off the Hook for Unpaid Internships," ProPublica, April 9, 2014, www.propublica.org/ article/how-the-labor-department-let-companies-off-hook-for-unpaid-internships.

107. Ibid. For more information about internships, go to the NACE website (www.naceweb.org) and click on the link to internships.

108. Anthony P. Carnevale, Tamara Jayasundera, and Dmitri Repnikov, "The Online College Labor Market: Where the Jobs Are, Georgetown University Center on Education and the Workforce, April 2014. "Analyses by the Georgetown University Center on Education and the Workforce have established that the Internet ads are disproportionately aimed at the college labor market. Hence, this report focuses solely on job opportunities for Bachelor's degree-holders."

109. Ibid.

13. DO UNTO OTHERS

110. Ron Fournier, "The Outsiders: How Can Millennials Change Washington if They Hate It?," *The Atlantic*, August 26, 2013.

111. Yonah Lieberman, interview by Rachel M. Cohen, June 23, 2014.

112. Laura Cowie, interview by Rachel M. Cohen, June 26, 2014.

113. "Untapped Potential: Findings from a New Survey of Alumni of All AmeriCorps Programs," June 2014, www.americorpsalums.org/?page=2014NationalSurvey.

114. The source for much of this information about the Peace Corps was gathered from several links accessed through the Peace Corps official website.

115. Alyson Ochs, e-mail message, June 23, 2014.

116. At Tufts University, "Military 101," about the structure and culture of the military, has been offered since 2011. This information, provided by the Center for a New American Security and compiled by Caerus Associates is part of that curriculum. See http://webcache .googleusercontent.com/search?q=cache:FqhPuF2-uicJ:www.tuftsgloballeadership.org/ sites/default/files/images/resources/1112AR.pdf+&cd=3&hl=en&ct=clnk&gl=us (page 89)

117. Phil Carter interview, June 17, 2014.

118. Jules Szanton, email message, June 25, 2014.

119. "Veterans' Preference," FedsHireVets, www.fedshirevets.gov/job/vetpref.

120. "The Pros of Working in Government," Go Government, http://gogovernment.org/government_101/pros_and_cons_of_working_in_government.php.

121. "Executive Order 13562: Recruiting and Hiring Students and Recent Graduates," December 27, 2010, www.whitehouse.gov/the-press-office/2010/12/27/executive-order -recruiting-and-hiring-students-and-recent-graduates.

122. Juny Canenguez, interview by Rachel M. Cohen, June 26, 2014.

123. Channing Martin, interview by Rachel M. Cohen, June 26, 2014.

124. Tim McManus, interview by Rachel M. Cohen, June 11, 2014.

125. U.S. Office of Personnel Management, "Frequently Asked Questions: Pay & Leave: Student Loan Repayment," www.opm.gov/FAQs/topic/payleave/index .aspx?cid=3504d1bb-6043-4299-9366-6526fa1e4764.

126. "If you work full-time in a public service job, you may qualify for Public Service Loan Forgiveness." Federal Student Aid website, https://studentaid.ed.gov/repay-loans/ forgiveness-cancellation/charts/public-service.

127. Mrim Boutla, interview by Rachel M. Cohen, June 17, 2014.